Essential PowerShell

ESSENTIAL POWERSHELL

Holger Schwichtenberg

Addison-Wesley

Upper Saddle River, NJ • Boston • Indianapolis • San Francisco
New York • Toronto • Montreal • London • Munich • Paris • Madrid
Cape Town • Sydney • Tokyo • Singapore • Mexico City

The publisher offers excellent discounts on this book when ordered in quantity for bulk purchases or special sales, which may include electronic versions and/or custom covers and content particular to your business, training goals, marketing focus, and branding interests. For more information, please contact:

U.S. Corporate and Government Sales
(800) 382-3419
corpsales@pearsontechgroup.com

For sales outside the United States please contact:

International Sales
international@pearson.com

Visit us on the Web: www.informit.com/aw

Library of Congress Cataloging-in-Publication Data

Schwichtenberg, Holger.
Essential PowerShell / Holger Schwichtenberg.
p. cm.
ISBN 978-0-672-32966-1
1. Windows PowerShell (Computer programming language) 2. Command languages (Computer science) 3. Scripting languages (Computer science) 4. Systems programming (Computer science) 5. Microsoft Windows (Computer file) I. Title.
QA76.73.W56S39 2008
005.4'2—dc22

2008020010

ISBN-13: 978-0-672-32966-1
ISBN-10: 0-672-32966-2

Text printed in the United States on recycled paper at RR Donnelley in Crawfordsville, Indiana.
First printing June 2008

This Book Is Safari Enabled

The Safari® Enabled icon on the cover of your favorite technology book means the book is available through Safari Bookshelf. When you buy this book, you get free access to the online edition for 45 days.

Safari Bookshelf is an electronic reference library that lets you easily search thousands of technical books, find code samples, download chapters, and access technical information whenever and wherever you need it.

To gain 45-day Safari Enabled access to this book:

- Go to http://www.informit.com/onlineedition
- Complete the brief registration form
- Enter the coupon code LJRM-BWZP-1HUA-KCPF-YA2S

If you have difficulty registering on Safari Bookshelf or accessing the online edition, please e-mail customer-service@safaribooksonline.com.

Editor-in-Chief
Karen Gettman

Executive Editor
Neil Rowe

Development Editor
Mark Renfrow

Managing Editor
Kristy Hart

Project Editor
Betsy Harris

Copy Editor
Keith Cline

Indexer
Publishing Works, Inc.

Proofreader
Paula Lowell

Technical Editor
Tony Bradley

Publishing Coordinator
Cindy Teeters

Cover Designer
Gary Adair

Compositor
Nonie Ratcliff

To Heidi, the woman I love.

Contents

PREFACE

Windows PowerShell is one of the most amazing products Microsoft has released in recent years, because it brings console-based system administration and scripting to the next level of abstraction. PowerShell is an excellent replacement for classic Windows shell commands and for Windows Script Host (WSH). PowerShell copies a lot of good features from UNIX shells and combines them with the power of the .NET Framework. In contrast to WSH, PowerShell enables consistent, straightforward, command-line system administration that does not require much software development knowledge.

Unfortunately, in the first version of PowerShell, the number of high-level commands is limited. For many tasks, lower-level concepts are required, especially the .NET Framework and Windows Management Instrumentation (WMI).

What Does This Book Cover?

This book covers the standard PowerShell commandlets, additional free commandlets (for example, PowerShell Community Extensions), and the direct use of classes from the .NET Framework, the Component Object Model (COM), WMI, and the Active Directory Service Interface (ADSI).

Because PowerShell is an extensive topic, this book cannot provide an exhaustive reference of all PowerShell commands and solutions for all possible administrative tasks. However, you will find a concise introduction to the most common command and scenarios. For more detailed information about PowerShell, refer to the Microsoft documentation for PowerShell, WMI, ADSI, and the .NET Framework (approximately 100,000 pages) as an additional source.

Who Should Read This Book?

The primary target audience comprises Windows administrators seeking a method of automated system administration that is more powerful than the classic Windows Shell but less complex than WSH and the associated COM components. After reading this book, administrators will be able to use PowerShell as their day-to-day command-line interface for all administrative tasks.

As a prerequisite, aside a good knowledge of the Windows operation system, you should have a basic understanding of object-oriented programming languages. Basic concepts of object orientation such as classes, objects, attributes, and methods are not explained in this book.

How This Book Is Structured

This book is organized into 24 chapters, some of which, based on your previous experience and knowledge of certain concepts, you might find easier to understand than others. The 24 chapters are split into two parts:

- **Part I: Getting Started with PowerShell.** Part I introduces the PowerShell architecture, all basic concepts (such as pipelining and navigation), the PowerShell Script Language, and the tools you should know.
- **Part II: Windows PowerShell in Action.** Part II covers PowerShell script solutions for day-to-day administrative tasks related to Windows services and Windows application, such as file system, processes, event logs, registry, networking, printers, documents, databases, Active Directory, and software installation. Each chapter contains dozens of self-contained examples.

The appendixes contain a list of all commandlets from PowerShell 1.0, the PowerShell Community Extensions 1.1.1, and the www.IT-Visions.de PowerShell Extensions 2.0. You will also find a short preview of the next version of Windows PowerShell (Version 2.0).

Throughout the text, you will find codes that match up to codes in Appendix C, "Bibliography." These codes are encased in brackets (for example, [MS01]). The appendix lists the code, the correlating subject, and a link that will provide you with more information.

Occasionally, when a line of code is too long to fit on one line in the printed text, a code-continuation character has been used to show that the line continues. For example

```
"{0} can be reached at {1}.
➥This information is dated: {2:D}." -f $a, $b, $c
```

This Book's Website

Many of the scripts are available for download from its website, www.Windows-Scripting.com. This website also contains errata for this book and the option to offer feedback to the author.

ACKNOWLEDGMENTS

Thanks to Dr. Regina Schymiczek who helped me to translate parts of this book from my previously published German book. Thanks to the entire editorial team at Addison-Wesley who gave me the opportunity to publish this book. Many thanks to Heidi, who gives me great support at work and in my private life.

About the Author

Dr. Holger Schwichtenberg holds a Master's degree and a Ph.D. in business informatics, both from the University Duisburg-Essen in Germany. He has had more than ten years experience as a lead developer and trainer. With his company IT-Visions.de, based in Germany, he works as a software architect, technology consultant, and trainer for leading companies throughout Europe.

Holger is one of Europe's well-known experts for .NET and Windows Scripting technologies, recognized by Microsoft as a Most Valuable Professional (MVP), a .NET Code Wise Member, a board member of codezone.de, an MSDN Online Expert, and a speaker for the International .NET Association (INETA). Based on his expertise in software development and the Windows operating system, Holger is one of the experts in the European Union versus Microsoft antitrust case.

He has published more than 30 books for Addison-Wesley and Microsoft Press in Germany, in addition to more than 400 journal articles, notably for the IT journals *iX*, *DOTNET Pro,* and *Windows IT Pro.* His community websites www.dotnetframework.de and www.windows-scripting.com are members of the Codezone Premier Website program.

Holger regularly speaks at professional conferences (for example, Microsoft TechEd, Microsoft IT Forum, Advanced Developers Conference, OOP, Net.Object Days, Online, BASTA, and DOTNET Conference).

Holger can be reached at hs@windows-scripting.com.

PART I

GETTING STARTED WITH POWERSHELL

CHAPTER 1

FIRST STEPS WITH WINDOWS POWERSHELL

In this chapter:

This chapter introduces Windows PowerShell and helps you set up your environment. In addition, the chapter provides a few easy examples that demonstrate how to use PowerShell.

What Is Windows PowerShell?

Windows PowerShell (WPS) is a new .NET-based environment for console-based system administration and scripting on Windows platforms. It includes the following key features:

- A set of commands called *commandlets*
- Access to all system and application objects provided by Component Object Model (COM) libraries, the .NET Framework, and Windows Management Instrumentation (WMI)
- Robust interaction between commandlets through pipelining based on typed objects

- A common navigation paradigm for different hierarchical or flat information stores (for example, file system, registry, certificates, Active Directory, and environment variables)
- An easy-to-learn, but powerful scripting language with weak and strong variable typing
- A security model that prevents the execution of unwanted scripts
- Tracing and debugging capabilities
- The ability to host WPS in any application

This book includes syntax and examples for these features, except the last one, which is an advanced topic that requires in-depth knowledge of a .NET language such as C#, C++/CLI, or Visual Basic .NET.

A Little Bit of History

The DOS-like command-line window survived many Windows versions in almost unchanged form. With WPS, Microsoft now provides a successor that does not just compete with UNIX shells, it surpasses them in robustness and elegance. WPS could be called an adaptation of the concept of UNIX shells on Windows using the .NET Framework, with connections to WMI.

Active Scripting with Windows Script Host (WSH, pronounced "wish") is much too complex for many administrators because it presupposes much knowledge about object-oriented programming and COM. The many exceptions and inconsistencies in COM make WSH and the associated component libraries hard to learn.

Even during the development of Windows Server 2003, Microsoft admitted that it had asked UNIX administrators how they administer their operating system. The short-term result was a large number of additional command-line tools included in Windows Server 2003. However, the long-term goal was to replace the DOS-like command-line window of Windows with a new, much more powerful shell.

Upon the release of the Microsoft .NET Framework in 2002, many people were expecting a "WSH.NET." However, Microsoft stopped the development of a new WSH for the .NET Framework because it foresaw that using .NET-based programming languages such as C# and Visual Basic .NET would require administrators to know even more about object-oriented software development.

Microsoft recognized the popularity of and satisfaction with UNIX shells and decided to merge the pipelining concept of UNIX shells with the .NET Framework. The goal was to develop a new shell that was simple to use but nearly as robust as a .NET program. The result: WPS.

In the first beta version, the new shell was presented under the code name Monad at the Professional Developer Conference (PDC) in October 2003 in Los Angeles. After the intermediate names Microsoft Shell (MSH) and Microsoft Command Shell, the shell received its final name, PowerShell, in May 2006. The final version of WPS 1.0 was released on November 11, 2006 at TechEd Europe 2006.

NOTE The main architect of WPS 1.0 was Jeffrey Snover. He is always willing to discuss his "baby" and answer questions. At large international Microsoft technical conferences, such as the Professional Developer Conference (PDC) and TechEd, you can easily find him; he is the only person at the Microsoft booths wearing a tie.

Why Use WPS?

If you need a reason to use WPS, here it comes. Just consider the following solution for one common administrative task in both the *old* WSH and the *new* WPS.

An inventory script for software is to be provided that will read the installed MSI packages using WMI. The script will get the information from several computers and summarize the results in a CSV file (*softwareinventory.csv*). The names (or IP addresses) of the computers to be queried are read from a TXT file (*computers.txt*).

The solution with WSH (Listing 1.1) requires 90 lines of code (including comments and parameterizing). In WPS, you can do the same thing in just 13 lines (Listing 1.2). If you do not want to include comments and parameterizing, you need just one line (Listing 1.3).

Listing 1.1 Software Inventory Solution 1: WSH

```
Option Explicit

' --- Settings
Const InputFileName = "computers.txt"
Const OutputFileName = "softwareinventory.csv"
```

(continues)

Listing 1.1 Software Inventory Solution 1: WSH *(continued)*

```
Const Query = "SELECT * FROM Win32_Product where not
➥Vendor like '%Microsoft%'"

Dim objFSO                ' Filesystem Object
Dim objTX                 ' Textfile object
Dim i                          ' Counter
Dim Computer           ' Current Computer Name
Dim InputFilePath     ' Path for InputFile
Dim OutputFilePath   ' Path of OutputFile

' --- Create objects
Set objFSO = CreateObject("Scripting.FileSystemObject")

' --- Get paths
InputFilePath = GetCurrentPath & "\" & InputFileName
OutputFilePath = GetCurrentPath & "\" & OutputFileName

' --- Create headlines
Print        "Computer" & ";" & _
      "Name" & ";" & _
     "Description" & ";" & _
     "Identifying Number" & ";" & _
     "Install Date" & ";" & _
     "Install Directory" & ";" & _
     "State" & ";" & _
     "SKU Number" & ";" & _
     "Vendor" & ";" & _
     "Version"

' --- Read computer list
Set objTX = objFSO.OpenTextFile(InputFilePath)

' --- Loop over all computers
Do While Not objTX.AtEndOfStream
     Computer = objTX.ReadLine
     i = i + 1
     WScript.Echo "=== Computer #" & i & ": " & Computer
       GetInventory Computer
Loop

' --- Close Input File
```

```
objTX.Close

' === Get Software inventory for one computer
Sub GetInventory(Computer)

Dim objProducts
Dim objProduct
Dim objWMIService

' --- Access WMI
Set objWMIService = GetObject("winmgmts:" &_
    "{impersonationLevel=impersonate}!\\" & Computer &_
    "\root\cimv2")
' --- Execeute WQL query
Set objProducts = objWMIService.ExecQuery(Query)
' --- Loop
For Each objProduct In objProducts
    Print _
    Computer & ";" & _
    objProduct.Name & ";" & _
    objProduct.Description & ";" & _
    objProduct.IdentifyingNumber & ";" & _
    objProduct.InstallDate & ";" & _
    objProduct.InstallLocation & ";" & _
    objProduct.InstallState & ";" & _
    objProduct.SKUNumber & ";" & _
    objProduct.Vendor & ";" & _
    objProduct.Version
Next
End Sub

' === Print
Sub Print(s)
Dim objTextFile
Set objTextFile = objFSO.OpenTextFile(OutputFilePath, 8, True)
objTextFile.WriteLine s
objTextFile.Close
End Sub

' === Get Path to this script
Function GetCurrentPath
GetCurrentPath = objFSO.GetFile (WScript.ScriptFullName).ParentFolder
End Function
```

Listing 1.2 Software Inventory Solution 2: WPS Script

```
# Settings
$InputFileName = "computers.txt"
$OutputFileName = "softwareinventory.csv"
$Query = "SELECT * FROM Win32_Product where not
➥Vendor like '%Microsoft%'"

# Read computer list
$Computers = Get-Content $InputFileName

# Loop over all computers and read WMI information
$Software = $Computers | foreach { get-wmiobject -query $Query -
computername $_ }

# Export to CSV
$Software | select Name, Description, IdentifyingNumber, InstallDate,
➥InstallLocation, InstallState, SKUNumber, Vendor, Version |
➥export-csv $OutputFileName -notypeinformation
```

Listing 1.3 Software Inventory Solution 3: WPS Pipeline Command

```
Get-Content "computers.txt" | Foreach {Get-WmiObject -computername
➥$_  -query "SELECT * FROM Win32_Product where not
➥Vendor like '%Microsoft%'" } |  Export-Csv "Softwareinventory.csv"
➥-notypeinformation
```

Downloading and Installing WPS

Windows Server 2008 is the first operating system that includes WPS on the DVD. However, it is an additional feature that can be installed through Add Feature in the Windows Server 2008 Server Manager.

WPS can be downloaded (see Figure 1.1) and installed as an add-on to the following operating systems:

- Windows XP for x86 with Service Pack 2
- Windows XP for x64 with Service Pack 2
- Windows Server 2003 for x86 with Service Pack 1

- Windows Server 2003 for x64 with Service Pack 1
- Windows Server 2003 for Itanium with Service Pack 1
- Windows Vista for x86
- Windows Vista for x64

Note that WPS is not included in Windows Vista, although Vista und WPS were released on the same day. Microsoft decided not to ship any .NET-based applications with Vista. Only the .NET Framework itself is part of Vista.

POWERSHELL DOWNLOAD PAGE www.microsoft.com/windowsserver2003/technologies/management/powershell/download.mspx

---

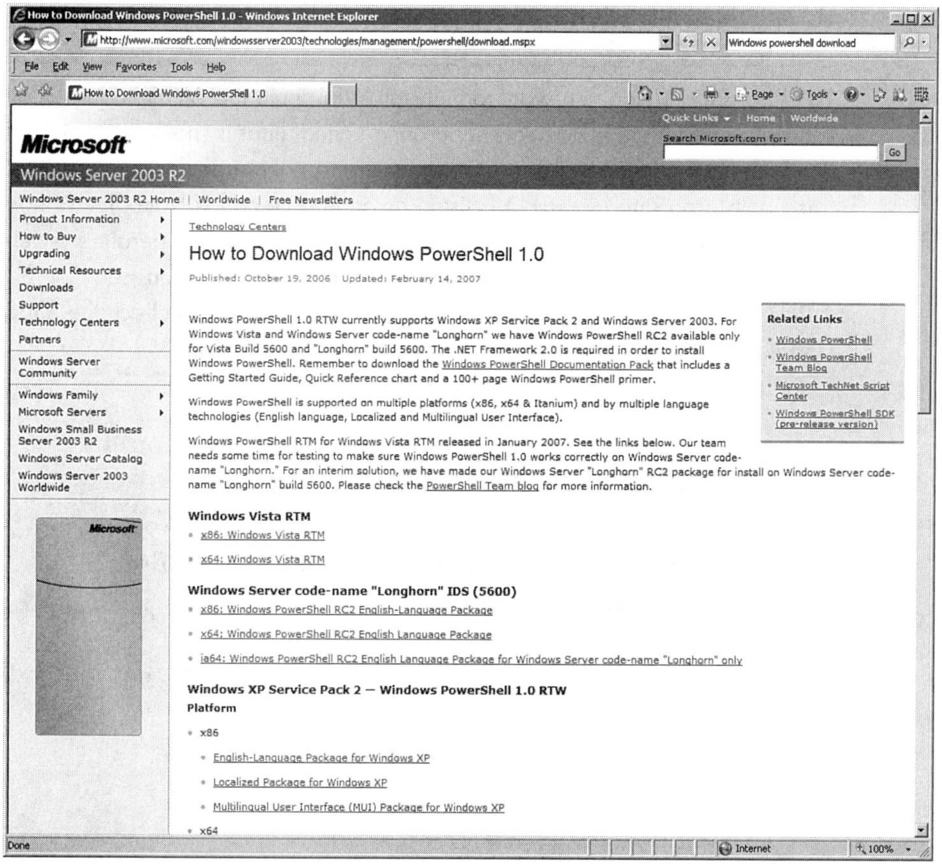

Figure 1.1 WPS download website

WPS requires that .NET Framework 2.0 or later be installed before running WPS setup. Because Vista ships with .NET Framework 3.0 (which is a true superset of 2.0), no .NET installation is required for it. However, on Windows XP and Windows Server, you must install .NET Framework 2.0, 3.0, or 3.5 first (if they are not already installed by another application).

MICROSOFT .NET FRAMEWORK 3.0 REDISTRIBUTABLE PACKAGE
www.microsoft.com/downloads/details.aspx?FamilyId=10CC340B-F857-4A14-83F5-25634C3BF043&displaylang=en

---

The setup routine installs WPS to the directory *%systemroot%\system32\WindowsPowerShell\V1.0* (on 32-bit systems) or *%systemroot%\Syswow64\WindowsPowerShell\V1.0* (for 64-bit systems). You cannot change this folder during setup.

TIP If for any reason you want to uninstall WPS, note that WPS is considered a software update to the Windows operating system (that is, not a normal application). Therefore, in the Add or Remove Programs control panel applet, it is not listed as a program; instead, it is listed as an update called Hotfix for Windows (KB *x*). The Knowledge Base (KB) number varies on different operating systems. However, you can identify WPS installation in the list by its icon (see Figure 1.2). On Windows XP and Windows Server 2003, you must check the Show Updates check box to see the WPS installation.

Taking WPS for a Test Run

This section includes some commands to enable you to try out a few WPS features. WPS has two modes, interactive mode and script mode, which are covered separately.

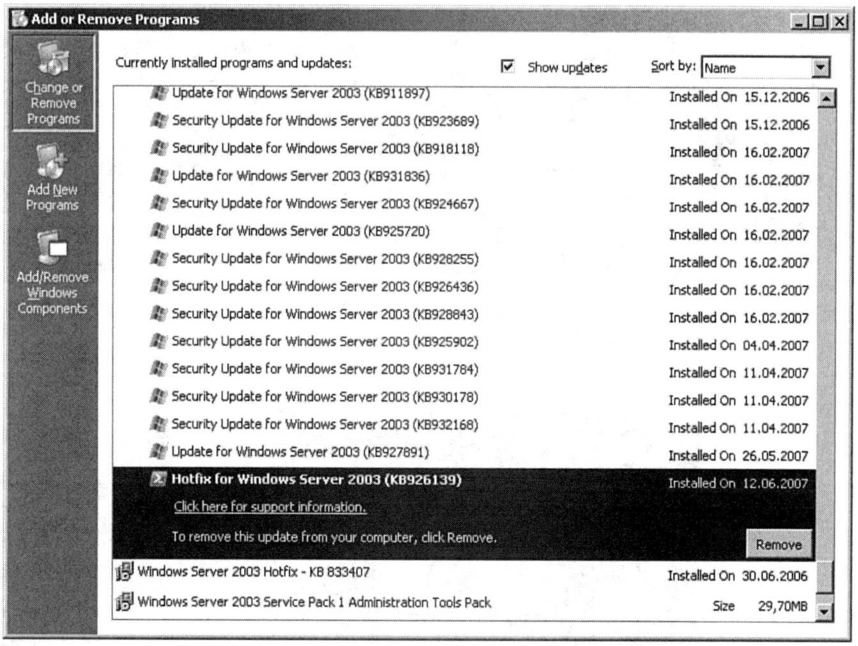

Figure 1.2 The uninstall option for WPS is difficult to find. (This screenshot is from Windows Server 2003.)

WPS in Interactive Mode

First, you'll use WPS in interactive mode.

Start WPS. An empty WPS console window will display (see Figure 1.3). At first glance, you might not see much difference between it and the traditional Windows console. However, there is much more power in WPS, as you will soon see.

At the command prompt, type **`get-process`** and then press the Return key. A list of all running processes on your local computer will display (see Figure 1.4). This was your first use of a simple WPS commandlet.

NOTE Note that the letter case does not matter. WPS does not distinguish between uppercase and lowercase letters in commandlet names.

Figure 1.3 Empty WPS console window

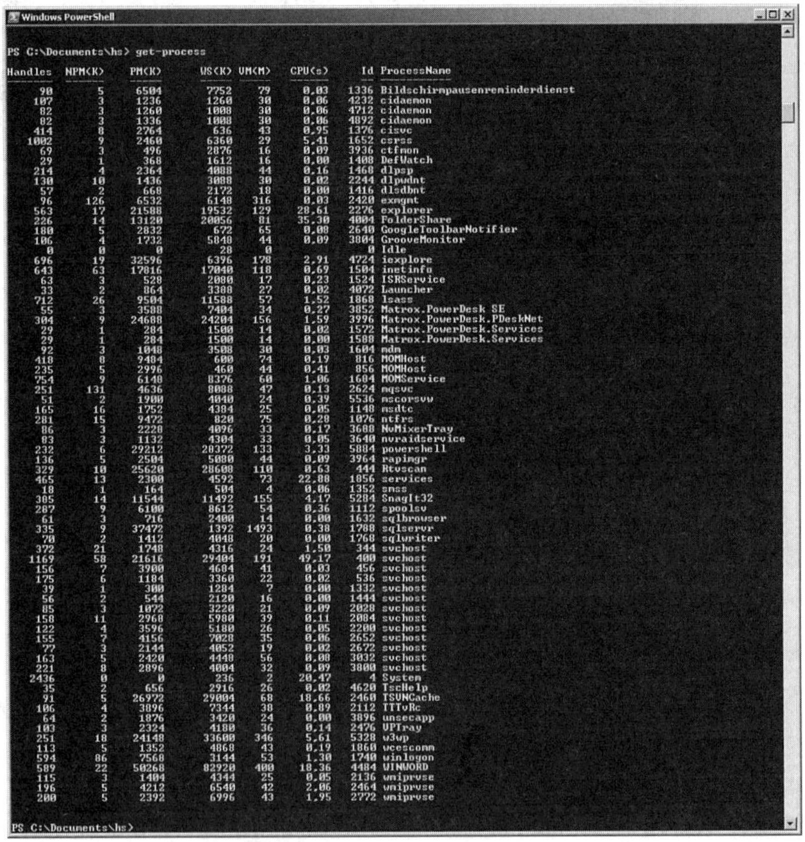

Figure 1.4 The `Get-Process` commandlet output

At the command prompt, type **`get-service i*`**. A list of all installed services with a name that begins with the letter *I* on your computer will display (see Figure 1.5). This was your first use of a commandlet with parameters.

Figure 1.5 A filtered list of Windows services

Type **`get-`** and then press the Tab key several times. You will see WPS cycling through all commandlets that start with the verb *get*. Microsoft calls this feature *tab completion*. Stop at `Get-Eventlog`. When you press Enter, WPS prompts for a parameter called LogName (see Figure 1.6). LogName is a required parameter. After typing **`Application`** and pressing Return, you will see a long list of the current entries in your Application event log.

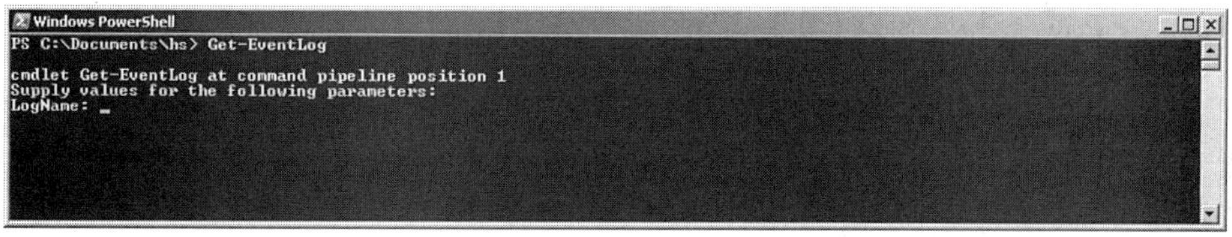

Figure 1.6 WPS prompts for a required parameter.

The last example in this section introduces you to the pipeline features of WPS. Again, we want to list entries from a Windows event log, but this time we want to get only some entries. The task is to get the most recent ten events that apply to printing. Enter the following command, which consists of three commandlets connected via pipes (see Figure 1.7):

```
Get-EventLog system | Where-Object { $_.source -eq "print" }
➥ | Select-Object -first 10
```

Note that WPS seems to get stuck for a few seconds after printing the first ten entries. This is the correct behavior because the first commandlet

(`Get-EventLog`) will receive all entries. The filtering is done by the subsequent commandlets (`Where-Object` and `Select-Object`). Unfortunately, `Get-EventLog` has no included filter mechanism.

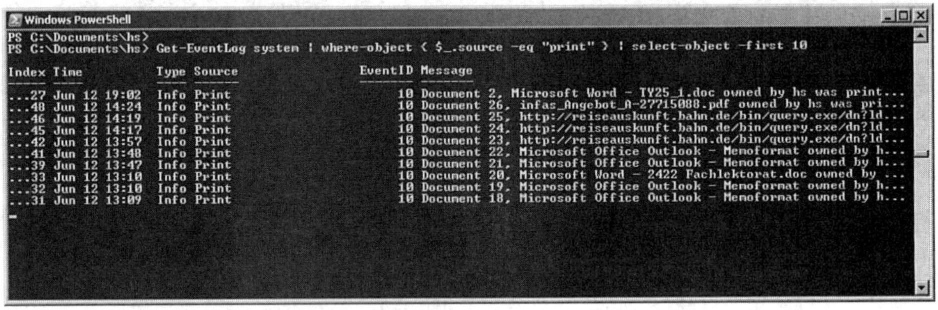

Figure 1.7 Filtering event log entries

WPS in Script Mode

Now it's time to try out PowerShell in script mode and incorporate a WPS script. A WPS script is a text file that includes commandlets/elements of PowerShell Script Language (PSL). The script in this example creates a new user account on your local computer.

Open Windows Notepad (or any other text editor) and enter the following lines of script code (which consists of comments, variable declarations, COM library calls, and shell output):

Listing 1.4 Create a User Account

```
### PowerShell Script
### Create local User Acount

# Variables
$Name = "Dr. Holger Schwichtenberg"
$Accountname = "HolgerSchwichtenberg"
$Description = "Author of this book / Website: www.windows-scripting.com"
$Password = "secret+123"
$Computer = "localhost"

"Creating User on Computer $Computer"
```

```
# Access to Container using the COM library
➥"Active Directory Service Interface (ADSI)"
$Container = [ADSI] "WinNT://$Computer"

# Create User
$objUser = $Container.Create("user", $Accountname)
$objUser.Put("Fullname", $Name)
$objUser.Put("Description", $Description)
# Set Password
$objUser.SetPassword($Password)
# Save Changes
$objUser.SetInfo()

"User created: $Name"
```

Save the text file with the name **createuser.ps1** into the directory *c:\temp*. Note that the file extension must be `.ps1`.

Now start WPS. Try to start the script by typing **c:\temp\createuser.ps1**. (You can use tab completion for the directory and filenames.) This attempt will fail because script execution is, by default, not allowed in WPS (see Figure 1.8). This is not a bug; it is a security feature. (Remember the Love Letter worm for WSH?)

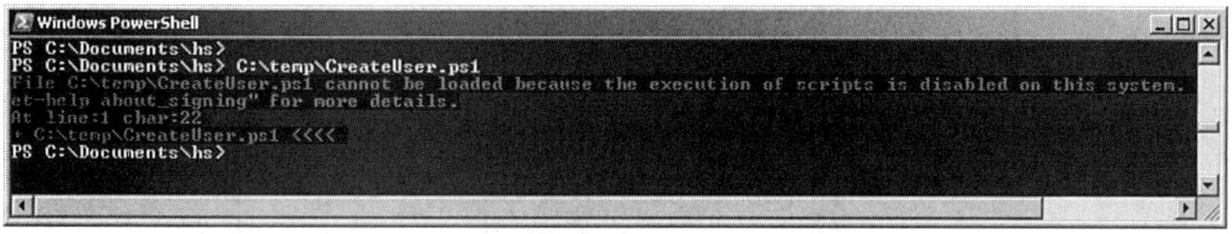

Figure 1.8 Script execution is prohibited by default.

For our first test, we will weaken the security a little bit (just a little). We will allow scripts that reside on your local system to run. However, scripts that come from network resources (including the Internet) will need a digital signature from a trusted script author. Later in this book you learn how to digitally sign WPS scripts. You also learn to restrict your system to scripts that you or your colleagues have signed.

To allow the script to run, enter the following:

```
Set-ExecutionPolicy remotesigned
```

Then, start the script again (see Figure 1.9). Now you should see a message that the user account has been created (see Figure 1.10).

Figure 1.9 Running your first script to create a user account

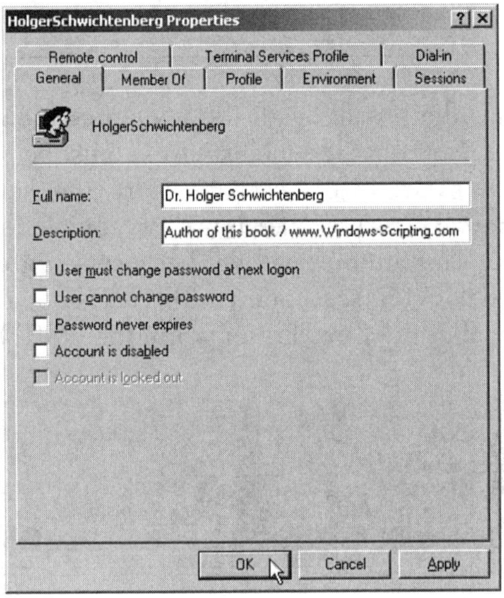

Figure 1.10 The newly created user account

Downloading and Installing PowerShell Community Extensions

WPS 1.0 includes only 129 commandlets. You might ask why I wrote *only*. You will notice soon that the most important commandlets are those with the verbs `get` and `set`. And the number of those commandlets is quite small compared to the large number of objects that Windows operating systems provide. All the other commandlets are, more or less, related to WPS infrastructure (for example, filtering, formatting, and exporting).

PowerShell Community Extensions (PSCX) is an open source project (see Figure 1.11) that provides additional functionality with commandlets such as `Get-DhcpServer`, `Get-DomainController`, `Get-MountPoint`, `Get-TerminalSession`, `Ping-Host`, `Write-GZip`, and many more. Microsoft leads this project, but any .NET software developer is invited to contribute. New versions are published on a regular basis. At the time of this writing, version 1.1.1 is the current stable release.

DOWNLOAD POWERSHELL COMMUNITY EXTENSIONS

www.codeplex.com/PowerShellCX

PSCX is provided as a setup routine that should be installed after WPS has been installed successfully.

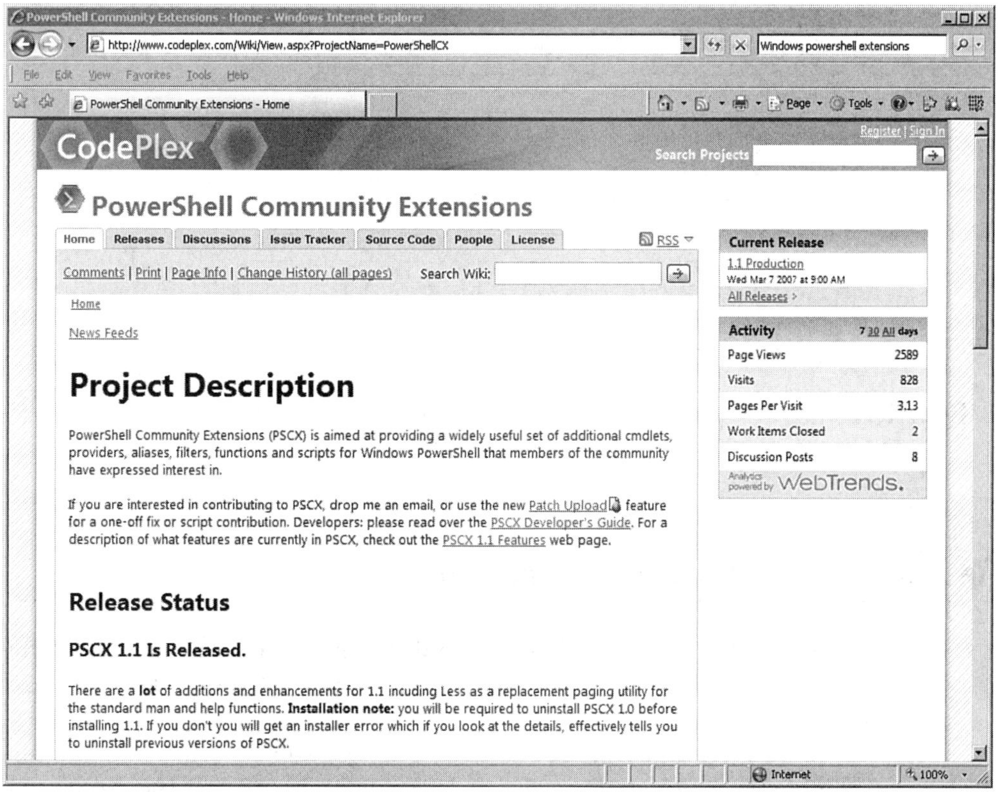

Figure 1.11 PowerShell Community Extension website

You can incorporate additional functionality of PSCX into WPS by using a profile script (see Figure 1.12). Just copy this profile script to your *My Documents/Windows PowerShell* directory, if you want, during PSCX setup. As a beginner, you should use this option.

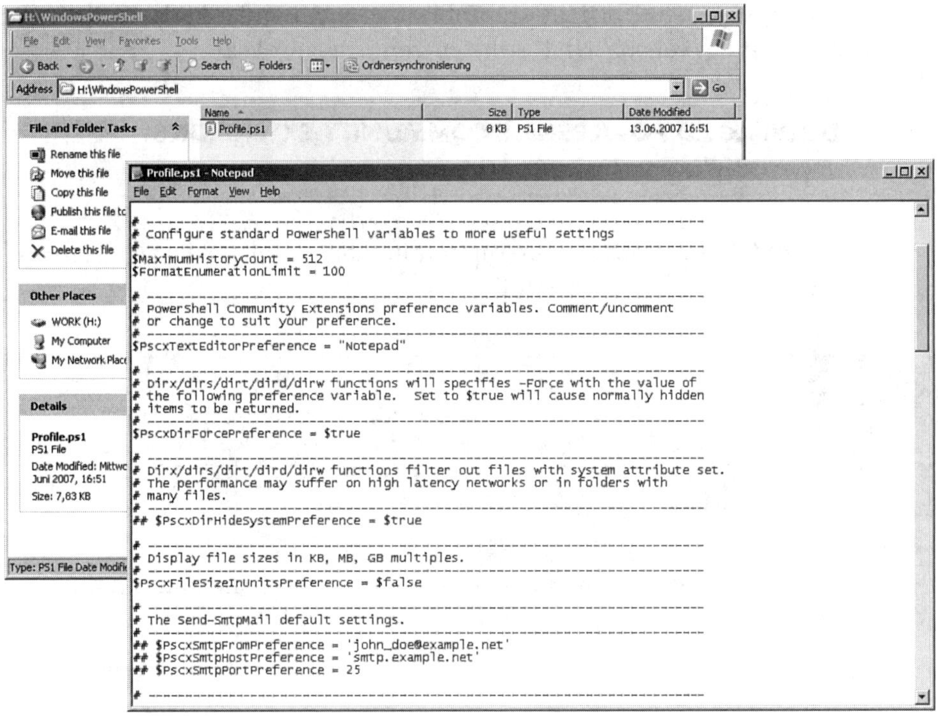

Figure 1.12 The PSCX profile script that was created during PSCX setup

Testing the PowerShell Extensions

The installation of PSCX changes the WPS console just a bit. Instead of the current path, the prompt now contains a counter. However, the path does display in the window's title.

Start WPS and type **`Get-DomainController`** (if your computer is a member of an Active Directory) or test PSCX by using **`Ping-Host`** with any computer on your network (see Figure 1.13).

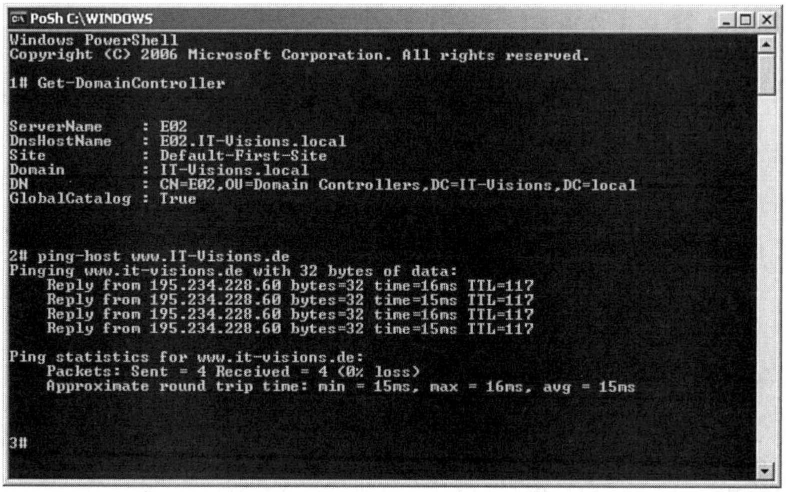

Figure 1.13 Testing `Get-DomainController` and `Ping-Host`

Downloading and Installing the PowerShellPlus

Unfortunately, Microsoft does not provide a script editor for WPS yet. However, a few third-party editors support WPS (see Chapter 9, "PowerShell Tools"). Throughout this book, we use PowerShellPlus Editor, which is free for noncommercial use.

A previous editor called PowerShell IDE from the same author was free even for commercial use. However, PowerShell IDE never made it to a final release and was discontinued.

The PowerShellPlus Editor is part of PowerShellPlus. PowerShellPlus consists of the editor and a console that provides IntelliSense while using the PowerShell interactively.

POWERSHELLPLUS WEBSITE www.powershell.com

PowerShellPlus does not need any setup. It is a true .NET application with XCopy deployment. You just unpack the ZIP file to the directory of your choice and start the `PowerShellPlus.exe` that is part of the package.

Testing the PowerShell Editor

The PowerShellPlus has, according to the WPS console, two modes: an interactive mode and a script mode (see Figure 1.14). After starting the PowerShellPlus, you will see the interactive mode. You can use any commandlet (or pipeline). When you press Return, the commandlet is executed, and the result displays in the same window. The handy feature is the IntelliSense. If you enter **`Get-P`**, you will see a drop-down list of the available commandlets that start with these letters.

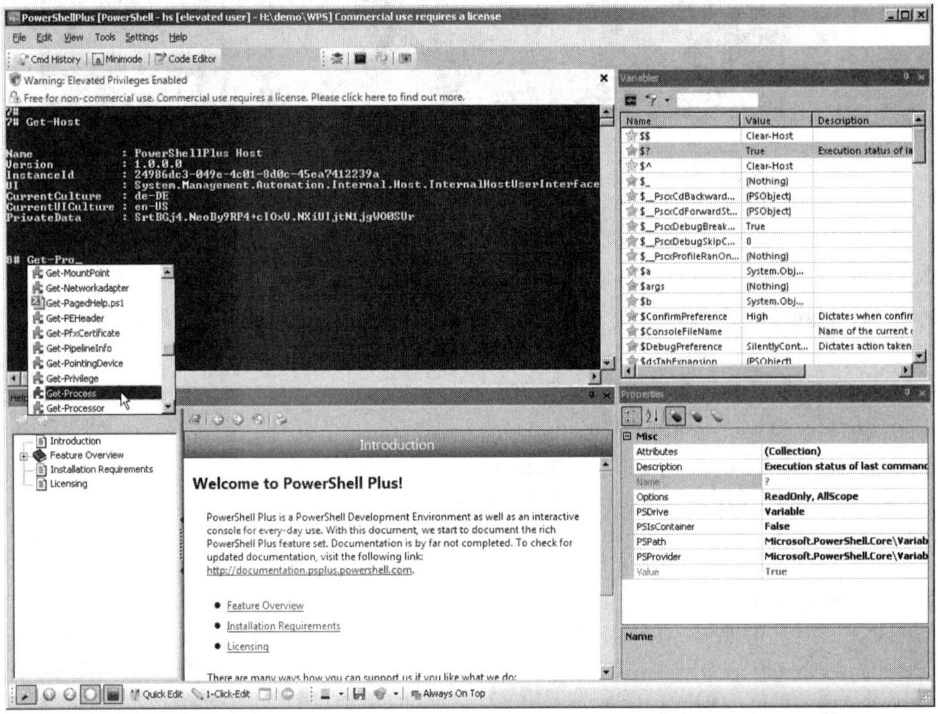

Figure 1.14 WPS IDE in interactive mode

To use the PowerShellPlus in script mode, click Code Editor and create a new script file (New/PowerShell Script) or open an existing script PS1 file (Open). Now open the script file `CreateUser.ps1` that you created earlier. You will see line numbers, and you will encounter the same IntelliSense features that you have in interactive mode. To run the script, click the Run symbol in the toolbar (see Figure 1.15). The result will display in the interactive Windows in the background.

WARNING Make sure the user account does not exist before running the script. Otherwise the script will fail with the error "The account already exists."

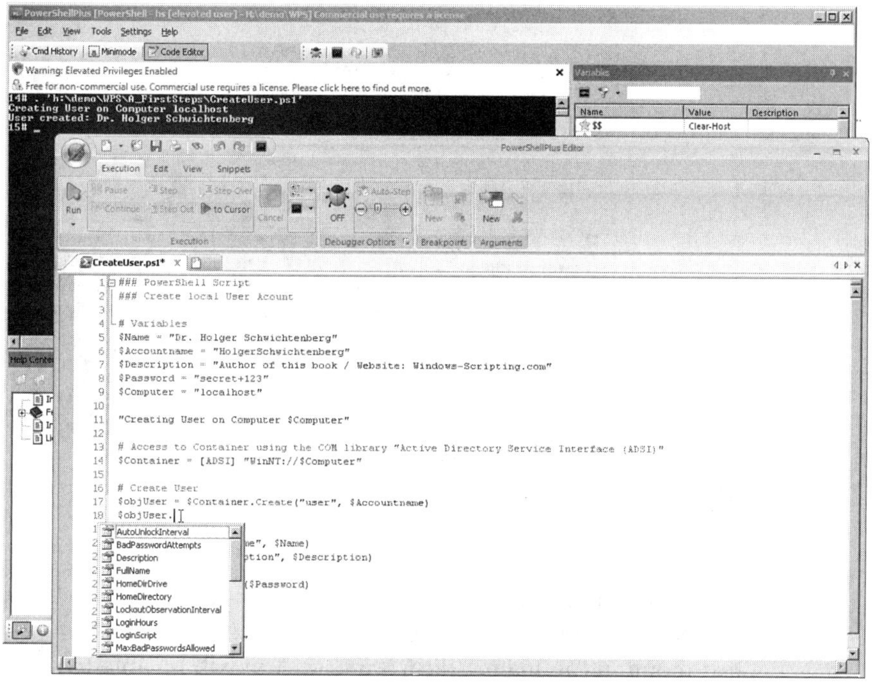

Figure 1.15 WPS IDE in script mode

Another great feature is debugging. Place the cursor on any line in your script and click the Debugging icon. Next, go to any line and press F9. This creates a red circle next to that line, called a *breakpoint*. Now run the script. You will see the PowerShellPlus Editor executing the script in slow motion, marking the current line yellow and stopping at the line with the breakpoint (see Figure 1.16). In the Variables Inspector window, you can inspect the current value of all variables. In the interactive window, you can type any WPS command that will be executed within the current context. That is, you can interactively access all script variables. To continue the script, press F8 or click the Continue icon in the toolbar.

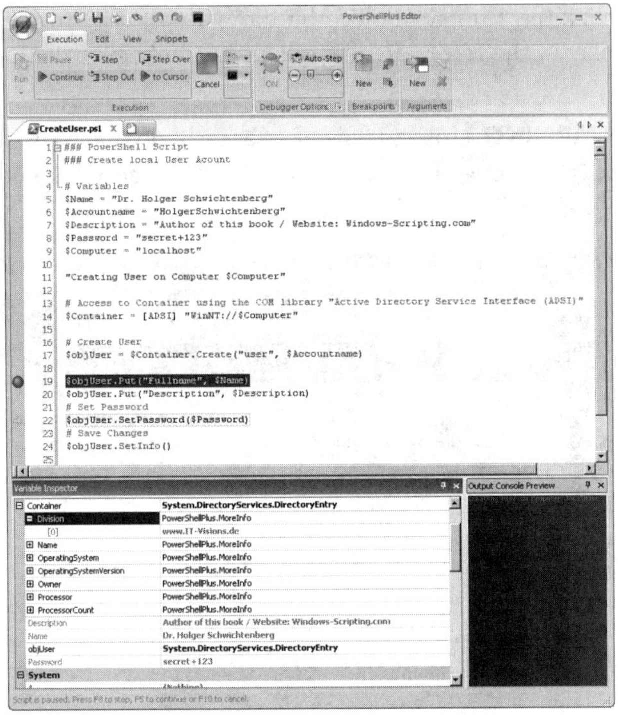

Figure 1.16 Script debugging with the WPS IDE

Code snippets are also a nice feature of the PowerShellPlus. In a script file, click Snippet/Insert on the toolbar or select Insert Snippet in the context menu in the main Editor window. You will be able to select a snippet. You can create you own snippets with the PowerShellPlus (via Snippets/New on the toolbar).

Summary

Windows PowerShell is a new .NET-based environment for scripting and is an interactive command-line shell. WPS is an optional feature on Windows Server 2008 and an add-on for Windows XP, Vista, and Server 2008. Commands in WPS are called commandlets. The PSCX extends WPS with additional commandlets.

The PowerShellPlus is an alternative shell for WPS commands and an editor for WPS scripts.

In the next chapter, you learn much more about commandlets and pipelines. You also learn how to get help if you are seeking a command or the available options for a commandlet.

CHAPTER 2

Commandlets

In this chapter:

Commands in Windows PowerShell (WPS) are called *commandlets.* This chapter introduces the concept of commandlets and discusses their common parameters. It also covers aliases and the available options for getting help.

Introducing Commandlets

A regular WPS command is called *commandlet* (cmdlet) or *function.* In this chapter, we first deal only with commandlets. A function offers an opportunity to create a command in WPS itself. Because the differences between commandlets and functions are partly academic from a user point of view, there will be no differentiation at this point.

A commandlet usually consists of three parts:

1. A verb
2. A noun
3. An (optional) parameter list

The verb and noun are separated by a hyphen (-), the optional parameters by spaces. Thus, the following composition is created:

```
Verb-noun [-parameter list]
```

The use of upper- or lowercase is irrelevant in commandlet names.
A simple example without parameters is the following:

```
Get-Process
```

This command retrieves a list of all processes.

TIP You can use tab completion in the WPS console with commandlets, when the verb and hyphen have already been typed in (for example, **`Export-`**`Tab`). You can also use placeholders. Entering **`Get-?e*`** and pressing Tab will show you `Get-Help` Tab `Get-Member` Tab `Get-Service`.

Parameters

Entering one parameter will get you only those processes whose names match the entered pattern:

```
Get-Process i*
```

Another example for a command with parameter is the following:

```
Get-ChildItem c:\Documents
```

`Get-ChildItem` lists all branches of the indicated object (*c:\Documents*), in this case all files and directories listed below this file.

Parameters are regarded as a string, even when they are not explicitly marked by quotation marks. Quotation marks are optional. Quotation marks are mandatory only in case of a blank within a parameter itself, because a blank serves as delimiter between parameters:

```
Get-ChildItem "C:\Program Files"
```

All commandlets have numerous parameters, differentiated by their names. In case no parameter names are indicated, predefined standard properties are used (that is, the sequence is essential):

```
Get-ChildItem C:\temp *.doc
```

means the same as

```
Get-ChildItem -Path C:\temp -Filter *.doc
```

If a commandlet has more than one parameter, either the sequence of the parameters is decisive or the user has to indicate the names of the parameters, too. All the following commands have the same meaning:

```
Get-ChildItem C:\temp *.doc
Get-ChildItem -Path C:\temp -Filter *.doc
Get-ChildItem -Filter *.doc -Path C:\temp
```

When indicating parameter names, you can change their sequence:

```
Get-ChildItem -Filter *.doc -Path C:\temp
```

The following, however, is wrong, because the parameters are not named and the sequence is incorrect:

```
Get-ChildItem *.doc C:\temp
```

Switches are parameters without any value. Using the parameter name activates the function (for example, the recursive run through a data file branch with `-recurse`):

```
Get-ChildItem h:\demo\powershell -recurse
```

Calculated Parameters

Parameters can be calculated (for example, combined out of substrings and merged by a plus sign). (This makes sense especially in connection with variables, which are discussed later in this book.)

The following syntax does not deliver the desired result, because here the delimiter before and after the + is a parameter delimiter at the same time:

```
Get-ChildItem "c:\" + "Windows" *.dll -Recurse
```

However, it also doesn't work without the two delimiters before and after the +. In this case, parentheses have to be used to ensure that the calculation is carried out first:

```
Get-ChildItem ("c:\" + "Windows") *.dll -Recurse
```

Another example follows demonstrating the calculation of numbers. The following command results in the process with the ID 2900:

```
Get-Process     -id (2800+100)
```

More Examples

The following shows those system services whose names don't start with the letters *K* to *Z:*

```
Get-Service -exclude "[k-z]*"
```

Commandlet parameters may also limit (filter) the output. The following command delivers only directory entries of type `user` of a certain Active Directory path (the example presupposes the installation of PSCX).

```
Get-ADObject -dis "LDAP://E02/ou=Management,dc=IT-Visions,
➥dc=de"-class user
```

TIP Tab completion also works with parameters. Try the following input at the WPS console:

```
Get-ChildItem -Tab
```

Placeholders

Often, placeholders (wildcards) are allowed in parameters. You get a list of all processes starting with the letter *I* as follows:

```
Get-Process i*
```

Other Aspects of Commandlets

Note that nouns used in commandlets are always used in the singular, even when a number of objects are asked for. However, the result doesn't always have to be a number of objects. For example, when entering

```
Get-Location
```

you get only one object with the recent path. With

```
Set-Location c:\windows
```

you change the recent path. This operation doesn't have any results.

NOTE The case of commandlet and parameter names (uppercase or lowercase) is irrelevant.

When started, WPS creates a process. All commandlets run within this process. This is difference from the classic Windows command shell, where executable files (`.exe`) run in separate processes.

Aliases

By using so-called aliases, you can shorten what you have to type for commandlets. For example, the aliases `ps` (for `Get-Process`) and `help` (for `Get-Help`) are predefined. Instead of `Get-Process i*`, you can also write `ps i*`.

Enumerating Aliases

With `Get-Alias` (or the relevant alias `aliases`), you receive a list of all predefined abbreviations in the form of instances of the class `System.Management.Automation.AliasInfo`.

When you add a name to `Get-Alias`, you receive the meaning of the alias:

```
Get-Alias pgs
```

However, if you want to know all aliases of a commandlet, you have to write the following:

```
Get-Alias | Where-Object { $_.definition -eq "get-process" }
```

Here you need to use a pipeline, which we discuss in detail in the next chapter.

Create a New Alias

The user can define a new alias with `Set-Alias` or `New-Alias`. For example

```
Set-Alias procs Get-Process
New-Alias procs Get-Process
```

The difference between `Set-Alias` and `New-Alias` is marginal: `New-Alias` creates a new alias and delivers a failure, when the alias to be created already exists. `Set-Alias` creates a new alias or overwrites an alias when the alias to be created already exists. You can use the parameter `-description` to create relevant description text.

You can use aliases not only for commandlets, but also for classical applications, such as the following:

```
Set-Alias np notepad.exe
```

WARNING When you create a new alias, the system does not check whether the respective commandlet or application exists. The failure will not appear until you call the new alias.

You cannot place any values on parameters via alias definitions. For example, if you want to define that the entering of Temp executes the action `Get-ChildItem c:\Temp`, you need a function to do so. This doesn't work with an alias.

```
Function Temp { get-childitem c:\temp }
```

Later on, we discuss functions in detail (see Chapter 7, "PowerShell Scripts"). WPS contains numerous predefined functions (for example, `c:`, `d:`, `e:`, `mkdir`, and `help`).

The newly defined aliases are valid only for the recent instance of the WPS console. You can, however, export your own alias definitions with `Export-Alias` and import them later with `Import-Alias` (see Table 2.1). As storage formats, the CSV format and the WPS script file format (PS1, see later chapters) are available. When you use the PS1 format, you must choose the script with dot sourcing to reimport your file.

Table 2.1 Importing and Exporting CSV

	File Format CSV	File Format PS1
Save	`Export-Alias c:\meinealias.csv`	`Export-Alias c:\meinealias.ps1 -as script`
Load	`Import-Alias c:\meinealias.csv`	`. c:\meinealias.ps1`

The number of aliases is, as standard, limited to 4,096. You can change this by using the variable `$MaximumAliasCount`.

Aliases are also defined as features. Instead of

```
Get-Process processname, workingset
```

you can also write

```
Get-Process name, ws
```

These aliases are defined in the file `types.ps1xml` in the installation dictionary of WPS (see Figure 2.1).

```
<Type>
    <Name>System.Diagnostics.Process</Name>
    <Members>
        <MemberSet>
            <Name>PSStandardMembers</Name>
            <Members>
                <NoteProperty>
                    <Name>SerializationDepth</Name>
                    <Value>1</Value>
                </NoteProperty>
                <PropertySet>
                    <Name>DefaultDisplayPropertySet</Name>
                    <ReferencedProperties>
                        <Name>Id</Name>
                        <Name>Handles</Name>
                        <Name>CPU</Name>
                        <Name>Name</Name>
                    </ReferencedProperties>
                </PropertySet>
            </Members>
        </MemberSet>
        <PropertySet>
            <Name>PSConfiguration</Name>
            <ReferencedProperties>
                <Name>Name</Name>
                <Name>Id</Name>
                <Name>PriorityClass</Name>
                <Name>FileVersion</Name>
            </ReferencedProperties>
        </PropertySet>
        <PropertySet>
            <Name>PSResources</Name>
            <ReferencedProperties>
                <Name>Name</Name>
                <Name>Id</Name>
                <Name>Handlecount</Name>
                <Name>WorkingSet</Name>
                <Name>NonPagedMemorySize</Name>
                <Name>PagedMemorySize</Name>
                <Name>PrivateMemorySize</Name>
                <Name>VirtualMemorySize</Name>
                <Name>Threads.Count</Name>
                <Name>TotalProcessorTime</Name>
            </ReferencedProperties>
        </PropertySet>
        <AliasProperty>
            <Name>Name</Name>
            <ReferencedMemberName>ProcessName</ReferencedMemberName>
        </AliasProperty>
        <AliasProperty>
            <Name>Handles</Name>
            <ReferencedMemberName>Handlecount</ReferencedMemberName>
        </AliasProperty>
        <AliasProperty>
            <Name>VM</Name>
            <ReferencedMemberName>VirtualMemorySize</ReferencedMemberName>
        </AliasProperty>
        <AliasProperty>
            <Name>WS</Name>
            <ReferencedMemberName>WorkingSet</ReferencedMemberName>
        </AliasProperty>
        <AliasProperty>
            <Name>PM</Name>
            <ReferencedMemberName>PagedMemorySize</ReferencedMemberName>
        </AliasProperty>
        <AliasProperty>
            <Name>NPM</Name>
            <ReferencedMemberName>NonpagedSystemMemorySize</ReferencedMemberName>
        </AliasProperty>
        <ScriptProperty>
            <Name>Path</Name>
            <GetScriptBlock>$this.Mainmodule.FileName</GetScriptBlock>
```

Figure 2.1 The content of the predefined file *types.ps1xml*

Expressions

Single WPS commands may also consist of (mathematical) expressions, such as the following:

```
10* (8 + 6)
```

or

```
"Hello "+ " " + "World"
```

Microsoft calls this the *expression mode* of WPS, in contrast to the command mode, which is used when you write the following:

```
Write-Output 10* (8 + 6)
```

WPS knows two command-processing modes: command mode and expression mode. In command mode, all input is treated as a string. In expression mode, numbers and operations are processed. You may mix command mode and expression mode.

You can integrate an expression in a command by using parentheses. Furthermore, a pipeline can start with an expression. Table 2.2 shows different examples of expressions.

Table 2.2 Expressions in WPS

Example	Meaning
`2+3`	It's an expression. WPS executes the calculation and writes 5.
`echo 2+3`	It's a pure command. `2+3` is regarded as a string and is shown without result on the screen.
`echo (2+3)`	It's a command with an integrated expression; 5 appears on the screen.
`2+3 | echo`	It's a pipeline starting with an expression. The screen shows 5.
`echo 2+3 | 7+6`	It's an invalid entry. An expression may be used only as the first element of a pipeline.
`$a = Get-Process`	It's an expression with an integrated command. The result is directed to a variable.
`$a | Get-Process`	It's a pipeline starting with an expression. The content of `$a` is passed on to `Get-Process` as parameter.
`Get-Process |`	It's an invalid entry. An expression may be used only as the first element of a pipeline.

External Commands

All entries that are not recognized as commandlets or mathematical formulas are treated as external applications. Classic command lines (such as `ping.exe`, `ipconfig.exe`, and `netstat.exe`) can be executed, as can Windows applications.

The entry of `c:\Windows\Notepad.exe` is thus possible to start the "popular" Windows Editor. Likewise, Windows Script WSH scripts may be started from WPS.

Figure 2.2 shows the call of `netstat.exe`. At first, the output remains unfiltered. In the second example, the commandlet `Select-String` has also been implemented. As a result, only those lines are shown that contain the term *LDAP*.

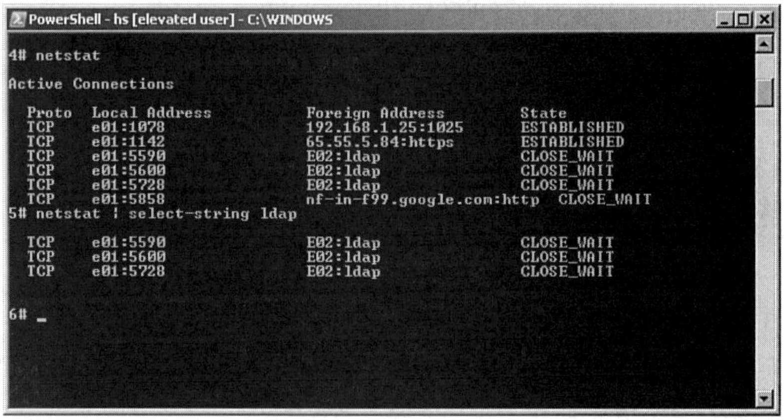

Figure 2.2 Execution of `netstat`

WARNING Sometimes an internal command of WPS (commandlet, alias, or function) will have the same name as an external command. In such a case, WPS does not warn you of this ambiguity. Instead, it executes the command according to the following preferences, in order:

1. Aliases
2. Functions
3. Commandlets
4. External commands

Filenames

According to Windows settings in the registry, the standard application gets started and the document is downloaded when file paths are entered. Filenames have to be marked by quotation marks only when they contain blanks.

Getting Help

Knowing how to get help is of primary importance when you begin using new software. This section describes the help functions included in the WPS console and external help files, too.

Getting a list of Available Commands

To get a list of all available commandlets, enter the following:

```
Get-Command
```

Patterns are also valid:

- `Get-Command get-*` delivers all commands starting with `get`.
- `Get-Command [gs]et-*` delivers all commands starting with `get` or `set`.
- `Get-Command *-Service` delivers all commands containing the noun `Service`.
- `Get-Command -noun Service` also delivers all commands containing the noun `Service`.

You can also use the commandlet `Get-Command` to gather information about what WPS regards as a command. `Get-Command` searches in commandlet names, aliases, functions, script files, and executable files (see Figure 2.3).

If you write the name of an `.exe` file after `Get-Command`, WPS shows the path where you can find the executable file. The search takes place only in paths that are included in the environment variable `%Path%`.

The following command shows a list of all directly callable executable files:

```
Get-Command *.exe
```

Getting Commandlet Help

You can request help text about a specific commandlet with `Get-Help commandletname` (for example, `Get-Help Get-Process`; see Figure 2.4).

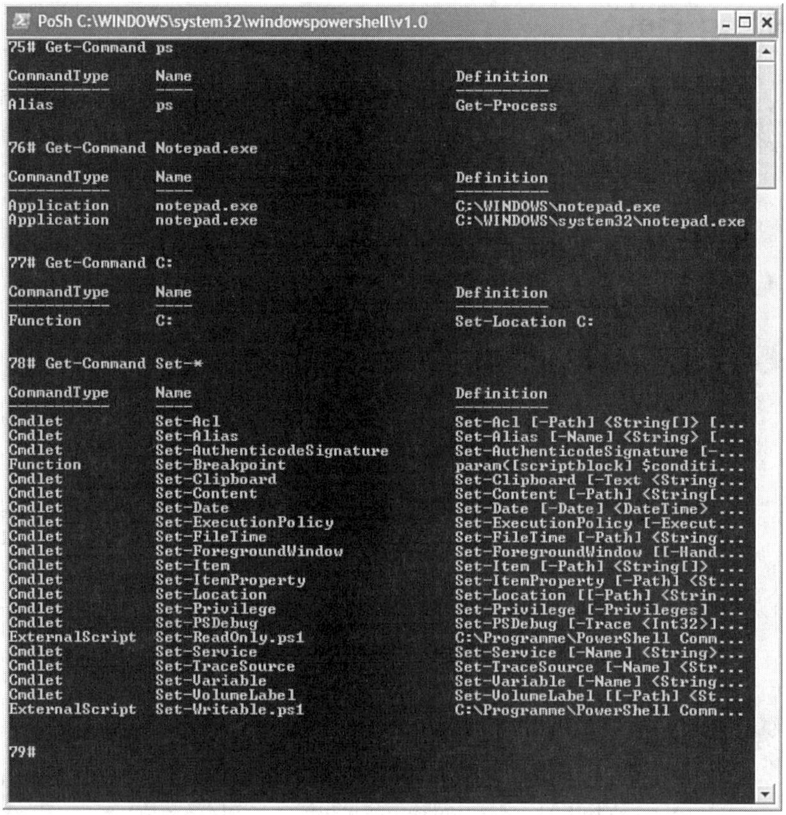

Figure 2.3 Example for the use of `Get-Command`

By using the parameters `-detailed` and `-full`, you can get more help. On the other hand, `Get-Help get` lists all commandlets that use the verb *get*. Help text language is based on the installed language version of WPS.

TIP Alternatively to calling `Get-Help`, you can also add the general parameter `-?` to the commandlet (for example, `Get-Process -?`). If you do so, you get a short version of help, but no option for the more detailed versions.

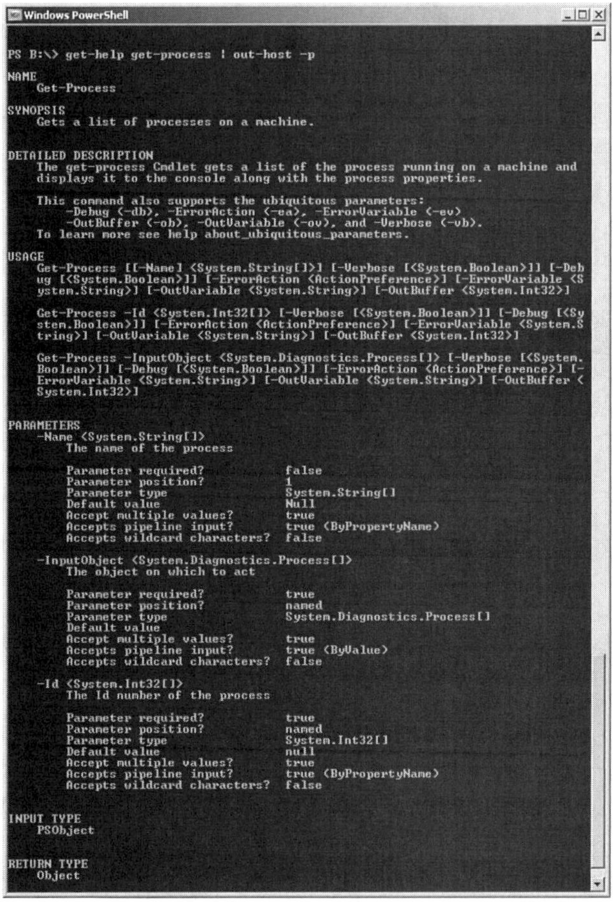

```
PS B:\> get-help get-process | out-host -p

NAME
    Get-Process

SYNOPSIS
    Gets a list of processes on a machine.


DETAILED DESCRIPTION
    The get-process Cmdlet gets a list of the process running on a machine and
    displays it to the console along with the process properties.

    This command also supports the ubiquitous parameters:
        -Debug (-db), -ErrorAction (-ea), -ErrorVariable (-ev)
        -OutBuffer (-ob), -OutVariable (-ov), and -Verbose (-vb).
    To learn more see help about_ubiquitous_parameters.

USAGE
    Get-Process [[-Name] <System.String[]>] [-Verbose [<System.Boolean>]] [-Deb
    ug [<System.Boolean>]] [-ErrorAction <ActionPreference>] [-ErrorVariable <S
    ystem.String>] [-OutVariable <System.String>] [-OutBuffer <System.Int32>]

    Get-Process -Id <System.Int32[]> [-Verbose [<System.Boolean>]] [-Debug [<Sy
    stem.Boolean>]] [-ErrorAction <ActionPreference>] [-ErrorVariable <System.S
    tring>] [-OutVariable <System.String>] [-OutBuffer <System.Int32>]

    Get-Process -InputObject <System.Diagnostics.Process[]> [-Verbose [<System.
    Boolean>]] [-Debug [<System.Boolean>]] [-ErrorAction <ActionPreference>] [-
    ErrorVariable <System.String>] [-OutVariable <System.String>] [-OutBuffer <
    System.Int32>]


PARAMETERS
    -Name <System.String[]>
        The name of the process

        Parameter required?           false
        Parameter position?           1
        Parameter type                System.String[]
        Default value                 Null
        Accept multiple values?       true
        Accepts pipeline input?       true (ByPropertyName)
        Accepts wildcard characters?  false

    -InputObject <System.Diagnostics.Process[]>
        The object on which to act

        Parameter required?           true
        Parameter position?           named
        Parameter type                System.Diagnostics.Process[]
        Default value
        Accept multiple values?       true
        Accepts pipeline input?       true (ByValue)
        Accepts wildcard characters?  false

    -Id <System.Int32[]>
        The Id number of the process

        Parameter required?           true
        Parameter position?           named
        Parameter type                System.Int32[]
        Default value                 null
        Accept multiple values?       true
        Accepts pipeline input?       true (ByPropertyName)
        Accepts wildcard characters?  false


INPUT TYPE
    PSObject


RETURN TYPE
    Object
```

Figure 2.4 Clipping from help text referring to the commandlet `Get-Process`

A graphic help file for WPS in CHM file format has been available since the end of May 2007 (half a year after the official launch of WPS 1.0) as a separate download at Microsoft.com. [MS01]

2. COMMANDLETS

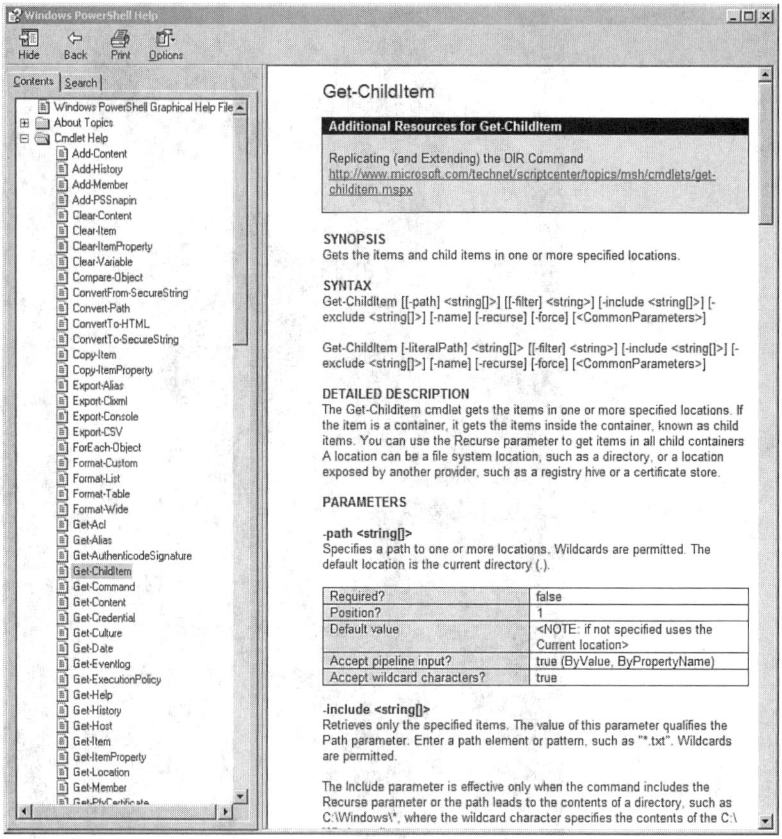

Figure 2.5 Help file for WPS

This CHM also contains advice about the manual transfer of VBScript code to WPS (see Figure 2.6).

Documentation of .NET Classes

For more information about.NET classes with which WPS works, check out the following resources:

- WPS documentation for the namespace `System.Management.Automation`
- .NET Framework software development kit or Windows software development kit for .NET 3.5 or Visual Studio 2008.

- Product-specific documentation (for example, Exchange Server 2007 documentation)

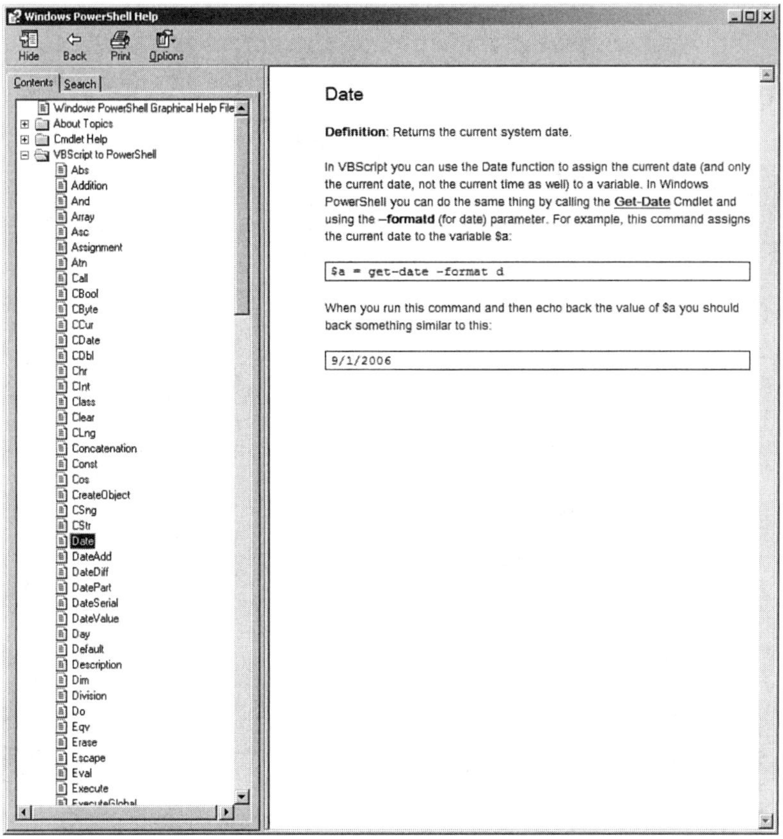

Figure 2.6 Help referring to the transfer of VBScript to WPS

The documentation shows the available class members (properties, methods, events, constructors; see Figure 2.7).

NOTE Because the documentation concerning .NET classes has been written for developers, it is often too detailed for WPS users. Unfortunately, there is currently no version in sight adapted to the needs of administrators.

Figure 2.7 shows the documentation of the class `Process` in the namespace `System.Diagnostics`. In the left branch, you will recognize different kinds of members: methods, properties, and events.

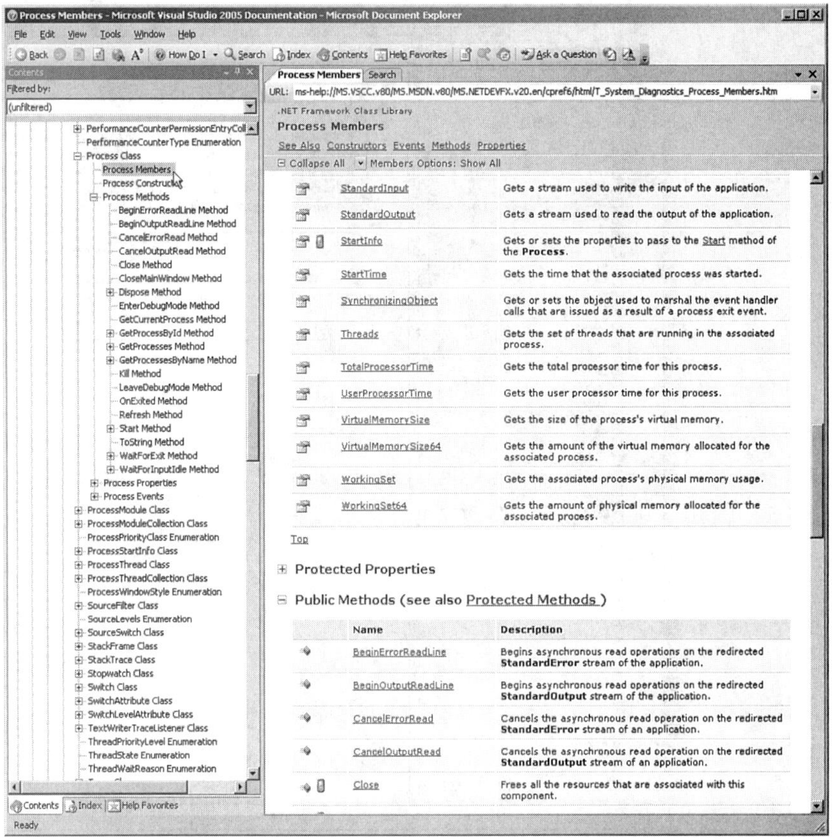

Figure 2.7 Clipping from the documentation of the .NET class `System.Diagnostics.Process`

Summary

A commandlet consists of a verb and noun separated by a hyphen. Placeholders can be used and parameters can be calculated. You have also learned that you can cut down on your typing by using aliases. A lot of aliases are predefined, but you can define as many as you want.

You have also learned that you can start classic command-line tools and Windows programs from the WPS console and that you can even use the console as a calculator.

You have become familiar with the commandlet `Get-Help`, which is one of the most important commandlets because it lists the contents of the XML help files that are available for most commandlets.

CHAPTER 3

PIPELINING

In this chapter:

Windows PowerShell (WPS) shows its real power through its object-oriented pipeline (that is, the passing of typed data from one commandlet to another). The pipeline in WPS contains structured objects, and the WPS provides a few commandlets for working with these objects, (for example, filtering, sorting, and calculating).

Pipelining Basics

To create a pipeline, you use the vertical line (|), as you would in UNIX shells and the normal Windows console.

The command

```
Get-Process | Format-List
```

means that the result of the `Get-Process` commandlets will be passed on to the commandlet `Format-List`. The standard output form of `Get-Process` is a table. When you use `Format-List`, the single properties of the listed processes are written one beneath the other rather than in columns.

Object Orientation

Object orientation is the outstanding feature of WPS: Commandlets can be linked to other commandlets by pipelines. In contrast to pipelines in UNIX shells, WPS commandlets do not exchange strings, but typed .NET objects. Object-oriented pipelining is, in contrast to string-based pipelining, common in UNIX shells and the normal Windows shell (`cmd.exe`), not dependent on the position of the information in the pipeline.

In a pipeline such as

```
Get-Process | Where-Object { $_.name -eq "iexplore" } |
➥Format-Table ProcessName, WorkingSet
```

the third commandlet is therefore not dependent on a certain positioning and formatting of the previous commandlets, but has direct access to the property of the objects via the so-called *reflection mechanism* (the built-in inspection mechanism of the .NET Framework).

NOTE To be exact, Microsoft calls this procedure *Extended Reflection* or *Extended Type System* (ETS), because WPS can add properties to objects that actually do not exist in the class definition.

Object Types and Data Members

In the preceding example `Get-Process` puts a .NET object of the type `System.Diagnostics.Process` in the pipeline for each running process. `System.Diagnostics.Process` is a class (alias type) from the .NET Framework class library; commandlets, however, can place any .NET object in the pipeline, even ordinary numbers or strings. As in .NET, there is no differentiation between elementary types and classes. However, to place a string in a pipeline will remain an exception, because the typed access to objects is much more robust against possible changes than the string evaluation with regular outputs.

The object-orientation approach becomes clearer when you use a number rather than a string. `WorkingSet64` is a numeric value of 64 bits that represents the recent cost of a process. All processes that currently need more than 20MB of RAM are listed with the following command:

```
Get-Process | Where-Object {$_.WorkingSet64 -gt 20*1024*1024 }
```

Instead of 20*1024*1024, you could also use the code 20MB. And you can shorten Where-Object with a question mark. The short version of the command is as follows:

```
ps | ? {$_.ws -gt 20MB }
```

When only one commandlet is used, the result is shown on the screen. When several commandlets are combined in a pipeline, the result of the last commandlet of the pipeline is also written on the screen. When the last commandlet doesn't deliver any data to the pipeline, however, you will see no result.

Executing Methods

The object pipeline has another advantage: According to the object-oriented paradigm, .NET objects not only have properties, they also have methods. Therefore, as a WPS user, you can also call the methods of objects in a pipeline. Objects of the type System.Diagnostics.Process, for example, have a method Kill(). In WPS, the call of this method is nested in the method Stop-Process.

The following WPS pipeline command ends all instances of Internet Explorer on your local system; the commandlet Stop-Process receives the instances of the relevant process from Get-Process:

```
Get-Process iexplore | Stop-Process
```

If you are an expert in .NET Framework, you may as well call the method directly. In this case, however, you need an explicit ForEach loop. Commandlets iterate automatically over all pipeline objects, whereas method calls don't. Note that the parentheses after the method name kill are mandatory. If you omit them, you get information about the method, but the method will not be executed.

```
Get-Process iexplore | Foreach-Object { $_.Kill() }
```

To abbreviate this, you can also use WPS aliases:

```
ps | ? { $_.name -eq "iexplore" } | % { $_.Kill() }
```

The application of the method Kill() was used only for demonstration purposes, to make clear that the pipeline really carries objects. In practice, you could perform the same more easily with the integrated Stop-Process.

However, this works well only when there are instances of Internet Explorer. If all of them have already been closed, Get-Process reports a failure, which might not be the desired behavior. With another pipeline, however, this failure can be prevented:

```
Get-Process | Where-Object { $_.Name -eq "iexplore" }
➥| Stop-Process
```

The second pipeline differs from the first. The filtering of the processes from the process list are now not executed by the Get-Process, but by a commandlet named Where-Object in the pipeline itself. Where-Object is more tolerant than Get-Process concerning the possibility that there might not be an adequate object.

ps is an alias for Get-Process, Kill for Stop-Process. Furthermore, Get-Process has an integrated filter function. To end all instances of Internet Explorer, you can either write

```
Get-Process | Where-Object { $_.Name -eq "iexplore" }
➥| Stop-Process
```

or

```
ps -p "iexplore" | Kill
```

Pipelining of Parameters

The pipeline can carry all kinds of information—not only complex objects, but also elementary data. Some commandlets support the fetching of parameters out of the pipeline. The following pipeline command creates a listing of all Windows system services starting with the letter *I:*

```
"i*" | Get-Service
```

Pipelining of Classic Command

Generally, you may as well use classic command-line applications in WPS. When you execute a command such as netstat.exe or ping.exe, they transfer a number of strings to the pipeline: Each line of output is an object of type System.String.

You can analyze these strings with the commandlet `Select-String`. `Select-String` allows only those lines to pass the pipeline that match the written regular expression (see Figure 3.1)

In the following example, only those lines of the expression of `netstat.exe` will be filtered that have an uppercase *E* followed by two numbers.

NOTE The syntax of regular expressions in .NET is not discussed in detail in this book. You can find good documentation in [MSDN08].

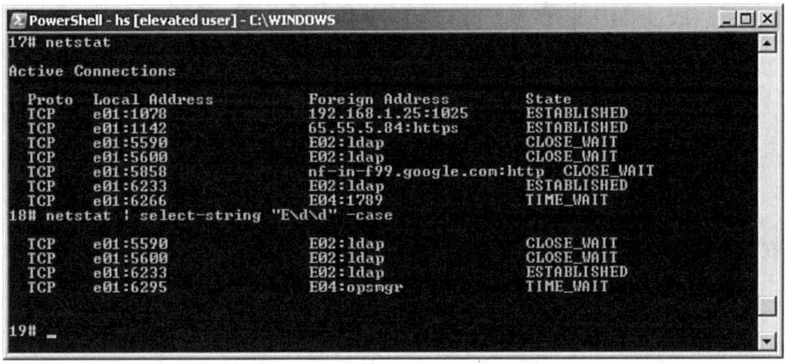

Figure 3.1 Use of `Select-String` for the filtering of expressions of classical command-line tools

Pipeline Processor

Responsible for the transfer of .NET objects to commandlets is the *PowerShell Pipeline Processor* (see Figure 3.2). The commandlets themselves do not have to worry about either object transfer or parameter evaluation.

NOTE As you can see Figure 3.2, the commandlet next in line immediately starts to work when it receives its first object from the pipeline. Sometimes, therefore, the first commandlet has not yet created all objects when the commandlets next in line start processing the first objects. A commandlet is immediately called as soon as the first object is ready.

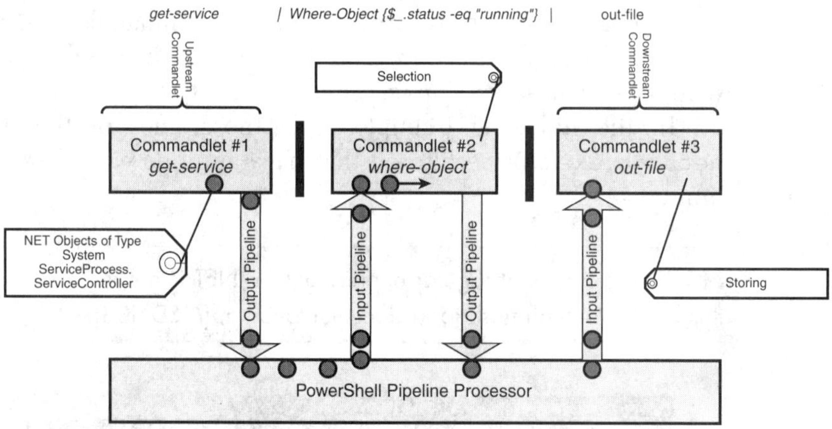

Figure 3.2 The PowerShell Pipeline Processor transfers objects from the downstream commandlet to the upstream commandlet.

Complex Pipelines

Users can define the length of a pipeline (that is, the number of commands in a single pipeline is unlimited). Here's an example for a more complex pipeline:

```
Get-ChildItem h:\Documents -r -filter *.doc
| Where-Object { $_.Length -gt 40000 }
| Select-Object Name, Length
| Sort-Object Length
| Format-List
```

`Get-ChildItem` identifies all Microsoft Word files in the directory *h:\Documents* and its children. The second commandlet (`Where-Object`) reduces the result to those objects where the property `Length` is greater than 40000. `Select-Object` cuts all properties from `Name` and `Length`. The fourth commandlet in the pipeline sorts the expression according to the property `Length`. Finally, the last commandlet creates a list format.

The sequence of the single commands, however, is not optional. You *cannot*, for example, put sorting after formatting in the preceding command; even though there is an object after the formatting, this object represents a text stream. `Where-Object` and `Sort-Object` could be exchanged; for reasons of resource use, however, it is wiser to limit the output first and sort the limited list after this.

You can access all properties and methods of .NET objects that have been placed by an earlier commandlet in the pipeline. Members of the objects can be used either via parameters of the commandlets (for example, in `Sort-Object Length`) or by an explicit reference to the recent pipeline object (`$_`) in a loop or condition (for example, `Where-Object { $_.Length -gt 40000 }`).

NOTE Not all sequences of commandlets make sense. Some sequences aren't even valid. A commandlet may expect certain kinds of input objects. Therefore, you should use commandlets that can process any kind of entry object.

Output

A regular commandlet should not create its own screen output, but should put a number of objects in the pipeline. Only certain commandlets are predefined to create an output, including the following:

- `Out-Default` Standard output according to WPS configuration (`DotNetTypes.Format.ps1xml`).
- `Out-Host` Same as `Out-Default` with additional option for pagewise output.
- `Out-Null` Pipeline objects are not transferred.
- `Format-Wide` Two-column list (see Figure 3.3)
- `Format-List` Detailed list (see Figure 3.4)
- `Format-Table` Table (see Figure 3.5)

NOTE Unfortunately, after the beta versions, Microsoft removed some commandlets that offered an output on a higher abstraction level. Therefore, the following commandlets are not available in WPS 1.0:

- Windows Forms data grid (`Out-Grid`)
- Excel chart (`Out-Excel`)
- E-mail (`Out-Email`)
- Column diagram (`Out-Chart`)

However, Microsoft has announced that at least a commandlet named `Out-GridView` will be available in WPS 2.0.

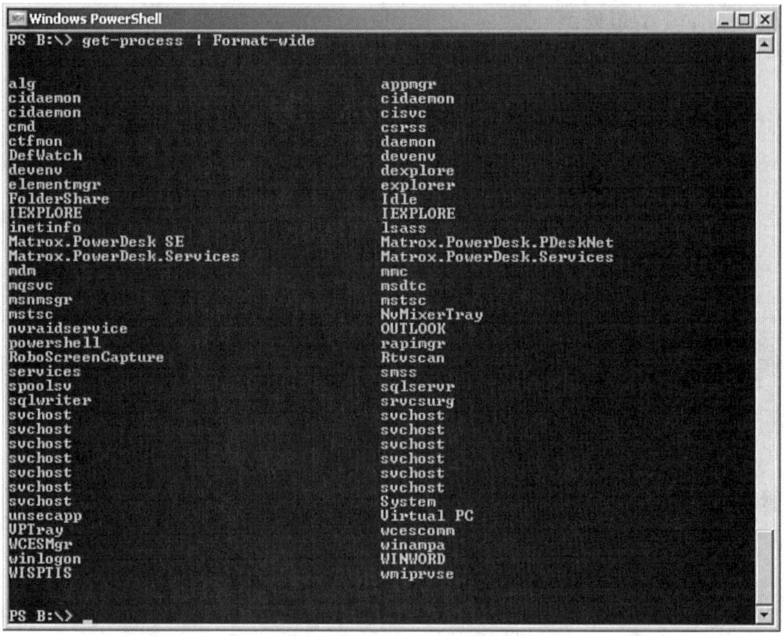

Figure 3.3 `Format-Wide` output

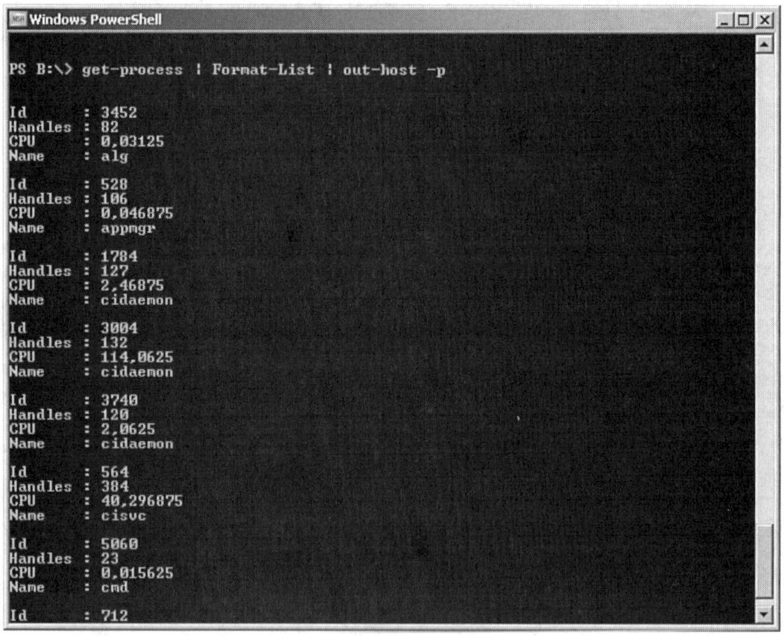

Figure 3.4 `Format-List` output

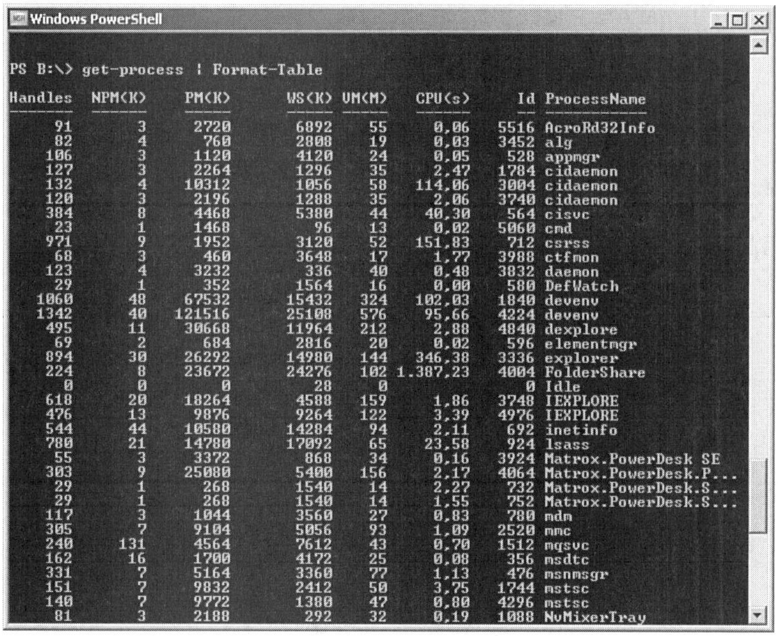

Figure 3.5 `Format-Table` output

Standard Output

When you do not name a format function at the end of a pipeline, WPS automatically uses the commandlet `Out-Default`. `Out-Default` uses a predefined output standard that is stored in `DotNetTypes.Format.ps1xml` in the installation directory of WPS. There, you can get the information that, for example, type `System.Diagnostics.Process` produces an output in an eight-column table (see Figure 3.6).

Pagewise Output

Often, output is too long to be presented on one screen page. Some output is even longer than the standard buffer of the WPS window (for example, `Get-Command | Get-Help`). You enforce the pagewise output with the parameter `-p` in the `Out-Host` commandlet. In this case, `Out-Host` has to be written as follows:

```
Get-Command | Get-Help | Out-Host -p
```

```
        <View>
            <Name>process</Name>
            <ViewSelectedBy>
                <TypeName>System.Diagnostics.Process</TypeName>
                <TypeName>Deserialized.System.Diagnostics.Process</TypeName>
            </ViewSelectedBy>
            <TableControl>
                <TableHeaders>
                    <TableColumnHeader>
                        <Label>Handles</Label>
                        <Width>7</Width>
                        <Alignment>right</Alignment>
                    </TableColumnHeader>
                    <TableColumnHeader>
                        <Label>NPM(K)</Label>
                        <Width>7</Width>
                        <Alignment>right</Alignment>
                    </TableColumnHeader>
                    <TableColumnHeader>
                        <Label>PM(K)</Label>
                        <Width>8</Width>
                        <Alignment>right</Alignment>
                    </TableColumnHeader>
                    <TableColumnHeader>
                        <Label>WS(K)</Label>
                        <Width>10</Width>
                        <Alignment>right</Alignment>
                    </TableColumnHeader>
                    <TableColumnHeader>
                        <Label>VM(M)</Label>
                        <Width>5</Width>
                        <Alignment>right</Alignment>
                    </TableColumnHeader>
                    <TableColumnHeader>
                        <Label>CPU(s)</Label>
                        <Width>8</Width>
                        <Alignment>right</Alignment>
                    </TableColumnHeader>
                    <TableColumnHeader>
                        <Width>6</Width>
                        <Alignment>right</Alignment>
                    </TableColumnHeader>
                    <TableColumnHeader />
                </TableHeaders>
                <TableRowEntries>
                    <TableRowEntry>
                        <TableColumnItems>
                            <TableColumnItem>
                                <PropertyName>HandleCount</PropertyName>
                            </TableColumnItem>
                            <TableColumnItem>
                                <ScriptBlock>[int]($_.NPM / 1024)</ScriptBlock>
                            </TableColumnItem>
                            <TableColumnItem>
                                <ScriptBlock>[int]($_.PM / 1024)</ScriptBlock>
                            </TableColumnItem>
                            <TableColumnItem>
                                <ScriptBlock>[int]($_.WS / 1024)</ScriptBlock>
                            </TableColumnItem>
                            <TableColumnItem>
                                <ScriptBlock>[int]($_.VM / 1048576)</ScriptBlock>
                            </TableColumnItem>
                            <TableColumnItem>
                                <ScriptBlock>
if ($_.CPU -ne $())
{
    $_.CPU.ToString("N")
}
                                </ScriptBlock>
                            </TableColumnItem>
                            <TableColumnItem>
                                <PropertyName>Id</PropertyName>
```

Figure 3.6 Clipping from the description of the standard output for type `System.Diagnostics.Process` in `DotNetTypes.Format.ps1xml`

Restricting the Output

The output commands allow specifications of object properties to be presented. For example

```
Get-Process | Format-Table -p id,processname,workingset
```

creates a table of processes with process ID, name of processes, and use of space. Names of properties can also be abbreviated with placeholder *, as follows:

```
Get-Process | Format-Table -p id,processn*,working*
```

NOTE You can get the same output when you use `Select-Object`:

```
Get-Process | Select-Object id, processname,
➥workingset | Format-Table
```

Output of Single Values

To display specific text or the content of a variable, you just have to write this on the console (see Figure 3.7). Alternatively, you can use the commandlets `Write-Host`, `Write-Warn`, and `Write-Error`. The commandlets `Write-Warn` and `Write-Error` create highlighted output.

With `Write-Host`, you can specify colors:

```
Write-Host "Hello Holger" -foregroundcolor red -backgroundcolor
➥white
```

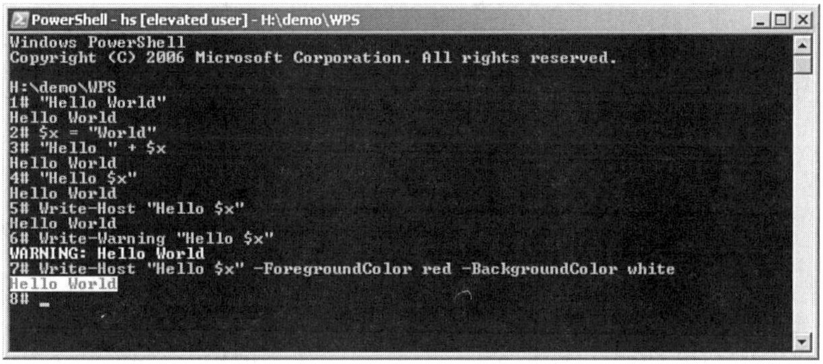

Figure 3.7 Output of constants and variables

To mix literals and variables in an output, you must either link them with +

```
$a + " can be reached at " + $b + ".
➥This information is dated: " + $c + "."
```

or integrate the variables directly in the string. In contrast to other languages, WPS evaluates the string and searches for he dollar sign (`$`) (variable resolution):

```
"$a can be reached at $b. This information is dated: $c."
```

You can also use placeholders and format markers common in .NET (for example, d = date in the long version). In addition, include the parameter `-f` after the string. Based on the format possibilities, this option is the most powerful:

```
"{0} can be reached at {1}.
➥This information is dated: {2:d}." -f $a, $b, $c
```

The following list summarizes the three equivalent possibilities:

```
$a = "Holger Schwichtenberg"
$b = "hs@windows-scripting.com"
$c = get-Date

# possibility 1
$a + " can be reached at " + $b + ".
➥This information is dated: " + $c + "."

# possibility 2
"$a can be reached at $b. This information is dated: $c."

# possibility 3
"{0} can be reached at {1}.
➥This information is dated: {2:D}." -f $a, $b, $c
```

Listing 3.1 Formatted Output (of the preceding script)

```
Holger Schwichtenberg can be reached at hs@windows-scripting.com.
➥This information is dated: 14.09.2007 16:53:13.
Holger Schwichtenberg can be reached at hs@windows-scripting.com.
➥This information is dated: 14.09.2007 16:53:13.
Holger Schwichtenberg can be reached at hs@windows-scripting.com.
➥This information is dated: Thursday, 14. September 2007.
```

Suppressing the Output

Because the standard output is in place, all return values of commandlet pipelines also display. This is not always desired.

You have three alternatives to suppress the output:

1. At the end of the pipeline, use `Out-Null`:
   `Commandlet | Commandlet | Out-Null`
2. Transfer the result of the pipeline to a variable:
   `$a = Commandlet | Commandlet`
3. Convert the result of the pipeline to type `[void]`:
   `[void] (Commandlet | Commandlet)`

Other Output Functions

The following list shows further output possibilities in WPS 1.0:

- With the commandlet `Out-Printer`, send the output to the printer.
- With `Out file`, you can write the content to a file.
- Output the process list to the standard printer:
  `Get-Process | Out-Printer`
- Output the process list to a specific printer:
  `Get-Process | Out-Printer "HP LaserJet PCL6 on E02"`
- Output the process list in a text file (overwriting existing content):
  `Get-Process | Out file "c:\temp\processlist.txt"`

- Output the process list in a text file (adding to existing content): `Get-Process | Out file "c:\temp\processlist.txt" -Append`

Getting User Input

Text input by the user may be received via `Read-Host`:

```
PS C:\Documents\hs> $name = read-host "Please enter username"
Please enter username: HS
PS C:\Documents\hs> $kennwort = read-host -assecurestring
➥"Please enter password"
Please enter password: ****
```

Input Dialog

A simple input box is provided by the function `InputBox()` (see Listing 3.2 and Figure 3.8); you might already be familiar with this input box from Visual Basic/VBScript. This function also exists in the .NET Framework in the class `Microsoft.VisualBasic.Interaction`. To use this function, you must load the assembly `Microsoft.VisualBasic.dll`. More details about loading assemblies and executing .NET methods directly are covered in a later chapter.

Listing 3.2 Simple Graphic Data Input in WPS

```
[System.Reflection.Assembly]::LoadWithPartialName
➥("Microsoft.Visual Basic")
$input = [Microsoft.Visual Basic.Interaction]::InputBox("Please
➥enter your name!")
"Hello $input!"
```

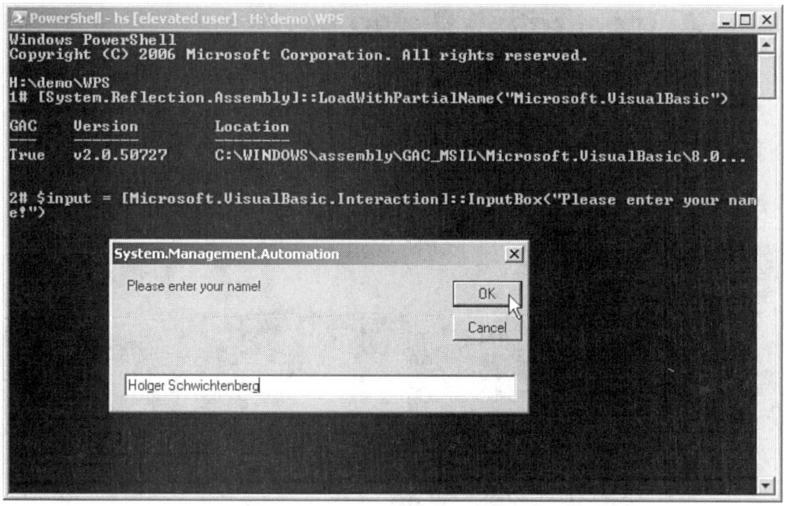

Figure 3.8 An input box in action

Dialog Boxes

To use dialog boxes, you can apply .NET classes. The script in Listing 3.3 asks the user for a decision within a dialog box (Yes/No).

Listing 3.3 Use of the Class `MessageBox` in WPS

```
[System.Reflection.Assembly]::LoadWithPartialName
➥("System.windows.forms")
[System.Console]::Beep(100, 50)
[System.Windows.Forms.MessageBox]::Show("We will ask you a
question","Advanced Warning", [System.Windows.Forms.MessageBoxKeys]::OK)

$answer = [System.Windows.Forms.MessageBox]::Show("Do you like
➥Windows PowerShell?","Headline",
➥[System.Windows.Forms.MessageBoxKeys]::YesNo)
if ($answer-eq "Yes")
{ "You agreed!" }
else
{ "You disagreed!" }
```

Authentication Dialog Box

A Windows authentication dialog box opens WPS with `Get-Credential` (see Figure 3.9). The result is an instance of `System.Management.Automation.PSCredential` with the username in plain text in `UserName` and the password coded in `Password`. In Chapter 14, "Processes and Services," you can see an example of how to use the entered credentials to start a process with a different identity.

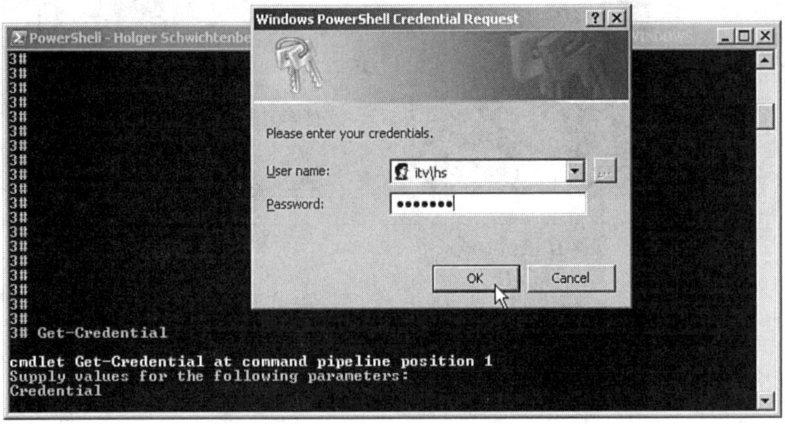

Figure 3.9 Use of `Get-Credential`

Summary

WPS commandlets can be connected through pipelines. One commandlet places objects into the pipeline, and other commandlets can access these objects. In contrast to classic shells, WPS pipelining is object oriented. This means that WPS pipelines carry structured objects rather than unstructured strings. Structured objects not only contain data, they also provide methods that can be executed.

CHAPTER 4

Advanced Pipelining

In this chapter:

This chapter includes advanced Windows PowerShell (WPS) pipelining features such as filtering, sorting, grouping, comparing, and calculating. The chapter introduces a few commandlets that are commonly used (for example, `Where-Object`, `Sort-Object`, `Group-Object`, and `Get-Member`).

Analyzing Pipeline Content

One of the greatest challenges in working with WPS is to answer the following two questions:

1. Which type do the objects, which are placed in the pipeline by a commandlet, have?
2. Which properties and methods do these objects have?

The commandlets' help is not always "helpful" here. In `Get-Service`, you can read the following:

```
RETURN TYPE
    System.ServiceProcess.ServiceController
```

But in `Get-Process`, it is not much help; it says only this:

```
RETURN TYPE
    Object
```

The WPS documentation ([MS01] and [MS02]) will not help you at all with the properties and methods of the resulting objects. You will find these only in the MSDN documentation about .NET Framework.

The following two helpful commandlets are introduced, which will help you in everyday work with WPS to learn what you really have in the pipeline:

```
Get-PipelineInfo
Get-Member
```

Get-PipelineInfo

The commandlet `Get-PipelineInfo` from the PowerShell Extensions of www.IT-Visions.de, delivers three important pieces of information about the pipeline contents (see Figure 4.1):

- Number of objects in the pipeline (the objects are numbered)
- Type of objects in the pipeline (name of .NET class)
- String representations of objects in the pipeline

The phrase *string representation* needs to be explained: Each .NET object has a method `ToString()`, which changes the object into a string, as `ToString()` is implemented in the "mother of all .NET classes," `System.Object`, and is passed on to all .NET classes and thus to all their instances. Whether `ToString()` delivers a sensible output depends on the relative class. In the case of `System.Diagnostics.Process`, the class name and process name are delivered. You can easily get this with `gps | foreach { $_.ToString() }` (see Figure 4.2). On the other hand, the conversion of class `System.ServiceProcess.ServiceController`, whose instances are delivered by `Get-Service`, is not so good, because the string contains only the class name, so the single instances cannot be diversified (see Figure 4.3).

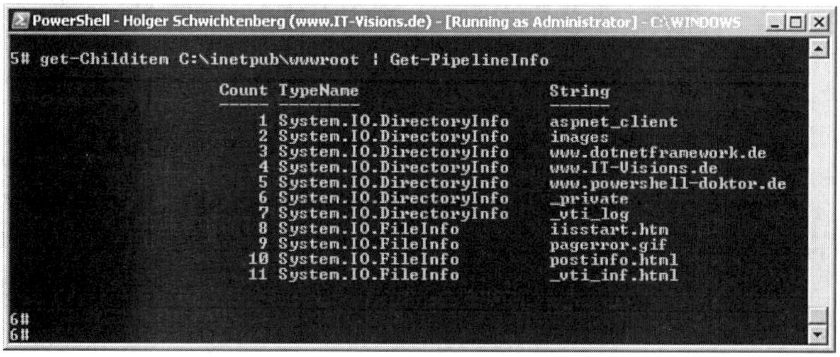

Figure 4.1 `Get_PipelineInfo` tells us that there are 11 objects in the data directory, 7 of which are subregistries (class `DirectoryInfo`) and 4 which are files (class `FileInfo`).

NOTE The conversion into the class name is the standard behavior, inherited from `System.Object`, and this standard behavior unfortunately is customary, because the developers of most of the .NET classes at Microsoft did not take the initiative to define a sensible string representation.

`ToString()` generally is not a serialization of the complete object content, but only mirrors the prime key of the object.

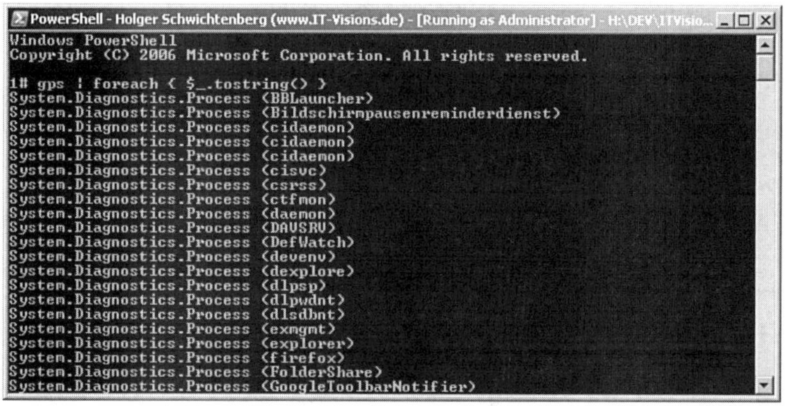

Figure 4.2 Use of `ToString()` on instances of class `System.Diagnostics.Process`

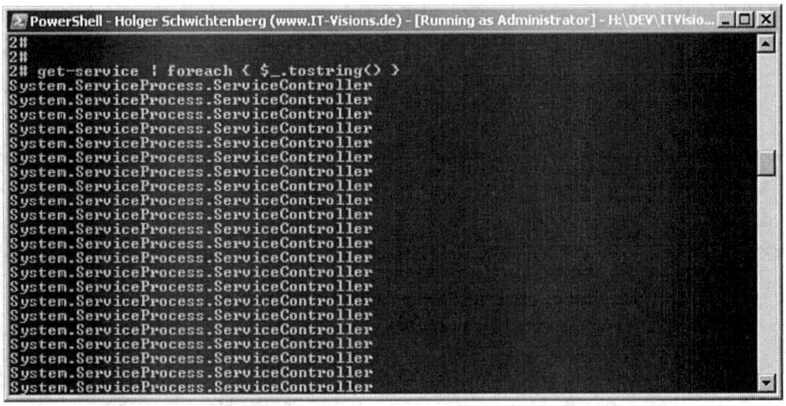

Figure 4.3 Use of `ToString()` on instances of class `System.ServiceProcess.ServiceController`

Get-Member

The commandlet `Get-Member` (alias `gm`) is another helpful commandlet: It shows the .NET class name of the objects in the pipeline and the properties and methods of this class. The output of `Get-Process | Get-Member` is so long that you need two screenshots for the presentation (see Figures 4.4 and 4.5). `Get-Member` is included in the basic WPS 1.0 commandlet set.

NOTE If there are different kinds of object types in the pipeline, members of all types are displayed, grouped according to the head section, starting with `TypeName`.

The output shows that from a WPS point of view, a .NET class has seven kinds of members:

- Methods
- Properties
- Property sets
- Note properties
- Script properties
- Code properties
- Alias properties

NOTE Concerning the previously mentioned member forms, only Method and Property are actual members of the .NET class. All other kinds of members are extensions, which WPS has added to the .NET object via the previously mentioned Extended Type System (ETS).

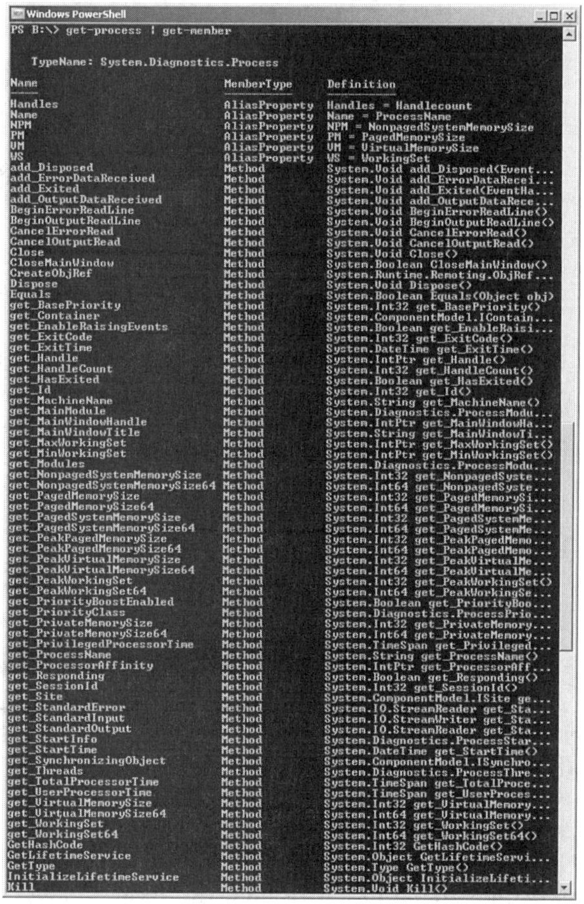

Figure 4.4 Part 1 of the output of `Get-Process | Get-Member`

4. Advanced Pipelining

Figure 4.5 Part 2 of the output of `Get-Process | Get-Member`

Methods are operations that you can call on an object and that will start an action, such as `Kill()`, which ends the process. Methods, however, may also display data or change data within an object.

WARNING To call a method, you must use parentheses at all times, even if there are no parameters. Without parentheses, you will get only information about the method; you will not call the method itself.

Properties are data elements that contain information about an object or with which information can be transferred to an object (for example, `MaxWorkingSet`). In the screenshots with the output of `Get-Process | Get-Member`, it is remarkable that there are two methods for each property (for example, `get_MaxWorkingSet()` and `set_MaxWorkingSet()`). The cause for this lies within the internals of the .NET Framework: Here properties (*not fields*) are mapped by a pair of methods—one method to fetch the data (called "get" method or Getter), and another method to set the data (called "set" method or Setter).

This means that for you, as the WPS user, you have two possibilities to call data:

- By using the property

  ```
  Get-Process | Where-Object { $_.name -eq "iexplore" } |
  Foreach-Object { $_.MaxWorkingSet }
  ```

- By using the relevant "get" method

  ```
  Get-Process | Where-Object { $_.name -eq "iexplore" } |
  Foreach-Object { $_.get_MaxWorkingSet() }
  ```

Likewise, you have the option to use the property as follows:

```
Get-Process | Where-Object { $_.name -eq "iexplore" } |
Foreach-Object { $_.MaxWorkingSet = 1413120 }
```

Alternatively, you can use the relevant "set" method:

```
Get-Process | Where-Object { $_.name -eq "iexplore" } |
Foreach-Object { $_.set_MaxWorkingSet(1413120) }
```

TIP The beginner might not be so happy about these options as they inflate the output; the advanced user will like it. In the end, there is a great advantage provided by the listing of getters and setters, besides the syntactical freedom. You can recognize which actions are possible on a property. If the setter is missing, the property cannot be changed (for example, `StartTime` in the class `Process`). If the getter is missing, you can set only one property. There is no example for this scenario in the class `Process`. Furthermore, this scenario is much rarer, but becomes evident with keywords, which cannot be regained because they were not saved in plain text, but only as hash values.

Property sets are a summary of a number of properties under one umbrella. For example, the property set `psRessources` covers all properties that refer to the resource use of a process. Therefore, you do not have to name the single property. You can write the following instead:

```
Get-Process | Select-Object psRessources | Format-Table
```

The developers of WPS thought of many things, but did not cover everything. For instance, for one process the preceding command leads to the failure report "Access is denied"; the pseudo-process "Idle" cannot be asked for `TotalProcessorTime` (see Figure 4.6).

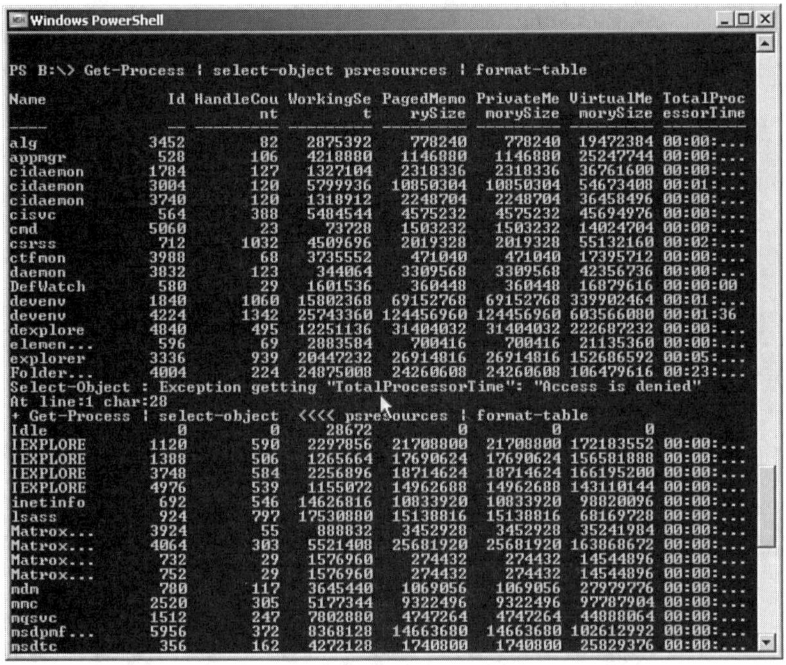

Figure 4.6 The WPS developers didn't address the special status of the pseudo-process "Idle."

Property sets do not exist in .NET Framework; they are a specialty of WPS and are defined in the file `types.ps1xml` in the installation directory of WPS (see Figure 4.7).

```
<PropertySet>
    <Name>PSConfiguration</Name>
    <ReferencedProperties>
        <Name>Name</Name>
        <Name>Id</Name>
        <Name>PriorityClass</Name>
        <Name>FileVersion</Name>
    </ReferencedProperties>
</PropertySet>
<PropertySet>
    <Name>PSResources</Name>
    <ReferencedProperties>
        <Name>Name</Name>
        <Name>Id</Name>
        <Name>Handlecount</Name>
        <Name>WorkingSet</Name>
        <Name>NonPagedMemorySize</Name>
        <Name>PagedMemorySize</Name>
        <Name>PrivateMemorySize</Name>
        <Name>VirtualMemorySize</Name>
        <Name>Threads.Count</Name>
        <Name>TotalProcessorTime</Name>
    </ReferencedProperties>
</PropertySet>
```

Figure 4.7 Definition of the property sets for the class `System.Diagnostics.Process` in `types.ps1ml`

Note properties are additional data elements that do not come from the data source, but have been added by the WPS infrastructure. In the class process, it's `__NounName`, which gives a shortened name to the class. Other classes have numerous note properties. Note properties do not exist in .NET Framework; they are a specialty of PowerShell.

A *script property* is a calculating property that is not saved within the object itself. This does not mean that the calculation has to be a mathematical one; it can also be the access to the properties of a subobject. The following command lists all processes with those products belonging to the relevant processes (see Figure 4.8):

```
Get-Process | Select-Object name, product
```

This is good to keep in mind when you are looking in your system at a process that you do not know and that you might take for a virus.

The information about the product cannot be found in the process (Windows does not list this information in the Task Manager either), but in the file, which contains the program code for the process. The .NET Framework offers access to this information via `MainModule.FileversionInfo.ProductName`. Microsoft offers a shortcut of the command:

```
Get-Process | Select-Object name,
➥Mainmodule.FileVersionInfo.ProductName
```

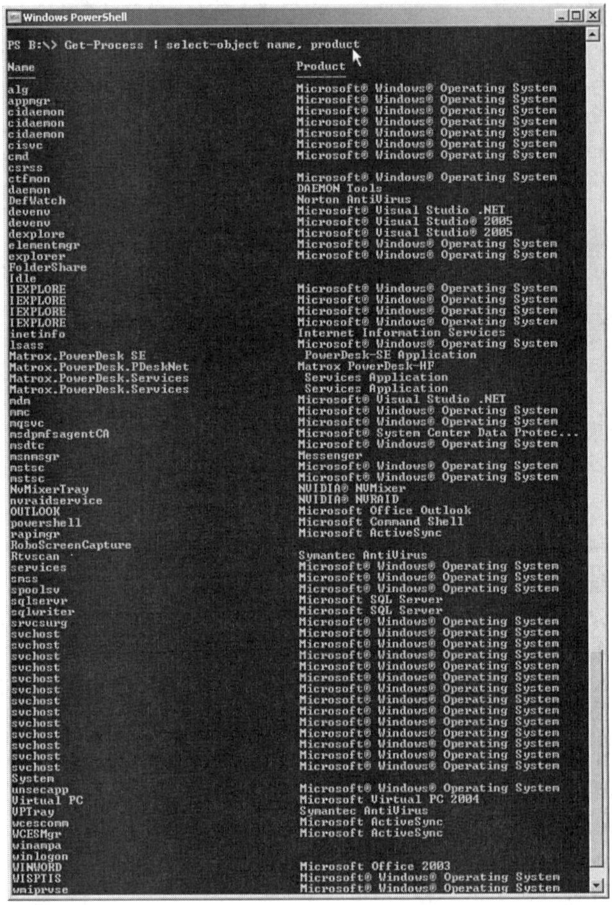

Figure 4.8 Listing of the calculating property Product

Microsoft offers this shortcut via the script property. This shortcut is defined in the file `types.ps1xml` in the installation directory of WPS (see Figure 4.9).

Script properties do not exist in .NET Framework; they are a specialty of WPS.

A *code property* equals a script property; the program code, however, is not given as script in WPS language, but as .NET code.

An *alias property* is a short form for a property. It is not based on a calculation, but on a shortening of the name. For example, `WS` is short for `WorkingSet`. The alias properties are also defined in the file `types.ps1xml` in the installation directory of WPS. Alias properties are also a WPS specialty.

```
<ScriptProperty>
    <Name>Product</Name>
    <GetScriptBlock>$this.Mainmodule.FileVersionInfo.ProductName</GetScriptBlock>
</ScriptProperty>
```

Figure 4.9 Definition of a script property in `types.ps1xml`

More Information about Get-Member

You can reduce the output of `Get-Member` by limiting it to a certain kind of members. You can accomplish this with the parameter `-Membertype` (or `-m`). The following command lists only properties:

```
Get-Process | Get-Member -Membertype Properties
```

Furthermore, you can set a name filter:

```
Get-Process | Get-Member *set*
```

The preceding command lists only those members of the class `Process` whose names contain the word *set*.

Extended Type System (ETS)

As already pointed out, WPS shows for many .NET objects more members than there are actually defined in the class. In some cases, however, members are suppressed. This is accomplished through the ETS.

The extension of members via ETS is applied to enable the WPS user to display data directly from some .NET classes, which are meta classes for the actual data (for example, `ManagementObject` for WMI objects, `ManagementClass` for WMI classes, `DirectoryEntry` for entries in directory services, and `DataRow` for data rows).

Members are suppressed when they are not usable in WPS or if there are better alternatives via extensions.

In the documentation, you find the following commentary from the WPS development team: "Some .NET object members are inconsistently named, provide an insufficient set of public members, or provide insufficient capability. ETS resolves this issue by introducing the ability to extend the .NET object with additional members." [MSDN04] Simply put, this means that the WPS team is not really satisfied with the development team's work with the .NET class library.

The ETS generally packs each object, which had been placed in the pipeline by a commandlet, into a WPS object, type `PSObject`. Then, the implementation of the class `PSObject` decides what remains visible for the following commandlets and commands.

This decision is influenced by different instruments:

- WPS object adapters that have been implemented for certain types, such as `ManagementObject`, `ManagementClass`, `DirectoryEntry`, and `DataRow`
- Declarations in the *types.ps1xml* file
- Members added in the commandlets
- Members added through the use of the commandlet `Add-Member`

Filtering Objects

Often, you will not process all objects displayed by a commandlet. Limitation criteria are conditions (for example, only processes with a cost greater than 10000000 bytes) or positions (for example, only the five processes with the greatest cost). As a means of limitation, you can use the commandlet `Where-Object` (alias `where`).

You can define limitations via conditions with `Where-Object`:

```
Get-Process | Where-Object {$_.ws -gt 10000000 }
```

Limitations via the position are defined with `Select-Object`. (In the following command, for the previously named example, an additional sorting is integrated, to get a sensible output.)

```
Get-Process | Sort-Object ws -desc | Select-Object -first 5
```

Likewise, you can display the process with lowest cost as follows:

```
Get-Process | Sort-Object ws -desc | Select-Object -last 5
```

You might find it difficult to get used to the syntax of the relational operators. Instead of >= you write `-ge` (see Tables 4.1 and 4.2). The use of regular expressions is possible with the operator `-Match`. (For example, the following expression lists all Windows services with a display name that consists of exactly two words separated by a white space; see Figure 4.10.)

```
Get-Service | Where-Object { $_.DisplayName -match
➥"^\w* \w*$" }
```

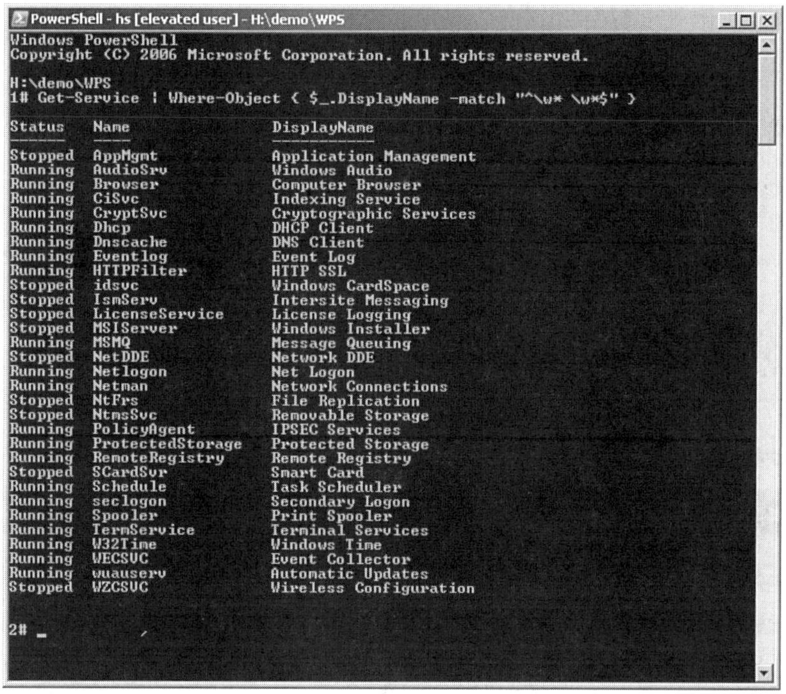

Figure 4.10 Services with two words in the display name

The syntax of regular expressions in .NET is not discussed in detail in this book. For more information about such, refer to [MSDN08].

Table 4.1 Relational Operators in WPS Syntax

Comparison with Case Sensitivity	Comparison with Case Insensitivity	Meaning
`-lt`	`-ilt`	Smaller
`-le`	`-ile`	Smaller or even
`-gt`	`-igt`	Greater
`-ge`	`-ige`	Greater or even
`-eq`	`-ieq`	Even
`-ne`	`-ine`	Not even
`-like`	`-ilike`	Similarity between strings, use of placeholders (`*` and `?`) possible
`-notlike`	`-inotlike`	No similarity between strings, use of placeholders (`*` and `?`) possible
`-match`		Comparison with regular expression
`-notmatch`		Does not comply with regular expression
`-is`		Type comparison

Table 4.2 Logical Operators in WPS Syntax

Logical Operator	Meaning
`-not` or `!`	Not
`-and`	And
`-or`	Or

Aggregation of Pipeline Content

The number of objects in the pipeline may be heterogeneous. For example, this is automatically the case when `Get-Childitem` is executed in the file system: The result contains `FileInfo` and `DirectoryInfo` objects.

You can also link two commands, which both send objects to the pipeline, so that the content of the pipeline looks like this (see Figure 4.11):

```
$( Get-Process ; Get-Service )
```

But this is only sensible when the following commands in the pipeline are able to handle heterogeneous pipeline content correctly. The standard expression can do this. In other cases, the type of the first object conditions the kind of processing in the pipeline (for example, with `Export-Csv`).

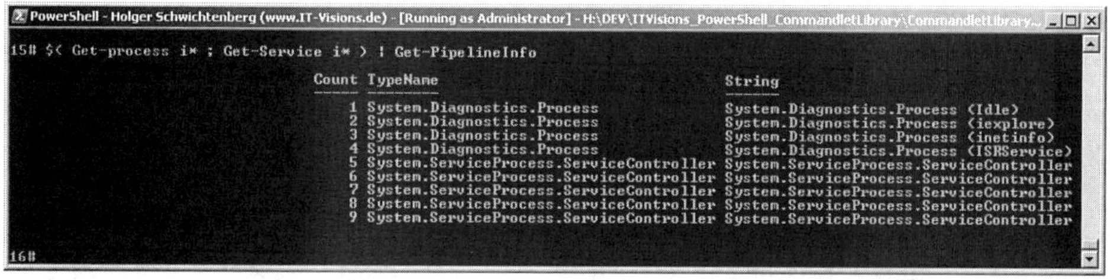

Figure 4.11 Use of `GetPipelineInfo` on a heterogeneous pipeline

Castrating Objects

The analysis of the pipeline content shows that there are often many members in the objects in the pipeline. Generally, however, you need only a few. Not only for reasons of space saving, but also because of concern for clarity, it is worth the effort to "castrate" objects in the pipeline.

With the command `Select-Object`, you can castrate an object in the pipeline. (that is, (almost) all object members are deleted from the pipeline, except those members explicitly mentioned behind `Select-Object`).

For example, the command

```
Get-Process | Select-Object processname, get_minworkingset,
➥ws | Get-Member
```

keeps only the members `processname` (property), `get_minworkingset` (method), and `workingset` (alias) of the `Process` objects in the pipeline (see Figure 4.12). As Figure 4.12 shows, castrating doesn't work without pain:

- `Get-Member` does not show the actual class name any longer, but instead shows `PSCustomObject`, a special class of WPS.
- All members are degraded to note properties.

That there are four more members in the list besides the three desired ones is easily explained. Each (that means really each single .NET object) has these four methods because they are derived from the basic class `System.Object` and inherited by each .NET class and thus each .NET object.

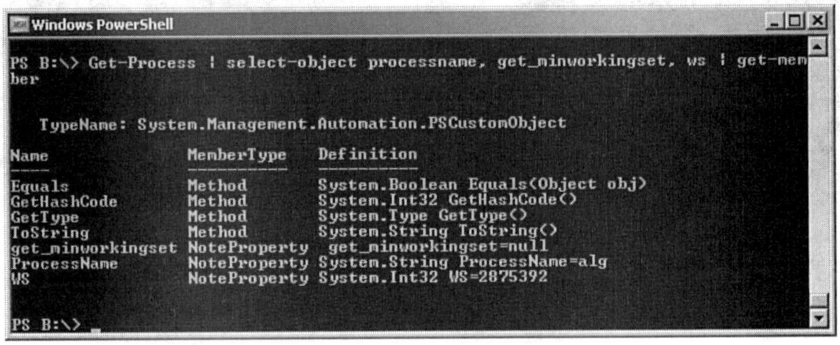

Figure 4.12 Effect of `Select-Object`

TIP With the parameter `-exclude`, you can also exclude single members in `Select-Object`.

Sorting Objects

With `Sort-Object` (alias `sort`), you can sort objects in the pipeline based on the properties previously mentioned. The standard sorting direction is in ascending order.

The following command sorts processes in a descending order according to their cost:

```
Get-Process | sort ws -desc
```

Grouping Objects

With `Group-Object`, you can group objects in the pipeline according to their properties.

With the following command, you can display how many system services are running and how many have been stopped:

```
PS B:\Scripte> Get-Service | Group-Object status
Count Name                    Group
----- ----                    -----
   64 Running                 {AeLookupSvc, ALG, AppMgmt, appmgr...}
   54 Stopped                 {Alerter, aspnet_state, ClipSrv,
                              ➥clr_optimiz...
```

The second example groups the files in the *System32* directory according to the file extension and sorts the grouping afterward in a descending order according to the number of files in each group (see Figure 4.13).

```
Get-ChildItem c:\windows\system32 | Group-Object Extension |
Sort -Object count -desc
```

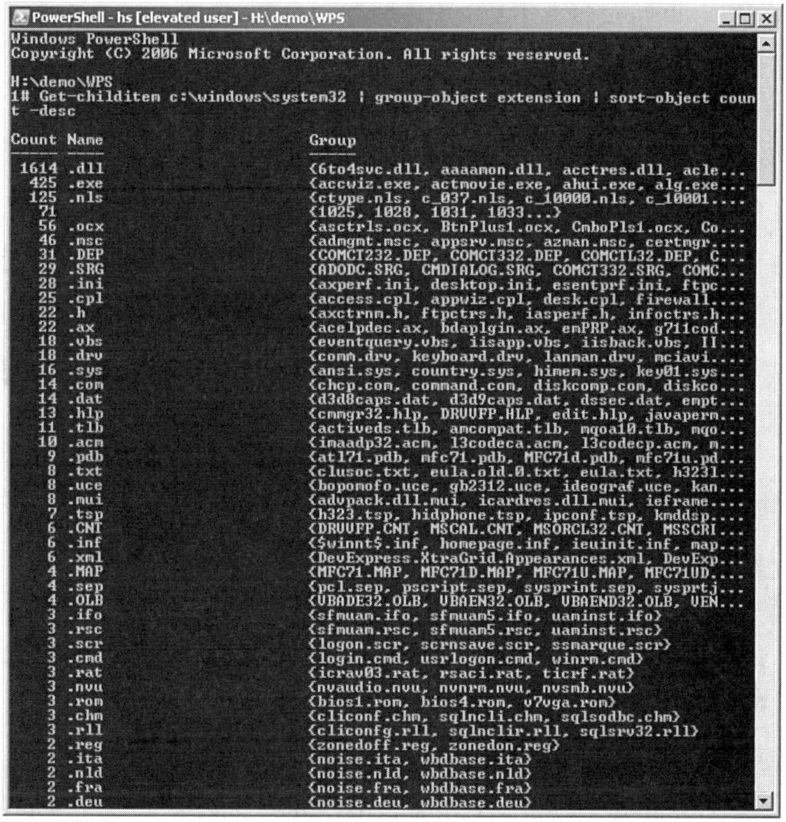

Figure 4.13 Use of `Group-Object` and `Sort-Object`

TIP When the only purpose is to display groups and not to determine the frequency of group elements, you can use `Select-Object` with the parameter `-unique` for grouping:

```
Get-ChildItem | Select-Object extension -Unique
```

Calculations

`Measure-Object` executes various calculations (number, average, sum, minimum, maximum) for objects in the pipeline. Here you should name the property that is the subject of the calculation, because the first property is a often text that cannot be processed mathematically.

For example, to access information about the files in *c:\Windows* use the following (see Figure 4.14):

```
Get-ChildItem c:\windows | Measure-Object -Property
➥length -min -max -average -sum
```

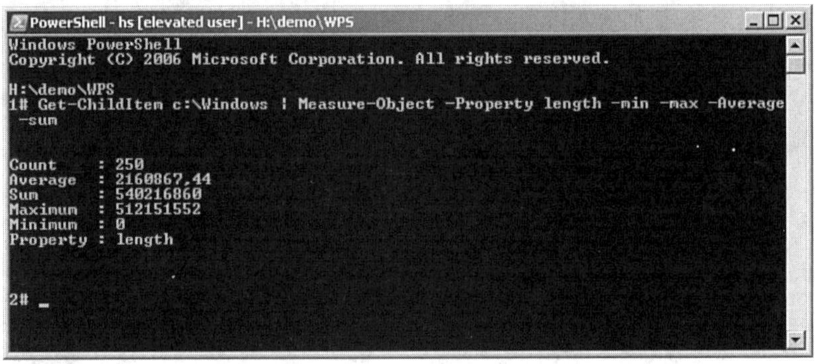

Figure 4.14 Example for the use of `Measure-Object`

Intermediate Steps in the Pipeline

A command in the pipeline may be as long as you want, and therefore also as complex. When a command becomes unclear or you want to have a closer look at the intermediate steps in the pipeline, you should buffer the content of the pipeline. WPS offers to file the content of the pipeline in variables. Variables are marked by a preceding dollar sign (`$`). Instead of

```
Get-Process | Where-Object {$_.name -eq "iexplore"} |
➥Foreach-Object { $_.ws }
```

you can also enter the following commands one after another in separate lines in the shell window:

```
$x = Get-Process
$y = $x | Where-Object {$_.name -eq "iexplore"}
$y | Foreach-Object { $_.ws }
```

The result is the same in both cases.

The access to variables without content does not produce a failure as long as you do not use commandlets later in the pipeline, where objects in the pipeline will definitely be anticipated (see Figure 4.15).

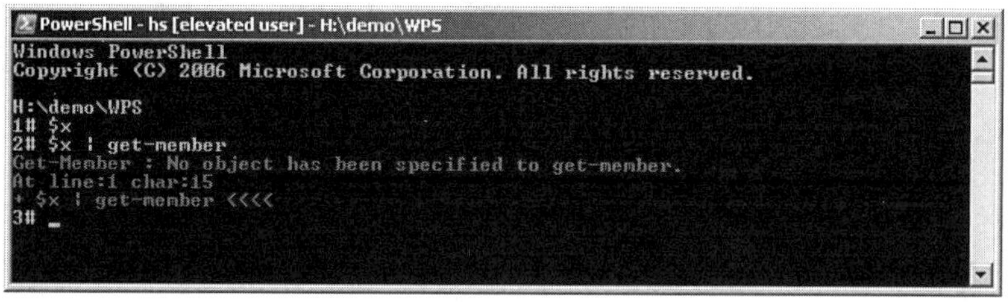

Figure 4.15 Access to variables without content

TIP A filled variable can be cleared with the commandlet `Clear-Variable`. Here, you should write the name of the variable without the dollar sign, as follows:

```
Clear-Variable x
```

Comparing Objects

With `Compare-Object`, you can compare the content of two pipelines. The following command sequence displays all processes started during a certain interim (see Figure 4.16):

```
$before = Get-Process
# Start a new process
$after = Get-Process
Compare-Object $before $after
```

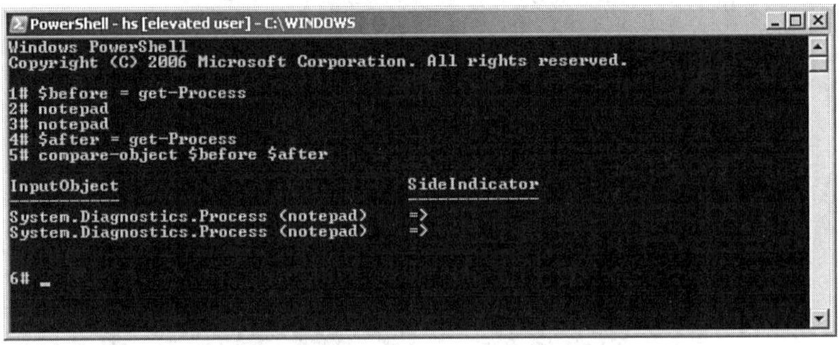

Figure 4.16 Comparison of two pipelines

Ramifications

Sometimes you want to pass on the result not only in the pipeline, but also in a variable or within the file system. The commandlet `Tee-Object` is used for ramifications within the pipeline, with the *Tee* standing for *ramify*. `Tee-Object` passes the content of the pipeline on in an unchanged condition to the next commandlet, but also offers to file the content of the pipeline in a variable or in the file system, according to your choice.

The following command uses `Tee-Object` two times for both use cases:

```
Get-Service | Tee-Object -var a | Where-Object { $_.Status
➥-eq "Running" } | Tee-Object -filepath g:\services.txt
```

After execution of the command, the variable `$a` provides a list of all services, and the TXT file `services.txt` has a list of all running services.

WARNING Note that when using `Tee-Object` with the parameter `-variable`, you must write the name of the variable without the usual variable marker `$`.

Summary

This chapter introduced you to some commandlets that provide helpful functions in WPS pipelines, including the following:

- `Where-Object` for filtering
- `Sort-Object` for sorting
- `Group-Object` for grouping
- `Measure-Object` for calculating sum, average, minimum, and maximum
- `Compare-Objects` for comparing pipelines

In addition, we discussed various WSP variables. You learned about the dollar sign (`$`) variable, for example, which enables you to store any content, including the full content of a pipeline. As discussed, you use variables to compare pipelines and to store the content of a pipeline for later use.

CHAPTER 5

The PowerShell Navigation Model

In this chapter:

Besides object pipelining, Windows PowerShell (WPS) has another interesting concept to offer: the uniform navigation paradigm for all kinds of data. The call of the command `Get-PSDrive` not only lists expected drives but also environment variables (`env`), the registry (`HKCU`, `HKLM`), Windows certificate store (`cert`), PowerShell aliases (`Alias`), PowerShell variables (`Variable`), and PowerShell functions (`Function`). WPS interprets this data also as drives. Consequently, you have to use a colon in the call: `Get-ChildItem Alias:` lists all defined aliases, just like `Get-Alias`.

Navigation through the Registry

In the registry, the administrator can work with the same commands as in the file system. Examples for valid registry commands include the following (see Figure 5.1):

- Navigation to *HKEY_LOCAL_MACHINE/Software*:

```
cd hklm:\software
```

This is the short form of the following:

```
Set-Location hklm:\software
```

- Listing of the subkeys of the current key:

```
Dir
```

This is an abbreviation for the following:

```
Get-ChildItem
```

- Creating a subkey with the name IT-Visions:

```
md IT-Visions
```

- Creating a subkey with a standard value:

```
New-Item  -Name  "Website" -Value "www.IT-Visions.de"
➥-type String
```

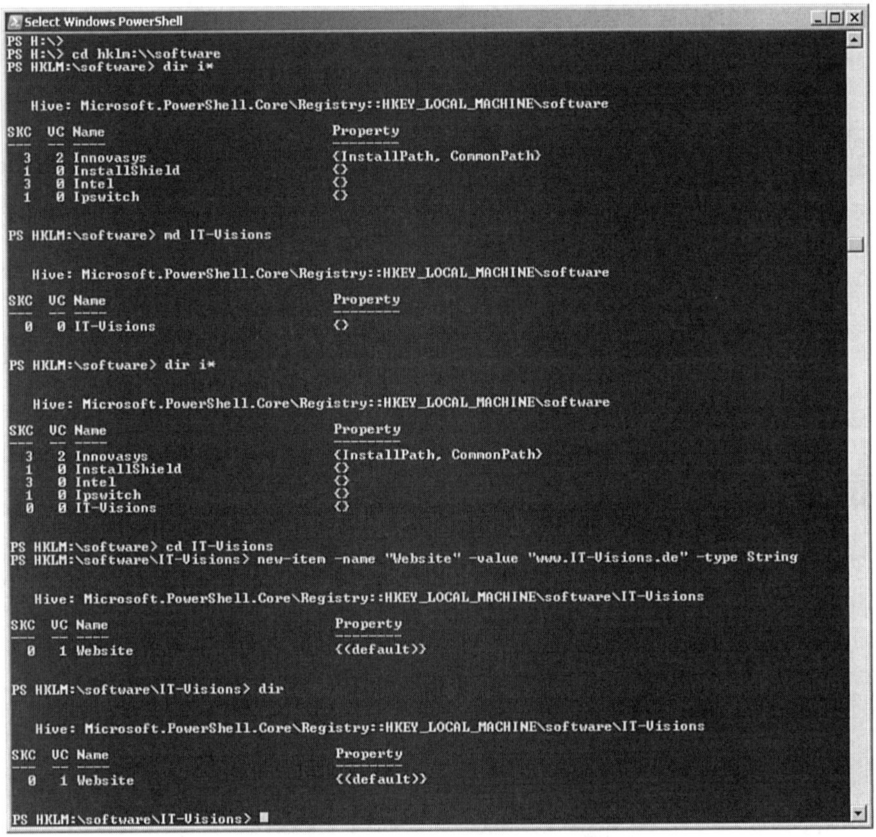

Figure 5.1 Navigation in and manipulation of the registry

Providers and Drives

`Get-PSDrive` shows that there are different "drive" providers. Normal drives belong to the provider FileSystem (FS). Microsoft calls the providers *navigation providers* or *commandlet providers*, and wants to treat all data equally with the same basic verbs (`Get`, `Set`, `New`, `Remove`, and so on), regardless of whether they are flat or hierarchical. The number of providers and the number of drives can be extended.

WPS 1.0 contains the following drives (see Figure 5.2):

- Windows file system (`A`, `B`, `C`, `D`, `E`, and so on)
- Windows registry (`HKCU`, `HKLM`)
- Windows environment variables (`env`)
- Windows certificate store (`cert`)
- Functions of PowerShell (`function`)
- Variables of PowerShell (`variable`)
- Aliases of PowerShell (`alias`)

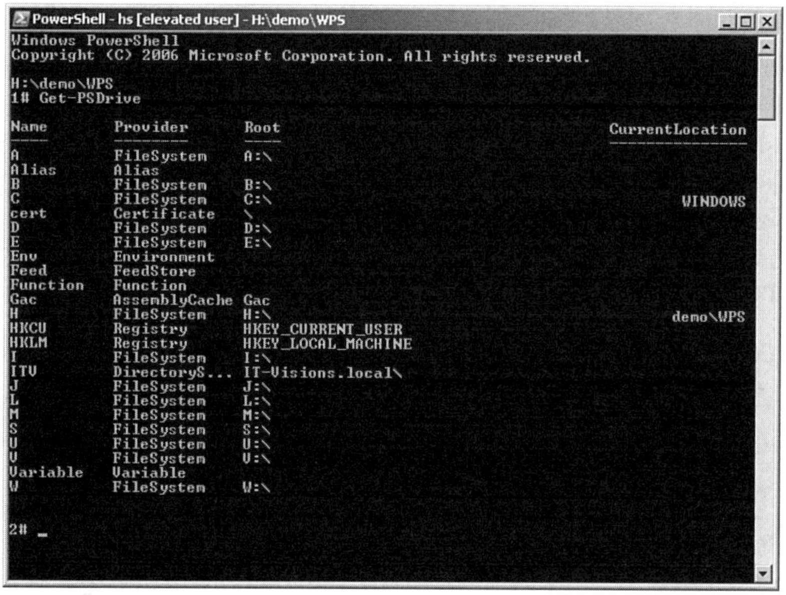

Figure 5.2 From the point of view of WPS, environment variables, aliases, and registries are drives, too.

The Active Directory can also be ruled by this navigation paradigm. Earlier beta versions of WPS contained a provider for this; however, it did not make it into the final version. The Active Directory provider is now available as part of the PowerShell Community Extensions (PCSX) [CODEPLEX01].

TIP You can see all installed providers with `Get-PSProvider`.

Table 5.1 Available WPS Providers

Provider	Source	Drives
Alias	WPS 1.0	Alias
Environment	WPS 1.0	Env
File system	WPS 1.0	A, B, C, D, and so on
Function	WPS 1.0	Function
Registry	WPS 1.0	HKLM, HKCU
Variable	WPS 1.0	Variable
Certificate	WPS 1.0	cert
RSS feed store	PCSX 1.1.1 [CODEPLEX01]	Feed
Assembly cache	PCSX 1.1.1 [CODEPLEX01]	Gac
Directory services	PCSX 1.1.1 [CODEPLEX01]	Windows NT 4.0-compatible name of domain
Windows SharePoint services or SharePoint Portal Server	WPS SharePoint provider [CODEPLEX02]	Any name

Navigation Commandlets

Table 5.2 shows the commandlets applicable for navigation.

Table 5.2 Navigation Commandlets

Commandlet	Aliases	Description
`Get-ChildItem`	`dir, ls`	Listing of children
`Get-Cwd`	`cd, pwd`	Change of location
`Get-Content`	`type, cat`	Call of element content
`New-Item`	`mkdir`	Creation of an item (branch or leave)
`Get-Location`		Call of the current location
`Set-Location`	`Cd`	Setting of the current location

Paths

Path indications in WPS support two different placeholders as well as the following:

- One dot (`.`) stands for the current directory.
- Two dots (`..`) stand for the parent directory.
- The tilde (~) stands for the profile directory of the current user (shown Figure 5.4).
- Brackets stand for one of the characters within the bracket.

Consider this example. The following command lists all files of a Windows directory that begin with the letter *A*, *B*, *C*, or *W* (see Figure 5.3):

```
Get-ChildItem c:\windows\[abcw]*.*
```

Alternatively you can also write the following:

```
Get-ChildItem c:\windows\[a-cw]*.*
```

Several commandlets offer support to navigate through WPS drives.

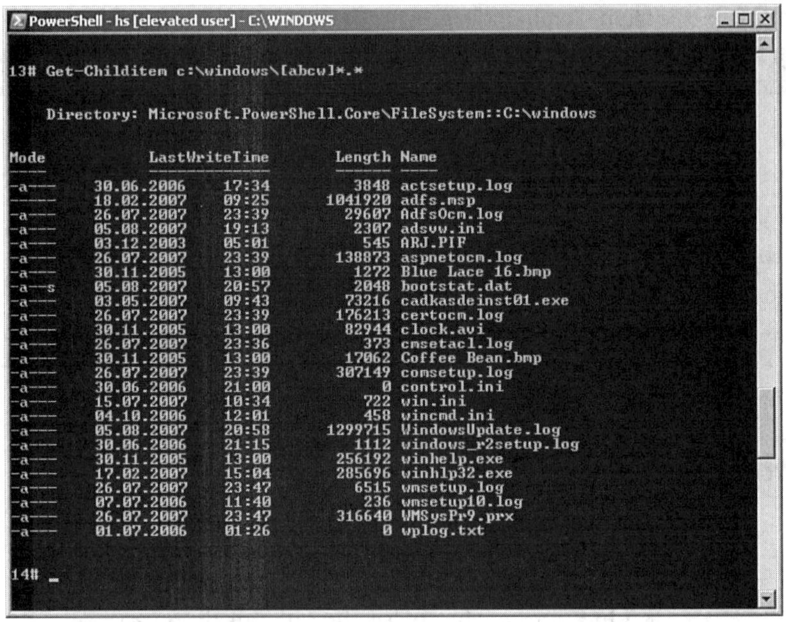

Figure 5.3 Use of placeholders

`Test-Path` checks whether there is a path. The result is `True` or `False` (`System.Boolean`):

```
Test-Path c:\temp
Test-Path HKLM:\software\IT-Visions
```

`Resolve-Path` resolves placeholders in paths and displays the resulting path as an object of the type `System.Management.Automation.PathInfo` (see Figure 5.4).

Many commandlets display path indications of the type `System.Management.Automation.PathInfo`. To convert this into a simple string (which, however, will be provider specific), you can use the commandlet `Convert-Path`.

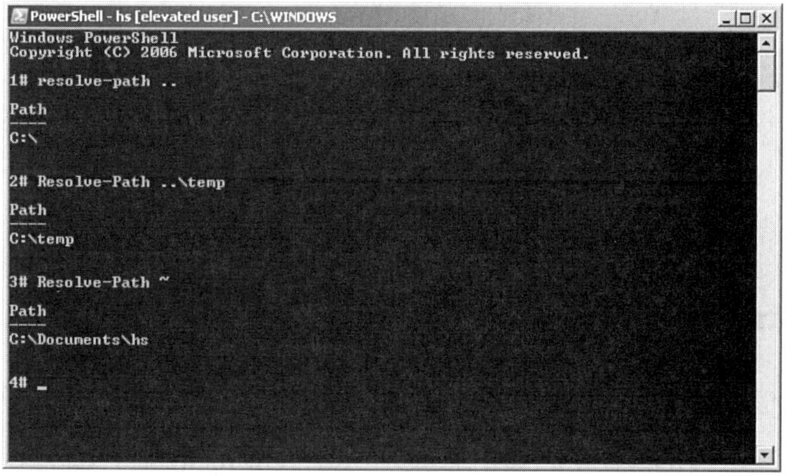

Figure 5.4 Use of `Resolve-Path`

Defining Drives

The navigation model of WPS allows the definition of new drives, which can then be used as shortcuts for (complex) paths.

The following command defines a new drive, Scripts, as an alias for a file system path:

```
New-PSDrive -Name Scripts -PSProvider FileSystem -Root
"h:\Scripts\PowerShell\"
```

After this, you can access the path by just writing the following:

```
Dir Scripts:
```

WARNING The newly defined drive functions only within WPS and is not applicable in other Windows applications. To be precise, the new drive functions only within the *current instance* of WPS. Two WPS windows do not share such declarations! If you like to have certain custom drives by default in all WPS consoles, you must add the `New -Drive` command to the WPS profile script (see Chapter 10, "Tips, Tricks, and Troubleshooting").

You can define shortcuts for the registry, too:

```
New-PSDrive -Name Software -PSProvider Registry -Root
HKLM:\SOFTWARE\Microsoft\Windows\CurrentVersion\Uninstall
```

The number of drives is by default limited to 4,096. You can change this with the variable `$MaximumDriveCount`.

Summary

After object-oriented pipelining, the navigation model is the second biggest innovation of WPS. The navigation model enables you to use different stores, such as the registry, environment variables, the certificate store, and even the variables in WPS to be treated as a file system, where you can navigate and operate with well-known commands such as `dir`, `cd`, `md`, and `rd`. These well-known commands, however, are just short forms (aliases or functions) for WPS commandlets.

CHAPTER 6

THE POWERSHELL SCRIPT LANGUAGE

In this chapter:

Besides the commandlet infrastructure, Windows PowerShell (WPS) offers its own scripting language for the creation of command sequences in the classic imperative programming style. The PowerShell Script Language (PSL) includes variables, loops, conditions, functions and error handling.

Microsoft did not use an existing script language as the basis for this new creation, but was, according to their own words, "inspired" by the UNIX shell languages, PERL, PHP, Python, and C#. As a consequence, the language uses curly brackets; semicolons, however, are not needed as separators.

Getting Help

The language constructs of WPS, just like the WPS commandlets, is explained in simple, purely text-based help documents that are installed along with WPS. Help documents for the language constructs begin with "About." For example, the command

```
Get-Help About_for
```

displays help for the `for` loop.

The command

```
Get-Help About
```

shows a list of all "About" documents.

Command Separation

Each line in WPS script is a command. A command may consist of several commandlets, separated by the pipe symbol (`|`). You can place several commands in one line, separated by a semicolon (`;`). You can also use the semicolons at the end of each line, just as in C++ und C#, but you do not have to.

Should one command fill several lines, the use of an inverted comma (`` ` ``) at the end of a line indicates that the next line should be added to the command:

```
gps | `
format-list
```

Comments

Comments are marked with the symbol #:

```
# Comment
```

Variables

Variables start with the variable symbol `$`. Variable names can consist of letters and numbers, as well as an underscore. Names, which have already been given to predefined variables, especially the name `$_`, are not valid.

Set the Type

Variables are either untyped

```
$a = 5
```

or explicitly typed on a WPS data type (also known as *type accelerator*) or any .NET class:

```
$a = [int] 5
$a = [System.DateTime] "1.8.1972"
```

You can use all .NET class names as type names, as well as some predefined WPS type names. For example, `[int]`, `[System.Int32]`, and `[int32]` are completely identical. `[int]` is the integrated WPS type indicator for whole numbers with a length of 32 bits. Internally, this is the .NET class `[System.Int32]`. This name, however, can be shortened to `[int32]`.

TIP The use of a type name in front of a variable assignment (for example, `[int] $a = 5`) limits the variable to accept only data of this type, and is thus related to the classic syntax in languages such as C++, Java und C#.

A variable is implicitly declared by an assignment of a value and is valid within the relevant scope in which it had been declared (for example, a block, a subroutine, or within the whole script). With `Remove-Variable`, you can remove a variable declaration.

If variables do not have to be declared explicitly, there is always the danger that typing errors may cause undesired effects. With the command `Set-PSDebug -Strict`, you can make sure that WPS reports a failure if you use a variable that has not yet been assigned a value.

In the following example, WPS reports a failure in the last command, because `$y` is valid only within the block marked by curly brackets:

```
Set-PSDebug -Strict
$x = 5
{
$y = 5
$x
}
$y
```

Available Types

Table 6.1 shows all available type accelerators. You will find descriptions of some of them (for example, `[WMI]` and `[ADSI]`) later in this book.

Table 6.1 WPS Type Accelerators

[int]	typeof(int)
[int[]]	typeof(int[])
[long]	typeof(long)
[long[]]	typeof(long[])
[string]	typeof(string)
[string[]]	typeof(string[])
[char]	typeof(char)
[char[]]	typeof(char[])
[bool]	typeof(bool)
[bool[]]	typeof(bool[])
[byte]	typeof(byte)
[double]	typeof(double)
[decimal]	typeof(decimal)
[float]	typeof(float)
[single]	typeof(float)
[regex]	typeof(System.Text.RegularExpressions.Regex)
[array]	typeof(System.Array)

[xml]	typeof(System.Xml.XmlDocument)
[scriptblock]	typeof(System.Management.Automation.ScriptBlock)
[switch]	typeof(System.Management.Automation.SwitchParameter)
[hashtable]	typeof(System.Collections.Hashtable)
[type]	typeof(System.Type)
[ref]	typeof(System.Management.Automation.PSReference)
[psobject]	typeof(System.Management.Automation.PSObject)
[wmi]	typeof(System.Management.ManagementObject)
[wmisearcher]	typeof(System.Management.ManagementObjectSearcher)
[wmiclass]	typeof(System.Management.ManagementClass)

Getting the Type

You can always get the data type of the variable, whether the variable has been explicitly typed or not. Untyped variables automatically take over the type of the last assigned value.

The method `GetType()` retrieves the data type in the form of a .NET object of the type `System.Type`. Because each WPS variable is an instance of a .NET class, each WPS variable owns the method `GetType()`, handed down to all .NET objects by the mother of all .NET classes, which is `System.Object`. In most cases, you will be interested only in the class name, returned from the property `Fullname` (including namespace) or `Name` (without namespace):

```
$b = [System.DateTime] "1.8.1972"
"$b has the type: " + $b.GetType().Fullname
```

Predefined Variables

WPS knows several predefined variables (also called *integrated variables* or *internal variables*). Table 6.2 shows only some of these variables.

Table 6.2 Predefined WPS Variables (Selection)

Variable	Meaning
`$true`	Value true
`$false`	Value false
`$OFS`	Separator for displaying object collection
`$Home`	Home directory of the entered user
`$PSHome`	Installation directory of the WPS host
`$Args`	Parameter (to be used in functions)
`$Input`	Current content of the pipeline (to be used in functions)
`$_`	Current object of the pipeline (to be used in loops)
`$StackTrace`	Current call sequence
`$Host`	Information about the WPS host
`$LastExitCode`	Return value of the last executed external Windows or console application
`$Error`	Complete list of all errors that have occurred since the start of WPS (maximum of errors saved is set by `$MaximumErrorCount`)

Example

Consider this example for the use of `$OFS`:
The command

```
$OFS="/" ; [string] ("a","b","c")
```

displays the following output:

```
a/b/c
```

TIP All declared variables, integrated and user defined, are listed by the command `Get-ChildItem Variable` (alias `Dir Variable:`).

`Dir Variable:p*` lists all variables that start with the letter *P* (uppercase or lowercase). `Get-Variable p*` has the same effect.

Constant Values

Some of the integrated variables cannot be changed. You can "lock" your own variables as follows:

```
Set-Variable variablename -Option readonly
```

WARNING Note that in this scenario, you must use the variable name without the dollar sign!

Variable Resolution

Variables are not only resolved in expressions, but also within strings. If you declare

```
[int] $count = 1
[string] $Computer = "E01"
```

then, instead of

```
$count.ToString() +". Access to Computer " + $Computer
```

you can write this shortcut:

```
"$count. Access to Computer $Computer"
```

In both cases, the result is the same:

```
"1. Access to Computer E01"
```

Variable resolution also works in parameters of commandlets. The following two commands have the same meaning (that is, in both cases the directory path *WinNT://E01* is called):

```
Get-DirectoryEntry ("WinNT://" + $Computer)
Get-DirectoryEntry "WinNT://$Computer"
```

The variable resolution is not just a resolution of variables, but a resolution of expressions. The dollar sign can also start any expression (see Figure 6.1). For example

```
"1+3=$(1+3)"
"Current Time: $((Get-Date).ToShortTimeString())"
```

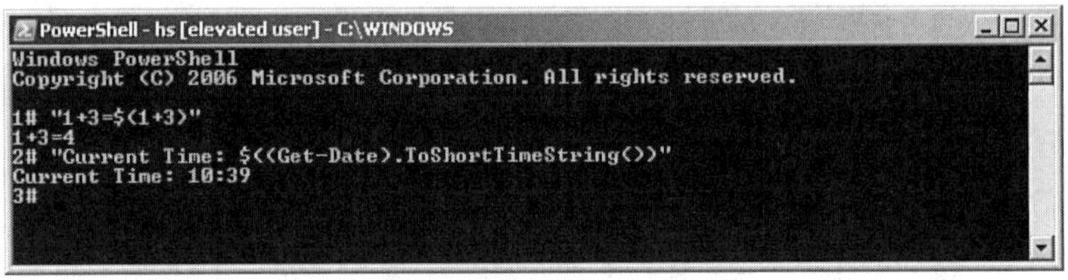

Figure 6.1 Output of the preceding examples

WARNING A variable resolution does not take place when the string is set in simple quotation marks:

```
'$count. Access to computer $Computer'.
```

Numbers

In WPS, you can write numbers as simple numbers, formulas, or as value ranges (see Figure 6.2). You can express hexadecimal numbers by prefixing `0X` (for example, `0Xff = 255`); you can then use them just as you use decimal numbers (for example, `0Xff+1 = 256`).

When assigning a number literal to an untyped variable, WPS creates an instance of the type `System.Int32`. If the value range of `Int32` is not sufficient, `Int64` or `Decimal` is created. If the number literal is a fraction (with a dot as separator for the internal decimal places), WPS creates `Double` or `Decimal`.

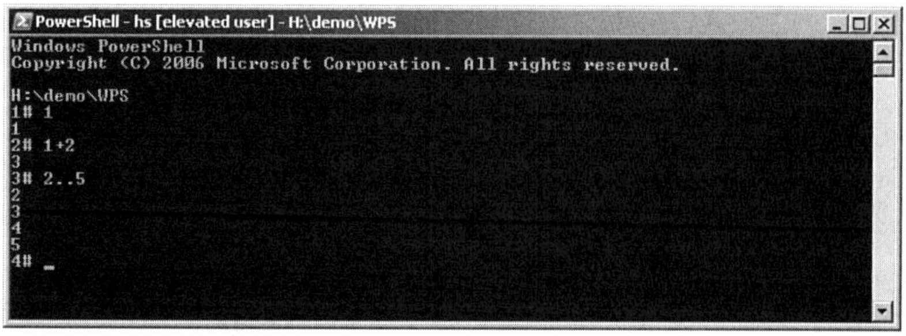

Figure 6.2 Numbers in WPS

If you want to have control over the data type of the variables, you must type the variable explicitly (for example, with `[Byte]` or `[Decimal]`). For `Decimal`, you have another option. You can also add the letter *D* to the literal (for example, `5.1d`):

```
# Implicit Integer
$i = 5
$i.GetType().Name

# Implicit Long
$i = 5368888888888888
$i.GetType().Name

# Implicit Decimal
$i = 53688888888888888888888888888
$i.GetType().Name

# Explicit Long (i.e. 64-bit integer)
[Int64] $l = 5
$l.GetType().Name

# Explicit Byte
[Byte] $b = 5
$b.GetType().Name

# Implicit Double
$d = 5.1
$d.GetType().Name
```

```
# Implicit Decimal
$d = 5.1d
$d.GetType().Name

# Explicit Decimal
[Decimal] $d = 5.1
$d.GetType().Name
```

When you explicitly set the type, you can choose whether you use the WPS types `[int]` and `[long]` or the corresponding .NET class names `[System.Int32]` and `[System.Int64]`.

WARNING With the short forms `KB`, `MB`, and `GB`, you can assign the units of measure kilobyte, megabyte, and gigabyte (for example, `5MB` stands for the number 5242880, 5 * 1024 * 1024).

These units of measure are valid starting with WPS 1.0 RC2. Before that, the short forms `M`, `K`, and `G` were used.

Random Numbers

You can create a random number with the commandlet `Get-Random`, which is part of the PowerShell Community Extensions (PSCX) [CODE-PLEX01]. `Get-Random` creates a number between 0 and 1. You can influence the range with the parameters `-Min` and `-Max` (see Figure 6.3).

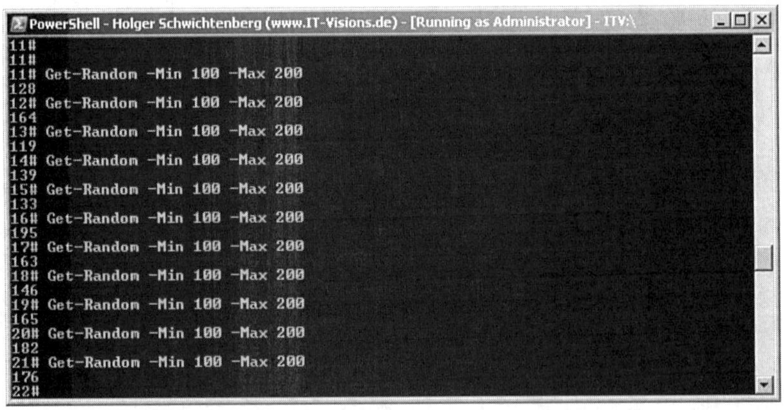

Figure 6.3 Use of `Get-Random` for the creation of random numbers 100 and 200

Strings

Strings exist in the WPS as instances of the .NET class `System.String`. They are marked by quotation marks or by @ at each end of the string. The last option, which also allows including line breaks, is called `Here-String`.

Listing 6.1 `Here-String` Example

```
#Here-String
@'
Long text
can be split
into different lines
using a specific separator
'@
```

In both cases, the strings may contain variables or expressions, which are automatically resolved.

Listing 6.2 Variable Resolution within a String

```
$a = 10
$b= "The current value is $a!"
Write-Warn $b
```

NOTE When you want to transfer parameters to commandlets, remember that you can surround strings with quotation marks *only;* otherwise, the parameter-separation would become unclear (for example, if there is a blank).

Working with Strings

WPS provides all processing options for strings of the class `System.String` (for example, `Insert()`, `Remove()`, `Replace()`, and `Split()`); see the list of members in Figure 6.4.

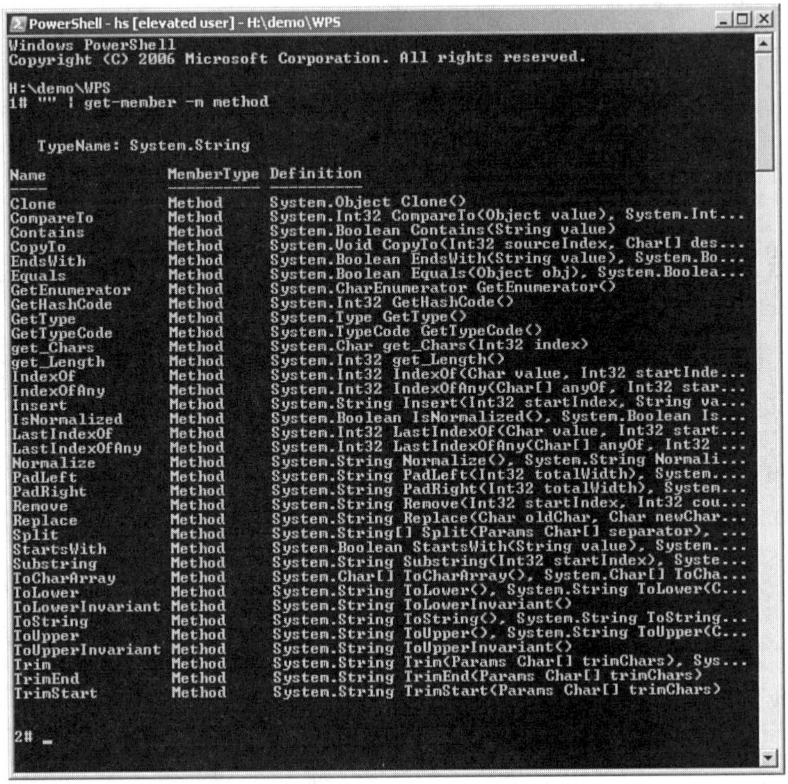

Figure 6.4 Methods of the class `System.String`

Listing 6.3 shows the following string operations:

- Changing all letters to capital letters
- Inserting text
- Extracting a portion of text as single characters

Listing 6.3 Changing Strings

```
# Convert to uppercase letters
$a = "Dr. Schwichtenberg"
$a.ToUpper()
$b
```

```
# Insert a string at a certain position
$a = $a.Insert(4, "Holger ")
$a

# Extract text parts
$c = $a[4..9]
$c
```

Figure 6.5 Output of the preceding script

Splitting and Joining Strings

Sometimes, you have to split a string (for example, `"Holger;Schwichtenberg;Essen;Germany;www.IT-Visions.de"`).

For this case, the .NET Framework offers the method `Split()` in the class `System.String` (see Listing 6.4).

Listing 6.4 Use of the Method `Split()`

```
System.String.
[String] $CSVString =
➥"Holger;Schwichtenberg;Essen;Germany;www.IT-Visions.de"
$CSVArray = $CSVString.Split(";")
$Surname = $CSVArray[1]
$Surname
```

Alternatively, you can use the commandlet `Split-String` from PSCX. This shortens things a bit (see Listing 6.5).

Listing 6.5 Use of the Commandlet `Split-String`

```
[String] $CSVString =
➥"Holger;Schwichtenberg;Essen;Germany;www.IT-Visions.de"
$CSVArray = Split-String $CSVString -Separator ";"
$Surname = $CSVArray[1]
$Surname
```

The counterparts for the joining of strings are the method `Join()` and the commandlet `Join-String` (see Listings 6.6 and 6.7). When you use `Join()`, keep in mind that this is a static method of the class `System.String`.

Listing 6.6 Use of the Static Method `Join()`

```
$Array = "Holger", "Schwichtenberg", "Essen", "Germany",
➥"www.IT-Visions.de"
$CSVString = [System.String]::Join(";", $Array)
$CSVString
```

Listing 6.7 Use of the Commandlet `Join-String`

```
$Array = "Holger", "Schwichtenberg", "Essen", "Germany",
➥"www.IT-Visions.de"
$CSVString = Join-String $Array -Separator ";"
$CSVString
```

Date and Time

The commandlet `Get-Date` creates an instance of the .NET class `System.DateTime`, which contains the current date and time.

```
Get-Date
```

You reduce the output to the date as follows:

```
Get-Date -displayhint date
```

You reduce the output to the time as follows:

```
Get-Date -displayhint time
```

You can also use `Get-Date` to create a specific date/time and to save this in a variable:

```
$a = Get-Date "8/1/1972 12:11:10"
```

You can calculate the difference between the current date and the date/time saved in a variable by calling the method `Subtract()`:

```
(Get-Date).Subtract((Get-Date "8/1/1972 12:11:10"))
```

Alternatively, you can simply use the minus operator:

```
(Get-Date) - (Get-Date "8/1/1972 12:11:10")
```

The preceding examples create the following output:

```
Days              : 12662
Hours             : 11
Minutes           : 56
Seconds           : 57
Milliseconds      : 927
Ticks             : 10940398179276185
TotalDays         : 12662,4978926808
TotalHours        : 303899,949424338
TotalMinutes      : 18233996,9654603
TotalSeconds      : 1094039817,92762
TotalMilliseconds : 1094039817927,62
```

Internally, WPS processes periods of time as instances of the class `System.TimeSpan`. You can also create periods of time by yourself with `New-TimeSpan` and use this to calculate, for example, the following:

```
$period = New-TimeSpan -Days 10 -hours 4 -minutes 3
➥-seconds 50
$now = Get-Date
$future = $now + $period
```

NOTE With `New-TimeSpan`, you can indicate the period only in days, hours, minutes, and seconds. An indication in months or years in not possible.

Remote Computers

You cannot get the time from a remote system with the commandlet `Get-Date`. You can do so only with assistance of the Windows Management Instrumentation (WMI) class `Win32_Currenttime`, as follows:

```
Get-Wmiobject Win32_CurrentTime -computername E02
```

The result of the preceding operation is not, however, a .NET object of the type `System.DateTime`, but a .NET object of the type `System.Management.ManagementObject`, which wraps a WMI object of the type `root\cimv2\Win32_LocalTime`.

Changing the Date and Time

You can set the current time on the local system with `Set-Date` (see Figure 6.6).

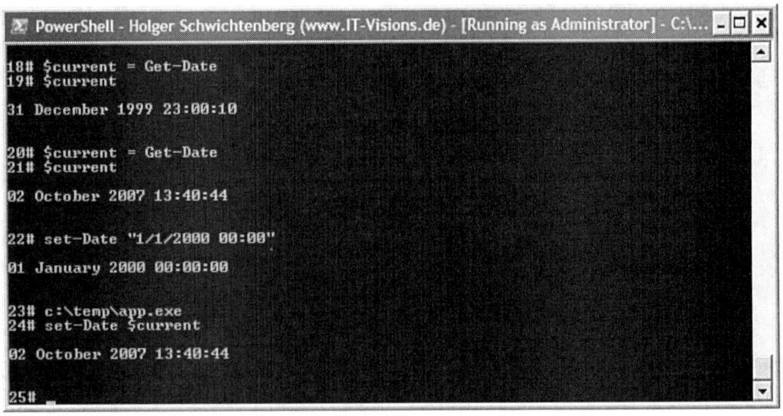

Figure 6.6 Use of `Set-Date` to start an application with a different date

Arrays

An array is declared by assigning a value set, separated by commas:

```
$a = 01,08,72,13,04,76
```

The array can also be declared explicitly with the WPS type identifier `[Array]`:

```
[Array] $b
$b = 1,2,3
```

If you want to define an array with only one element, you have to start the list with a comma or declare the array explicitly:

```
$a = ,"Only one element"
[Array] $a = "Only one element"
```

To list an array, you can use the commandlet `Foreach-Object`, but you do not have to. If an array is the output of the last commandlet in the pipeline, the array is displayed (see Figure 6.7).

The property `Count` delivers the number of elements in the array:

```
[array] $b
$b = 1,2,3
$b.Count
```

To access elements, you must set an index (starting with 0) or an index range in brackets. The index range has to be separated by two dots (for example, `$a[3..6]`). The operator += completes an element at the end of an array (see Figure 6.7). The removal of elements is not possible. (You can only copy the elements into another array.)

You can join two arrays with the plus operator:

```
$DomainControllers = "E01", "E02", "E03"
$MemberServers = "E04", "E05", "E06"
$AllServers = $DomainControllers + $MemberServers
$AllServers.Count # Result: 6 !
```

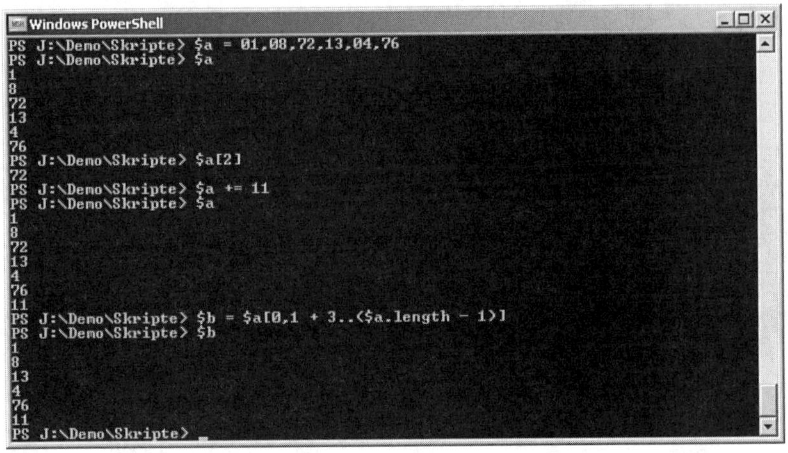

Figure 6.7 Output of an array

Multidimensional arrays are possible, when you surround the elements with parentheses. The following example shows the creation of a two-dimensional array. The elements of the first dimension contain arrays with three elements each. In this scenario, you can also complete the collection with the plus operator:

```
$DomainControllers = ("E01", "192.168.1.10", "Building 1"),
➥("E02", "192.168.1.20", "Building 2"),
➥("E03", "192.168.1.30", "Building 3")
"Number of Computers: " + $DomainControllers.Count
"IP Address of Computer 2: " + $DomainControllers[1][1]
➥# 192.168.1.20
"Building of Computer 2: " + $DomainControllers[1][2]
➥# Building 3
$DomainControllers += ("E04", "192.168.1.40", "Building 4")
"Building of Computer 4: " + $DomainControllers[3][2]
➥# Building 4
```

Associative Arrays (Hash Tables)

Besides the arrays, WPS also supports named (associative) lists in the form of so-called hash tables. Elements in a hash table are not identified by their position, but by a distinct marker (called a *key*). You can find this concept in other languages, too, where it is often called an *associative array*. The basic concept for this is the .NET class `System.Collections.Hashtable`.

To define a hash table, you have to use the `@` sign, followed by an element list in curly brackets (`{}`). You must use a semicolon (`;`) to separate each element. Each element consists of an element name and an element value, which have to be separated by an equals sign (=). The element name must *not* be set in quotation marks. If you want to explicitly indicate the data type, use `[Hashtable]`.

```
# Implicit Hash Table
$Computers = @{ E01 = "192.168.1.10"; E02 = "192.168.1.20";
➥E03 = "192.168.1.30"; }

# Explicit Hash Table
[Hashtable] $Computers = @{ E01 = "192.168.1.10"; E02 =
➥"192.168.1.20"; E03 = "192.168.1.30"; }
```

Hash tables can be accessed both via the notation with square brackets as simple arrays and via the dot operator. This makes working with hash tables rather elegant:

```
# Get IP Address of Computer E02
$Computers["E02"]
$Computers.E02
```

You can also write to the elements directly:

```
# Change on Element
$Computers.E02 = "192.168.1.21"
```

It is very convenient that a new element is created when you write a value to this element. Thus, you can also create a hash table step by step (that is, you can start with an empty list). An empty list is expressed with `@{ }`, as follows:

```
# Add a new Element
$Computers.E04 = "192.168.1.40"

# Start with an empty list
$MoreComputers = @{ }
```

```
$MoreComputers.E05 = "192.168.1.50"
$MoreComputers.E06 = "192.168.1.60"
$MoreComputers.Count # Result = 2
```

You can join two hash tables just as you can join two arrays. However, this works only when each element name appears only once in both lists. If there are duplicates, a runtime error is generated:

```
# Add two hash tables
$AllComputers = $Computers + $MoreComputers
$AllComputers.Count # Result = 6
```

You can use hash tables not only for real lists, but also for a simple definition of your own data structures (for example, to save information about a person):

```
# Use a hash table as a custom data structure
$Author = @{ Name="Dr. Holger Schwichtenberg";
➥Age=35; Country="Germany" }
$Author.Name
$Author.Age
$Author.Country
```

Operators

WPS supports the basic arithmetic operators `+`, `-`, `*`, `/`, and `%` (modulo operation, alias division remainder). The plus sign (`+`) is used in addition and in the linking of strings. Even lists (arrays, hash tables) can be linked. The star operator (`*`) is used in multiplication, but also has another meaning: You can multiply a string as well as an array with this sign. Therefore, signs or elements are repeated as often as necessary. However, it lies in the nature of a hash table that elements cannot be multiplied, because this would lead to doubled element names, which is invalid:

```
# Multiply a string
$String = "abcdefghijklmnopqrstuvwxyz"
$LongString = $String * 20
"Count: " + $LongString.Length # = 520
```

```
# Multiply an Array
$a = 1,2,3,4,5
$b = $a * 10
"Count: " + $b.Count # = 50
```

The equals sign (=) is used as an assignment operator. Of special interest are cross-assignments, which enable you to elegantly exchange the contents of two variables. Normally, you need an interim variable to do this. In WPS, however, you can just write `$x, $y = $y, $x` (see Figure 6.8).

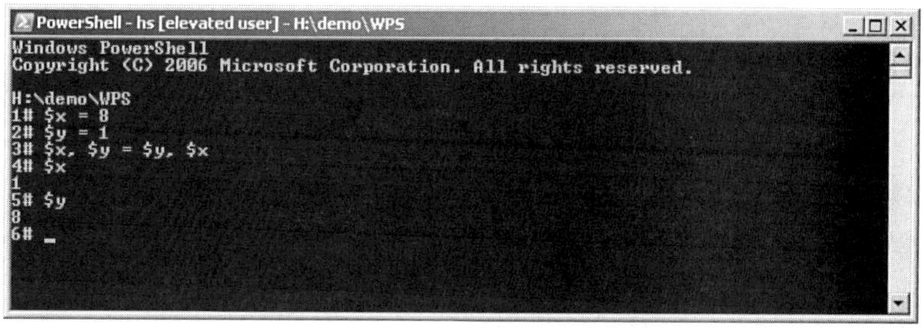

Figure 6.8 Cross-assignments for the exchange of variables in WPS

Another interesting operator is the ampersand (`&`). You can use it to execute a string as a command, thus enabling you to write dynamic and self-modifying program code.

Here's an example:

```
$What = "Process"
& ("Get-"+$What)
```

The preceding command sequence leads to the execution of the commandlet `Get-Process`. You could get the content of the variable `$What` from another source, too (for example, a user input).

Alternatively, you can use the commandlet `Invoke-Expression` rather than the operator `&`:

```
$UserEntry = "Process"
invoke-expression("Get-"+$UserEntry)
```

WARNING Keep in mind that dynamic code execution raises a safety risk when user entries are processed directly in commands. You could get the impression from the preceding example that the risk is limited, because the `Get` command is always executed. However, it is not, as the following script shows:

```
$UserEntry = "Process | Stop-Process"
invoke-expression("Get-"+$UserEntry)
```

Control Structures

The PowerShell Script Language (PSL) contains the following control structures:

```
if (condition) {...} else {...}
switch ($var) {value {...} value {...} default {..} } }
while(condition) { ... }
do { ... } while (condition)
do { ... } until (condition)
foreach ($var in $collection) {...}
function name {...}
break
continue
return
exit
trap failure class { ... } else { ... }
throw "failure text"
throw failure class
```

NOTE You can find more information about the commands in WPS help documents. In this book, we avoid a detailed description of these basic constructs in favor of other content, specifically because their functioning is quite similar to other programming languages. `Throw` and `Trap` are discussed separately in Chapter 7, "PowerShell Scripts."

Loops

Listing 6.8 shows self-explanatory examples for the constructs `for`, `while`, and `foreach`.

Listing 6.8 Loops

```
# Loops from 1 to 5
"for:"
for ($i = 1; $i -lt 6; $i++) { $i }

"While:"
$i = 0
while($i -lt 5)
{ $i++
$i
}

"Foreach:"
$i = 1,2,3,4,5
foreach ($z in $i) { $z }
```

Conditions

Listing 6.9 shows self-explanatory examples for the use of `if` and `switch`.

Listing 6.9 Conditions

```
if ($i -lt 10)
{ "Smaller than 10" }
else
{ "Greater than 10" }

switch ($i)
{
    1 {"one"}
    5 {"five"}
    10 {"ten"}
    default { "other" }
}
```

Subroutines

Listing 6.10 shows self-explanatory examples for subroutines with parameters and return values.

Listing 6.10 Subroutines

```
function UnnamedParameter()
{
"To this functions has been given: $args[0] and $args[1]"
return  $args[0] + $args[1]
}

UnnamedParameter 1 2

function NamedParameter([int] $a, [int] $b)
{
"To this function has been given: $a and $b"
return  $b + $a
}

NamedParameter 1 4
```

TIP WPS has several integrated functions (see Figure 6.9). The installation of PSCX adds even more. The execution of the command `dir function:` lists all functions and demonstrates that even some commands, such as `C:` and `Dir`, retained for backward compatibility with the classic Windows console, are realized as integrated functions.

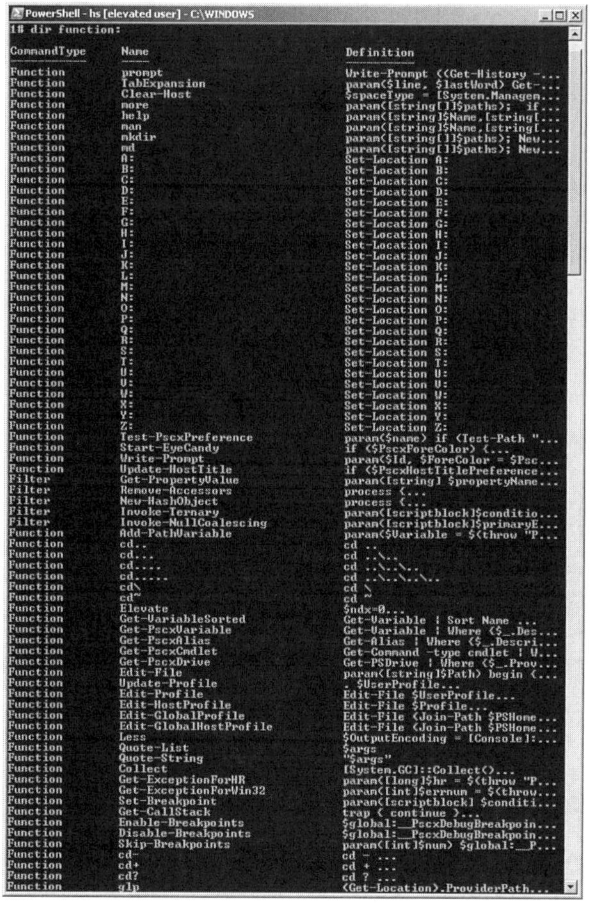

Figure 6.9 List of integrated functions (including PCSX)

Summary

PowerShell Script Language (PSL) does not use the exact same syntax as any other existing programming language, but it is very similar to PERL, PHP, Python, and C#. Variables can be typed or untyped. All used types are classes from the .NET Framework class library, even basic types such as `string` and `int` have a corresponding class in the .NET Framework. Therefore, the whole functionality for manipulation of types (for example, string functions) is available to the WPS user.

Variables can contain single values or an array of values. An array can be accessed via a numeric index or distinct marker.

In addition to variables, WPS supports all the important syntax constructs for structured programming (for example, conditions, loops, and subroutines).

CHAPTER 7

PowerShell Scripts

In this chapter:

Command sequences can be saved as Windows PowerShell (WPS) scripts in the file system and executed later (with or without observation by any user). These scripts are pure text files and have the file extension `.ps1`. The number 1 here stands for version 1.0 of WPS. Regarding longevity of many scripts, Microsoft provided the possibility that different versions of WPS with different script file formats can coexist on one system.

A First PowerShell Script Example

Listing 7.1 shows a script that files a hierarchy of keys in the registry. The simple addition of numbers is here intentionally contained in a subroutine, to show the return of values to the caller with the `return` command. Literals and expressions, which are in the script without a commandlet, display at the console.

Listing 7.1 A PowerShell Script to Manipulate the Registry

```
#########################################
# PowerShell Script
# The script creates a key hierarchy in the registry.
# (C) Dr. Holger Schwichtenberg
#########################################

# === Subroutine, executing an addition
function Addition
{
return $args[0] + $args[1]
}

# === Subroutine, creating a key in the registry.
function CreateEntry
{
"Create entry..."

New-Item  -Name ("Eintrag #{0}" -f $args[0]) -value $args[1]
➥-type String

}

# === Major routine
"PowerShell Registry Script (C) Dr. Holger Schwichtenberg 2006"

# Navigation in the Registry
cd hklm:\software

# Check, if entry \software\IT-Visions exists
$b = Get-Item IT-Visions
if ($b.childName -eq "IT-Visions")
{ # Delete existing entry with all sub-keys
"Key already exists, delete..."
cd hklm:\software
del IT-Visions -force -recurse
}
# Create new entry "IT-Visions"
"Create IT-Visions..."
md IT-Visions
```

```
cd IT-Visions

# Create subkey
for($a=1;$a -lt 5;$a++)
{
$result =  Addition $a $a
CreateEntry $a $result
}
```


Start a PowerShell Script

Jeffrey Snover, leading architect of WPS, called the fact that a WPS script cannot be started with a double-click on the symbol in Windows a "top-security function." Basically, you can add this start option, but it is not contained in the standard WPS installation.

A WPS script is started by entering the filename with or without the file extension. Moreover, the prefaced commandlet `Invoke-Expression` or the operator `&` are optional. You can use a relative or an absolute path:

`ScriptName` or

`ScriptName.ps1` or

`& ScriptName.ps1` or

`Invoke-Expression ScriptName.ps1`

Alternatively, you can start a WPS script out of the normal Windows command-line window via a link from the Windows desktop or as login script by prefacing the following:

```
powershell.exe:
powershell.exe ScriptName
```

WARNING WPS scripts are subject to the same limitations and workarounds as WSH scripts, as far as Vista user account control (User Account Control, UAC) is concerned.

Including Scripts

Dot sourcing describes a possibility to call a script and to make the definitions included in this script permanently available in the current WPS console. The difference to the previously mentioned possibilities of starting a script is that after dot sourcing all variables declared in the script, all WPS functions contained in the script are available for later operations outside the script. Dot sourcing is an easy way to extend the functionality of WPS. Dot sourcing is activated by a pre-positioned dot followed by a blank space:

```
. ScriptName.ps1
```

NOTE When a dot-sourced script contains "free" commands (that is, commands that are not part of a function), these commands are executed immediately.

You can also integrate one script into others with dot sourcing:

Listing 7.2 A WPS Script That Exists Only to Integrate and to Call Other Scripts

```
# Demo User Management
# Include three scripts
. ("H:\demo\PowerShell\ADS\Localuser_Create.ps1"
. ("H:\demo\PowerShell\ADS\LocalGroup.ps1")
. ("H:\demo\PowerShell\ADS\Localuser_Delete.ps1")
```

Scripting Security

Active Scripting via scripting features in Internet Explorer, Outlook, and Windows Script Host (WSH) raised security concerns. In contrast, however, and according to Microsoft documentation, WPS is "by default a secure environment." [MS02] When you try to use the WPS console either interactively or to start a script, you will soon notice that no script can be executed (see Figure 7.1). The execution policy does not accept any scripts whatsoever. In the following pages, you learn how to change this behavior.

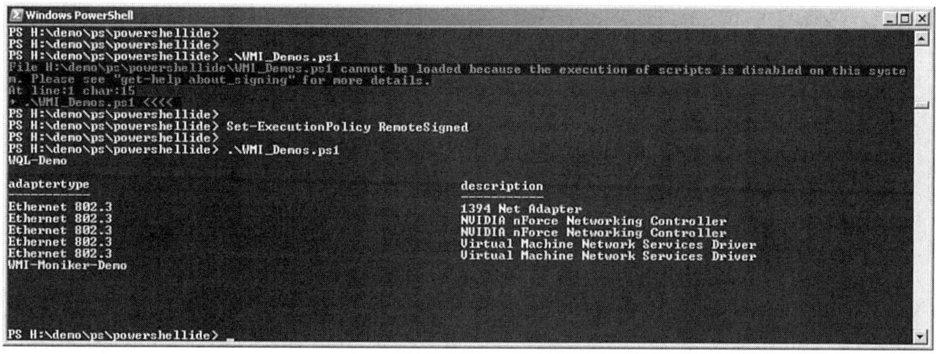

Figure 7.1 At first, script execution has to be activated explicitly in WPS.

Even before the final launching of WPS, intended WPS viruses were reported. However, these were only a threat if started explicitly. [MSSec01]

Security Policy

A user can use WPS interactively only after lowering the security level on the execution policy via the commandlet `Set-Executionpolicy`. The following modes are available:

- **Restricted.** This is the default value and prevents execution of any script.
- **AllSigned.** Only signed scripts of trusted sources can start.
- **RemoteSigned.** A trusted signature is needed only for scripts from the Internet (via browsers, Outlook, and Messenger) and other network resources; local scripts also start without a signature.
- **Unrestricted.** All scripts can run.

You (I hope) do not want to use Unrestricted; the Unrestricted mode opens the door to "evil" scripts that might be transferred as e-mail attachments, for instance. In the long run, you should opt for AllSigned. However, if you don't want to delve into the complex process of digital signing, the option RemoteSigned is a compromise.

The security policy is stored in the registry, on system level and user level, in the keys *HKEY_CURRENT_USER\Software\Microsoft\PowerShell\1\ShellIds\Microsoft.PowerShell\ExecutionPolicy* and *HKEY_LOCAL_MACHINE\SOFTWARE\Microsoft\PowerShell\1\ShellIds\Microsoft.PowerShell\ExecutionPolicy* (see Figure 7.2).

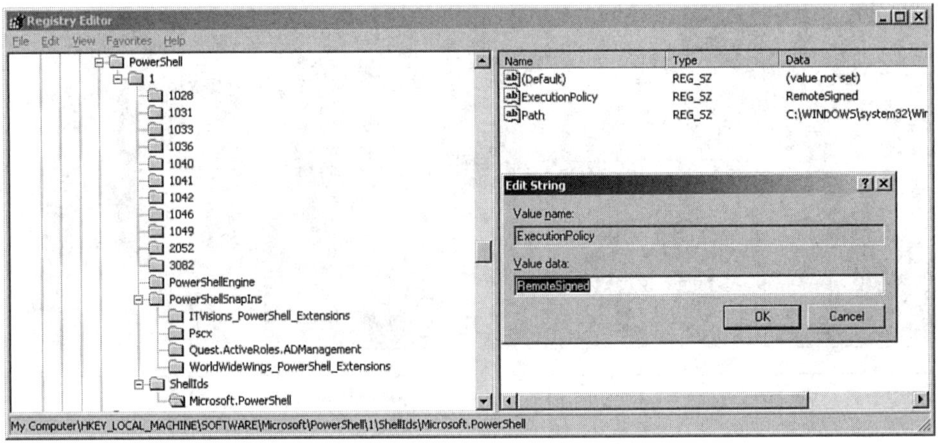

Figure 7.2 Persisting of the security policy in the registry

WARNING Note that the storing of the security policy in the registry under Windows Vista can be changed only when the console runs under elevated rights.

Signing of Scripts

When used within companies, digital signatures are adequate. For the signing of scripts, WPS offers the commandlet `Set-AuthenticodeSignature`. To sign a script, follow these steps (also see Figure 7.3):

1. If you do not have a digital certificate to sign code, you must create a certificate (for example, with the command-line tool `makecert.exe`).
2. List your own Windows certificates in the WPS console:

   ```
   dir cert:/currentuser/my
   ```

3. Display the position of the certificate that you want to use, and save this certificate in a variable. (Note that the counting starts with 0!)

   ```
   $cert = @(dir "cert:/currentuser/my/")[1]
   ```

4. Sign the script:

```
Set-AuthenticodeSignature scriptname.ps1 $cert
```

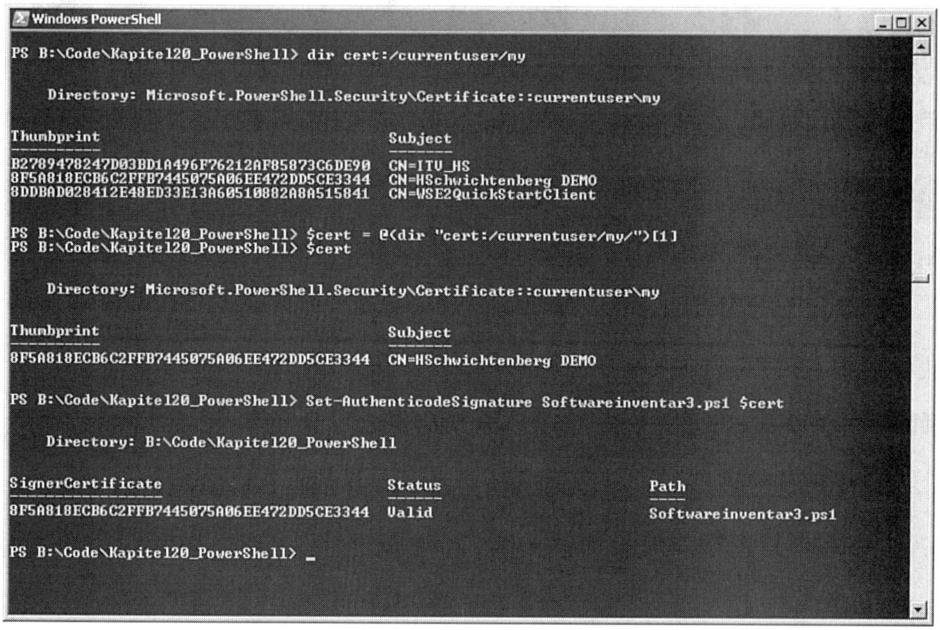

Figure 7.3 Signing of a WPS script

Now, if you write

```
Set-AuthenticodeSignature AllSigned
```

the WPS script signed by you should run; no other scripts will run.

WARNING If WPS prompts asking whether you really want to start the script (see Figure 7.4), this is a sign that the script has been signed by somebody, the issuing certificate authority is known in your regular certificate authority, but you do not yet explicitly trust this script author. If you choose the option Always Run, the script author is added to the list of trustworthy publishers in the certificate management console.

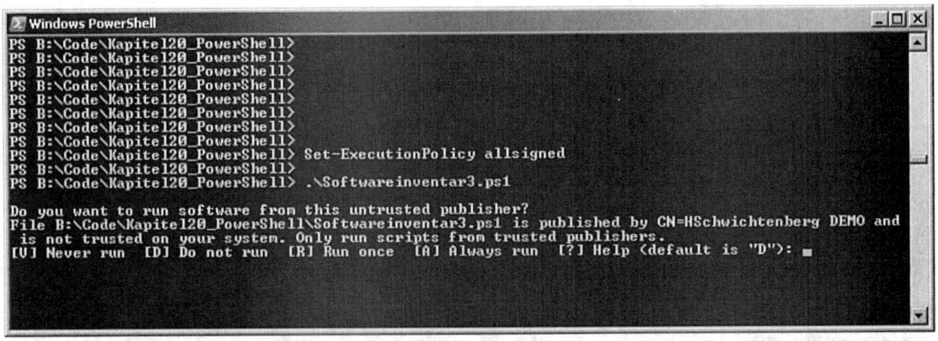

Figure 7.4 Prompt at script start

Letting a Script Sleep

You can pause a WPS script for a while. The time is counted in milliseconds or seconds.

To make a script sleep for 10 milliseconds, add the following:

```
Start-Sleep -m 10
```

To make a script sleep for 10 seconds, add this:

```
Start-Sleep -s 10
```

Errors and Error Treatment

WPS differentiates between errors where the termination of an execution is mandatory (*terminating error*) and errors where the execution may be continued with the next command (*nonterminating error*). Terminating errors can be caught with `Trap` commands. Nonterminating errors, on the other hand, can be changed into terminating ones.

`Trap` catches occurring terminating errors and executes the indicated code (see Table 7.1). In the error handling code, the variable `$_` contains information about the error in the form of an instance of the .NET class `System.Management.Automation.ErrorRecord`. The subobject

$_.Exception is the actual error in the form of an instance of an error class that inherits from System.Exception. Via $_.Exception.GetType().FullName, you get the error type. Via $_.Exception.Message, you display the error text.

With the statements Break or Continue, the error handler is told whether the script will be continued after the error. The default procedure is Continue. With Exit, you can cause a definite immediate ending of the whole script.

Example

With Listing 7.3, you can test WPS error behavior and experiment with the different reaction options. The error is resolved by the call Copy-Item with a wrong path (a nonterminating error) and Get-Dir. (This commandlet does not exist; it's a terminating error.)

Listing 7.3 Script for Testing the Trap Statement

```
# Example for the testing of error trapping

trap {
                      Write-Host ("### trapped ERROR: " +
$_.Exception.Message)
          #Write-Error ("Fehler: " + $_.Exception.Message)
          #continue
          #break
          #exit
          #throw "test"
}

"Example for the testing of error trapping "
"At first, everything works fine..."
copy g:\Documents\Suppliers c:\temo\Documents
"Then it doesn't work so fine anymore (false path)"
copy g:\Documents\Suppliers k:\Documents\Suppliers
"And then an unknown commandlet follows"
Get-Dir k:\Documents\Suppliers
"End of Script"
```

Table 7.1 Reaction of WPS to Errors When `Trap` Is Used

Trap	Reaction
Not existing	WPS shows error reports for `Copy-Item` ("drive does not exist") and `Get-Dir` ("not recognized as a cmdlet, function, program, or script file") and continues the execution until the end of the script.

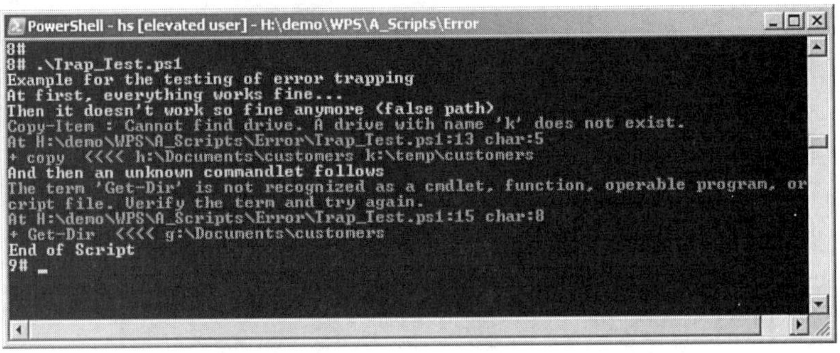

Trap	Reaction
Existing, only with `Write-Host`	In addition to the WPS error report, the `Trap` block reports its own error text.

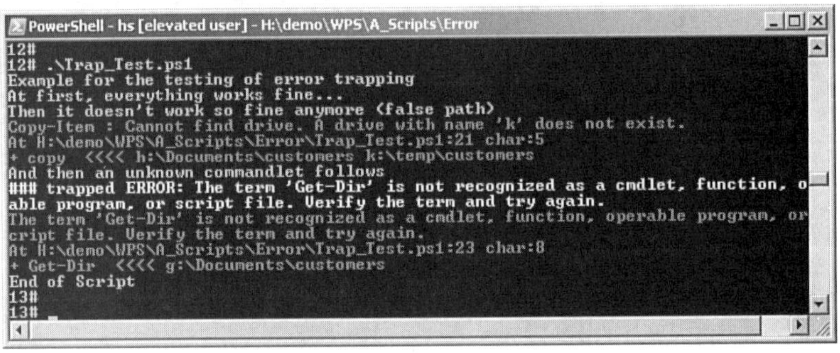

Trap	Reaction
Existing, with continue	Just the error text from the `Trap` block displays.

Trap	Reaction

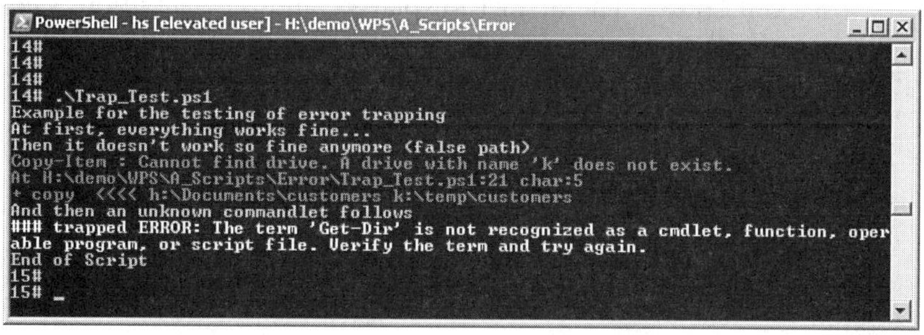

Trap	Reaction
Existing, with break	The terminating error results first in its own error text, followed by a WPS error text display. After that, the script is terminated (i.e., the output "End of Scripts" does not display).

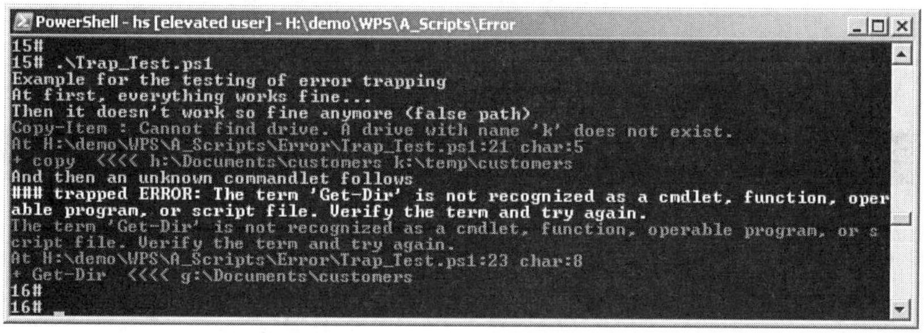

Trap	Reaction
Existing, with exit	The terminating error results first in its own error text. Then the execution stops immediately.

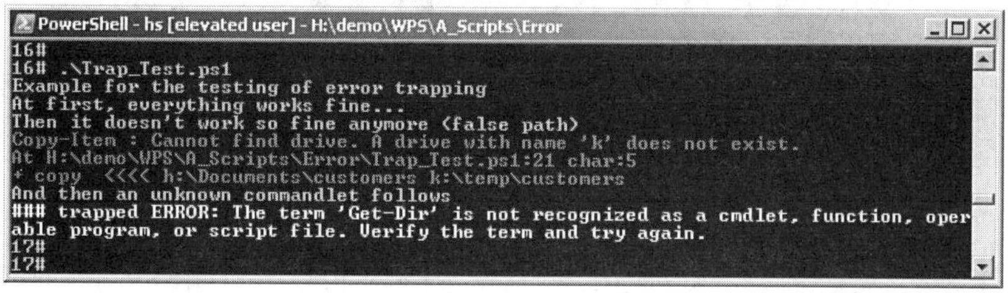

Individual Reactions to Errors

The options vary even more because each single commandlet can decide via the parameter `-ErrorAction` (or `-ea`) how errors will be handled:

- `Stop` The error is displayed, and the execution is terminated (all nonterminating errors thus *become* terminating errors).
- `Continue` The error is displayed, and the execution is continued.
- `SilentlyContinue` The error is not displayed, and the execution is continued.
- `Inquire` Users are asked whether they want to continue the execution despite the error.

All the possible combinations of `-ErrorAction` and `Trap` are beyond the scope of this book. Therefore, this text contains just sample cases (see Table 7.2).

NOTE The application of `-ErrorAction` has an effect only on existing commandlets. The nonexisting commandlet `Get-Dir`, which is used in the example, would not be able to react.

Table 7.2 WPS Reaction to Errors When `Trap` and `-ErrorAction` Are Used

Trap	`ErrorAction`	Reaction
Not existing	`-ErrorAction silentlycontinue`	An error report for the path error does not appear any longer with `Copy-Item`. The problem will be further reported with `Get-Dir`.

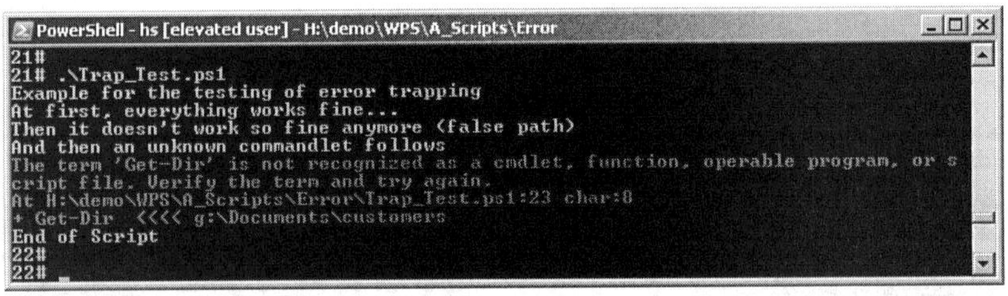

Trap	`ErrorAction`	Reaction
Existing, with continue	`-ErrorAction silentlycontinue`	A standard WPS error report doesn't appear at all, but only the user-defined report from the `Trap` block for the nonexisting commandlet.

Trap	ErrorAction	Reaction

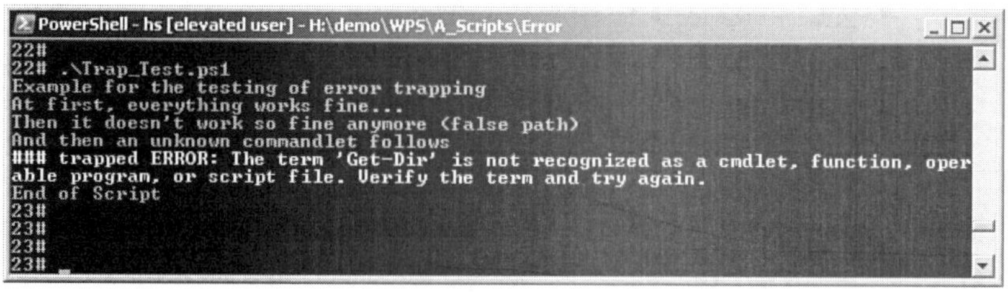

Trap	ErrorAction	Reaction
Not existing	`-ErrorAction stop`	The execution is terminated with a WPS error report, directly after the first nonexecutable `Copy` command.

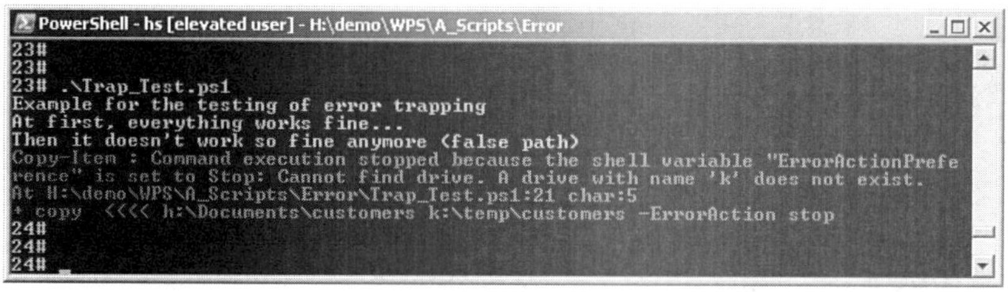

Trap	ErrorAction	Reaction
Existing, with continue	`-ErrorAction stop`	For both errors, just the error text from the `Trap` block displays.

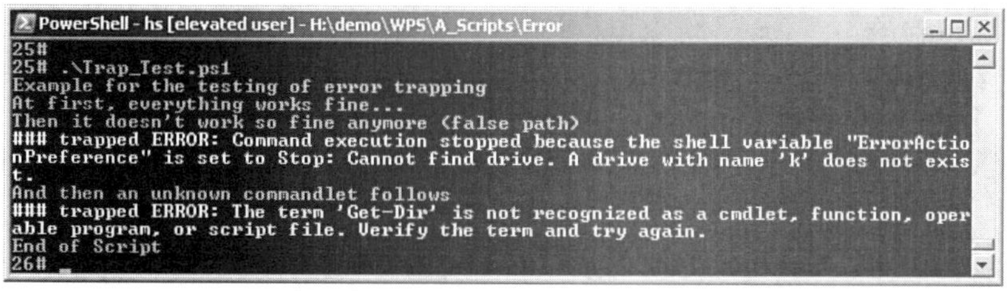

Further Options

WPS offers us even more with regard to error treatment:

- Via the global integrated variable `$ErrorActionPreference`, you can set the standard reaction `-ErrorAction` for all commandlets. This is in the standard setting Continue.

- `$Error` contains the complete history of errors in the form of objects that belong to error classes (for example, `System.Management.Automation.CommandNotFoundException`).
- `Trap` blocks can be limited to certain error groups by indicating an error type in square brackets (error class). Therefore, one script can contain several `Trap` blocks.
- With `Throw`, you can create any error of your own within or outside of `Trap` blocks. `Throw` creates a terminating error of the class `System.Management.Automation.RuntimeException`. You can also name another error class in square brackets. The class has to be a class that derives from `System.Exception`.

```
throw "error text"
throw [System.ApplicationException] "error text"
```

Summary

WPS scripts are text files with the extension `.ps1`, and you can start a script in several different ways. And although the default security restrictions in WPS prevent all scripts from executing, you can use the commandlet `Set-Executionpolicy` to lower the security settings on the execution policy. Instead of allowing all scripts to run, you should use WPS modes that require digitally signed scripts.

The second big topic in this chapter was error treatment, which is important in scripts. This chapter examined the differences between terminating errors and nonterminating errors. The chapter also provided numerous examples that showed how to catch an error with the `Trap` statement and how to configure the error behavior (reaction) of commandlets with the parameter `ErrorAction`.

CHAPTER 8

Using Class Libraries

In this chapter:

Microsoft enabled Windows PowerShell (WPS) to access different application programming interfaces (APIs)—specifically, class libraries based on the .NET Framework, the Component Object Model (COM), and Windows Management Instrumentation (WMI). These class libraries enable you to perform additional functions within WPS. However, they require at least a basic understanding of object-oriented programming.

NOTE WPS offers a special treatment for WMI (`System.Management`), ADSI (`System.DirectoryServices`), and ADO.NET (`System.Data`). Objects from these libraries are shown simplified by the object adapter to the user. Collaboration data objects (CDOs) for access to Microsoft Exchange are not yet supported in a special way by WPS 1.0.

Using .NET Classes

With the commandlet `New-Object`, the administrator can create an instance of any class from the .NET class library (or a COM class, see the next chapter).

Creating Instances

The following example creates an instance of the .NET class `System.Net.WebClient` and then calls its method `DownloadString()`(see Figure 8.1):

```
$wc = (new-object System.Net.WebClient)
$wc.DownloadString("http://www.windows-scripting.com")
```

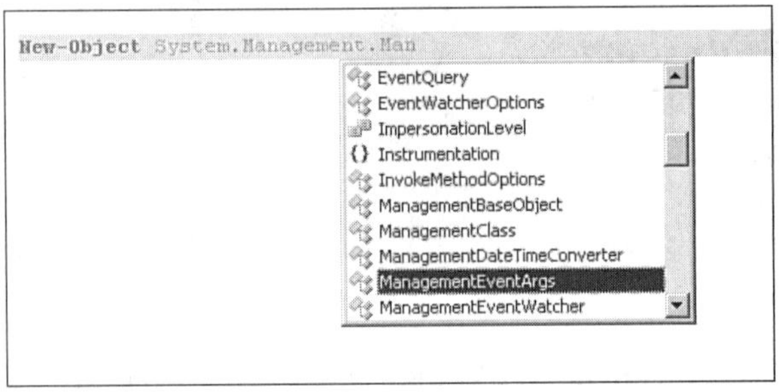

Figure 8.1 PowerShell IDE and PowerShellPlus offer IntelliSense-like input support for .NET class names after `New-Object`

Constructors with Parameters

A constructor is a special piece of program code in a class that is called when a class is instantiated. .NET classes can expect parameters in the constructors. These can be declared with or without parentheses after the class name:

```
$o = New-Object
➥System.Directoryservices.DirectoryEntry("LDAP://E02")
```

or

```
$o = new-object System.Directoryservices.DirectoryEntry
➥"LDAP://E02"
```

Static Members in .NET Objects/Static .NET Classes

.NET classes know the concept of their static members (class members), which can be called without creating an instance. Some of these classes are also static classes (that is, they have only static members). Such classes do not have a constructor. Therefore, the commandlet `New-Object` is not applicable to static classes.

```
# This does not work:
#(New-Object System.Console).Beep(100,50)
```

For this case, WPS has another construct, which asks you to set the .NET class name in square brackets and separate the name of the member with two colons. The following command uses the static method `Beep()` in the static .NET class `System.Console` to create a sound:

```
# correct:
[System.Console]::Beep(100, 50)
```


Loading Additional Assemblies

You can only instantiate .NET classes via `New-Object` and the notation in square brackets when the corresponding software component (assembly), where they are located, has been loaded into memory. Some assemblies are loaded automatically by WPS. In other cases, you have to request loading of the assembly via the class `System.Reflection.Assembly`. Therefore, to display a dialog window, you first have to load `System.Windows.Forms.dll`. Because this assembly is located in the so-called Global Assembly Cache (GAC) of .NET, you do not have to indicate a path:

```
[System.Reflection.Assembly]::LoadWithPartialName
➥("System.Windows.Forms")
[System.Windows.Forms.MessageBox]::Show("Text","Heading",
[System.Windows.Forms.MessageBoxCases]::OK)
```

TIP Instead of the notation with square brackets, you can also use the integrated WPS type `[Type]`, which creates a .NET `type` object based on a string. Therefore, you can write the preceding example in the following way:

```
([Type] "System.Reflection.Assembly")::LoadWithPartialName
➥("System.Windows.Forms")
$msg = [Type] "System.Windows.Forms.MessageBox"
$msg::Show("test")
```

Object Analysis

With the help of the commandlet `Get-Member`, which has previously been used in this book to analyze pipeline contents, you can also analyze the content of a variable containing an object instance. You have to keep in mind, however, that the object has to be sent either in a pipeline to `Get-Member` (that is, `$Variable | Get-Member`) or that you have to use the parameter name `-InputObject` (`Get-Member -InputObject $Variable`). Not only for `Get-Member`, but for most of the commandlets, it does not matter whether there are a number of objects in the pipeline or just a single object.

Enumerations

When using some .NET classes (for example, `FileSystemRights`), you must combine different flags with a binary `or` operation. If you repeat the name of the listing in which the flag is defined with each flag, you're really overworking your fingertips.

WPS can pick the respective flag values in the enumeration out of a string with comma separators and link them with a binary `or`. So, instead of

```
$Rights= [System.Security.AccessControl.FileSystemRights]::
➥Read `
-bor [System.Security.AccessControl.FileSystemRights]::
➥ReadExtendedProperties `
-bor [System.Security.AccessControl.FileSystemRights]::
➥ReadProperties `
-bor [System.Security.AccessControl.FileSystemRights]::
➥ReadPermissions
```

you can use the following abbreviation:

```
$Rights = [System.Security.AccessControl.FileSystemRights]
➥"ReadData, ReadExtendedProperties,
➥ReadProperties, ReadPermissions"
```

Using COM Classes

This section examines the basic mechanisms for accessing COM objects.

Create an Instance

The commandlet `New-Object` is also used for instantiating classes defined within the Component Object Model (see Figure 8.2). In this case, the name of the COM class has to be preceded by the parameter `–comobject` (short, `-com`). The programmatic identifier (ProgID) has to be indicated as `Name`. The COM class must be listed in the registry of the local system. `New-Object` complies with `CreateObject()` in Visual Basic/VBScript.

Listing 8.1 shows the call of the method `GetTempName()` from the COM class `Scripting.FileSystemObject`. This method creates a name for a temporary file.

Listing 8.1 `com.ps1`

```
$fso = new-object -com "scripting.filesystemobject"
$fso.GetTempName()
```

With Listing 8.2, you open Internet Explorer with a specific website.

Listing 8.2 Creating an Instance of a COM Class

```
$ie = new-object -com "InternetExplorer.Application"
$ie.Navigate("http://www.windows-scripting.com")
$ie.visible = $true
```

NOTE You do not have to load COM components (COM components are *not* called assemblies) because the COM infrastructure automatically loads the appropriate DLLs based on the data stored in the registry when the COM component was installed. So, you can access all public classes in all installed COM components.

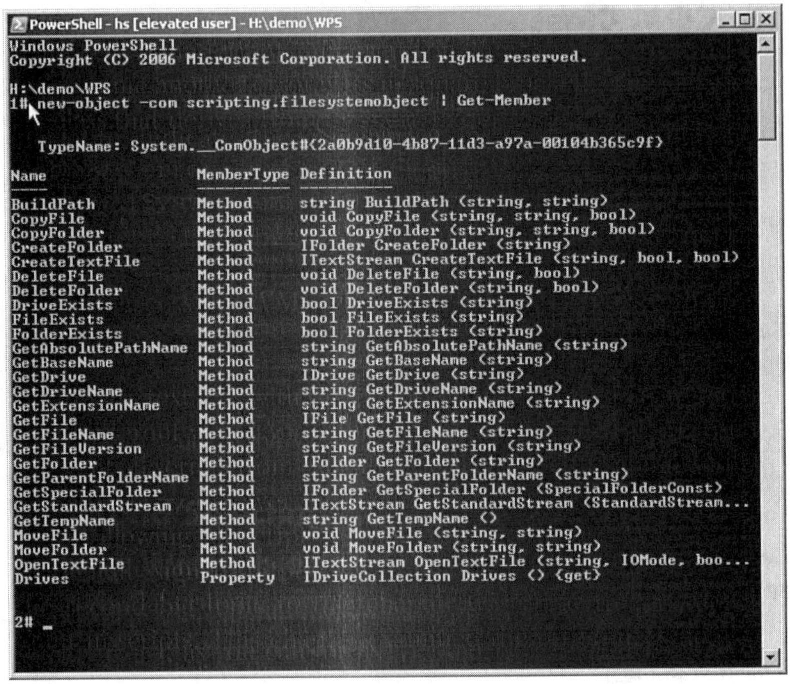

Figure 8.2 Instantiation of a COM object in WPS

Get an Existing Instance

A direct equivalent for `GetObject()` from VB/VBScript to activate an existing object is not available in WPS. However, you can load the assembly for Visual Basic .NET and use the method `GetObject()`, which is available there for compatibility reasons.

Listing 8.3 shows a document in Microsoft Word on the screen and writes some text in the document:

Listing 8.3 Getting an Existing Instance of a COM Class

```
$doc = [microsoft.visualbasic.interaction]::
➥GetObject("C:\temp\document.doc")
$doc.application.visible = $true
$doc.application.selection.typetext("You successfully
➥created an instance of Word!")
```

Using COM Objects

After instantiation, accessing COM objects is the same as accessing .NET objects, with two exceptions:

- COM objects do not have constructors with parameters.
- COM objects do not have static members.

Using WMI Classes

The commandlet `Get-WmiObject` and the integrated WPS types `[WMI]`, `[WMICLASS]`, and `[WMISEARCHER]` open the world of mighty Windows Management Instrumentation (WMI), which offers almost all modules of modern Windows operating systems in an object-oriented manner.

NOTE This chapter assumes that you have a basic knowledge of WMI.

System.Management

Windows WPS uses the .NET assembly `System.Management.dll` with the namespace `System.Management` to access WMI. Therein, a meta object model for access to WMI objects is realized. However, access to WMI using COM classes is also possible; it is just more cumbersome and is not covered in this book.

Central classes of the object model (see Figure 8.3) of `System.Management` are as follows:

- `ManagementObject`
  This class represents a WMI object.
- `ManagementClass`
  This class represents a WMI class. `ManagementClass` is derived from `ManagementObject`.
- `ManagementBaseObject`
  Both classes are derived from `ManagementBaseObject`. This class is not abstract, but is also used at different places within the object model.

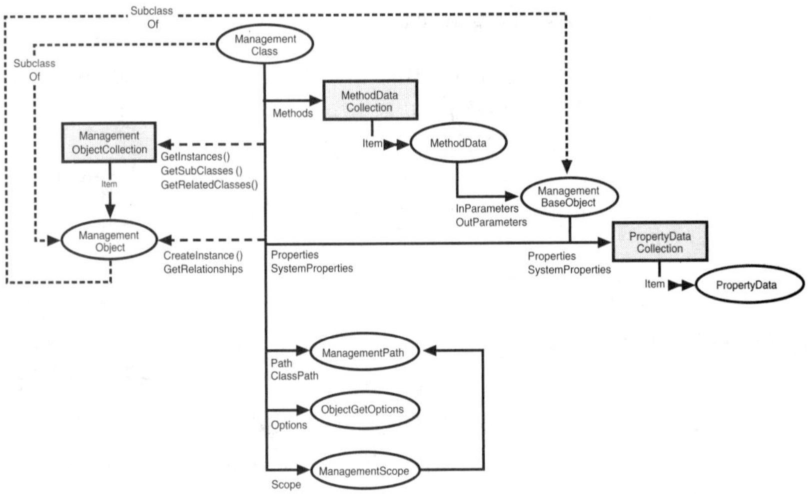

Figure 8.3 Object model of `System.Management`

In `System.Management.dll`, the class `ManagementObject` serves as the meta class for all WMI classes (that is, an instance of `ManagementObject` is mapped to a WMI object during its creation via a WMI path and consequently displays this). Unfortunately, this mapping is not as easy to handle as one would want, because all properties have to be called via `PropertyDataCollection` (refer to Figure 8.3) and method calls must be made cumbersomely via `InvokeMethod()`.

NOTE In the following sections, you will see that WPS extremely simplifies the access to COM by providing a WPS object adapter.

WMI Support in WPS

WPS offers the option to access the local WMI repository, and WMI repositories on remote systems, too.

For this purpose, WPS offers the following constructs:

- The commandlet `Get-WmiObject` (alias `gwmi`)
- The integrated WPS type indicators `[WMI]`, `[WMICLASS]`, and `[WMISEARCHER]`
- The WPS WMI object adaptor, which simplifies the access to WMI objects

Accessing WMI Objects

To access a WMI object, you have three options:

- Use of the commandlet `Get-WmiObject` with a filter and optionally with the indication of a computer name
- Use of the integrated WPS types `[WMI]` and `[WMIClass]` with WMI paths
- Direct instantiation of the classes `System.Management.ManagementObject` (that is, `System.Management.ManagementClass` with respective indication of a WMI path in the constructor)

TIP Classes, which can have only one instance anyway, can be called without any filter (see Figure 8.4):

```
Get-WmiObject Win32_ComputerSystem
Get-WmiObject Win32_OperatingSystem
```

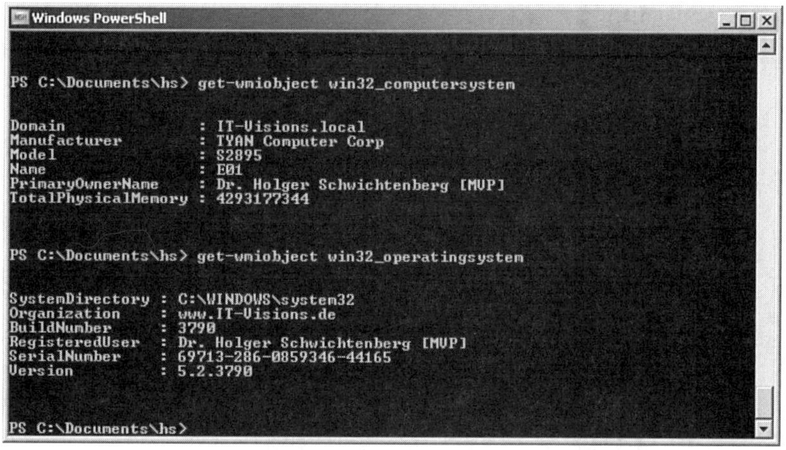

Figure 8.4 `Win32_Computersystem` and `Win32_OperatingSystem` exist only once in the WMI repository.

Table 8.1 Accessing Single WMI Objects

	`Get-WmiObject` with Filter	Integrated WPS Types	Direct Instantiating
WMI Object of a WMI Class with One Key Property	`Get-WmiObject Win32_LogicalDisk -Filter "DeviceID='C:'"`	`[WMI] "\\.\root\cimv2: Win32_LogicalDisk. DeviceID='C:'"`	`New-Object System.Management. ManagementObject("\\. \root\cimv2:Win32_ LogicalDisk.DeviceID='C:'")`
WMI Object of a WMI Class with Two Key Properties	`Get-WmiObject Win32_Account -filter "name='hs' and domain='itv'"`	`[WMI] "\\.\root\cimv2: Win32_UserAccount. Domain='ITV', Name='hs'"`	`New-Object System.Management. ManagementObject("\\.\root\ cimv2:Win32_UserAccount. Domain='ITV',Name='hs'")`
WMI Object on a Remote System	`Get-WmiObject Win32_LogicalDisk -Filter "DeviceID='C:'" -computer "E02"`	`[WMI] "\\E02\root\cimv2: Win32_UserAccount. Domain='ITV', Name='hs'"`	`New-Object System.Management. ManagementObject("\\E02\ root\cimv2: Win32_UserAccount. Domain='ITV',Name='hs'")`
WMI Class	*Not possible*	`[WMICLASS] "\\.\root\ cimv2:Win32_ UserAccount"`	`New-Object System.Management. ManagementClass("\\E01\ root\cimv2:Win32_ UserAccount")`

NOTE A fundamental difference between `Get-WmiObject` and `New-Object` is that `Get-WmiObject` displays all existing instances of a WMI class (for example, all processes), whereas `New-Object` creates a new instance. The semantics of `Get-WmiObject` do not apply to COM and .NET objects because a central directory for instances does not exist. Instead, WMI has the WMI repository. How to display a list of all instances in COM and .NET classes depends on the structure of the respective classes and cannot be expressed generally in WPS.

Type Indicators

When using the type indicators `[WMI]` and `[WMIClass]`, users often forget to set the path name in parentheses when it is a composite name. The type indicators have a stronger binding than the plus operator (+).

Wrong:

```
$Computer = "E01"
[WMI] "Win32_PingStatus.Address='"+ $Computer + "`"
```

Right:

```
$Computer = "E01"
[WMI] ("Win32_PingStatus.Address='"+ $Computer + "`")
```

The WMI Object Adapter

The normal access to WMI objects via .NET is not really "smooth" because you always have to cumbersomely call `PropertyDataCollection`. Here, WPS offers a simplification based on Extended Type System (ETS); WPS dynamically creates objects via the integrated WMI object adapter that comply with the WMI classes. Figure 8.5 shows this complex relationship.

NOTE To answer the question, why you, as WPS user, have to know this mechanism, there are three answers:

1. To be able to transfer code examples that use WSH or .NET to WPS
2. To understand in which documentation you have to look
3. To find the cause if something does not work

WMI is not the only component for which WPS offers such a WPS object adapter. The access to directory services, databases, and XML documents works similarly.

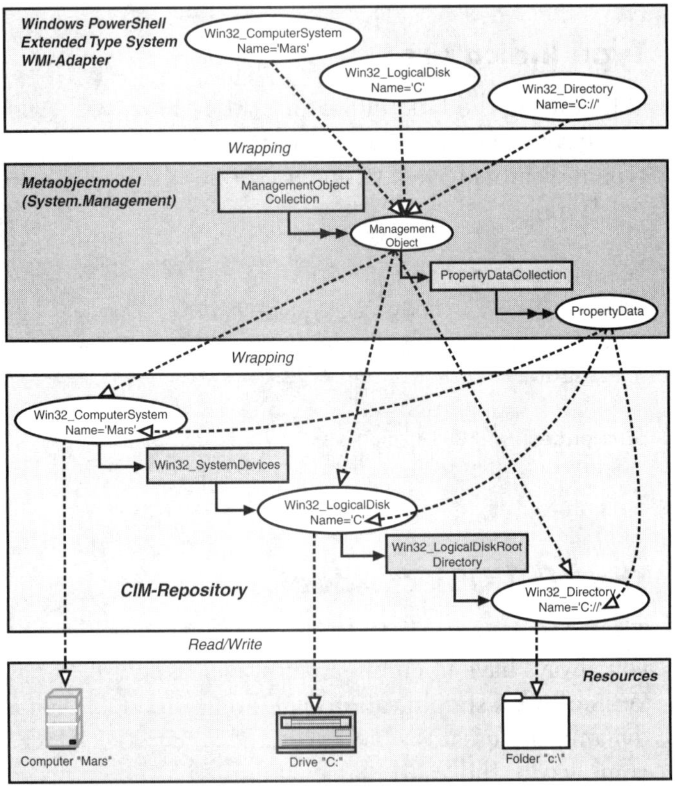

Figure 8.5 Architecture of the WMI in WPS

Analyzing WMI Objects

You can display all available properties and methods in WMI objects with `Get-Member`, just as you can for .NET objects. Although the members of a WMI class (for example, `Win32_Videocontroller`) are not at the same time members of the .NET meta class that packs the WMI class (`System.Management.ManagementObject`), `Get-Member` nevertheless lists the members of both abstraction levels.

WPS has its own way to name classes created by the WMI object adapter. It uses the name of the .NET meta class (`System.Management.ManagementObject`) and the path of the WMI class, separated by the hash sign (#):

```
System.Management.ManagementObject#root\cimv2\Win32_LogicalDisk
```

Figure 8.6 shows the commandlet `Get-Member` displaying such type names.

Figure 8.6 Listing of the pipeline content with `Get-Member` when there are WMI objects in the pipeline

WARNING The properties and methods displayed by `Get-Member` are not members of the .NET class `ManagementObject`, but of the WMI class `Win32_LogicalDisk`. When you search for help information about the objects in the pipeline, you consequently have to consult the documentation of the WMI schema [MSDN05], not the documentation of `System.Management` [MSDN06].

Accessing WMI Members

You can access the properties and the methods of WMI classes just as you access members of .NET classes. WPS abstracts from the meta object model implementation in the .NET class `System.Management.ManagementObject`. The complicated access to the property `Properties` and the method `Invokemethod()` is thus not necessary.

Both the access to single objects and to collections, display a long output list. By default, `Format-List` lists the numerous properties of the displayed WMI objects (see Figure 8.7).

An output with the commandlet `Format-Table` does not help either. True, it makes the output a bit shorter, but also much broader. It would be great to "cut down" the resulting object to its interesting properties with `Select-Object`:

```
Get-WmiObject Win32_VideoController |
Select-Object name,installeddisplaydrive
```

Also, for some WMI classes, there is a definition within the *types.ps1xml* file that properties are to be displayed. There is no such setting for `Win32_Videocontroller`; therefore, all properties display. Figures 8.8 and 8.9, however, show the effect of the declarations for the WMI class `Win32_CDROMDrive`.

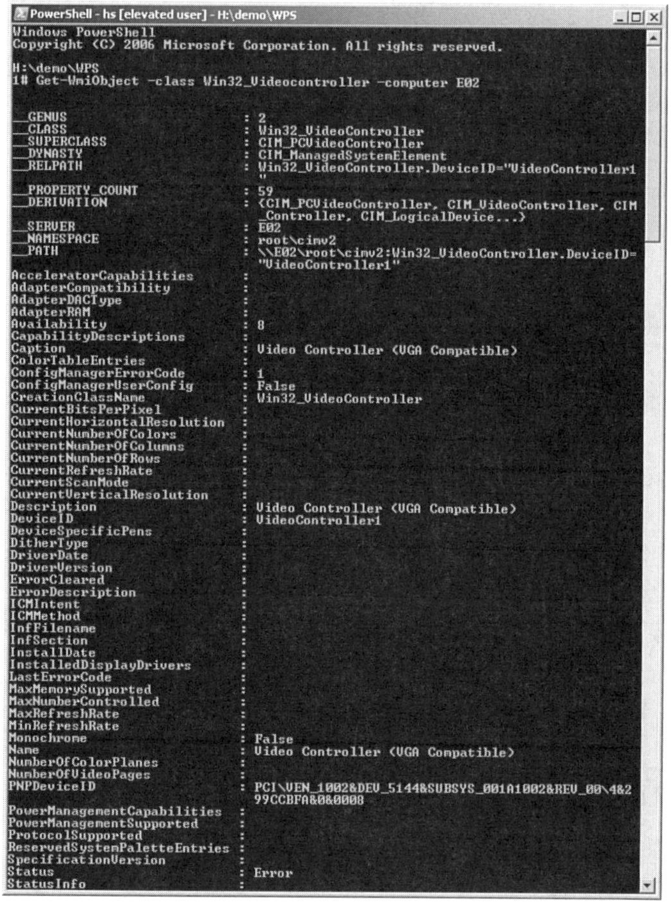

Figure 8.7 Properties of the class `Win32_VideoController`

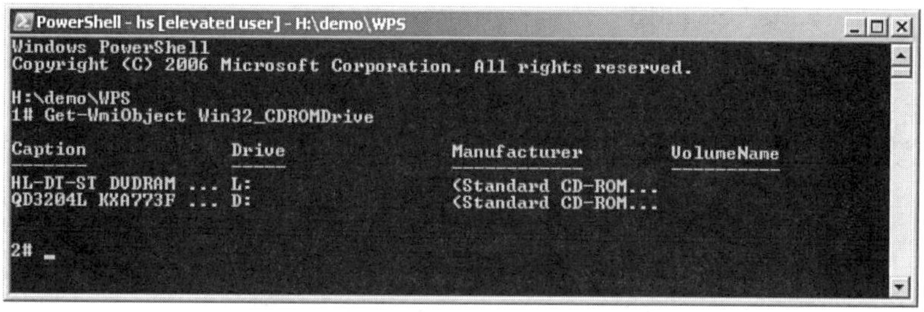

Figure 8.8 Standard output of the command `Get-WmiObject Win32_CDRomDrive`

```
<Type>
    <Name>System.Management.ManagementObject#root\cimv2\Win32_CDROMDrive</Name>
    <Members>
        <PropertySet>
            <Name>PSStatus</Name>
            <ReferencedProperties>
                <Name>Availability</Name>
                <Name>Drive</Name>
                <Name>ErrorCleared</Name>
                <Name>MediaLoaded</Name>
                <Name>NeedsCleaning</Name>
                <Name>Status</Name>
                <Name>StatusInfo</Name>
            </ReferencedProperties>
        </PropertySet>
        <MemberSet>
            <Name>PSStandardMembers</Name>
            <Members>
                <PropertySet>
                    <Name>DefaultDisplayPropertySet</Name>
                    <ReferencedProperties>
                        <Name>Caption</Name>
                        <Name>Drive</Name>
                        <Name>Manufacturer</Name>
                        <Name>VolumeName</Name>
                    </ReferencedProperties>
                </PropertySet>
            </Members>
        </MemberSet>
    </Members>
</Type>
```

Figure 8.9 Setting of the displayed properties for WMI class `Win32_CDRomDrive`

Listing 8.4 shows further examples for the use of `Get-WmiObject` in cooperation with commandlets for the pipeline control.

Listing 8.4 Using `Get-WmiObject`

```
# Name and free bytes on all drives
Get-WmiObject Win32_logicaldisk | Select-Object
➥deviceid,freespace

# Name and domain of the user accounts, whose names
➥never become invalid
Get-WmiObject Win32_account | Where-Object
➥{$_.Passwordexpires -eq 0 } | Select-Object Name,Domain
```

Static Class Members

In contrast to the handling of .NET objects, WPS does not make any syntactic differences between static methods and instance methods in WMI (that is, you always have to use the simple dot operator; in .NET objects, the colon has to be used for static methods). As far as WMI is concerned, the WPS type [WMIClass] refers only to the WMI path of the WMI class, not to a precise instance.

For example:

```
([WMIClass] "Win32_Product").Install("c:\name.msi")
```

Date and Time

In WMI, date and time are saved as a string in the form of `yyyymmddHHMMSS.mmmmmmsUUU`; in this rather self-explanatory short form, `mmmmmm` stands for the number of milliseconds, and `UUU` stands for the number of minutes. The local time differs from the universal coordinated time (UTC). `UUU` is the three-digit offset indicating the number of minutes that the originating time zone deviates from UTC.

The static method `ToDateTime()` in the class `System.Management.ManagementDateTimeConverter` is available for the conversion of a WMI date format into a normal date format of WPS (class `System.DateTime`):

Listing 8.5 Converting WMI Date Formats to an Instance of `System.DateTime`

```
$cs = Get-WMIObject -Class Win32_OperatingSystem
"Starting time of the system in WMI format: " + $cs.LastBootUpTime
[System.DateTime] $starting time =
➥[System.Management.ManagementDateTimeConverter]::
➥ToDateTime($cs.LastBootUpTime)
"Starting time of the system in normal format: " + $starting time
```

With the PowerShell Community Extensions installed, the class `ManagementObject` possesses the additional method `ConvertToDateTime()`, which can perform the conversion:

Listing 8.6 Another Option for Converting a WMI Date Format to an Instance of `System.DateTime`

```
$cs = Get-WMIObject -Class Win32_OperatingSystem -property
LastBootUpTime
$cs.ConvertToDateTime($cs.LastBootUpTime)
```

Accessing WMI Collections

The use of Get-WmiObject with a WMI class name

```
Get-WmiObject WMIClassname
```

displays all instances of the indicated WMI class (if the WMI class exists on the local system).

For example, the following

```
# Name and drive for all graphic cards in this computer
Get-WmiObject Win32_VideoController
```

displays all installed video cards.

This is the short form for

```
Get-WmiObject -class Win32_VideoController
```

If the class is not declared in the standard namespace root\cimv2, you have to indicate the namespace explicitly with the parameter -Namespace:

```
Get-WmiObject IISwebserver -Namespace root\microsoftIISv2
```

You can also access the WMI schema on remote systems with the parameter -Computer:

```
Get-WmiObject -class Win32_VideoController -computer E02
```

Filtering and Selecting

If you do not want to display all instances, but only selected ones that adhere to special criteria, you can use these alternative options:

- Use of a filter in the commandlet Get-WmiObject
- Use of WQL queries with the parameter -Query in the commandlet Get-WmiObject
- Use of WQL queries with the type indicator [WMISEARCHER]
- Use of WQL queries with the .NET class System.Management.ManagementObjectSearcher

Filtering with `Get-WmiObject`

With the commandlet `Get-WmiObject`, you can filter objects as soon as they are called. You have to insert the criteria after the parameter `-Filter` in a string.

Consider these examples:

- All user-accounts from the domain ITV
  `Get-WmiObject Win32_account -filter "domain='itv'"`
- All user accounts whose name starts with *H* from the domain ITV
  `Get-WmiObject Win32_account -filter "domain='itv' and name like 'h%'"`

WQL Queries

Queries written in WMI Query Language (WQL) can be executed in WPS with the parameter `-Query` in the commandlet `Get-WmiObject` or with the WPS type indicator `[WMISEARCHER]` (see Figures 8.10 and 8.11).

The following command selects all network adapters that contain the number 802 in the network card type:

```
Get-WmiObject -query "Select * from Win32_Networkadapter
➥where adaptertype like '%802%'" | select
➥adaptertype,description
```

Alternatively, you can execute this query with the type indicator `[WMISearcher]`:

```
([WmiSearcher] "Select * from Win32_Networkadapter where
➥adaptertype like '%802%'").get()| select
➥adaptertype,description
```

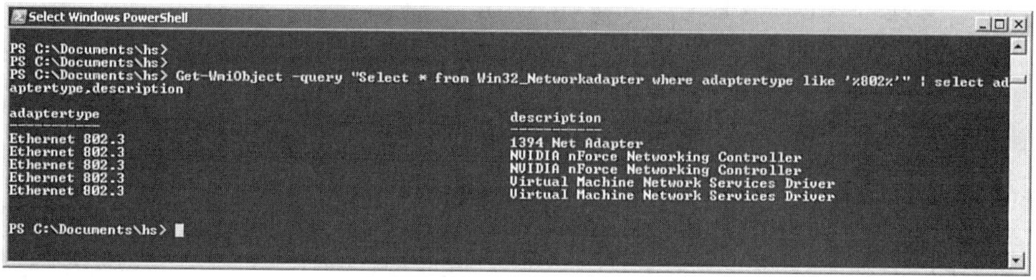

Figure 8.10 Execution of a WMI query

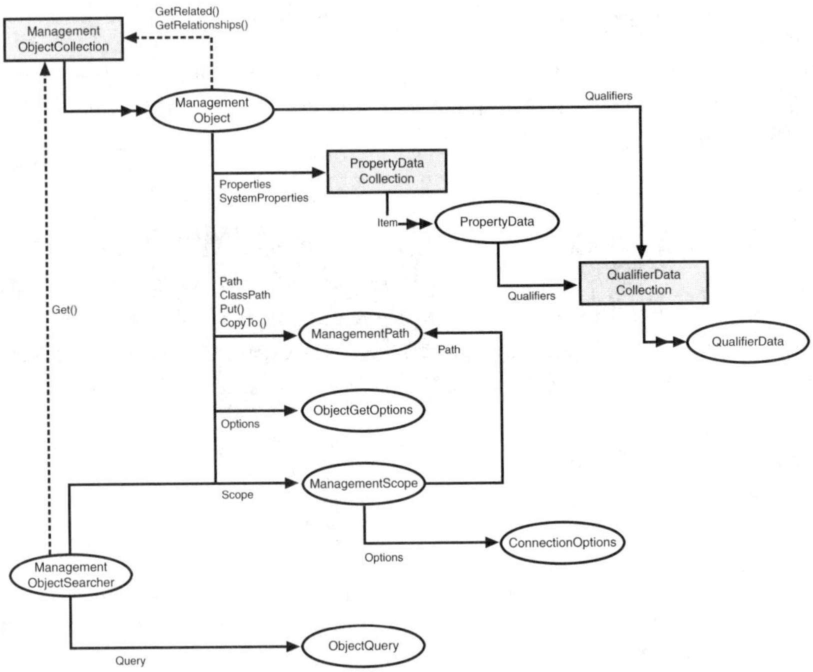

Figure 8.11 Object model for searching via `[WMISearcher]` or `System.Management.ManagementObjectSearcher`

List of All WMI Classes

You can display a list of all available WMI classes on one system with the parameter `-List` in the commandlet `Get-WmiObject`. Here, a class name may not be indicated.

```
Get-WmiObject -list
```

If not indicated otherwise, the namespace `"root\cimv2"` is used. You can also indicate a namespace explicitly:

```
Get-WmiObject -list -Namespace
➥root/cimv2/Anwendungs/microsoftIE
```

You can access the WMI repository of a specific computer because all classes are dependent on the drive and on the installed applications:

```
Get-WmiObject -list -Computer E02
```

Creating New Instances of WMI Classes

Many WMI classes are structured in such a way that a new instance of a class has to be instantiated for the creation of a new system element. For this purpose, static methods with the name `Create()` are provided on class level (see Figure 8.12).

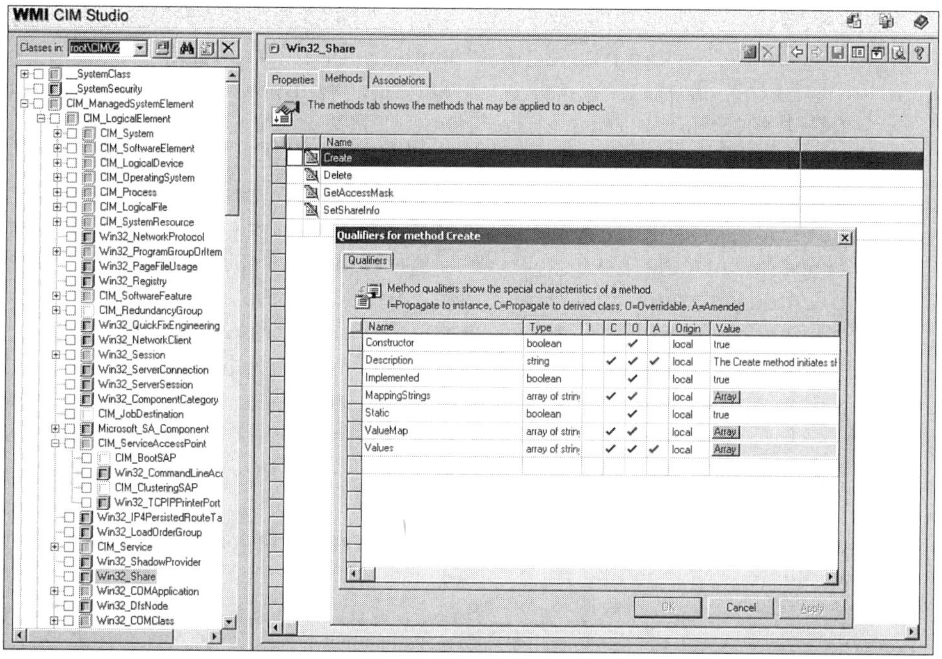

Figure 8.12 Methods of the class `Win32_Share`

Listing 8.7 shows the creation of a file share with standard rights. The creation of file share with specific permission is a more complex matter, and is discussed later in this book.

Listing 8.7 Creating a New Share with Default Permissions

```
# Create Win32_Share
$class = [WMIClass] "ROOT\CIMV2:Win32_Share"
$Access = $Null
$R = $class.Create($pfad, $Sharename, 0, 10, $Comment, "", $Access)
if ( $R.ReturnValue -ne 0) { Write-Error "Error in creating:
➥"+ $R.ReturnValue; Exit}
"Clearance is created!"
```

Summary

Microsoft does not provide commandlets for all administrative tasks yet.

In this chapter, you have learned how to use classes defined with the .NET Framework class library, with COM components, and with WMI. .NET and COM libraries can be used though the commandlet `New-Object`. WMI objects are received accessible via `Get-WmiObject`.

Using class libraries is more difficult than using commandlets (especially because with class libraries you must have knowledge of object-oriented programming). However, because Microsoft provides only a small number of commandlets for accessing the Windows infrastructure, in many cases using a class library is the only way to perform certain actions within WPS.

In contrast to .NET and COM, the classes in WMI are accessed through a meta model. This makes the understanding of the *modus operandi* of this library a little more difficult. On the other hand, the meta model provides common approaches for accessing objects, members, and collections that can be used for all classes.

CHAPTER 9

PowerShell Tools

In this chapter:

This chapter discusses the Windows PowerShell (WPS) console provided by Microsoft and useful tools from other vendors. So far, Microsoft does not provide an editor for PowerShell scripts.

NOTE As far as external tools are concerned, keep in mind that most of the tools implement their own hosting of WPS. Therefore, the tools have the same functional power as the WPS console, but do not share a common declaration space. Definitions of aliases, drives, and new script-based commandlets are therefore relevant only for the respective current execution environment.

PowerShell Console

Speculation about a WPS console with IntelliSense did not become reality because the WPS development team for version 1.0 put their focus strictly on the WPS infrastructure. They gave very little attention to supporting tools.

The WPS console offers only a little more input support than the classic command shell in Windows. Version 1.0 of the WPS console, however, is far from reaching the support level of the development environment in Visual Studio.

Console Functions

The WPS console offers the following functions:

- The size and design of the window can be controlled via the properties of the console window (see Figure 9.1).
- The Windows clipboard is only cumbersomely available via the menu (see Figure 9.2); that is, via the so-called quick edit mode. The key combinations Ctrl+C/X/V do not work.
- Command and path input and class names and object member can be completed with the Tab key.
- A return to the last 64 commands (number is variable) is possible (command history).
- The last commands are shown using the key F7 (see Figure 9.3).
- Callback of the last command can be performed completely with the key F3 or sign-wise via F1.
- The termination of a running command can be performed with the key combination Ctrl+C.

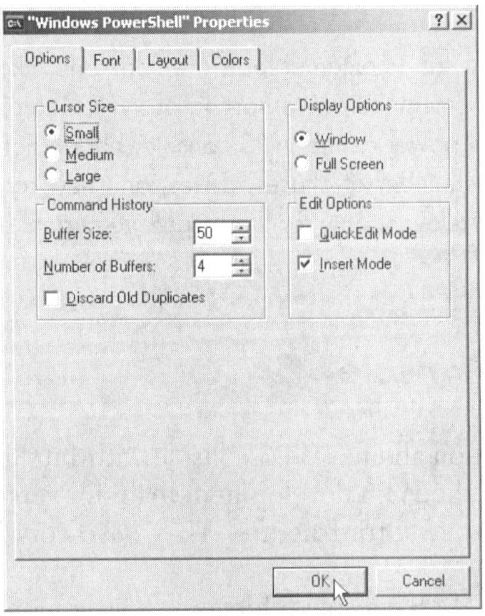

Figure 9.1 Window properties for the WPS console

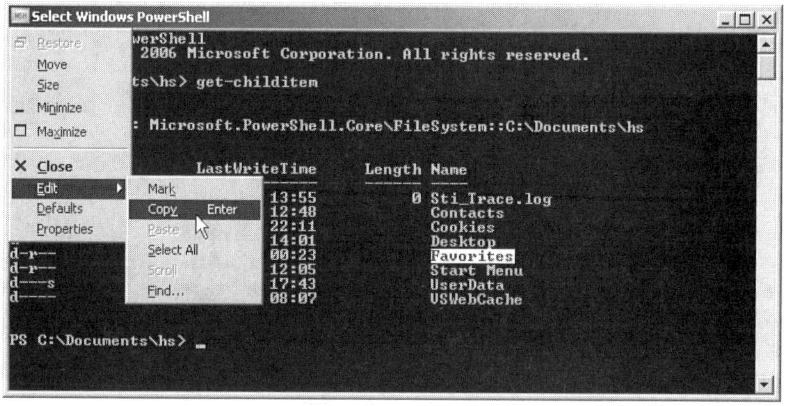

Figure 9.2 Use of the cache in the WPS console

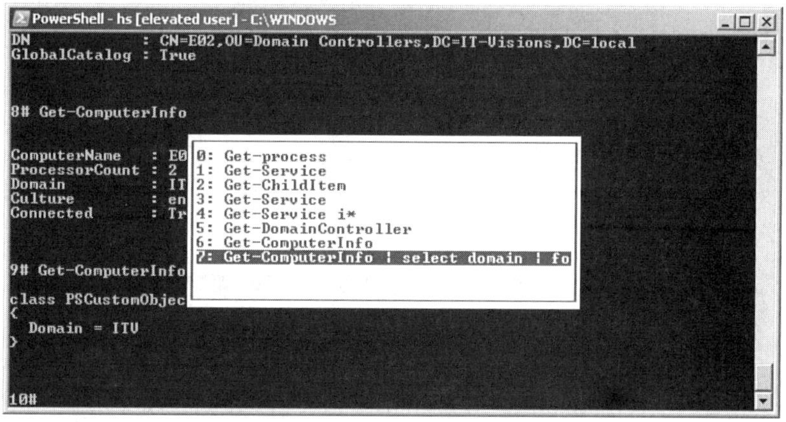

Figure 9.3 Output of the command history with F7

Tab Completion

For commandlets, parameters, and object properties, WPS supplies a function already common in the classic command-line window. In the DOS command-line window, you can run through the available files and subdirectories with the Tab key (called *Tab completion* in developer talk) after typing one or several letters. In WPS, this also works with commandlets, their parameters, and the properties of objects in the pipeline (see Figures 9.4 through 9.6).

Figure 9.4 Input of the beginning of a word

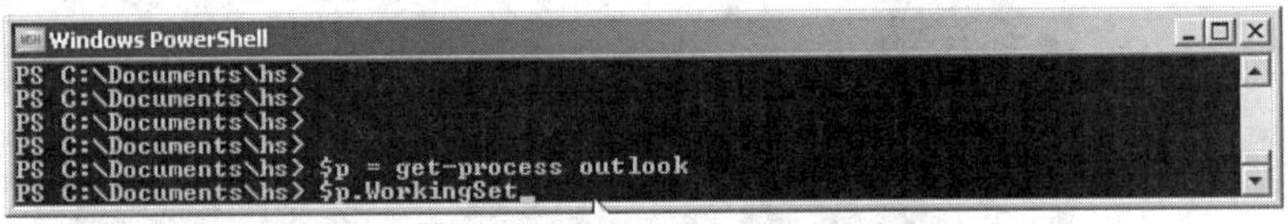

Figure 9.5 After you press the Tab key, the first alternative appears.

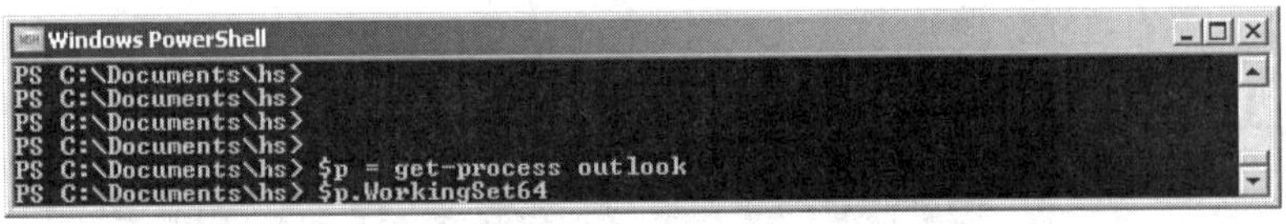

Figure 9.6 After you press the Tab key again, the second alternative appears.

Command Mode Versus Interpreter Mode

Generally, the console executes all commands immediately after you press Enter. If, however, an incomplete command had been entered (for example, a command ending with the pipeline symbol, |), the WPS console changes to the so-called interpreter mode, where commands are not executed immediately. The interpreter mode is indicated by the prompt >> (see Figure 9.7). The interpreter mode is valid as long as you make a blank entry (see Figure 9.8). Then the command is executed.

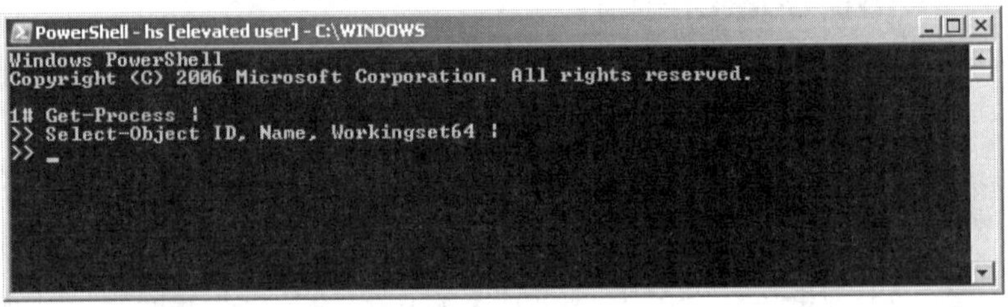

Figure 9.7 The console is in interpreter mode.

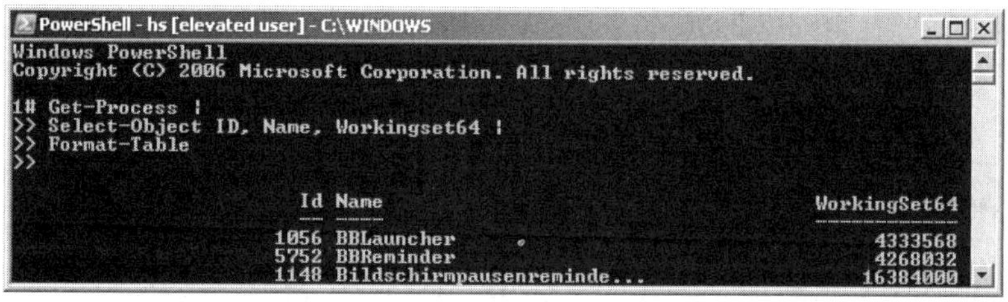

Figure 9.8 The interpreter mode has been left via a blank entry.

User Account Control in Windows Vista

WPS, as well as all other applications, is subject to Vista's user account control and is therefore started with limited permissions. To start WPS with full permissions, select Execute as Administrator in the context menu under the application icon. After that, Vista will ask for confirmation of the elevation of permissions.

In contrast to the classic Windows shell, WPS thereafter does not indicate in the titles list that it now runs under administrative rights.

TIP To show the elevation status in the titles list of the WPS console and to affect other adjustments of the display, if applicable (as shown in Figure 9.9), you can write a WPS profile script. In Chapter 10, "Tips, Tricks, and Troubleshooting," you learn how to write such a script (as well as the script used to display the elevation status).

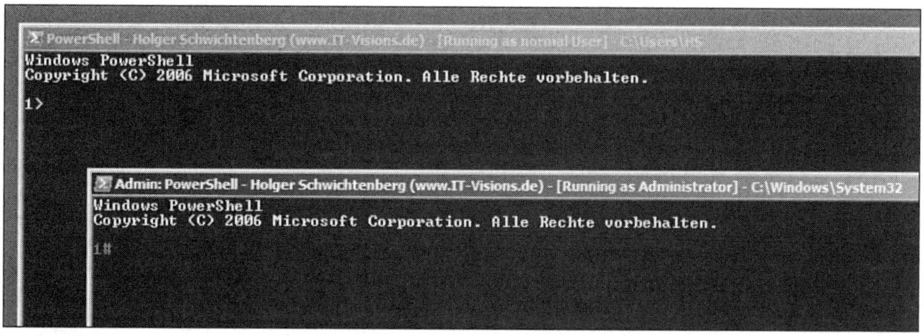

Figure 9.9 Two WPS instances with different rights

In addition, you can use the Windows command-line tool *whoami.exe* with the option `/all` to check which permission a running console has.

PowerTab

PowerTab extends the WPS console capabilities, proposing possible commands to the user when the user presses the Tab key. PowerTab especially makes proposals for members of .NET classes.

PowerTab	
Vendor	Marc van Orsouw (short "MoW")
Price	Free of charge
URL	http://thepowershellguy.com/blogs/posh/pages/powertab.aspx

PowerShell IDE

The preliminary version of the PowerShell IDE, which was available at the time of this writing, offers IntelliSense for commandlets, parameters, .NET classes, and class members.

PowerShell IDE	
Vendor	ScriptInternals—Dr. Tobias Weltner
Price	Beta version free of charge
URL	www.powershell.de

PowerShell IDE offers two modes:

- In the interactive mode, all commands are executed immediately, just like in the WPS console. The advantage of IDE, however, is that syntax color highlighting and selection lists are available in a separate editor. In a separate window, the user can see the current status of all variables.
- In the script mode, the user writes, also with IntelliSense-like functions, complex command sequences in WPS language, which can be saved under the file extension `.ps1` and started at a later date.

`.ps1` is the official file extension for WPS scripts, which can also be understood by the WPS console. The PowerShell IDE user can also save interactive recordings of interactive sessions in the form of XML files with the file extension `.brain`. This format, however, is understood only by the PowerShell IDE. The user can also save the content of the output window by clicking the symbol Hardcopy.

- Debugging in script mode is interesting. PowerShell IDE, just like other modern IDEs, allows users to set breakpoints. Upon stopping, the Variables window shows the currently valid values.

So far, according to its author, the PowerShell IDE is an "experimental editor." The real product will be Windows PowerShell Plus. Many functions in the PowerShell IDE, including help and the intended community function for the exchange of source code, are not implemented yet. Sometimes, for example, you get a system crash rather than help. Nevertheless, working with the PowerShell IDE is clearly easier than direct input at the WPS console (see Figure 9.10).

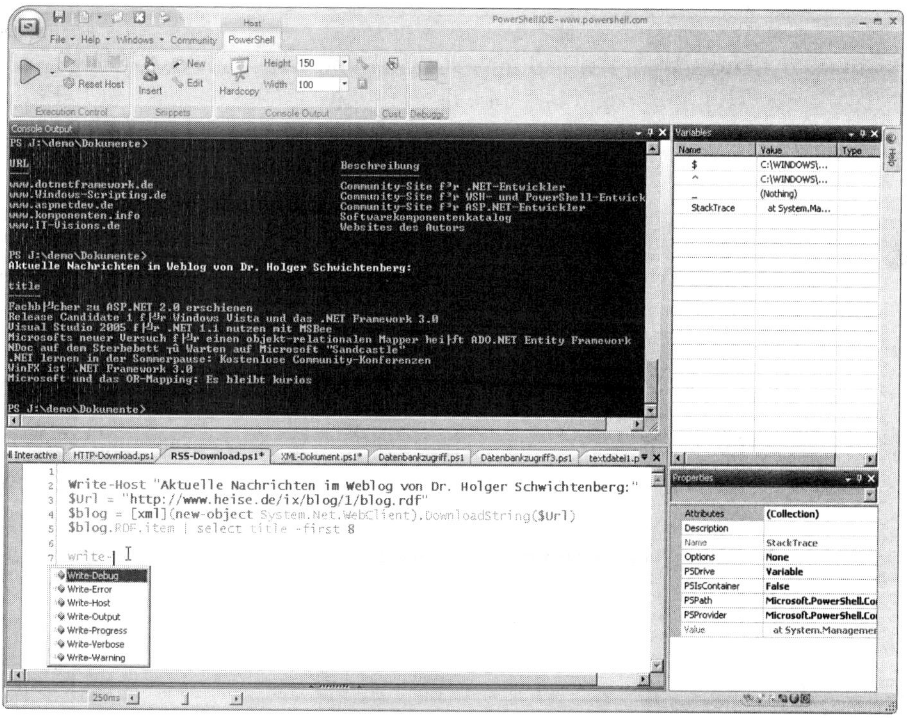

Figure 9.10 PowerShell IDE 1.0 for WPS 1.0

Windows PowerShellPlus

PowerShellPlus is the commercial enhancement of the PowerShell IDE. PowerShellPlus consists of an improved WPS console (PowerShellPlus Host) that directly supports IntelliSense and a related editor (PowerShellPlus Editor).

PowerShellPlus	
Vendor	Shell Tools, LLC
Price	$79
URL	www.powershell.com

Notable functions of PowerShellPlus include the following:

- The console is an enhancement of the WPS console and thus understands all commands that are understood by the WPS console delivered by Microsoft.
- In contrast to the classic Windows console, this console supports copying and inserting via Ctrl+C and Ctrl+V.
- The editor and console are integrated. The console and editor are shown in two separate windows when a script is started, but the script is shown in the console. A quick change is possible with Ctrl+W.
- IntelliSense exists in the console and in the editor for commandlet names, commandlet parameters, variable names, path names, .NET class names and .NET class members (see Figures 9.11 through 9.18).
- Code editor with syntax highlighting.
- Debugging with single-step mode (see Figure 9.19).
- Use and administration of reusable code snippets.
- Recording of console entries, which can be recalled via hot keys.
- Display of current variables and details of their contents (see Figure 9.20).
- Transparent display of console window (optional).
- Direct edit of WPS profile scripts.

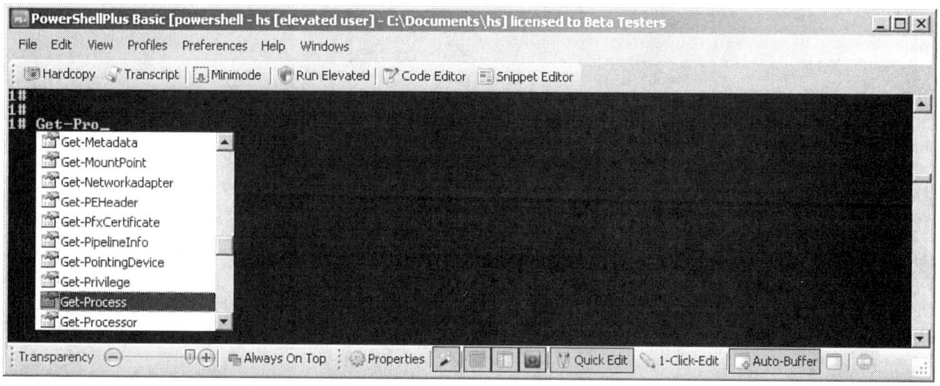

Figure 9.11 IntelliSense for commandlet names

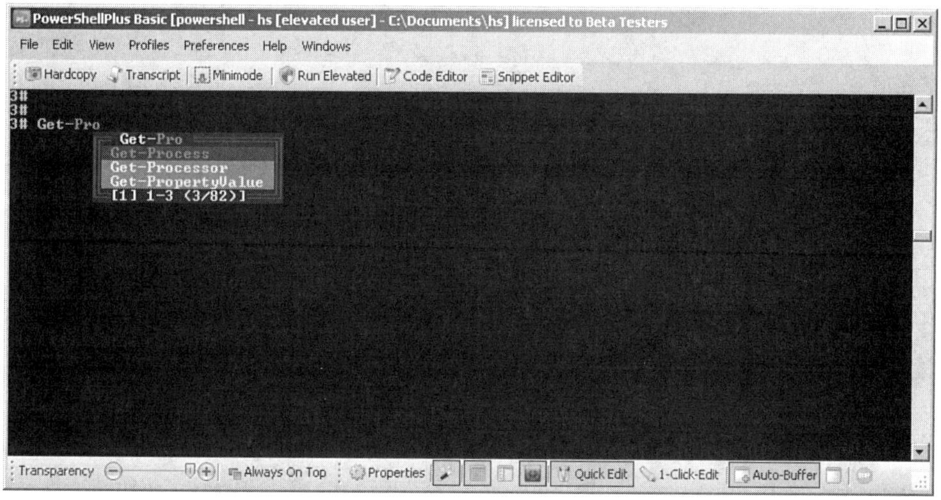

Figure 9.12 An alternative IntelliSense for commandlet names

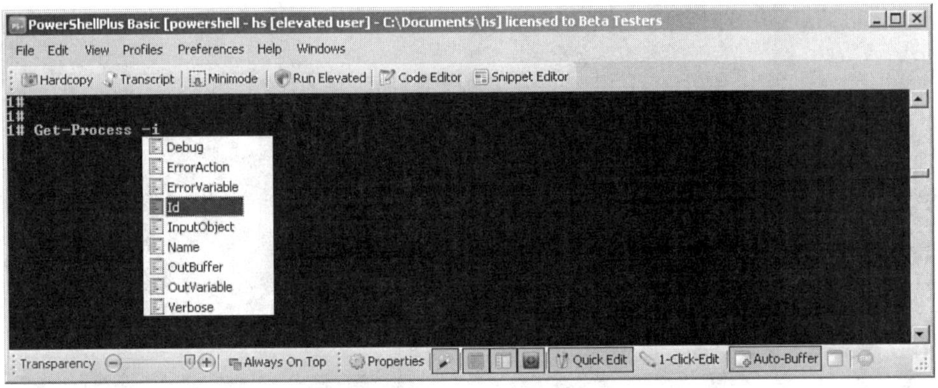

Figure 9.13 IntelliSense for commandlet parameters

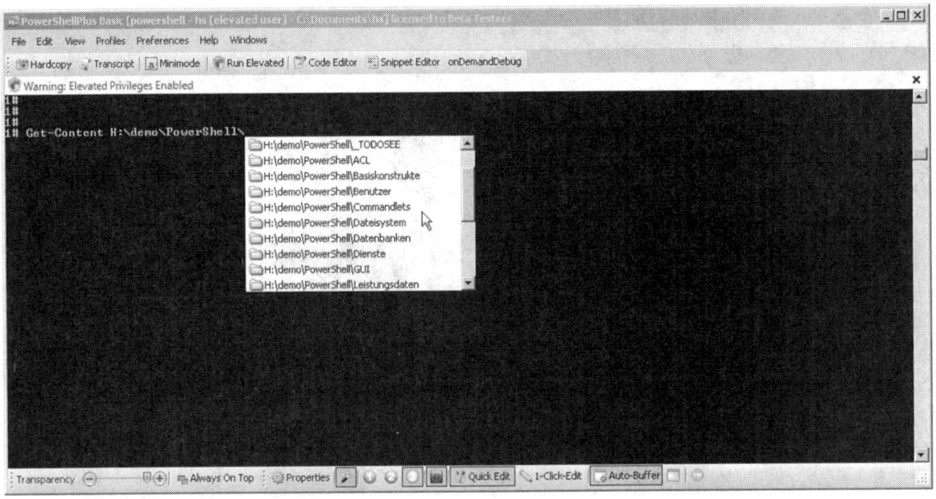

Figure 9.14 IntelliSense for path names

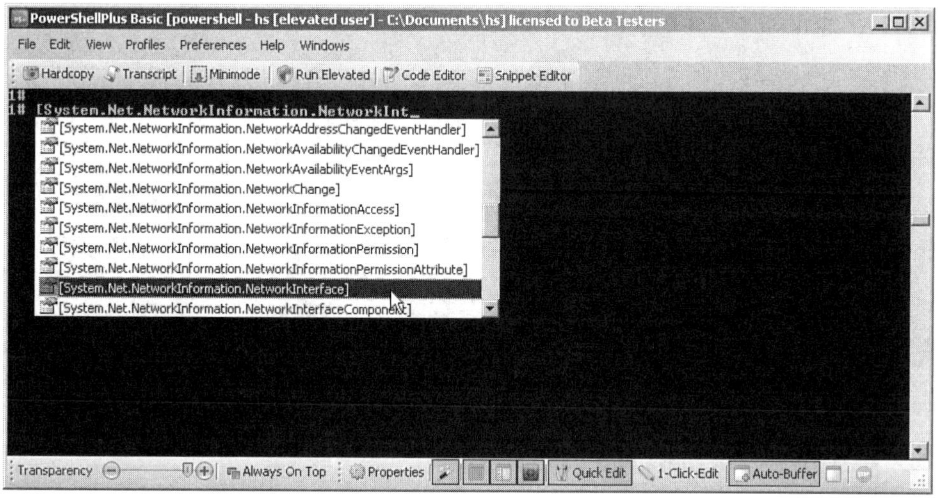

Figure 9.15 IntelliSense for .NET class names

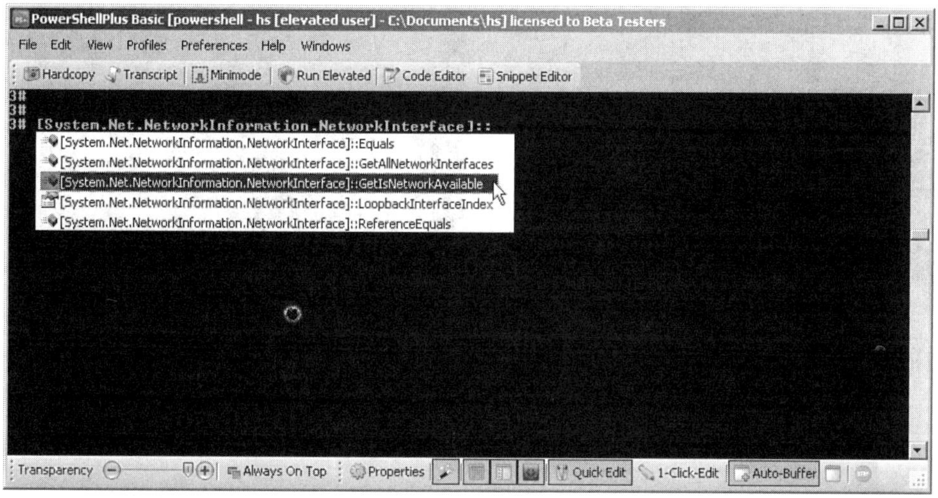

Figure 9.16 IntelliSense for .NET class members

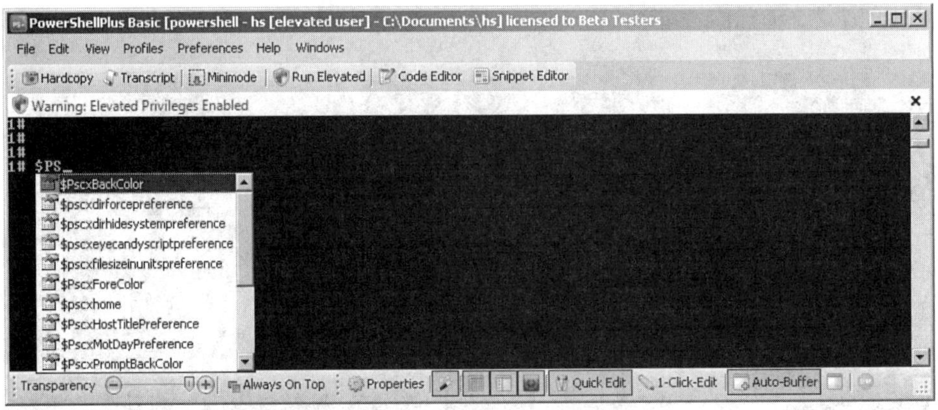

Figure 9.17 IntelliSense for variable names

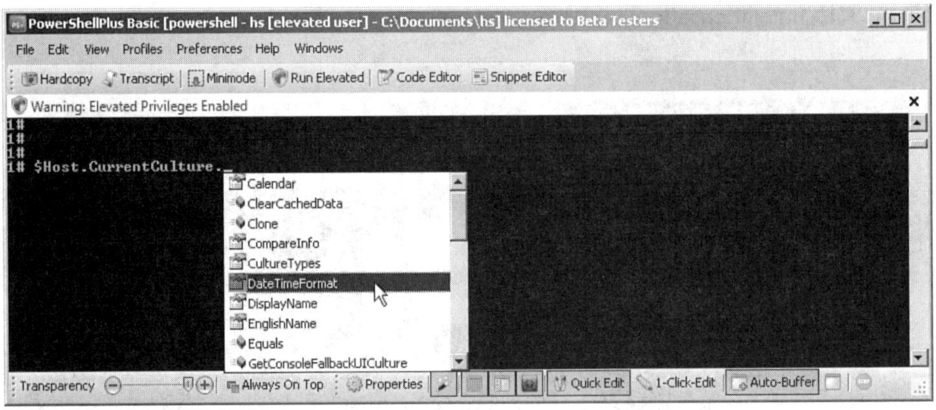

Figure 9.18 IntelliSense for variable members

TIP In the PowerShellPlus Editor, debugging is used not only for error searching, but also for improving the IntelliSense support. Because a commandlet does not declare which objects are in the pipeline, and the output of a commandlet can depend on the context, the editor cannot know the available options as long as the script has not been run at least once. When you are running the debugger, the PowerShellPlus Editor remembers the content of the pipelines and the variables and will provide IntelliSense thereafter.

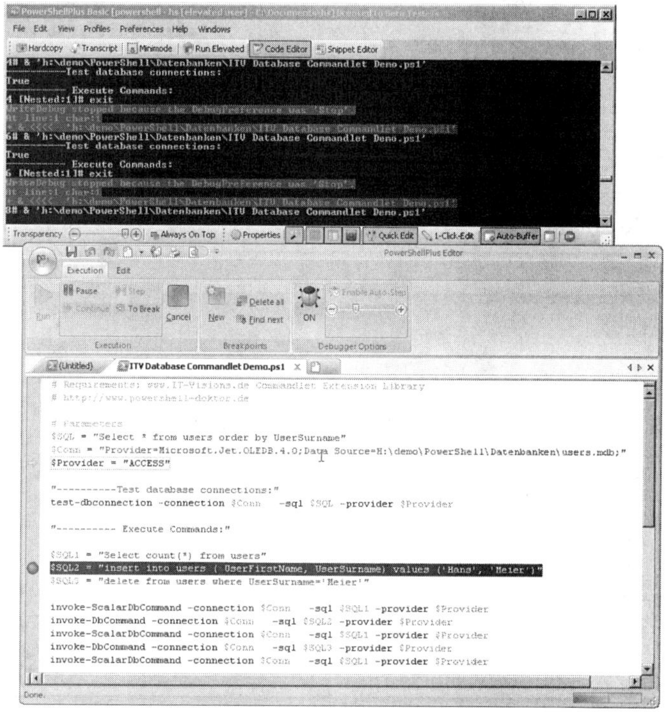

Figure 9.19 Debugging with single-step mode

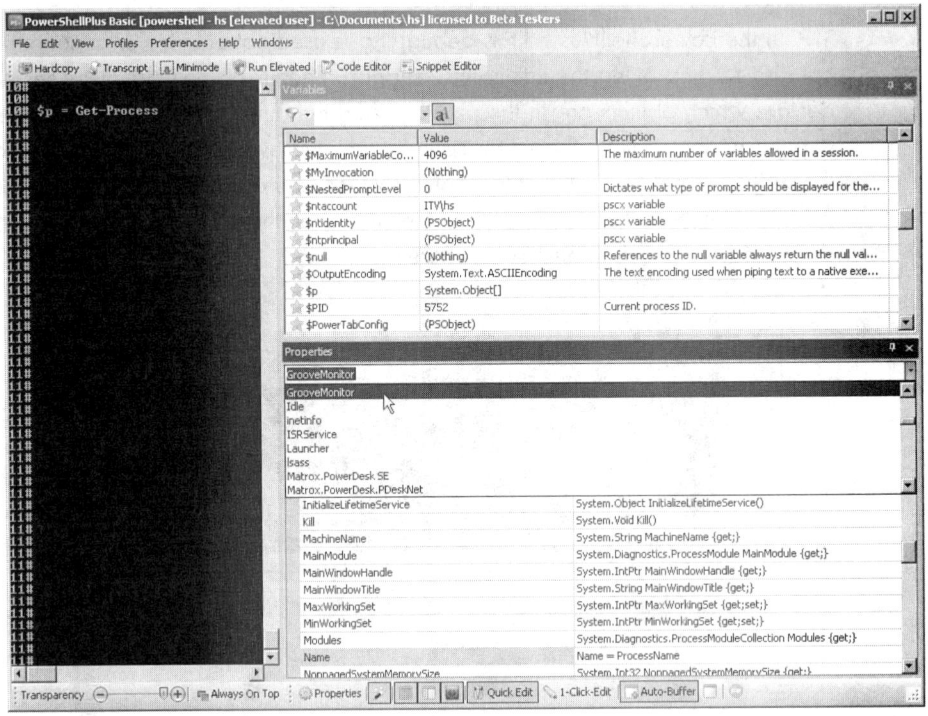

Figure 9.20 Display of all current variables and their content

PowerShell Analyzer

The Windows PowerShell Analyzer by Karl Prosser, an owner of Shell Tools, enables you to display pipeline objects in a table (see Figure 9.21) or diagram. These are several separated run spaces in which WPS commands can be executed independently. However, two important editor functions are missing here: IntelliSense for classes and class members (see Figure 9.21) and a debugger.

PowerShell Analyzer	
Vendor	Shell Tools, LLC
Price	$129
URL	www.powershellanalyzer.com

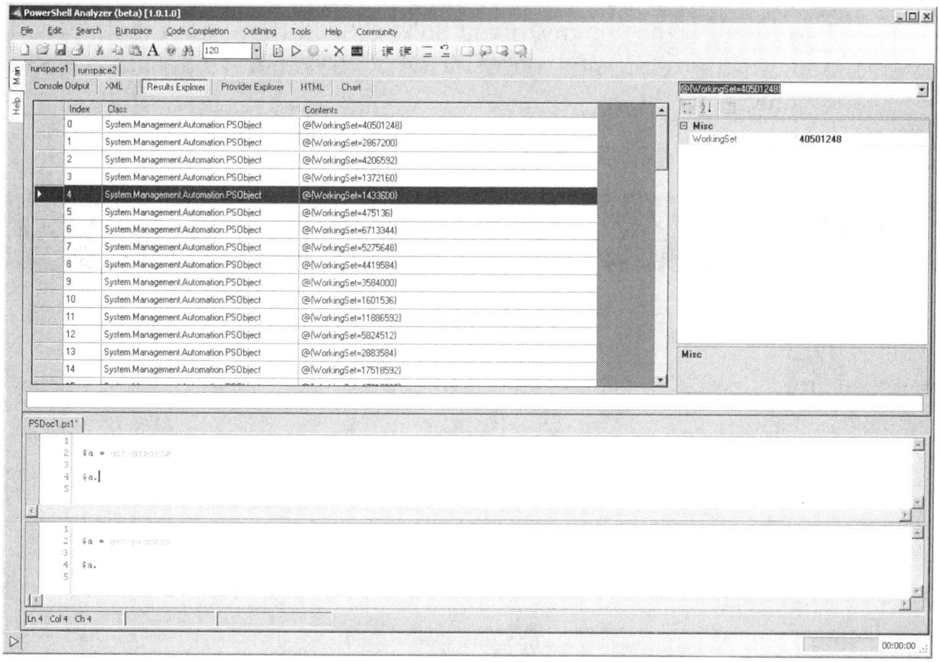

Figure 9.21 Windows PowerShell Analyzer 1.0 for WPS 1.0

PrimalScript

The universal editor PrimalScript supports editing WPS scripts starting with version 4.1 (see Figure 9.22). For further information, refer to the website of the vendor, Sapien.

PrimalScript	
Vendor	Sapien
Price	From $179
URL	www.primalscript.com/

Table 9.1 compares PrimalScript 4.5 with PowerShellPlus 1.0 and the PowerShell IDE, demonstrating on one hand that PowerShellPlus offers more functions for WPS, but showing on the other hand that PrimalScript is a universal editor.

Table 9.1 Comparison of PrimalScript 4.5 and PowerShellPlus 1.0

	PowerShellPlus 1.0	PowerShell IDE 1.0	PrimalScript 4.5
Console for interactive input	Yes	No	No
Script editor	Yes	Yes	Yes
IntelliSense for commandlets (see Figure 9.23)	Yes	Yes	Yes
IntelliSense for parameters (see Figure 9.24)	Yes	Yes	Yes
IntelliSense for class names	Yes	Yes	Yes
IntelliSense for .NET class members	Yes	No	No
IntelliSense for variable names (see Figure 9.25)	Yes	No	No
IntelliSense for variable members	Yes	No	No

	PowerShellPlus 1.0	PowerShell IDE 1.0	PrimalScript 4.5
IntelliSense for path names	Yes	No	No
Debugging	Yes	Yes	Yes
Support for other types of files	XML	N/A	WSH, ActionScript, AWK, AutoIt, Batch, HTA, Kixtart, LotusScript, Perl, Python, Rebol, REXX, Ruby, SQL, Tcl, WinBatch, ASP, HTML, JSP, PHP, XML, XLST, XSD, C#, C++, VB, ColdFusion u.a.

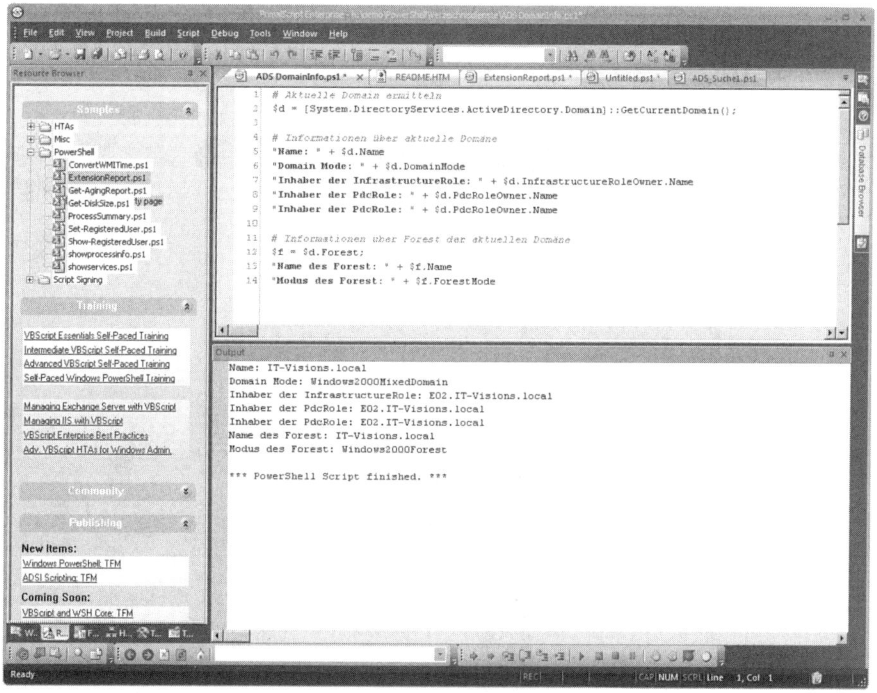

Figure 9.22 Output of a WPS script in PrimalScript 2007

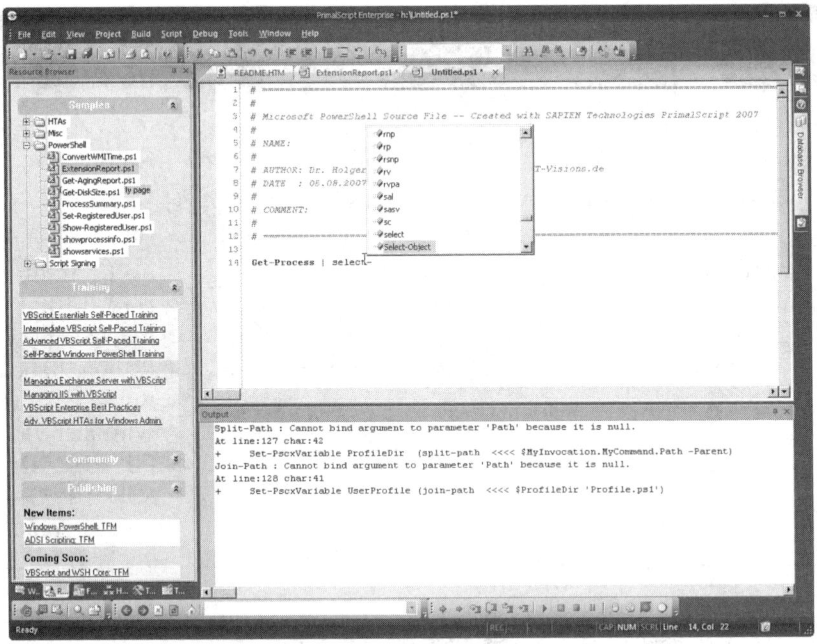

Figure 9.23 IntelliSense for commandlets

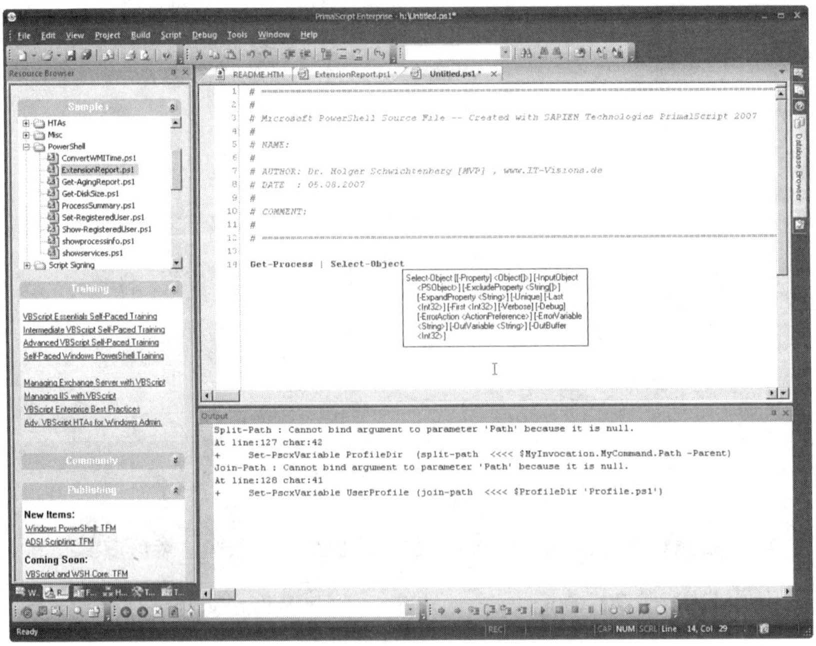

Figure 9.24 IntelliSense for parameters

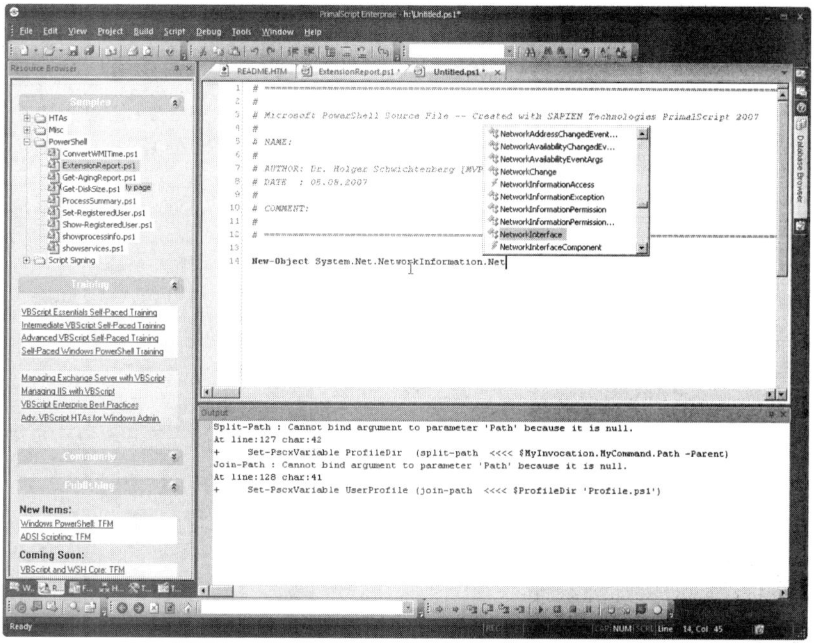

Figure 9.25 IntelliSense for class names

PowerShell Help

PowerShell Help is a simple tool to show the stored help text for commandlets stored in XML files (see Figure 9.26).

PowerShell Help	
Vendor	Sapien
Price	Free
URL	www.primalscript.com/Free_Tools/index.asp

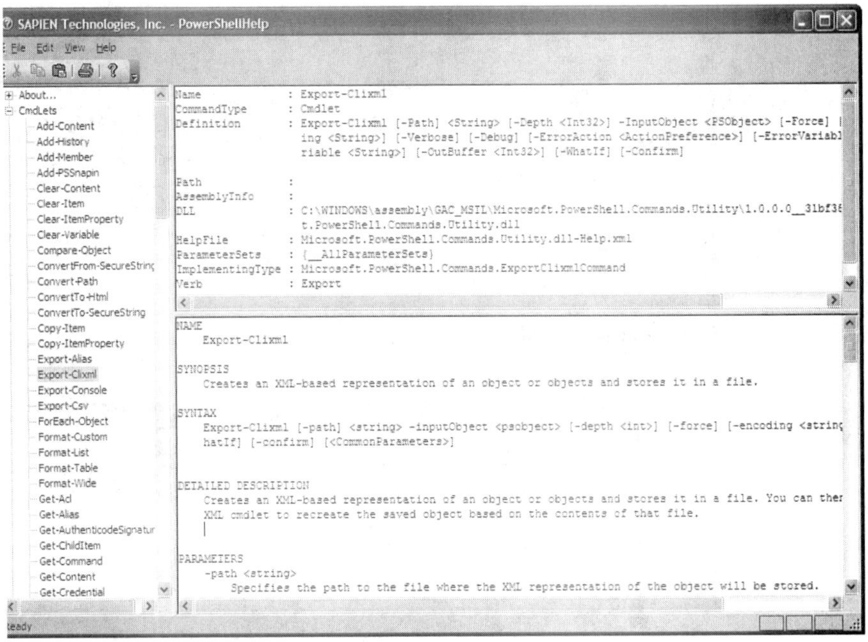

Figure 9.26 PowerShell Help for WPS 1.0

Summary

In this chapter, you learned that the WPS console is basically the same as the classic Windows console, with just a few more features. You can add input support with the free PowerTab tool. The third-party tool PowerShellPlus provides full IntelliSense support for the console.

Microsoft does not provide an editor for WPS scripts. For such, you can choose between the free, albeit incomplete PowerShell IDE and the commercial products PowerShellPlus Editor and PrimalScript.

CHAPTER 10

TIPS, TRICKS, AND TROUBLESHOOTING

In this chapter:

This chapter contains a few tips for your work with Windows PowerShell (WPS), including debugging, installing commandlet extensions, using profile scripts and the command history, and displaying user interfaces. The chapter also introduces a few of the available commandlet extensions from third-party vendors and the open source community.

Debugging and Tracing

Regarding debugging, the commandlets offer a few common parameters:

- With the parameters `-Verbose` and `-Debug`, the administrator gets more output than usual.
- With `-Confirm`, the administrator requests that all actions that make any changes have to be reconfirmed by the user.
- To be on the safe side, you can simulate actions with `-WhatIf` before starting the real execution.

WARNING The parameters `-Confirm` and `-WhatIf` are not supported by all commandlets.

When you use `-WhatIf` with the commandlet `Stop-Service`, WPS lists in detail which services Windows will really stop, according to existing service dependencies.

`-WhatIf` is also very helpful when you use a command with a placeholder. Figure 10.1 shows which services would be stopped when `Stop-Service a*` is executed.

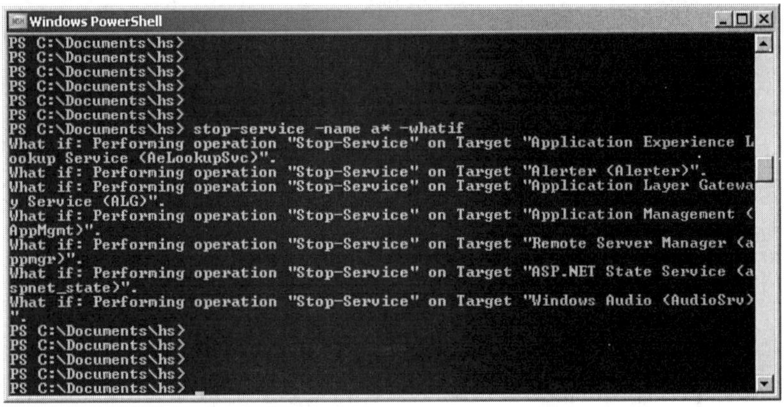

Figure 10.1 Operations with placeholders can have severe consequences; `-WhatIf` demonstrates which services would be affected.

Verbose Execution

Detailed information about a single commandlet can be gathered via the standard parameter `–verbose`. If you want to get the same for whole scripts, use `Set-PsDebug -trace 1` or `Set-PsDebug -trace 2`. Figure 10.2 shows the output of `-trace 1`. With `-trace 2`, the output would be even more detailed.

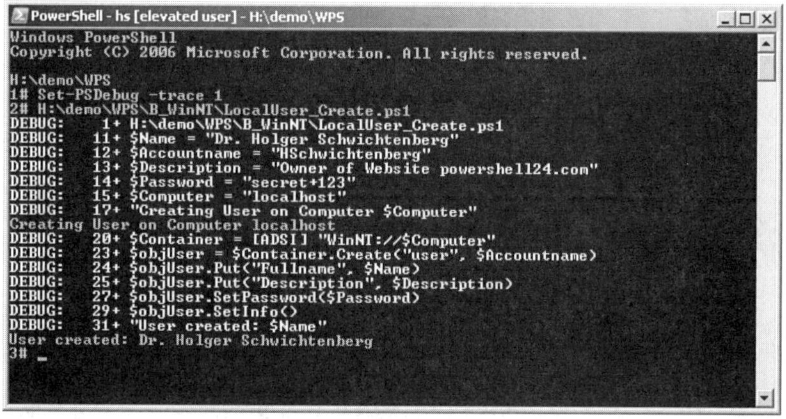

Figure 10.2 Protocoling a script execution

Single-Step Mode

With the commandlet `Set-PsDebug -step`, you can execute a script step by step. WPS not only executes the steps, it also asks after each step whether you want to continue the execution (see Figure 10.3).

Measuring Execution Time

The commandlet `Measure-Command` shows, in the form of a `TimeSpan` object, how much time a command needs for execution.

For example

```
Measure-Command { Get-Process | Foreach-Object { $_.ws } }
```

Tracing

You can activate a trace with the commandlet `Set-TraceSource`, which displays internal information about each step processed within the WPS environment. `Get-TraceSource` lists all traceable sources. By default, there are 176 sources. This shows the complexity of the matter, which goes far beyond the scope of this book.

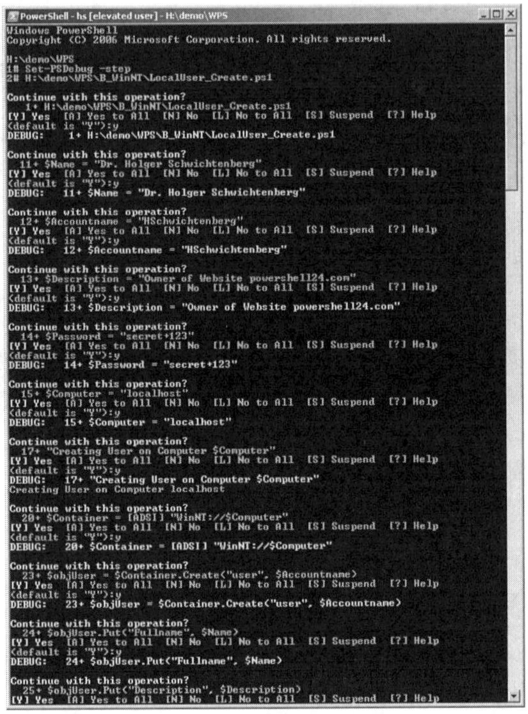

Figure 10.3 Execution of a script in single steps with confirmation

---

WARNING When experimenting with `Set-TraceSource`, you might soon reach the point where you cannot see the real actions because of all those protocols displayed. To deactivate the tracing, use `Set-TraceSource` with the parameter `-RemoveListener`.

Commandlet Extensions

WPS does not have a fixed set of commandlets. Additional commandlets can be added when WPS is started or at any time during its operation. Additional commandlets are either implemented as WPS script files, which are added via dot sourcing (see Chapter 8, "Using Class Libraries") or via installation of a snap-in (described in the following text).

Adding Snap-Ins

Commandlet extensions are delivered in the form of a snap-in DLL. They have to be integrated in WPS in two steps:

1. Registering the DLL (alternatively called *assembly*) that contains the commandlets
2. Loading the snap-in to the WPS console

DLL Registration

Registration of the DLL is performed with the command-line tool *installutil.exe,* which is installed together with the .NET Framework. You will find the tool in the installation directory of the .NET Framework (usually *c:\Windows\Microsoft .NET\Framework\v x.y*). WPS has implemented this path automatically as a search path for the command.

When using `installutil.exe`, you must indicate the filename of the extension DLL, including the path (in case the WPS console does not already have this exact path as the current path).

```
installutil.exe
➥G:\PowerShell_Commandlet_Library\PowerShell_Commandlets.dll
```

Figure 10.4 shows how the tool displays the successful installation.

The registration has the effect that the DLL is added to the registry key *HKEY_LOCAL_MACHINE\SOFTWARE\Microsoft\PowerShell\1\PowerShellSnapIns.*

Loading of Snap-Ins to the PowerShell Console

To load a snap-in, you must use the commandlet `Add-PSSnapin` in the WPS console. This commandlet needs the name of the snap-in, not the name of the DLL. If you do not know the name of a snap-in, see the section "Listing Snap-Ins" later in this chapter.

```
Add-PSSnapin PowerShell_Commandlet_Library
```

Figure 10.4 Output of `Installutil.exe`

Whereas registration of a DLL is necessary only once, the WPS console discards a loaded snap-in each time it is terminated. If you want WPS to always start with certain extensions, you have two options:

- Add the relevant `Add-PSSnapIn` commands in your system-wide or user-specific profile file (`Profile.ps1`, see "PowerShell Profiles" in this chapter and Figure 10.5).
- Export a console configuration file with `Export-Console` (see Figure 10.6). At first, however, you have to add the snap-in to the current console, and then you can export this current console. This creates an XML file with the filename extension `.psc1`. The PSC file has to be handed to WPS with the command-line parameter `-PSConsoleFile` when it is started.

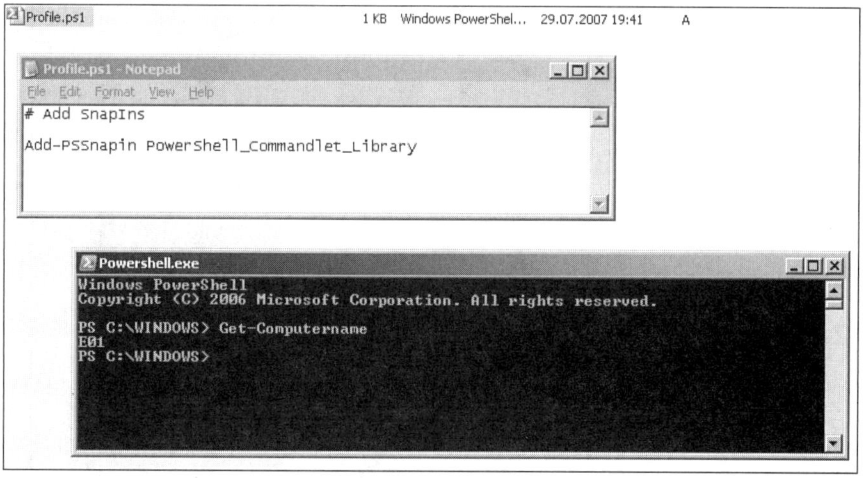

Figure 10.5 Loading a snap-in in the profile file

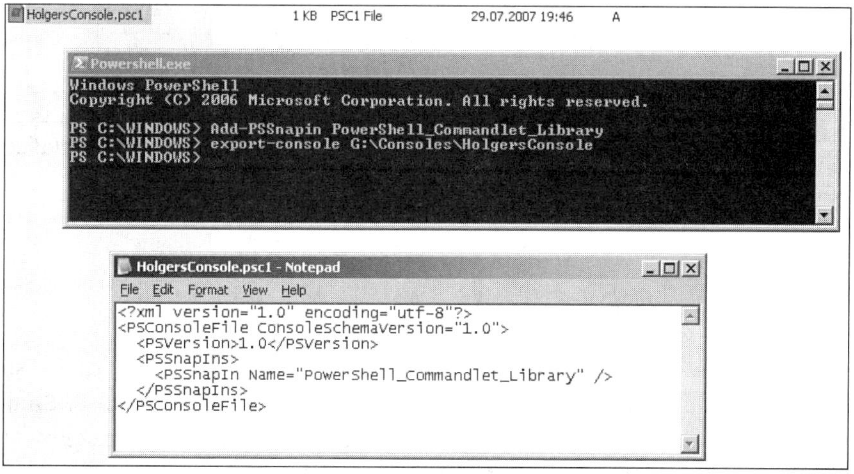

Figure 10.6 Exporting a console configuration file

The best thing to do is to create a link in your file system with the following destination (see Figure 10.7):

```
%SystemRoot%\system32\WindowsPowerShell\v1.0\powershell.exe
➥-PSConsoleFile "G:\Consoles\HolgersConsole.psc1"
```

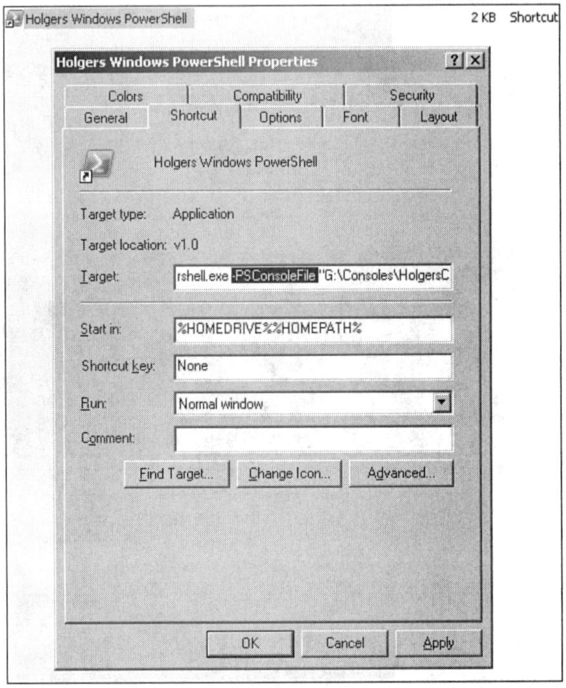

Figure 10.7 Creating a link to the WPS console; the link automatically loads a certain console configuration file

Listing Snap-Ins

The commandlet `Get-PSSnapIn` usually lists only those snap-ins that already have been added to the WPS by using the `Add-PSSnapIn`. Among these, there are also the standard commandlet packages, starting with `Microsoft.PowerShell.*` (see Figure 10.8).

`Get-PSSnapin -registered`, however, lists all registered snap-ins, regardless of whether they are active in the current console. Figure 10.9 shows the snap-in `WorldWideWings_PowerShell_Extensions`, which is not active in the console (see Figure 10.9).

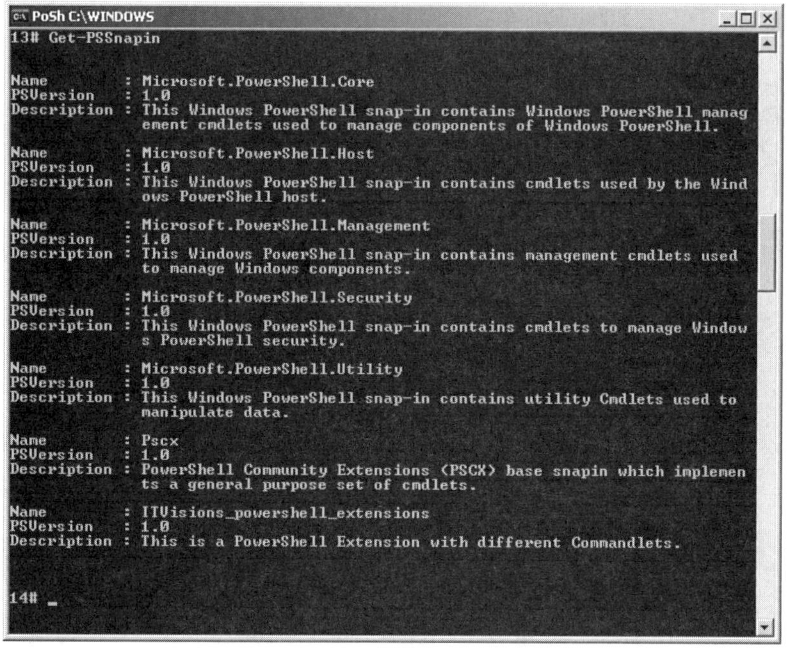

Figure 10.8 Active PowerShell snap-ins

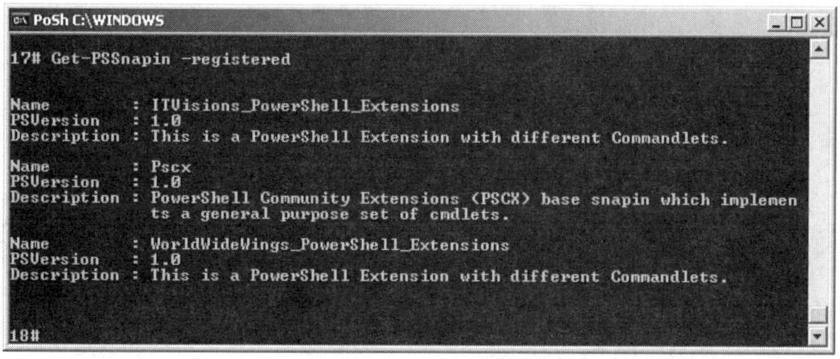

Figure 10.9 All commandlets registered on the system

List of Available Commandlets

To get a list of all commandlets in a specific snap-in, you can filter for the property `PSSnapIn` in the class `CmdletInfo`, as follows:

```
Get-command | where { $_.pssnapin -like "Pscx" }
```

or

```
Get-command | where { $_.pssnapin -like
➥"ITVisions_PowerShell_Extensions" }
```

or

```
Get-command | where { $_.pssnapin -like
➥"quest.activeroles.admanagement" }
```

Ambiguous Commandlets

It might happen that you activate different snap-ins that define commandlets with the same name, because there is no central registry for commandlets. When you encounter this problem, WPS answers the call of ambiguous commandlets with an error (see Figure 10.10).

WARNING Note that this error actually occurs during operation, not when the WPS console is started.

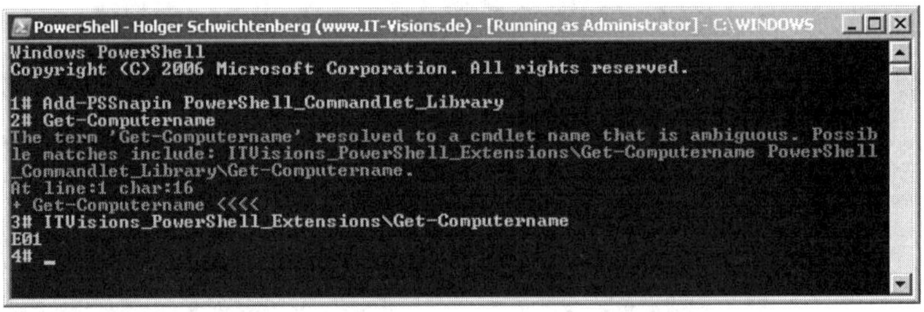

Figure 10.10 A commandlet name has been assigned twice.

To differentiate between the two commandlets with the same name in different snap-ins, you have to preface the name of the snap-in to the commandlet (separated by a backslash), as follows:

```
ITVisions_PowerShell_Extensions\Get-Computername
```

Available Commandlet Extensions

Important commandlet extensions (some free, some not) include the following:

- PowerShell Community Extensions by Microsoft.
- PowerShell Extensions by www.IT-Visions.de.
- Quest offers commandlets for Active Directory scripting.
- Group policy administration with PowerShell is offered by the company FullArmor.
- Commandlets for network management with PowerShell are offered by the company /n Software.
- The company PowerGadget offers, under the same name, a collection of additional commandlets to display WPS pipeline content.

PowerShell Community Extensions

You can find additional commandlets and providers for WPS 1.0 from Microsoft in Windows PowerShell Community Extensions (PSCX).

PSCX	
Vendor	Microsoft/Open Source Community Project
Price	Free
URL	www.codeplex.com/PowerShellCX

PSCX 1.1.1 contains the following commandlets:

```
ConvertFrom-Base64
ConvertTo-Base64
ConvertTo-MacOs9LineEnding
ConvertTo-UnixLineEnding
ConvertTo-WindowsLineEnding
Convert-Xml
Disconnect-TerminalSession
Export-Bitmap
```

```
Format-Byte
Format-Hex
Format-Xml
Get-ADObject
Get-Clipboard
Get-DhcpServer
Get-DomainController
Get fileVersionInfo
Get-ForegroundWindow
Get-Hash
Get-MountPoint
Get-PEHeader
Get-Privilege
Get-PSSnapinHelp
Get-Random
Get-ReparsePoint
Get-ShortPath
Get-TabExpansion
Get-TerminalSession
Import-Bitmap
Join-String
New-Hardlink
New-Junction
New-Shortcut
New-Symlink
Out-Clipboard
Ping-Host
Remove-MountPoint
Remove-ReparsePoint
Resize-Bitmap
Resolve-Assembly
Resolve-Host
Select-Xml
Send-SmtpMail
Set-Clipboard
Set fileTime
Set-ForegroundWindow
Set-Privilege
Set-VolumeLabel
Split-String
Start-Process
Start-TabExpansion
Stop-TerminalSession
Test-Assembly
Test-Xml
Write-BZip2
Write-Clipboard
Write-GZip
Write-Tar
Write-Zip
```

PSCX commandlets have their own installation routines. During installation, you are asked whether you want to create a profile file that integrates the PSCX snap-in and creates various variables and functions. When you do not want to do this (because you already have your own profile file), you have to integrate PSCX manually in your own profile file or execute the PSCX snap-in, via the following command, each time you start the console:

```
Add-PSSnapin PSCX
```

www.IT-Visions.de PowerShell Extensions

The PowerShell extensions provided for free by the author's company offer functions in the areas of

- Directory administration (`Get-DirectoryEntry`, `Get-DirectoryChildren`, `Add-DirectoryEntry`, `Remove-DirectoryEntry`, and so on)
- Hardware information (`Get-Processor`, `Get-Memorydevice`, `Get-NetworkAdapter`, `Get-CDRomDrive`, `Get-Videocontroller`, `Get-USBController`, and more)
- Database access (`Get-DbTable`, `Get-DbRow`, `Set-DbTable`, `Invoke-DbCommand`, and so forth)

www.IT-Visions.de WPS Extensions	
Vendor	www.IT-Visions.de
Price	Free
URL	www.IT-Visions.de/scripting/powershell/PowerShellcommandletExtensions.aspx

The snap-in has to be installed manually with `installutil.exe`:

```
installutil.exe ITVisions_PowerShell_Extensions.dll
```

After that, the extension has to be loaded into the console. (It is best to add this to `Profil.ps1`.)

```
Add-PSSnapin ITVisions_PowerShell_Extensions
```

Quest Management Shell for Active Directory

Quest offers commandlets for Active Directory administration and a custom WPS console (Quest Management Shell for Active Directory).

Quest Management Shell for Active Directory	
Vendor	Quest
Price	Free
URL	www.quest.com/activeroles-server/arms.aspx

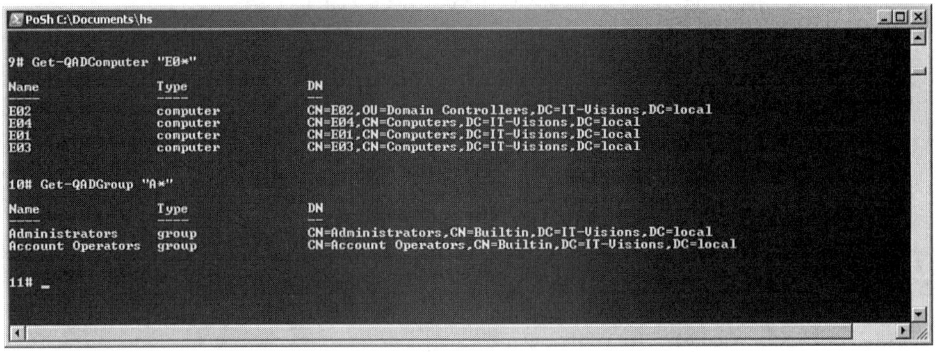

Figure 10.11 Quest Management Shell for Active Directory

Quest commandlets can be integrated into the Quest management console in the standard WPS via `Add-PsSnapin Quest.Activeroles.AdManagement`.

The Quest extensions in the current version, 1.0.4, contain the following commandlets:

```
Add-QADGroupMember
Connect-QADService
Disconnect-QADService
Get-QADComputer
Get-QADGroup
Get-QADGroupMember
Get-QADObject
Get-QADUser
New-QADGroup
New-QADObject
New-QADUser
Remove-QADGroupMember
Set-QADObject
Set-QADUser
```

Microsoft Exchange Server 2007

Microsoft Exchange Server 2007 is the first Microsoft product using WPS for administration. The Exchange management shell (a custom version of the WPS console), delivered together with the Exchange Server, and a number of commandlets enable you to effectively execute all the administrative tasks of Exchange Server right from the command line (see Figure 10.12).

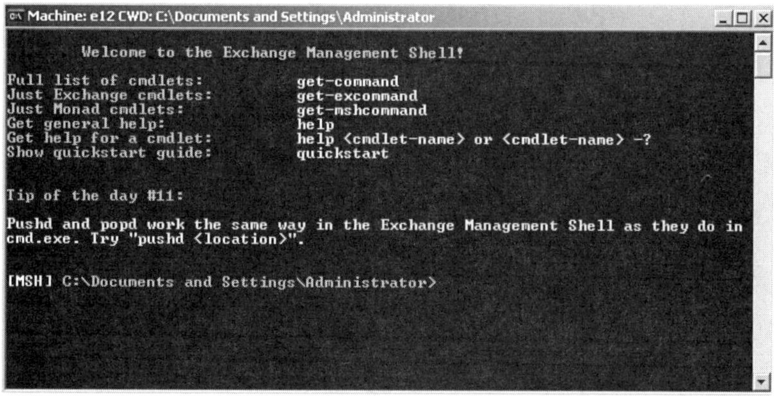

Figure 10.12 Exchange Server 2007 management shell

Among others, the following commandlets are provided in this snap-in:

```
Get-ExchangeServer          Get-UMMailbox
Enable-Mailcontact          New-MailboxDatabase
Enable-Mailbox              New-StorageGroup
Disable-Mailbox             New-SendConnector
Get-Mailbox                 Suspend-Queue
Get-MailboxStatistics       Resume-Queue
New-SystemMessage           Set-RecipientFilterConfig
Get-Recipient               New-JournalRule
```

NOTE For further information, refer to [TNET01] and [TNET02].

System Center Virtual Machine Manager 2007

System Center Virtual Machine Manager (SCVMM) 2007 is an administration tool for virtual systems based on Microsoft Virtual Server. This

SCVMM is completely based on WPS commandlets, so all action of the SCVMM can also be executed via commandlets or script.

Among others, the following commandlets are provided here:

```
New-VirtualNetworkAdapter
New-VirtualDVDDrive
New-HardwareProfile
Get-VirtualHardDisk
Add-VirtualHardDisk
New-VM
Get-VMHost
Get-FloppyDrive
Get-DVDDrive
```

Command History

By default, the WPS console saves the last 64 entered commands in a command history. You can get a list of those saved commands with the commandlet `Get-History`. Via the parameter `Count`, you can look at a certain number of commands (that is, the last *n* commands will be shown):

```
Get-History -count 10
```

You can distinctly call a command via its position:

```
Invoke-History 9
```

You can increase the number of the saved commands through the integrated WPS variable `$MaximumHistoryCount`.

You can export the command history either as script file or as an XML file (see Table 10.1). A script file is used when the commands entered will be executed automatically in the same sequence as entered. The XML file format is used when the command history of a former session will be restored without simultaneously executing all the commands.

Table 10.1 Export Options for the WPS Command History

	Script Files (.ps1)	XML Format
Exporting	`Get-History -Count 10 | format-table commandline -HideTableHeader | Out-File "c:\MyScript.ps1"`	`Get-History | Export-CliXml "b:\Scripts\History.xml"`
Importing / Executing	`. "c:\MyScript.ps1"`	`Import-CliXml "b:\Scripts\History.xml" | Add-History`

`Clear-Host` (alias `clear`) deletes the display in the WPS console, but it does not delete the command history.

System and Host Information

The commandlet `Get-Host` and the integrated variable `$Host` deliver information about the current WPS environment. The commandlet and the variable display the same instance of the class `System.Management.Automation.Internal.Host.InternalHost`. `InternalHost` contains information and also allows modifications through its subobject `UI.RawUI`, as follows:

- `$Host.Name` Name of the host. (This makes a differentiation of the environment possible; for example, WPS Plus Host delivers a different value than the default WPS console.)
- `$Host.Version` Version number of the host.
- `$Host.UI.RawUI.WindowTitle = "Title"` Setting the title of the window.
- `$Host.UI.RawUI.ForeGroundColor = [System.ConsoleColor]::White` Setting the foreground text color.
- `$Host.UI.RawUI.BackgroundColor = [System.ConsoleColor]::DarkBlue` Setting the text background color.

Example

Listing 10.1 produces a headline in which not only the name of the current user is displayed but also whether he is an administrator. The code is extremely useful on Windows Vista and should be included in your profile script.

Listing 10.1 A Profile Script for a Meaningful Title Line

```
# PowerShell Profile Script - Title with Username and Status
# Holger Schwichtenberg 2007

# ------------- Window Title

$WI = [System.Security.Principal.WindowsIdentity]::GetCurrent()
$WP = New-Object System.Security.Principal.WindowsPrincipal($wi)
if ($WP.IsInRole([System.Security.Principal.WindowsBuiltInRole]::
➥Administrator))
{
 $Status = "[elevated user]"
}
else
{
 $Status = "[normal User]"
}

$Host.UI.RawUI.WindowTitle  = "PowerShell - " +
[System.Environment]::UserName  + " " + $Status
```

`Get-Culture` (or `$Host.CurrentCulture`) and `Get-UICulture` (or `$Host.CurrentUICulture`) deliver information about the current language in the form of single instances of the .NET class `System.Globalization.CultureInfo`. `Get-Culture` refers to the output of date, time, and currency (compare to regional settings of Windows system control). `Get-UICulture` refers to the language of the user interface. Generally, both settings are similar; a user, however, could set these differently (see Figure 10.13).

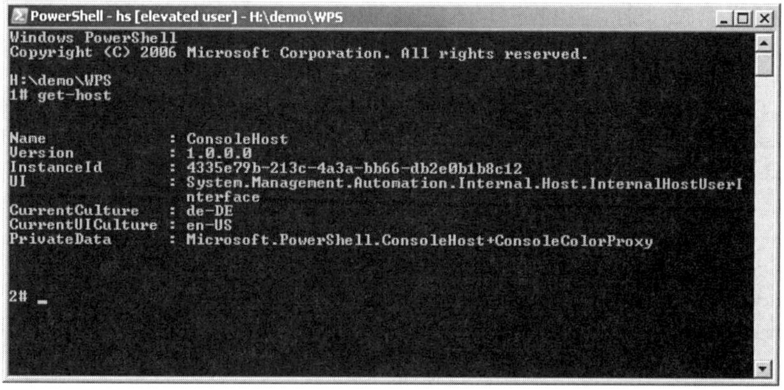

Figure 10.13 Execution of `Get-Host`

PowerShell Profiles

When a WPS console is terminated, it forgets all its settings (for example, loaded snap-ins, defined aliases, defined functions, integrated WPS providers, and the command history). With the help of so-called profile files, you can reinstall WPS console's memory during startup. Profiles are WPS scripts with the name *Profile* and the filename extension `.ps1`.

A `Profile.ps1` can exist on two levels:

- **Globally for all users.** This file resides within the WPS installation directory (generally, *C:\Windows\System32\WindowsPowerShell\v1.0*).
- **User related.** This file resides in the file system directory (under Vista usually in *c:\User\(Username)\documents\Windows PowerShell;* on older systems, under *c:\documents and settings\(username)\documents\WindowsPowerShell*).

Figure 10.14 shows storing a profile in Windows Vista.

NOTE The PowerShell Command Extensions (PSCX) create such a user-specific profile file, with numerous settings during the installation process (see Listing 10.2).

Listing 10.2 Slightly Adapted Version of the Profile File from PSCX

```
# ---------------------------------------------------------------------------
# Author: Keith Hill, jachymko
# Desc:   Simple global profile to get you going with PowerShell.
# Date:   Nov 18, 2006
# Site:   http://www.codeplex.com/PowerShellCX
# Usage:  Copy this file to your Windows PowerShell directory e.g.:
#
#  Copy-Item "$Env:PscxHome\Profile\Profile.ps1"
➥(Split-Path $Profile -Parent)
#
# ---------------------------------------------------------------------------
# Adapted by Holger Schwichtenberg, July 2007


# ---------------------------------------------------------------------------
# Configure standard PowerShell variables to more useful settings
# ---------------------------------------------------------------------------
$MaximumHistoryCount = 512
$FormatEnumerationLimit = 100

# ---------------------------------------------------------------------------
# PowerShell Community Extensions preference variables.
➥Comment/uncomment
# or change to suit your preference.
# ---------------------------------------------------------------------------
$PscxTextEditorPreference = "Notepad"

# ---------------------------------------------------------------------------
# Dirx/dirs/dirt/dird/dirw functions will specify
➥-Force with the value of
# the following preference variable. Set to $true
➥will cause normally hidden
# items to be returned.
# ---------------------------------------------------------------------------
$PscxDirForcePreference = $true

# ---------------------------------------------------------------------------
# Dirx/dirs/dirt/dird/dirw functions filter out files with
➥system properties set.
# The performance may suffer on high latency networks or in
➥folders with
```

```
# many files.
# ---------------------------------------------------------------------
## $PscxDirHideSystemPreference = $true

# ---------------------------------------------------------------------
# Display file sizes in KB, MB, GB multiples.
# ---------------------------------------------------------------------
$PscxFileSizeInUnitsPreference = $false

# ---------------------------------------------------------------------
# The Send-SmtpMail default settings.
# ---------------------------------------------------------------------
## $PscxSmtpFromPreference = 'john_doe@example.net'
## $PscxSmtpHostPreference = 'smtp.example.net'
## $PscxSmtpPortPreference = 25

# ---------------------------------------------------------------------
# Uncomment this to create a transcript of the entire
➥PowerShell session.
# ---------------------------------------------------------------------
## $PscxTranscribeSessionPreference = $true

# ---------------------------------------------------------------------
# You can modify every aspect of the PSCX prompt appearance by
# creating your own eye-candy script.
# ---------------------------------------------------------------------
## $PscxEyeCandyScriptPreference = '.\EyeCandy.Jachym.ps1'
$PscxEyeCandyScriptPreference = '.\EyeCandy.Keith.ps1'

# ---------------------------------------------------------------------
# The following functions are used during processing of the
➥PSCX profile
# and are deleted at the end of loading this profile.
# !! Do not modify or remove the functions below !!
# ---------------------------------------------------------------------
function Set-PscxVariable($name, $value)
{
  Set-Variable $name $value -Scope Global -Option AllScope,ReadOnly
➥-Description "PSCX variable"
}

function Set-PscxAlias($name, $value, $type = 'cmdlet',
➥[switch]$force)
```

(continues)

Listing 10.2 Slightly Adapted Version of the Profile File from PSCX *(continued)*

```
{
  Set-Alias $name $value -Scope Global -Option AllScope -Force:$force
➥-Description "PSCX $type alias"
}

function Test-PscxPreference($name)
{
  if (Test-Path "Variable:$name")
  {
    (Get-Variable $name).Value
  }
  else
  {
    $false
  }
}
# -------------------------------------------------------------------
# !! Do not modify or remove the functions above !!
# -------------------------------------------------------------------

if (!(Test-Path Variable:__PscxProfileRanOnce))
{
  # -------------------------------------------------------------------
  # This should only be run once per PowerShell session
  # -------------------------------------------------------------------
  Add-PSSnapin Pscx
  Start-TabExpansion

  # -------------------------------------------------------------------
  # Load ps1xml files which override built-in PowerShell defaults.
  # -------------------------------------------------------------------
  Update-FormatData -PrependPath
"$Env:PscxHome\FormatData\FileSystem.ps1xml"
  Update-FormatData -PrependPath
"$Env:PscxHome\FormatData\Reflection.ps1xml"

  # -------------------------------------------------------------------
  # Create $UserProfile to point to the user's non-host specific profile
➥script
  # -------------------------------------------------------------------
```

```
  Set-PscxVariable ProfileDir  (split-path
➥$MyInvocation.MyCommand.Path -Parent)
  Set-PscxVariable UserProfile (join-path
➥$ProfileDir 'Profile.ps1')

  # ---------------------------------------------------------------
  # Create PSCX convenience variables, identity variables used by
➥EyeCandy.*.ps1
  # ---------------------------------------------------------------
  Set-PscxVariable PscxHome    ($env:PscxHome)
  Set-PscxVariable PscxVersion ([Version](Get fileVersionInfo
➥(Get-PSSnapin Pscx).ModuleName).ProductVersion)
  Set-PscxVariable Shell       (new-object
➥-com Shell.Application)
  Set-PscxVariable NTIdentity  ([Security.Principal.WindowsIdentity]
[ic:ccc[::GetCurrent())
  Set-PscxVariable NTAccount
($NTIdentity.User.Translate([Security.Principal.NTAccount]))
  Set-PscxVariable NTPrincipal (new-object
Security.Principal.WindowsPrincipal $NTIdentity)
  Set-PscxVariable IsAdmin
($NTPrincipal.IsInRole([Security.Principal.WindowsBuiltInRole]::
➥Administrator))
}
else
{
  # ---------------------------------------------------------------
  # This should be run every time you want apply changes to
➥your type and format
  # files.
  # ---------------------------------------------------------------
  Update-FormatData
  Update-TypeData
}

# ---------------------------------------------------------------
# PowerShell Community Extensions utility functions and filters.
# Comment out or remove any dot sourced functionality that
➥you don't want.
# ---------------------------------------------------------------
```

(continues)

Listing 10.2 Slightly Adapted Version of the Profile File from PSCX *(continued)*

```
Push-Location (Join-Path $Env:PscxHome 'Profile')
. '.\TabExpansion.ps1'
. '.\GenericAliases.ps1'
. '.\GenericFilters.ps1'
. '.\GenericFunctions.ps1'
. '.\PscxAliases.ps1'
. '.\Debug.ps1'
. '.\Environment.VirtualServer.ps1'
. '.\Environment.VisualStudio2005.ps1'
. '.\Cd.ps1'
. '.\Dir.ps1'
. '.\TranscribeSession.ps1'
. $PscxEyeCandyScriptPreference
Pop-Location

# ---------------------------------------------------------------------
# Add PSCX Scripts dir to Path environment variable to allow
➥scripts to be executed.
# ---------------------------------------------------------------------
Add-PathVariable Path $env:PscxHome,$env:PscxHome\Scripts

# ---------------------------------------------------------------------
# Remove functions only required for the processing of the
➥PSCX profile.
# ---------------------------------------------------------------------
Remove-Item Function:Set-PscxAlias
Remove-Item Function:Set-PscxVariable

# ---------------------------------------------------------------------
# Keep track of whether or not this profile has run already
➥and remove the
# temporary functions
# ---------------------------------------------------------------------
Set-Variable __PscxProfileRanOnce

# ---------------------------------------------------------------------
# Additions from Dr. Holger Schwichtenberg
# ---------------------------------------------------------------------

# Snap-Ins laden
```

```
Add-PSSnapin ITVisions_PowerShell_Extensions

# Title
$Wi = [System.Security.Principal.WindowsIdentity]::GetCurrent()
$wp = New-Object System.Security.Principal.WindowsPrincipal($wi)
if ($wp.IsInRole([System.Security.Principal.WindowsBuiltInRole]
➥::Administrator))
{
 $Status = "[elevated user]"
}
else
{
 $Status = "[normal User]"
}
$PscxWinx
dowTitlePrefix  = "PowerShell - " + [System.Environment]::UserName
➥+ " " + $Status + " - "
```


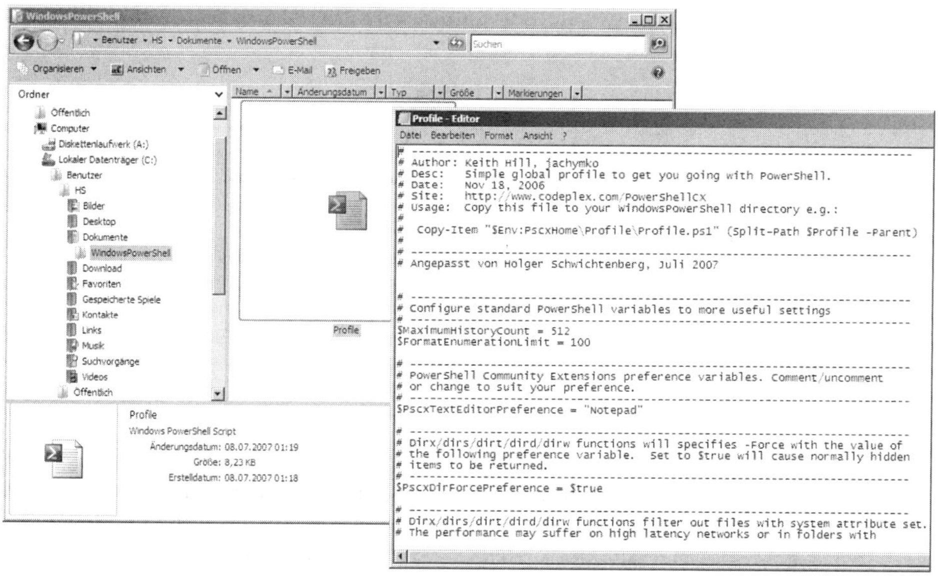

Figure 10.14 Storing the profile file in Windows Vista

Graphical User Interfaces

Microsoft Shell does not possess commandlets for the presentation of graphical user interfaces. However, there's no reason why you shouldn't use the `System.Windows.Forms` library (Windows Forms or WinForms) of .NET directly.

NOTE There's no space in this book for a detailed explanation of the Windows Forms library (some hundred classes!). Nevertheless, two examples will explain the approach.

Input Dialog

The following script creates an input mask for three values. For the sake of simplification, input fields are arranged automatically and not positioned absolutely (flow layout panel, compare HTML) (see Figure 10.15).

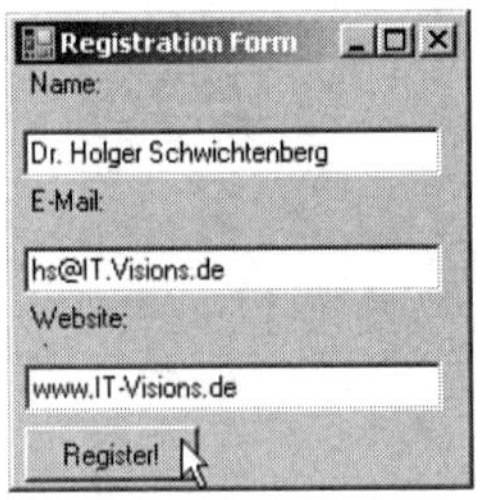

Figure 10.15 An input window created with WPS

The WPS script in Listing 10.3 shows the example, where a form (`Form`), a flow layout panel (`FlowLayoutPanel`), three labels (`Label`), and three text boxes (`Textbox`) are used. It's important that the section fills the form (`[System.Windows.Forms.DockStyle]::Fill`) and that you correctly add the controls to the control tree one after the other in the order you like them to appear on the screen (`Controls.Add()`).

Listing 10.3 Show and Evaluate the Input Window

```
########################################
# PowerShell Script: Display a GUI
# (C) Dr. Holger Schwichtenberg
# http://www.windows-scripting.com
#########################################


# Load Windows Forms Library
[System.Reflection.Assembly]::LoadWithPartialName
➥("System.windows.forms")

# Create Window
$form = new-object "System.Windows.Forms.Form"
$form.Size = new-object System.Drawing.Size @(200,200)
$form.topmost = $true
$form.text = "Registration Form"

# Create Flow Panel
$panel = new-object "System.Windows.Forms.flowlayoutpanel"
$panel.Dock = [System.Windows.Forms.DockStyle]::Fill
$form.Controls.Add($panel)

# Create Controls
$L1 = new-object "System.Windows.Forms.Label"
$L2 = new-object "System.Windows.Forms.Label"
$L3 = new-object "System.Windows.Forms.Label"
$T1 = new-object "System.Windows.Forms.Textbox"
$T2 = new-object "System.Windows.Forms.Textbox"
$T3 = new-object "System.Windows.Forms.Textbox"
$B1 = new-object "System.Windows.Forms.Button"

# Set labels
$L1.Text = "Name:"
$L2.Text = "E-Mail:"
$L3.Text = "Website:"
$B1.Text = "Register!"

# Set size
$T1.Width = 180
$T2.Width = 180
```

(continues)

Listing 10.3 Show and Evaluate the Input Window *(continued)*

```
$T3.Width = 180

# Add controls to Panel
$panel.Controls.Add($L1)
$panel.Controls.Add($T1)
$panel.Controls.Add($L2)
$panel.Controls.Add($T2)
$panel.Controls.Add($L3)
$panel.Controls.Add($T3)
$panel.Controls.Add($B1)

# Event Binding
$reg = $false
$B1.add_Click({$reg = $true; $Form.close()})

# Show window
$form.showdialog()

# Display result
if ($reg)
{
"You have entered: " + $T1.Text + ";" + $T2.Text + ";" + $T3.Text
}
else
{
"You have canceled the dialog!"
}
```

Displaying Objects

When you want to display an object with many attributes, the preceding procedure with the individual creation of Windows Forms elements is extremely laborious. It is much easier with `PropertyGrid`, a control defined in Windows Forms, to which any optional .NET object can be connected and which also saves changes to the object (see Figure 10.16 and Listing 10.4).

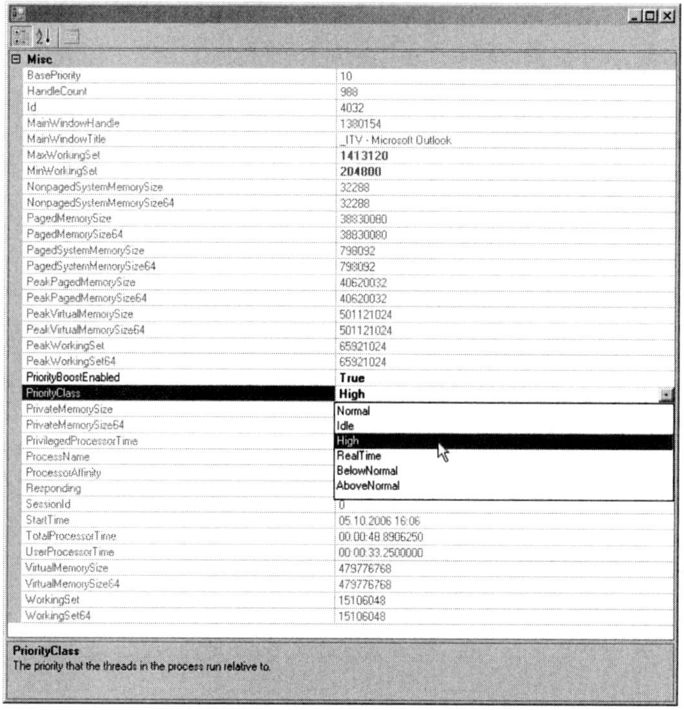

Figure 10.16 Display and change of process objects with a Windows Forms `PropertyGrid`

Listing 10.4 Display and Change of a Process Object with a Windows Forms PropertyGrid

```
# Download Windows Forms
[System.Reflection.Assembly]::LoadWithPartialName
➥("System.windows.forms")

# Create window
$form = new-object "System.Windows.Forms.Form"
$form.Size = new-object System.Drawing.Size @(700,800)
$form.topmost = $true
```

(continues)

Listing 10.4 Display and Change of a Process Object with a Windows Forms `PropertyGrid` *(continued)*

```
# Create PropertyGrid
$PG = new-object "System.Windows.Forms.PropertyGrid"
$PG.Dock = [System.Windows.Forms.DockStyle]::Fill
$form.Controls.Add($PG)

# Assign content to PropertyGrid
$i = Get-process "outlook"
$PG.selectedobject = $i

# Display Window
$form.showdialog()
```

Windows Clipboard

For filling and displaying the cache, you have the following commandlets at hand in PSCX:

`Write-Clipboard`	see Figure 10.17
`Set-Clipboard`	see Figure 10.18
`Get-Clipboard`	

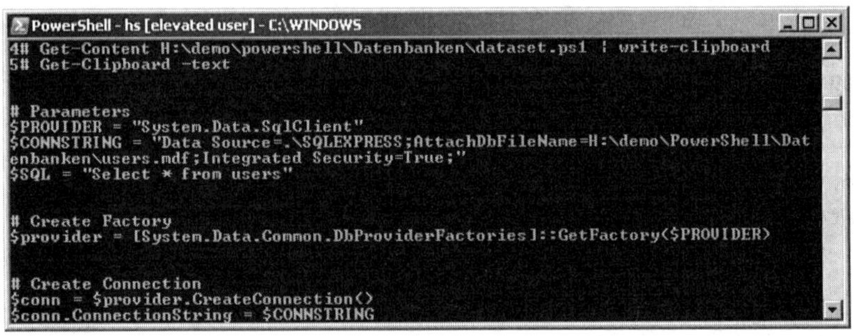

Figure 10.17 Use of the commandlet `Write-Clipboard`

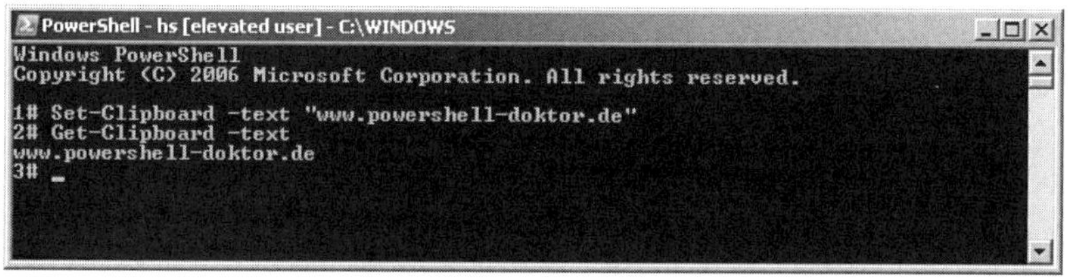

Figure 10.18 Use of the commandlet `Set-Clipboard`

Summary

In this chapter, you have learned different tips and tricks, including the following:

- Debugging with the parameters `verbose`, `whatif`, and `confirm`
- The installation of commandlet extensions (snap-ins) through `installutil.exe` and `Add-PSSnapIn`
- Using the command history of WPS with `Get-History` and `Invoke-History`
- Getting information about your WPS host from commandlets and integrated variables
- Using WPS profile files (`Profile.ps1`)

PART II

WINDOWS POWERSHELL IN ACTION

CHAPTER 11

FILE SYSTEMS

In this chapter:

Windows PowerShell (WPS) provides access to the Windows file system through PowerShell Navigation Provider. There are also .NET classes and WMI classes that support the administration of file systems. Samples in this chapter include the enumeration of directory content, file system operations such as copying and deleting, the management of links in the file systems, file compression, and the creation of file shares.

Available Commandlets for File System Administration

Table 11.1 enumerates the relevant commandlets and their counterparts in the classic Windows shell and Unix shells.

Table 11.1 Important Commandlets for Working with the Windows File System

WPS Commandlet	WPS Alias	Classic UNIX Shell	sh	Description
`Clear-Item`	`cli`	N/A	N/A	Clear content of a file
`Copy-Item`	`cpi, cpp, cp, copy`	`copy`	`cp`	Copy file or folder
`Get-Content`	`gc`	`type`	`cat`	Get the content of a file
`Get-Location`	`gl, pwd`	`pwd`	`pwd`	Get the current directory
`Move-Item`	`mi, move, mv, mi`	`move`	`mv`	Move file or folder
`New-Item`	`ni, md`	N/A	N/A	Create file or folder
`Remove-Item`	`ri, rp, rm, rmdir, del, erase, rd`	`del, rd`	`rm, rmdir`	Delete file or folder
`Rename-Item`	`rni, ren`	`rn`	`ren`	Rename file or folder
`Set-Content`	`sc`	`>`	`>`	Set file content
`Set-Item`	`si`	N/A	N/A	Set file content
`Set-Location`	`Sl, cd, chdir`	`cd, chdir`	`cd, chdir`	Set current directory

Drives

To list all drives, you have four options:

1. Use the commandlet `Get-PSDrive` (commandlet of WPS 1.0).
2. Use the commandlet `Get-Disk` (commandlet of the www.IT-Visions.de extensions).
3. Static method `GetDrives()` of the .NET class `System.IO.DriveInfo` (see Figure 11.1).

4. Display the instances of the WMI class `Win32_LogicalDisk` (see Figure 11.2).

`Get-PSDrive` lists all WPS drives, including variables and the registry (see the discussion about navigation providers in Chapter 5, "The PowerShell Navigation Model"). If you want a list of all file system drives only, you have to limit `Get-PSDrive` to the provider file system as follows:

```
Get-PSDrive -psprovider filesystem
```

The result consists of objects of the type `System.Management.Automation.PSDriveInfo`. One of the attributes of this class is `Root`, which contains the root directory of each drive.

WARNING The WPS class `PSDriveInfo` does not contain any information about size and free space of the drives, because this is a generic concept for all kinds of navigable object collections, and such values would not make sense for some drives (for example, environment variables).

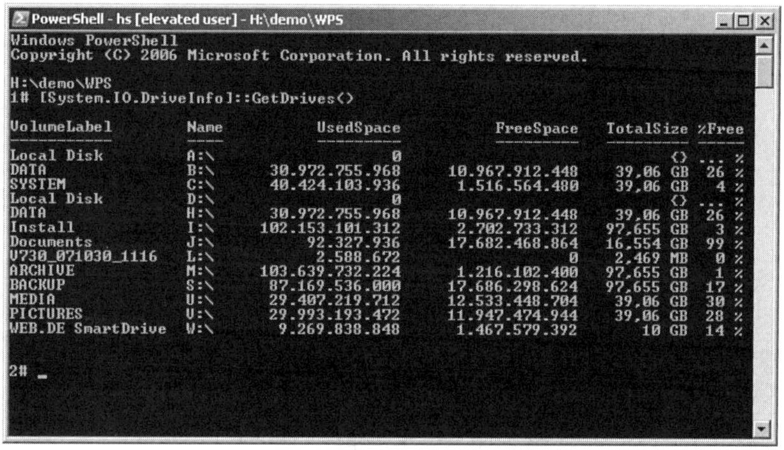

Figure 11.1 Use of the method `GetDrives()`

11. FILE SYSTEMS

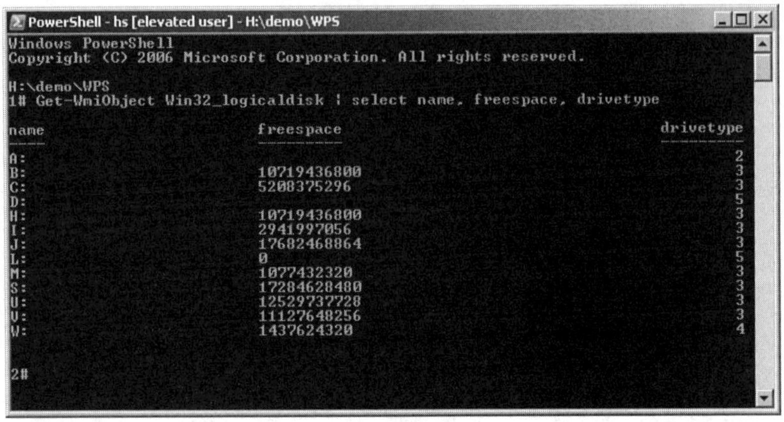

Figure 11.2 Use of `Win32_LogicalDisk`. Drive types are 3 = local disk, 4 = network drive, 5 = CD/DVD.

Free Space

To display the free space of the file system drives, you have the following options (see Listings 11.1 through 11.6):

- Property `TotalFreeSpace` in the .NET class `System.IO.DriveInfo`
- Property `Freespace` in the WMI class `Win32_LogicalDisk`
- Use of the commandlet `Get-Disk` (commandlet of www.IT-Visions.de), which internally works with WMI

Listing 11.1 Displaying the Free Space of the C: Drive by Using .NET Class `System.IO.DriveInfo`

```
$drive = new-object System.IO.DriveInfo("C")
$drive.TotalFreeSpace
```

Listing 11.2 Displaying the Free Space of the C: Drive by Using WMI Class `Win32_LogicalDisk`

```
Get-WmiObject Win32_logicaldisk -Filter "DeviceID = 'c:'" |
➥Select FreeSpace
```

Listing 11.3 Displaying the Free Space of All Drives by Using WMI Class `Win32_LogicalDisk`

```
Get-WmiObject Win32_logicaldisk | Select-Object
➥deviceid,size,freespace
```

The script in Listing 11.4 shows one way to display this data in a better format.

Listing 11.4 Fetching the Free Space of the Drives

```
$Computer = "localhost"
$drives = Get-WmiObject Win32_LogicalDisk -computer $computer
" drive          size(MB)     free space(MB)"
ForEach ($drive in $drives)
{
"     {0}         {1,15:n}     {2,15:n}" -f $drive.DeviceID,
➥($drive.Size/1mb), $($drive.freespace/1mb)
}
```

The use of the WMI class `Win32_LocigalDisk` has two advantages:

- You can also call remote systems (see example).
- With the help of a WQL, you may also filter your call explicitly (see example).

Listing 11.5 Fetching the Free Space of the C: Drive of a Remote Computer by Using WMI Class `Win32_LogicalDisk`

```
Get-WmiObject Win32_logicaldisk -Filter "DeviceID = 'c:'"
➥-Computer E02 | Select DeviceID, FreeSpace
```

Listing 11.6 Displaying Drives with Little Free Space by Using a WQL Call via the WMI Class `Win32_LogicalDisk`

```
([WMISearcher] "Select * from Win32_LogicalDisk where Freespace
➥< 1000000000").Get()  | Select DeviceID, FreeSpace
```

Drive Labels

To fetch and change drive names, you can use `VolumeLabel` of the class `DriveInfo`.

Listing 11.7 Changing Drive Names

```
$drive = new-object System.IO.DriveInfo("C")
"old name:"
$drive.VolumeLabel
"new name:"
$drive.VolumeLabel = "SYSTEM"
$drive.VolumeLabel
```

Alternatively, you can use the commandlet `Set-Volumelabel` from PSCX (although there does not yet exist the counterpart `Get-VolumeLabel`).

```
Set-VolumeLabel "c:" "Systeml drive"
```

Network Drives

You can display information about the mapped network drives of the logged-in user via the WMI class `Win32_MappedLogicalDisk`:

```
Get-WmiObject Win32_MappedLogicalDisk | select caption,
providername
```

Directory Content

You can get the content of a directory listed with `Get-ChildItem` (alias `dir`).

Without parameters, Get-ChildItem lists the current path. You can, however, explicitly indicate a path:

```
Get-ChildItem c:\temp\Scripts
```

The resulting volume consists of .NET objects of the types System.IO.DirectoryInfo (for subdirectories) and System.IO.FileInfo (for files).

The parameter -Filter limits the output volume to files with a distinct name pattern:

```
Get-ChildItem c:\temp\Scripts -filter "*.ps1"
```

Alternatively, you can use -include for filter purposes and indicate various file extensions at the same time:

```
Get-ChildItem c:\temp\Scripts -include *.ps1,*.vbs
```

The commandlet usually works only on the indicated level. It can, however, also search the subdirectories recursively:

```
Get-ChildItem c:\temp\Scripts -filter "*.ps1" -recurse
```

With Measure-Object, you can execute calculations regarding an object volume. The following command shows the number of files in *c:\Windows*, the total size of all files, the size of the biggest and of the smallest file, and the average file size:

```
Get-ChildItem c:\windows | Measure-Object -Property length
➥-min -max -average -sum
```

With the following command, a list of big Word files on drive H and its subdirectories is created, and a list of the names and sizes, sorted according to size, is exported to a CSV file:

```
Get-ChildItem h:\ -filter *.doc | Where-Object
➥{ $_.Length -gt 40000 } | Select-Object Name, Length
➥| Sort-Object Length | export-csv
➥p:\LargeWordDocuments.csv -notype
```

The -notype at the end prevents the type name of the .NET class from being exported. If you would export the type name, you could later re-import the data with Import-CSV and process that data as an object pipeline.

TIP The short name of a file or directory, according to the old 8+3 notation, can be displayed with the commandlet Get-ShortPath from PSCX.

File System Operations

To copy files and folders, use the commandlet Copy-Item (aliases copy or cp):

```
Copy-Item j:\demo\documents\profile.pdf
c:\temp\profile_HSchwichtenberg.pdf
```

To move file system objects, Move-Item (alias move) is used:

```
Move-Item j:\demo\documents\profil.pdf
c:\temp\profile_HSchwichtenberg.pdf
```

The commandlet Rename-Item (alias Rename) renames a file system object:

```
Rename-Item profile.pdf profile_HS.pdf
```

To delete a file, use the commandlet Remove-Item (alias del):

```
Remove-Item j:\demo\profile_HS.pdf
```

TIP -WhatIf is a useful function for working with Remove-Item, because you can see the simulated behavior before actually executing the command (see Figure 11.3).

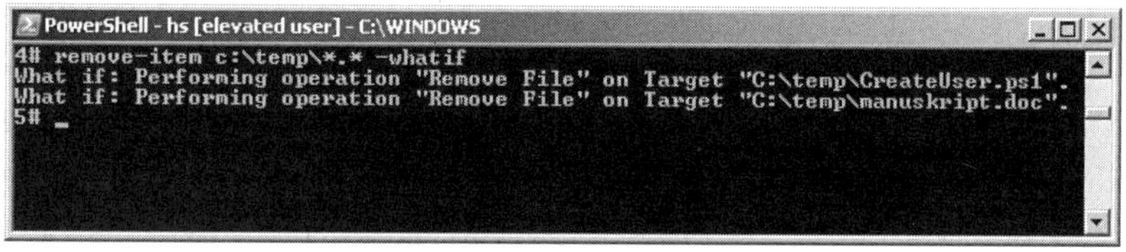

Figure 11.3 Use of `-WhatIf` with `Remove-Item`

The following command deletes all files older than 30 days:

```
Get-ChildItem c:\temp -recurse | where-object {($now -
➥$_.LastWriteTime).Days -gt 30} | remove-item
```

Reading and Writing File Properties

Information about a file system object (for example, name, size, last changes, and properties) is displayed with the commandlet `Get-Item`:

```
Get-Item j:\demo\profile_HSchwichtenberg.pdf
```

This will provide an instance of `System.IO.FileInfo` for a file. You can get the same effect with the following:

```
Get-ItemProperty j:\demo\profile_HSchwichtenberg.pdf
```

Single data (for example, `length` and `attributes`) can be called as follows:

```
Get-ItemProperty Data.txt -name length
Get-ItemProperty Data.txt -name attributes
```

NOTE Do not get confused about the word *attribute*. Classes such as `FileInfo` have attributes (for example, `name` and `length`) that provide containers for the information that are stored in the classes' instances. In the class `FileInfo`, one of these attributes has the name `attributes`. The `attributes` attribute contains the information about the file attributes.

With `Set-ItemProperty`, you can initiate a change of file properties. The following command sets the bit flags, stored in `Attributes`. The .NET class library defines the possible flags in the listing `System.IO.FileAttributes`. It is important that the elements of the listing are called like static members (that is, with the `::` operator) and linked with a binary exclusive Or (`-bxor`):

```
Set-ItemProperty Data.txt -name attributes -value
➥([System.IO.FileAttributes]::ReadOnly -bxor
➥ [System.IO.FileAttributes]::Archive)
```

Times

The `FileInfo` class offers information about the creation date and the date of the last access of the file:

```
dir $dir | select name, creationtime, lastaccesstime,
➥lastwritetime
```

With `Set-FileTime` (contained in the PSCX), you can manipulate this data (for example, if you do not want someone to know how old a file really is):

Listing 11.8 Setting of All Times of All Files in a Directory to the Current Date and Current Time

```
$dir = "c:\temp"
$time = [DateTime]::Now

dir $dir | Set fileTime -Time $time -SetCreatedTime -SetModifiedTime
dir $dir | select name, creationtime, lastaccesstime, lastwritetime
```

Properties of Executables

PSCX offers some special commandlets for executable files:

- `Test-Assembly` Displays `true` when the file is a .NET assembly (only applicable to DLL files)

- `Get-FileVersionInfo` Displays information about the product name, manufacturer, and file version
- `Get-PEHeader` Displays the head information of the Portable Executable (PE) formats for any executable files
- `Get-ExportedType` Displays the list of instanceable classes for a .NET assembly

The WPS script in Listing 11.9 displays all executable DLLs created with .NET in the Windows directory and shows version information about these DLLs.

Listing 11.9 Search for .NET Assemblies

```
"Search .NET Assemblies"

foreach ( $d in (Get-ChildItem c:\Windows\ -include "*.dll" -recurse))
{
$a = $d.Fullname | Test-assembly -ErrorAction SilentlyContinue
if ($a) { Get fileVersionInfo $d.Fullname }
}
```

The following example displays the PE header information about the Windows Editor (see Figure 11.4):

```
Get-PEHeader  C:\windows\system32\notepad.exe
```

With the commandlet `Resolve-Assembly`, you can check which versions of a .NET software component are available or whether a distinct version exists.

```
# Show all versions of this assembly
Resolve-Assembly System.Windows.Forms
# Check, whether version 3.0 is available
Resolve-Assembly System.Windows.Forms -Version 2.0.0.0
```

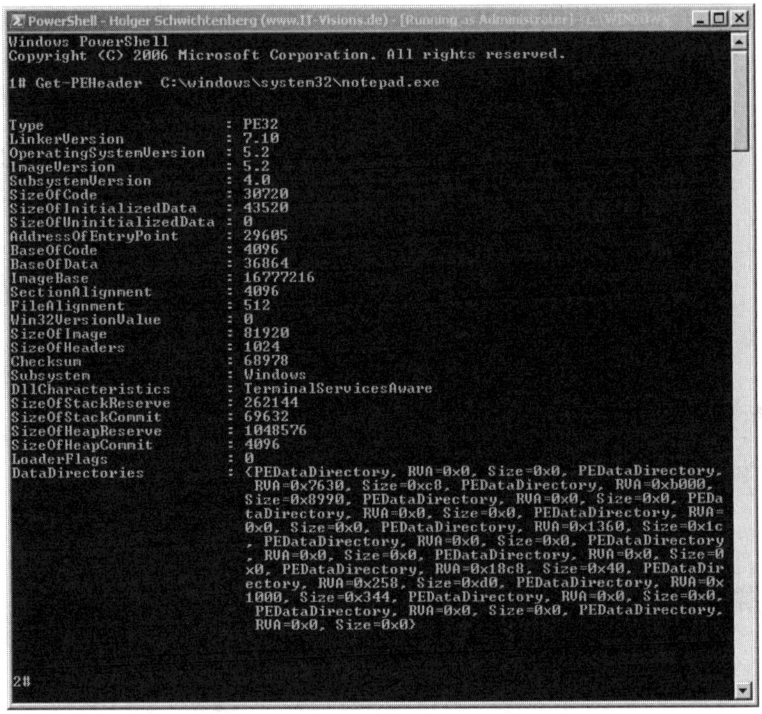

Figure 11.4 Output of PE head information

File System Links

Commandlets for the creation of links in the file system can be found in the PSCX.

Explorer Links

Starting with Windows 95, Windows Explorer supported links in the file system with `.lnk` files. These `.lnk` files contain either a file or a directory as the link destination. They are created in Windows Explorer via the context menu functions Create Link or New, Link. Windows does not show the filename extension of `.lnk` files. Instead, you see the symbol of the target object with an arrow in Windows Explorer. A double-click directs Windows Explorer, or a file dialog supporting `.lnk` files, to the target.

These Explorer links are created with the commandlet `New-Shortcut`, with the first parameter being the path to the `.lnk` file to be created, and the second parameter being the target path:

```
New-Shortcut "j:\books" "j:\projects\books"
```

WARNING If the link already exists, it is overwritten without prior warning.

Unfortunately, there are three serious disadvantages regarding Explorer links based on `.lnk` files:

- Windows Explorer does not show links to folders according to the folder hierarchy on the left side, but sorts them into the file list on the right side (see Figure 11.5).
- Links do not work at the command-line level (Windows shell).
- Windows does not track the target during renaming/re-moving, but starts to search only when the target is no longer traceable; as a consequence, the right target is not always finally found.

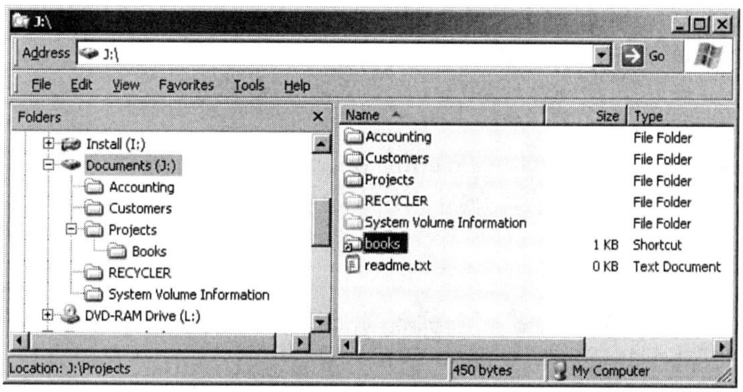

Figure 11.5 Windows Explorer displays Explorer links to folders in the file list but not in the tree view

Hardlinks

Users of UNIX, however, know better kinds of links in the form of hardlinks and symbolic links (symlinks). Under Windows, the user of the

NTFS file system can use similar concepts. The NTFS supports fixed links to any kind of files in the form of so-called hardlinks and to folders in the form of junction points. Unfortunately, both functions are not supported directly in the Windows Explorer, but only via command-line tools or tools from other suppliers.

A hardlink is a fixed link to a file. For this purpose, Microsoft provides in Windows XP and Windows Server 2003 the command-line tool *fsutil.exe.* In the WPS extensions, you can find the commandlet `New-Hardlink`.

The syntax for the creation of a hardlinks reads as follows:

```
New-Hardlink <new filename> <existing filename>
```

For example

```
New-Hardlink "j:\MyProjects.csv" "j:\projects\content.csv"
```

Afterward, the file appears in both directories, without a link arrow. Nevertheless, this is not a copy; both entries in the directory tree point to the same spot on the drive, and therefore the file can be manipulated at both places. You will not have any problems with moving the file. The file content is only lost when both entries in the directory tree have been deleted.

There are two flaws to be aware of:

- Folder links cannot be created.
- Links can be created only to files on the same drive.

NOTE To delete a hardlink, you have to delete the link file. The target file remains unaffected:

```
Remove-Item "j:\MyProjects.csv"
```

Junction Points

Junction points are the equivalents to hardlinks for folders. In contrast to hardlinks, junction points also work on other drives. The commandlet you want to use here is `New-Junction`, which, however, is available only through the additional resource kits of the different Windows versions. When you use `linkd.exe`, you have to name the source first and then the target, in contrast, to `fsutil.exe`.

For example, the command

```
New-Junction "j:\books" "j:\projects\books\"
```

consequently creates a link that shows the directory *s:\books* as subdirectory *backup* in the folder *j:\project*. Junction points also work on the command line. Thus, the command

```
dir j:\books
```

shows *j:\projects\books*.

Windows Explorer places a junction point, just like a folder, in the folder hierarchy on the left side (see Figure 11.6).

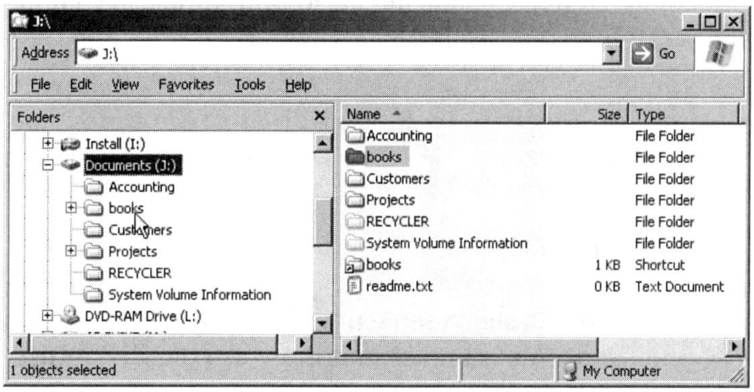

Figure 11.6 The junction point books shows on both sides of Windows Explorer.

You can see the target of a junction point with the commandlet `Get-ShortPath`, as follows:

```
Get-ReparsePoint j:\books
```

To delete a junction point, use the following:

```
Remove-ReparsePoint "j:\books"
```

WARNING If the actual target folder is deleted earlier than the junction point, an orphaned junction point is created. Unfortunately, Windows does not notice the moving of a file, so that in this case, too, the remaining junction point leads to the void.

Symbolic Links in Windows Vista

The new symbolic links, which Microsoft introduced with Windows Vista, can be created with the PSCX commandlet `New-Symlink`.

Compression

You can find commandlets for the creation of compressed file archives in PSCX. Here are commandlets for four different compression formats (ZIP, GZIP, TAR, and BZIP2):

```
Write-Zip
Write-GZip
Write-Tar
Write-BZip2
```

Table 11.2 shows some practical examples that explain the syntax of the commands. All examples uniformly use the ZIP format. All other formats work analogically with the relevant commandlet.

Table 11.2 Practical Examples for `Write-Zip`

`Write-zip Content.csv`	Compresses the file `Content.csv` into the archive `Content.csv.zip`
`Write-zip Content.csv Content.zip`	Compresses the file `Content.csv` to Content.zip
`"Content.csv", "Pricelist.doc", "Projectguidelines.doc" | Write-Zip`	Compresses the three indicated files individually in `Content.csv.zip`, `Priceliste.doc.zip`, and `Projectguidelines.doc.zip`
`"Content.csv", "Pricelist.doc", "Projectguidelines.doc" | Write-Zip -Outputpath J:\projects.zip`	Compresses the three indicated files together in `Clients.zip`
`Write-Zip j:\projects -Outputpath J:\projects.zip`	Compresses the whole content of the folder *j:\projects* to `Clients.zip`
`dir g:\data -Filter *.doc -Recurse | Write-zip -Output g:\Data\docs.zip`	Searches in the folder *g:\Data* and all its subfolders for Microsoft Word files and compresses these together in *g:\Data\docs.zip*

NOTE When the target file already exists, the new files are also integrated in the archive. Existing files are not deleted.

The compression commandlets have some additional options, including the following:

- `-RemoveOriginal` Deletes the original file after it has been integrated into the archive.
- `-Level` Compression rate from 1 to 9 (standard is 5).
- `-FlattenPaths` No path information is stored in the archive.

File Shares

Access to file shares is affected via the WMI class `Win32_Share` (see Figure 11.7). Important members of this class are as follows:

- `Name` Name of the file share
- `Path` Path in the file system that leads to the file share
- `Description` Description of the files shared
- `MaximumAllowed` Maximum number of simultaneous users
- `SetShareInfo()` Setting the property `Description`, `MaximumAllowed`, and authorizations for file shares
- `GetAccessMask()` Fetching the access control list for the share
- `Create()` A static method of the class `Win32_Share` to create new file shares

---

WARNING The attribute `AccessMask` is always empty (see Figure 11.7) because Microsoft declared it obsolete. The setting and reading of authorizations is affected via the methods `Create()`, `SetShareInfo()`, and `GetAccessMask()`. These methods create the respective associations.

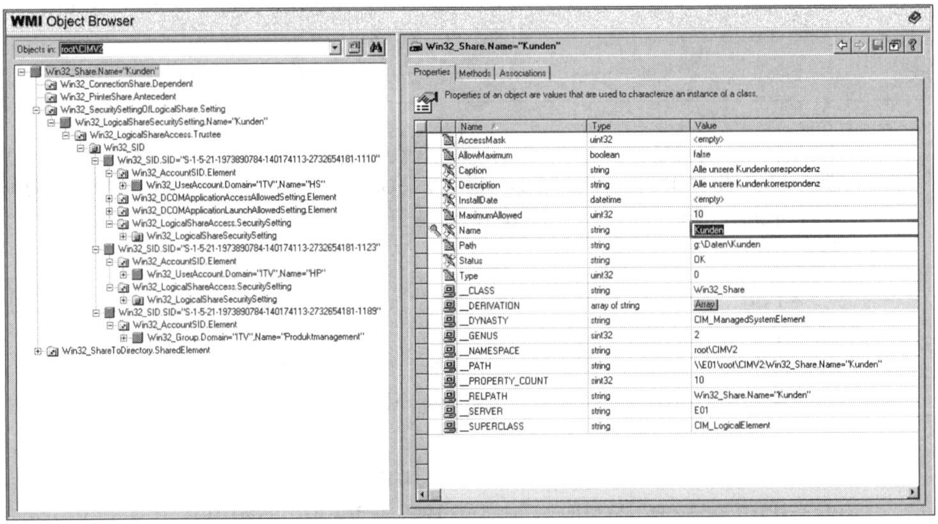

Figure 11.7 Depiction of an instance of the class `Win32_Share` in the WMI object browser

The most complicated parts of file shares are the authorizations, as you can see from the associations in the WMI object browser.

Enumerating File Shares

To enumerate files shared, you have to use the instances of the WMI class `Win32_Share` (see Figure 11.8):

```
Get-WmiObject Win32_Share
```

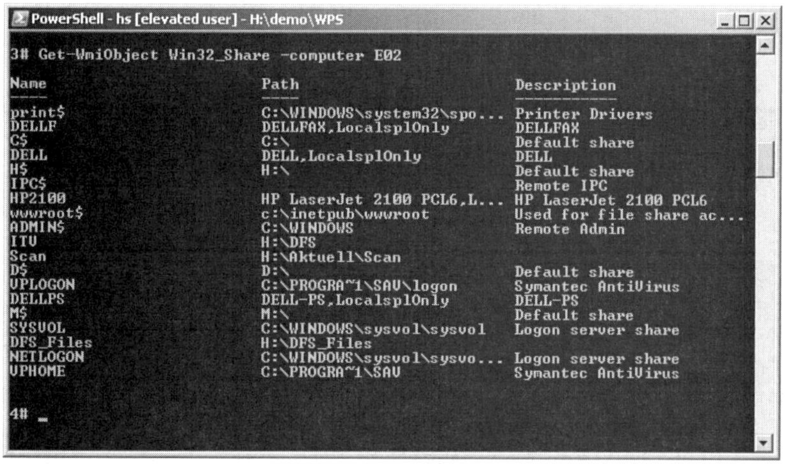

Figure 11.8 Listing of the file share system directories

Via the name of the file share, you can distinctly call the file share (even on a remote system):

```
Get-WmiObject Win32_Share -Filter "Name='C$'" -computer E02 |
➥Select Name, Path, Description, MaximumAllows | Format-List
```

Creating File Shares

The creation of a file share is a more elaborate matter, at least when you also want to set the access privilege list. Unfortunately, you cannot use a .NET class to grant privileges; you have to use the WMI classes instead.

For didactic reasons, the script in Listing 11.10 creates a share without explicitly defining access rules. Therefore, the file shares get standard rights (unrestricted access for everybody). To create a file share, the static method `Create()` of the class `Win32_Share` is called. In this case, `$null` is transferred for AccessMask. When starting, the script checks whether a file share already exists and deletes it if necessary to enable a new creation. You can see the result in Figure 11.9.

NOTE `Create()` has several error codes specific to it (for example, 22 = name of file share already exists, and 21 = false parameters).

Listing 11.10 Creating a File Share with Standard Privileges

```
############################################
# New-Share (without permissions)
# (C) Dr. Holger Schwichtenberg
############################################

# Parameters
$Computer = "E01"
$ShareName = "customers"
$Path = "j:\customers"
$Comment = "Customer Documents"

# before
"Before:"
Get-WmiObject Win32_Share -Filter "Name='$ShareName'"

Get-WmiObject Win32_Share -Filter "Name='$ShareName'" |
➥foreach-object { $_.Delete() }

# Win32_Share
$MC = [WMIClass] "ROOT\CIMV2:Win32_Share"
$Access = $Null
$R = $mc.Create($Path, $Sharename, 0, 10, $Description, "", $Access)

if ( $R.ReturnValue -ne 0) { Write-Error ("Error: "+ $R.ReturnValue);
Exit}
"Share has been created!"

# after
"After:"
Get-WmiObject Win32_Share -Filter "Name='$ShareName'"
```

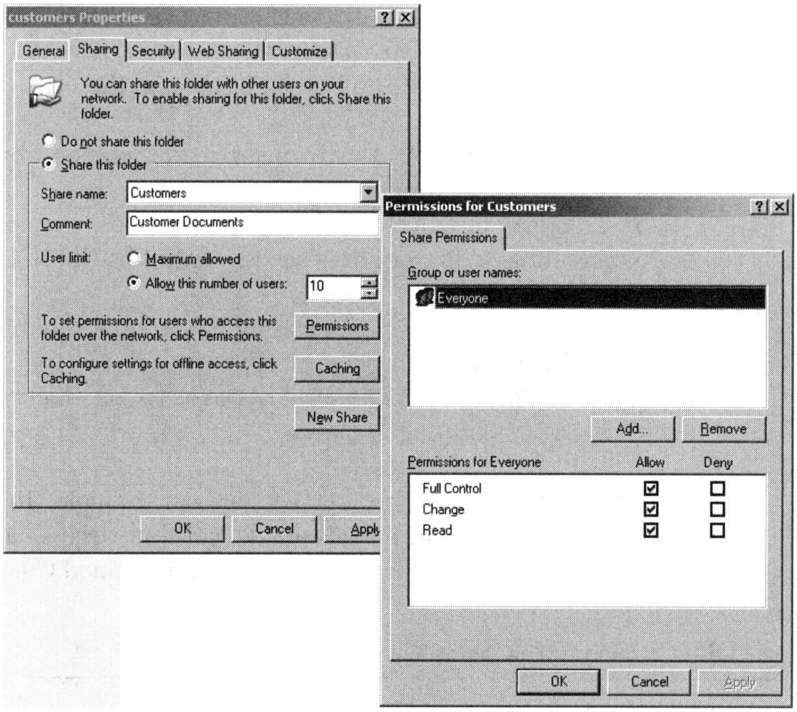

Figure 11.9 A file share created with standard privileges

Setting Permissions on File Shares

To set access control on file shares, you have to correctly assemble a Windows security descriptor (SD). An SD consists of an access control list (ACL) with various access control entries (ACEs), with each ACE permitting or refusing a number of privileges for a user (trustee) or a group of users.

In particular, the following steps are necessary:

1. Receive the security identifier (SID) for each user/each group intended to receive access (in this case, with the help of the Windows NT provider of the Active Directory Service Interface, which, despite its name, also works with Windows systems without Active Directory).

2. Create an instance of `Win32_Trustee` for each user/each group intended to receive access.
3. Create appropriate ACEs via instancing the class `Win32_ACE` for each ACE.
4. Fill the `Win32_ACE` with the `Win32_Trustee` object, the ACL, and any other properties you want.
5. Create an instance of `Win32_SecurityDescriptor.`
6. Assemble a discretionary access control list (DACL) consisting of all the ACEs.
7. Fill the `Win32_SecurityDescriptor` object with the newly created DACL.
8. Transfer the `Win32_SecurityDescriptor` object to the method `Create()` of `Win32_Share`.

Listing 11.11 and Figure 11.10 show an example. In this case, the groups Management and Consultants get full access, and the group Developers gets read access for the a file share named Customers.

Listing 11.11 Creating a New Share with Permissions

```
###########################################
# New-Share (with permissions)
# (C) Dr. Holger Schwichtenberg
###########################################

# Parameters
$Computer = "E01"
$ShareName = "customers"
$Path = "j:\customers"
$Comment = "Customer Documents"

# Constants
$SHARE_READ = 1179817
$SHARE_CHANGE = 1245462
$SHARE_FULL = 2032127
$SHARE_NONE = 1

$ACETYPE_ACCESS_ALLOWED = 0
$ACETYPE_ACCESS_DENIED = 1
$ACETYPE_SYSTEM_AUDIT = 2
```

```
$ACEFLAG_INHERIT_ACE = 2
$ACEFLAG_NO_PROPAGATE_INHERIT_ACE = 4
$ACEFLAG_INHERIT_ONLY_ACE = 8
$ACEFLAG_INHERITED_ACE = 16
$ACEFLAG_VALID_INHERIT_FLAGS = 31
$ACEFLAG_SUCCESSFUL_ACCESS = 64
$ACEFLAG_FAILED_ACCESS = 128

# Get Trustee
function New-Trustee($Domain, $User)
{
$Account = new-object system.security.principal.ntaccount("itv\hs")
$SID = $Account.Translate([system.security.principal.securityidentifier])
$useraccount = [ADSI] ("WinNT://" + $Domain + "/" + $User)
$mc = [WMIClass] "Win32_Trustee"
$t = $MC.CreateInstance()
$t.Domain = $Domain
$t.Name = $User
$t.SID = $useraccount.Get("ObjectSID")
return $t
}

# Create ACE
function New-ACE($Domain, $User, $Access, $Type, $Flags)
{
$mc = [WMIClass] "Win32_Ace"
$a = $MC.CreateInstance()
$a.AccessMask = $Access
$a.AceFlags = $Flags
$a.AceType = $Type
$a.Trustee = New-Trustee $Domain $User
return $a
}

# Create SD
function Get-SD
{

$mc = [WMIClass] "Win32_SecurityDescriptor"
$sd = $MC.CreateInstance()
$ACE1 = New-ACE "ITV" "Developers" $SHARE_READ
➥$ACETYPE_ACCESS_ALLOWED $ACEFLAG_INHERIT_ACE
```

(continues)

Listing 11.11 Creating a New Share with Permissions *(continued)*

```
$ACE2 = New-ACE "ITV" "Consultants" $SHARE_FULL
➥$ACETYPE_ACCESS_ALLOWED $ACEFLAG_INHERIT_ACE
$ACE3 = New-ACE "ITV" "Management" $SHARE_FULL
➥$ACETYPE_ACCESS_ALLOWED $ACEFLAG_INHERIT_ACE
[System.Management.ManagementObject[]] $DACL = $ACE1 , $ACE2, $ACE3


$sd.DACL = $DACL
return $sd
}

# before
"Before:"
Get-WmiObject Win32_Share -Filter "Name='$ShareName'"

Get-WmiObject Win32_Share -Filter "Name='$ShareName'" |
➥foreach-object { $_.Delete() }

# Win32_Share anlegen
$MC = [WMIClass] "ROOT\CIMV2:Win32_Share"
$Access = Get-SD
$R = $mc.Create($Path, $Sharename, 0, 10, $Comment, "", $Access)

if ( $R.ReturnValue -ne 0) { Write-Error ("ERROR: "
➥+$R.ReturnValue)  ; Exit}
"Share has been created!"

# after
"After:"

Get-WmiObject Win32_Share -Filter "Name='$ShareName'" |
➥foreach { $_.GetAccessMask()  } | gm
```

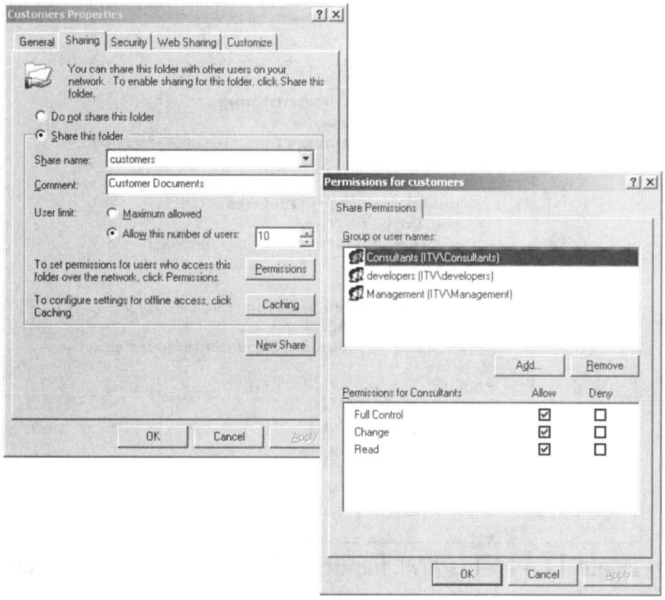

Figure 11.10 Result of the preceding script for the creation of a file share with explicit access rules

Mass Creation of Shares

You may often want to create a bunch of file shares at once. Figure 11.11 shows an XML file describing different file shares. The WPS script in Listing 11.12 reads the XML file (see Figure 11.11) and creates the corresponding file shares (see Figures 11.12 and 11.13).

At first, the XML file is read with `Get-Content`. The file content is then converted to the built-in WPS file type `[XML]`, thus creating a new instance of the .NET class `System.Xml.XmlDocument`. With the method `SelectNodes()`, you get access to the *<Share>* nodes contained in the document. By means of the built-in XML adapter, WPS encapsulates the single nodes in such a way that the subnodes appear as properties of the WPS variables (here, `$Share`). The method `Create()` of the WMI class `Win32_Share` is then fed with this data, with the tasks (including the possible earlier deletion of a file share with the same name), being encapsulated in a subroutine (`New-Share`).

```
<?xml version="1.0" encoding="utf-8" ?>
- <Shares>
    <!-- This document describes a list of shares to be created. -->
  - <Share>
      <Path>h:\documents\customers</Path>
      <Name>Customers</Name>
      <Description>Customers Documents</Description>
    </Share>
  - <Share>
      <Path>h:\documents\Projects</Path>
      <Name>Projects</Name>
      <Description>Projects Files</Description>
    </Share>
  - <Share>
      <Path>h:\documents\Accounting</Path>
      <Name>Accounting</Name>
      <Description>Accounting Documents</Description>
    </Share>
  - <Share>
      <Path>i:\</Path>
      <Name>Software</Name>
      <Description>Setup Files</Description>
    </Share>
  </Shares>
```

Figure 11.11 This XML file describes file shares to be created.

Listing 11.12 Creating a Bunch of Shares with Explicit Access Control

```
###########################################
# Create a bunch of shares with permissions
# (C) Dr. Holger Schwichtenberg, www.IT-Visions.de
###########################################

# Parameters
$Computer = "."

# Subs

# Constants
$SHARE_READ = 1179817
$SHARE_CHANGE = 1245462
$SHARE_FULL = 2032127
$SHARE_NONE = 1

$ACETYPE_ACCESS_ALLOWED = 0
$ACETYPE_ACCESS_DENIED = 1
$ACETYPE_SYSTEM_AUDIT = 2

$ACEFLAG_INHERIT_ACE = 2
$ACEFLAG_NO_PROPAGATE_INHERIT_ACE = 4
```

```
$ACEFLAG_INHERIT_ONLY_ACE = 8
$ACEFLAG_INHERITED_ACE = 16
$ACEFLAG_VALID_INHERIT_FLAGS = 31
$ACEFLAG_SUCCESSFUL_ACCESS = 64
$ACEFLAG_FAILED_ACCESS = 128

# Get Trustee
function New-Trustee($Domain, $User)
{
$Account = new-object system.security.principal.ntaccount("itv\hs")
$SID = $Account.Translate([system.security.principal.securityidentifier])
$useraccount = [ADSI] ("WinNT://" + $Domain + "/" + $User)
$mc = [WMIClass] "Win32_Trustee"
$t = $MC.CreateInstance()
$t.Domain = $Domain
$t.Name = $User
$t.SID = $useraccount.Get("ObjectSID")
return $t
}

# Create ACE
function New-ACE($Domain, $User, $Access, $Type, $Flags)
{
$mc = [WMIClass] "Win32_Ace"
$a = $MC.CreateInstance()
$a.AccessMask = $Access
$a.AceFlags = $Flags
$a.AceType = $Type
$a.Trustee = New-Trustee $Domain $User
return $a
}

# Create SD
function Get-SD
{

$mc = [WMIClass] "Win32_SecurityDescriptor"
$sd = $MC.CreateInstance()
$ACE1 = New-ACE "ITV" "Management" $SHARE_READ
➥$ACETYPE_ACCESS_ALLOWED $ACEFLAG_INHERIT_ACE
$ACE2 = New-ACE "ITV" "Sales" $SHARE_FULL $ACETYPE_ACCESS_ALLOWED
➥$ACEFLAG_INHERIT_ACE
```

(continues)

Listing 11.12 Creating a Bunch of Shares with Explicit Access Control *(continued)*

```
$ACE3 = New-ACE "ITV" "Productmanagement" $SHARE_FULL
➥$ACETYPE_ACCESS_ALLOWED $ACEFLAG_INHERIT_ACE
[System.Management.ManagementObject[]] $DACL = $ACE1 , $ACE2, $ACE3

$sd.DACL = $DACL
return $sd
}

Function New-Share($Computer,$ShareName, $Path, $Comment, $Access)
{
# Info
"Creating Share $ShareName for $Path..."

# Delete if exists
Get-WmiObject Win32_Share -ComputerName $Computer -Filter
"Name='$ShareName'" | foreach {
 Write-Warning "Deleting existing share $($_.Name)..."
$_.Delete()
}

# Create Win32_Share
$MC = [WMIClass] "ROOT\CIMV2:Win32_Share"
$Access = Get-SD
$R = $mc.Create($Path, $Sharename, 0, 10, $Comment, "", $Access)

# Result
if ( $R.ReturnValue -ne 0) { Write-Error ("Error creating share: " +
$R.ReturnValue); Exit}
"Share was created!"

}

# Get XML file
$doc = [xml] (Get-Content -Path
h:\demo\powershell\datasystem\shares.xml)
$shares = $doc.SelectNodes("//Share")

# Loop
foreach ($share in $shares)
{
New-Share $Computer $share.Name $share.Path $share.description
}
```

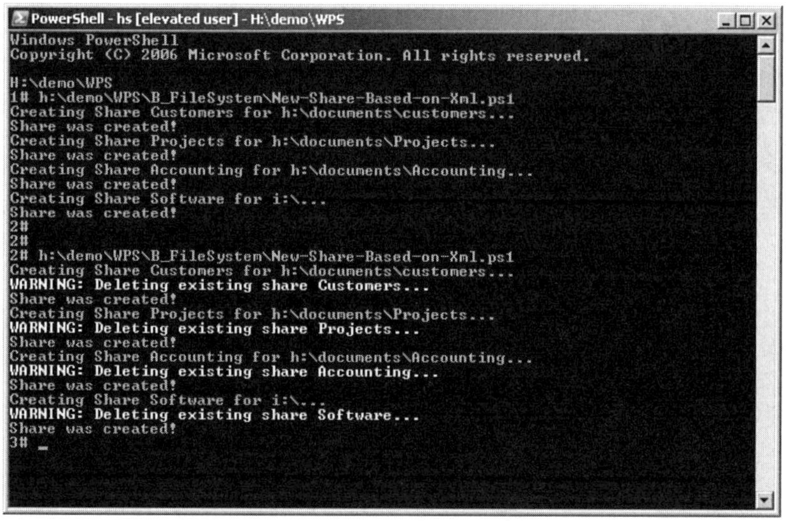

Figure 11.12 Creation of a bunch of shares with standard access control

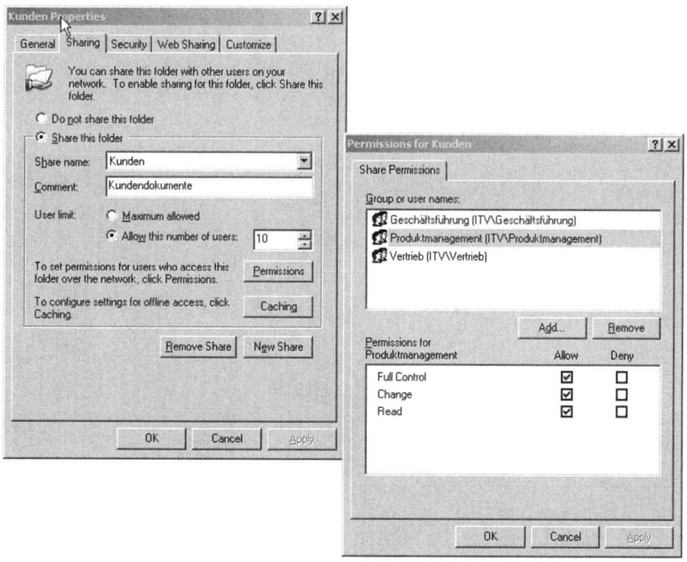

Figure 11.13 Result of access control

Summary

In this chapter, you learned about using WPS to administer file systems. WPS contains many commandlets for standard operations such as copying files (`Copy-Item`), moving files (`Move-Item`), deleting files (`Remove-Item`) and enumerating the content of folders (`Get-ChildItem`). Also, file properties can be accessed through the commandlets `Get-ItemProperty` and `Set-ItemProperty`. However, there are operations that require WMI, that is, the management of file shares. The PowerShell Community Extensions provide additional commandlets for file compression and the management of file system links.

CHAPTER 12

MANAGING DOCUMENTS

In this chapter:

This chapter discusses the creation and use of different document types: text files, binary files, CSV files, and XML files. Examples in this chapter include searching in files, importing and exporting data in the CSV format, as well as reading, changing, transforming, and formatting XML documents.

Text Files

For reading files, Windows PowerShell (WPS) provides the commandlet `Get-Content`. By default, `Get-Content` reads the complete file.

Listing 12.1 demonstrates the entering of a text file and the row-by-row output using the commandlet `Foreach-Object`.

Listing 12.1 Row-wise Entering of a Text File

```
$file = Get-Content j:\documents\protocol.csv
$a = 0
$file | Foreach-Object { $a++; "Row" + $a + ": " + $_ }
"Total number of rows: " + $a
```

If you are interested in displaying only the number of rows, you can get this information in a much shorter way:

```
Get-Content j:\documents\protocol.csv | Measure-Object
```

Writing Files

Writing to a text file in the file system is possible with a few commandlets, especially `Set-Content` and `Add-Content`. `Set-Content` exchanges the content, `Add-Content` adds contents (see Listing 12.2).

Listing 12.2 Creation of and Adding to a Text File

```
$file = "j:\documents\protocol.txt"
"Start of new protocol file " | Set-Content $file

"New entry " | Add-content $file
"New entry " | Add-content $file
"New entry " | Add-content $file

"Content of file is now:"
Get-content $file
```

`Clear-Content` deletes the content of a file, but leaves the empty file in the file system.

Another option to create a text file is to use `New-Item`:

```
New-Item . -name data.txt -type "file" -value "This is the
➥content!" -force
```

In this case, however, there is only the option to create the file as a new one (without `-force`) or to overwrite an already existing file (with `-force`).

A third option to write 1a file is the commandlet `Out-File`, as follows:

```
Get-Process | Out-File c:\temp\processes1.txt
Get-Process | Set-Content c:\temp\processes2.txt
```

As you can see in Figures 12.1 and 12.2, there is a difference between using `Out-File` and `Set-Content`: `Out-File` will use the standard formatting that you would also see in the WPS console, whereas `Set-Content` just calls `ToString()` on each object in the pipeline.

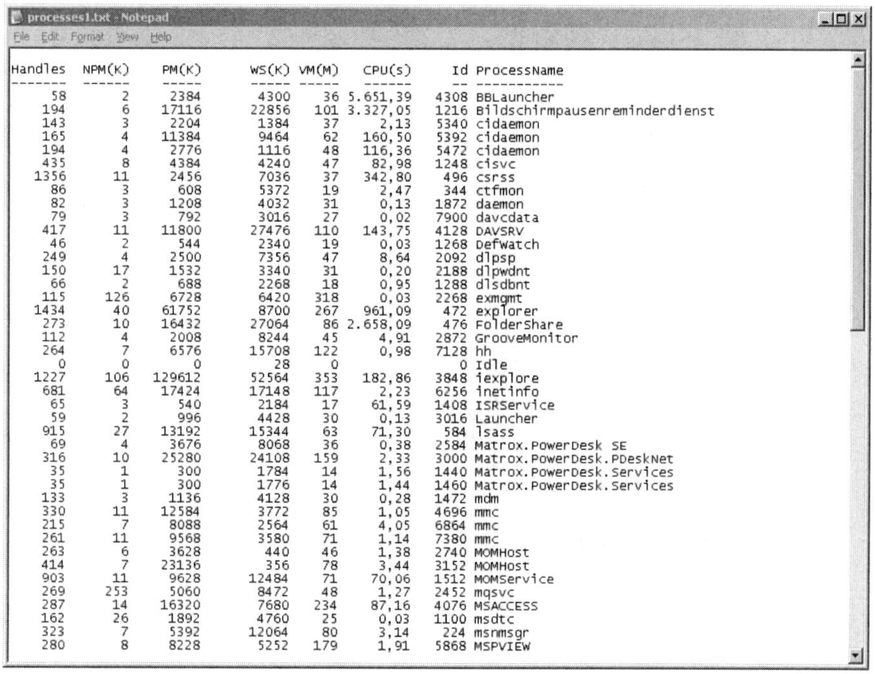

Handles	NPM(K)	PM(K)	WS(K)	VM(M)	CPU(s)	Id	ProcessName
58	2	2384	4300	36	5.651,39	4308	BBLauncher
194	6	17116	22856	101	3.327,05	1216	Bildschirmpausenreminderdienst
143	3	2204	1384	37	2,13	5340	cidaemon
165	4	11384	9464	62	160,50	5392	cidaemon
194	4	2776	1116	48	116,36	5472	cidaemon
435	8	4384	4240	47	82,98	1248	cisvc
1356	11	2456	7036	37	342,80	496	csrss
86	3	608	5372	19	2,47	344	ctfmon
82	3	1208	4032	31	0,13	1872	daemon
79	3	792	3016	27	0,02	7900	davcdata
417	11	11800	27476	110	143,75	4128	DAVSRV
46	2	544	2340	19	0,03	1268	DefWatch
249	4	2500	7356	47	8,64	2092	dlpsp
150	17	1532	3340	31	0,20	2188	dlpwdnt
66	2	688	2268	18	0,95	1288	dlsdbnt
115	126	6728	6420	318	0,03	2268	exmgmt
1434	40	61752	8700	267	961,09	472	explorer
273	10	16432	27064	86	2.658,09	476	FolderShare
112	4	2008	8244	45	4,91	2872	GrooveMonitor
264	7	6576	15708	122	0,98	7128	hh
0	0	0	28	0		0	Idle
1227	106	129612	52564	353	182,86	3848	iexplore
681	64	17424	17148	117	2,23	6256	inetinfo
65	3	540	2184	17	61,59	1408	ISRService
59	2	996	4428	30	0,13	3016	Launcher
915	27	13192	15344	63	71,30	584	lsass
69	4	3676	8068	36	0,38	2584	Matrox.PowerDesk SE
316	10	25280	24108	159	2,33	3000	Matrox.PowerDesk.PDeskNet
35	1	300	1784	14	1,56	1440	Matrox.PowerDesk.Services
35	1	300	1776	14	1,44	1460	Matrox.PowerDesk.Services
133	3	1136	4128	30	0,28	1472	mdm
330	11	12584	3772	85	1,05	4696	mmc
215	7	8088	2564	61	4,05	6864	mmc
261	11	9568	3580	71	1,14	7380	mmc
263	6	3628	440	46	1,38	2740	MOMHost
414	7	23136	356	78	3,44	3152	MOMHost
903	11	9628	12484	71	70,06	1512	MOMService
269	253	5060	8472	48	1,27	2452	mqsvc
287	14	16320	7680	234	87,16	4076	MSACCESS
162	26	1892	4760	25	0,03	1100	msdtc
323	7	5392	12064	80	3,14	224	msnmsgr
280	8	8228	5252	179	1,91	5868	MSPVIEW

Figure 12.1 Result of using `Out-File`

Searching

The searching of text files is possible with the commandlet `Select-String`. The following command displays the information about which script files of a directory hierarchy contain the word *Where*:

```
Get-ChildItem j:\Scripts -Filter *.ps1 -Recurse |
➥Select-String "Where"
```

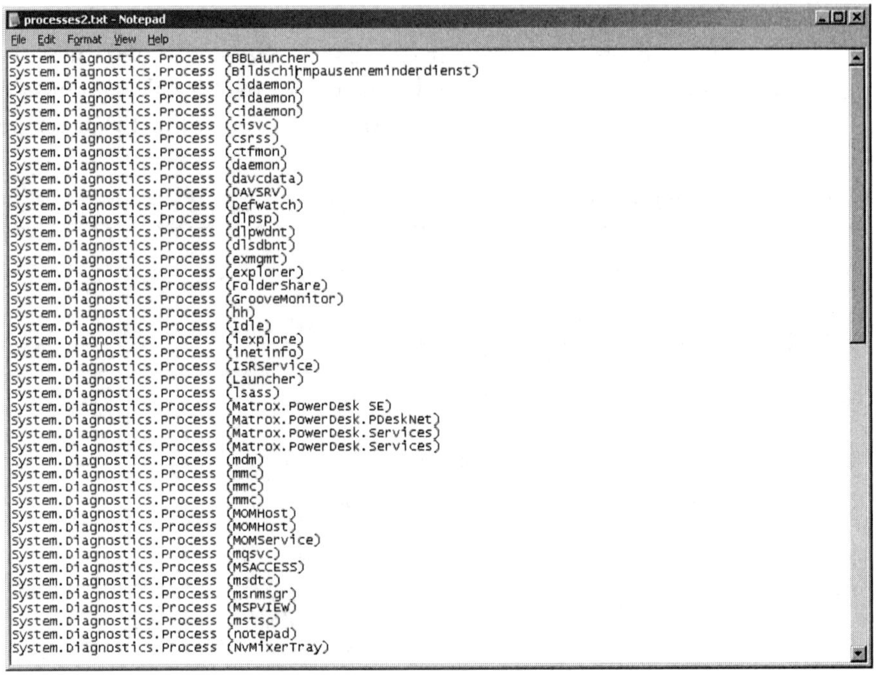

Figure 12.2 Result of using `Set-Content`

Binary Files

Binary files can also be read with `Get-Content` and written with `Set-Content` or `Add-Content`. The parameter to be added, respectively, is `-encoding Byte` (see Listing 12.3).

Listing 12.3 Fetching and Writing a Binary File

```
# --- Read binary file
$a = Get-Content H:\images\www.IT-Visions.de_Logo.jpg -encoding byte

# --- Write binary file
$a | Set-Content "g:\Data\Logo.jpg" -encoding byte
```

CSV Files

To enable the import and export of files in CSV (comma-separated value) format, WPS offers the commandlets `Export-Csv` and `Import-Csv`.

CSV Export

There are two alternatives for exporting. You can create a common CSV file without meta data (see Figure 12.3):

```
Get-Service | Where-Object {$_.status -eq "running"} |
Export-Csv j:\administration\services.csv -NoTypeInformation
```

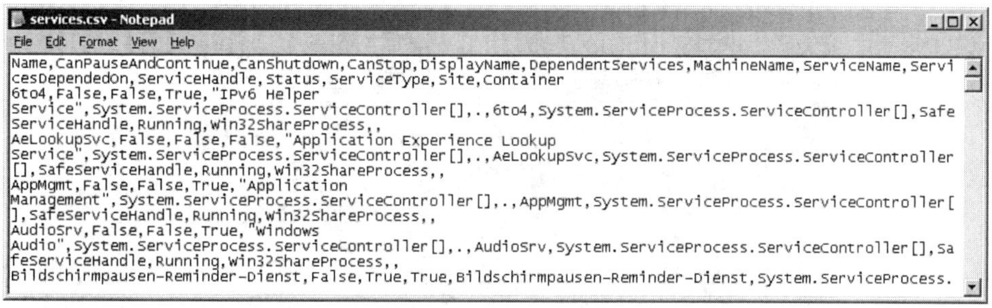

```
services.csv - Notepad
File Edit Format View Help
Name,CanPauseAndContinue,CanShutdown,CanStop,DisplayName,DependentServices,MachineName,ServiceName,Servi
cesDependedOn,ServiceHandle,Status,ServiceType,Site,Container
6to4,False,False,True,"IPv6 Helper
Service",System.ServiceProcess.ServiceController[],.,6to4,System.ServiceProcess.ServiceController[],Safe
ServiceHandle,Running,Win32ShareProcess,,
AeLookupSvc,False,False,False,"Application Experience Lookup
Service",System.ServiceProcess.ServiceController[],.,AeLookupSvc,System.ServiceProcess.ServiceController
[],SafeServiceHandle,Running,Win32ShareProcess,,
AppMgmt,False,False,True,"Application
Management",System.ServiceProcess.ServiceController[],.,AppMgmt,System.ServiceProcess.ServiceController[
],SafeServiceHandle,Running,Win32ShareProcess,,
AudioSrv,False,False,True,"Windows
Audio",System.ServiceProcess.ServiceController[],.,AudioSrv,System.ServiceProcess.ServiceController[],Sa
feServiceHandle,Running,Win32ShareProcess,,
Bildschirmpausen-Reminder-Dienst,False,True,True,Bildschirmpausen-Reminder-Dienst,System.ServiceProcess.
```

Figure 12.3 Exporting without type information

Alternatively, you can create a CSV file in which persisted object types are indicated in the first rows after the hash symbol (see Figure 12.4):

```
Get-Service | Where-Object {$_.status -eq "running"} |
➥Export-Csv j:\administration\services.csv
```

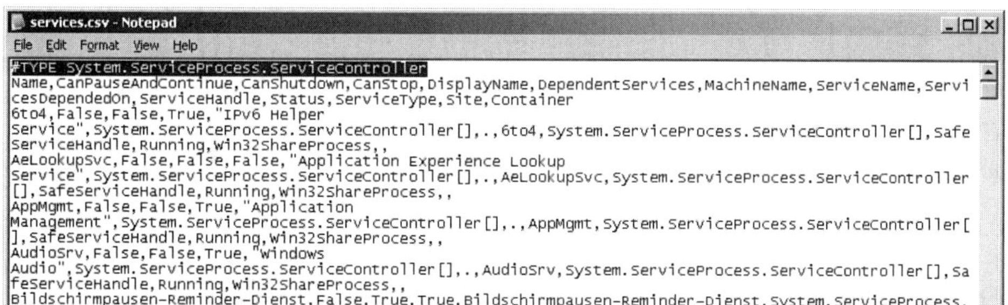

```
services.csv - Notepad
File Edit Format View Help
#TYPE System.ServiceProcess.ServiceController
Name,CanPauseAndContinue,CanShutdown,CanStop,DisplayName,DependentServices,MachineName,ServiceName,Servi
cesDependedOn,ServiceHandle,Status,ServiceType,Site,Container
6to4,False,False,True,"IPv6 Helper
Service",System.ServiceProcess.ServiceController[],.,6to4,System.ServiceProcess.ServiceController[],Safe
ServiceHandle,Running,Win32ShareProcess,,
AeLookupSvc,False,False,False,"Application Experience Lookup
Service",System.ServiceProcess.ServiceController[],.,AeLookupSvc,System.ServiceProcess.ServiceController
[],SafeServiceHandle,Running,Win32ShareProcess,,
AppMgmt,False,False,True,"Application
Management",System.ServiceProcess.ServiceController[],.,AppMgmt,System.ServiceProcess.ServiceController[
],SafeServiceHandle,Running,Win32ShareProcess,,
AudioSrv,False,False,True,"Windows
Audio",System.ServiceProcess.ServiceController[],.,AudioSrv,System.ServiceProcess.ServiceController[],Sa
feServiceHandle,Running,Win32ShareProcess,,
Bildschirmpausen-Reminder-Dienst,False,True,True,Bildschirmpausen-Reminder-Dienst,System.ServiceProcess.
```

Figure 12.4 Exporting with type information

CSV Import

When a CSV file is imported with

```
Import-Csv j:\administration\services.csv | where
➥{ $_.Status -eq "Running" }
```

the type information decides which object type will be constructed. With type information, the respective type is then created. Without type information, instances of the class `System.Management.Automation.PSCustomObject` are created (see Figures 12.5 and 12.6).

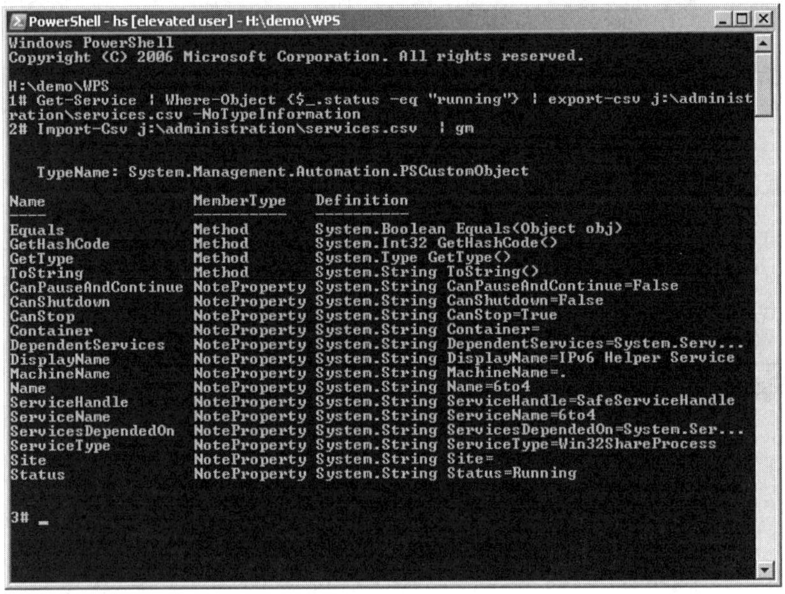

Figure 12.5 Pipeline content after importing a CSV file without type information

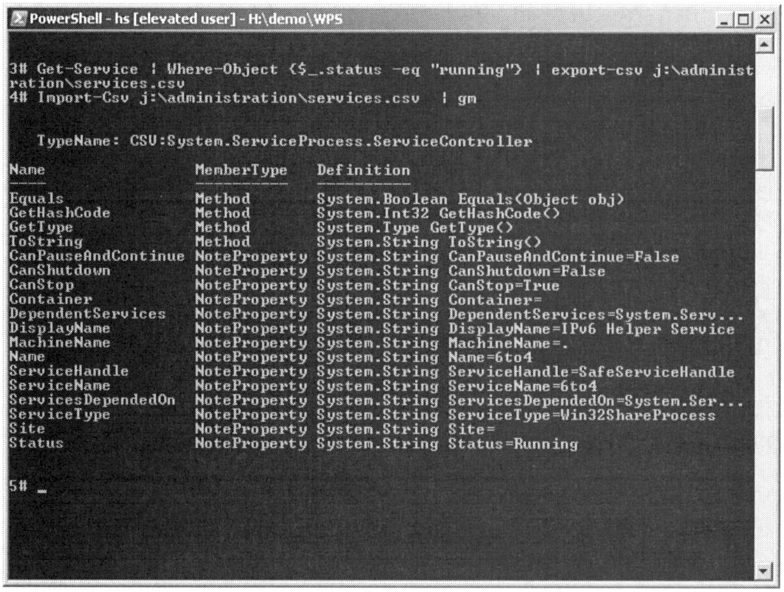

Figure 12.6 Pipeline content after importing a CSV file with type information

XML Files

WPS offers a very easy option to read XML documents through the WPS XML adapter.

Reading XML Documents

XML element names can be accessed just like the attributes of .NET objects. When `$doc` contains the XML document shown in Figure 12.7, `$doc.Websites.Website` displays the volume of XML nodes named *<Website>*.

```
<?xml version="1.0" encoding="utf-8"?>
<Websites>
  <Website ID="1">
    <URL>www.sams.com</URL>
    <Description>Publisher</Description>
  </Website>
  <Website ID="2">
    <URL>www.IT-Visions.de</URL>
    <Description>Website of the Authors Consulting Company</Description>
  </Website>
  <Website ID="3">
    <URL>www.powershell24.com</URL>
    <Description>Companion website for this book</Description>
  </Website>
  <Website ID="4">
    <URL>www.microsoft.com/windowsserver2003/technologies/management/powershell/default.mspx</URL>
    <Description>Microsofts PowerShell Website</Description>
  </Website>
</Websites>
```

Figure 12.7 Example for an XML document

The preceding document can be evaluated as shown in Listing 12.4 and Figure 12.8.

Listing 12.4 Fetching of an XML file

```
$doc = [xml] (Get-Content -Path j:\documents\websites.xml)
$Sites = $doc.Websites.Website
$Sites | select URL, description
```

NOTE To use the special XML support of WPS, WPS needs to know which variables an XML document contains. Therefore, the type conversion with `[xml]` in the first row is of great importance.

Checking XML Documents

If you try to convert an invalid XML document (which lacks, for instance, a closing tag) into the type `[Xml]`, you will get an error report from WPS (see Figure 12.9).

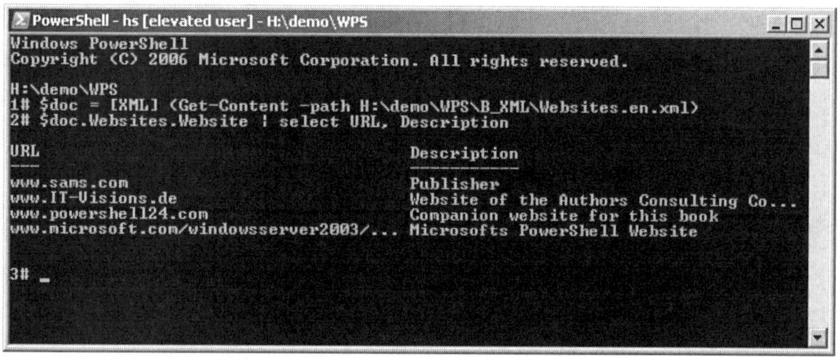

Figure 12.8 Result of the evaluation of the XML document

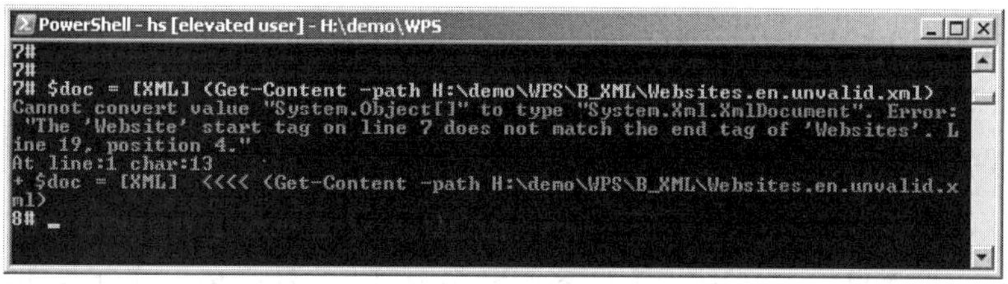

Figure 12.9 Error report, when a closing tag is missing

You can check in advance whether a document is valid with the commandlet `Test-Xml` (from PSCX). `Test-Xml` displays `True` or `False`.

```
Test-Xml h:\demo\powershell\xml\websites_invalid.xml
```

By default, `Test-Xml` checks only XML well formedness. As an option, it is possible to validate against an XML schema (for example, Figure 12.10). Here, after `-SchemaPath`, you have to indicate the path to the XML schema file (*.xsd*). Alternatively, you can also indicate an array with several paths.

```
Test-Xml h:\demo\powershell\xml\websites.xml -SchemaPath
➥h:\demo\powershell\xml\websites.xsd
```

```
Websites.xsd*
<?xml version="1.0" encoding="utf-8"?>
<xs:schema attributeFormDefault="unqualified" elementFormDefault="qualified" xmlns:
xs="http://www.w3.org/2001/XMLSchema">
 <xs:element name="Websites">
  <xs:complexType>
   <xs:sequence>
    <xs:element maxOccurs="unbounded" name="Website">
     <xs:complexType>
      <xs:sequence>
       <xs:element name="URL" type="xs:string" />
       <xs:element name="Beschreibung" type="xs:string" />
      </xs:sequence>
      <xs:attribute name="ID" type="xs:unsignedByte" use="required" />
     </xs:complexType>
    </xs:element>
   </xs:sequence>
  </xs:complexType>
 </xs:element>
</xs:schema>
```

Figure 12.10 XML schema for the Websites file

Formatting

XML documents do not have to be formatted (that is, insertions of the XML elements according to the respective level are not necessary). In PSCX, there is the possibility to display nonformatted XML documents as formatted, or to adapt the formatting to the output with the commandlet `Format-Xml`.

The following command displays a formatted output of an XML document, where each level is inserted with a dot and four spaces (see Figure 12.11).

```
Format-Xml h:\demo\powershell\xml\websites.xml -IndentString
➥".    "
```

XPath

For searching in XML documents with the help of XPath (XPath is a W3C standard; see [W3C01]) the class `XmlDocument` supports the methods `SelectNodes()` and `SelectSingleNode()`. In PSCX, there is the commandlet `Select-Xml` (see Table 12.1).

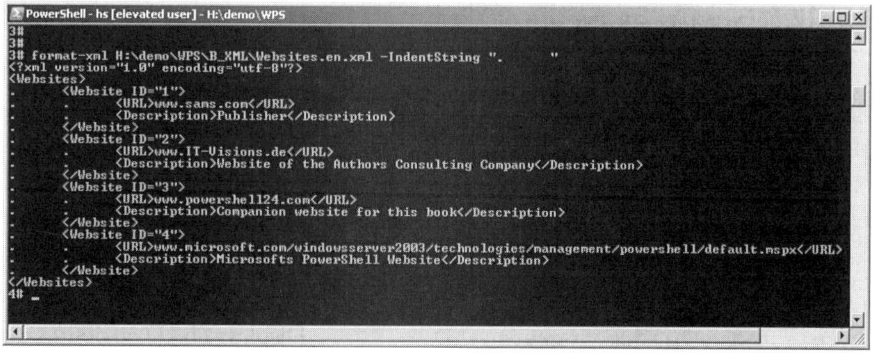

Figure 12.11 Use of `Format-Xml`

WARNING `SelectNodes()` and `SelectSingleNode()` display instances of the classes `System.Xml.XmlElement` and `System.Xml.XmlAttribute`. `Select-Xml`, however, displays instances of `MS.Internal.Xml.Cache.XPathDocumentNavigator`. Therefore, the output is very different. To receive the same output with both commands, you must send the result of `Select-Xml` to `Select-Object InnerXml` (see Figure 12.12).

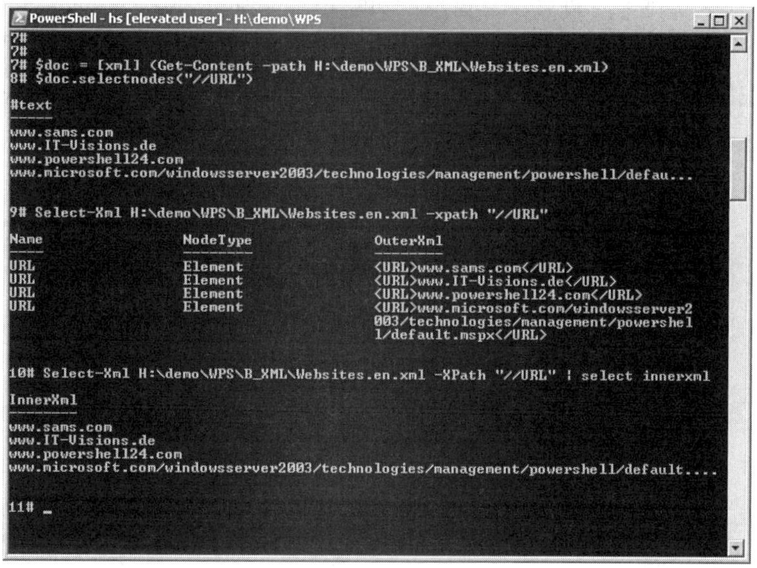

Figure 12.12 Comparing the output of `SelectNodes()` and `Select-Xml`

Table 12.1 Examples for the Use of XPath

`$doc.SelectNodes("//URL")` or `select-Xml h:\demo\powershell\xml\websites.xml -XPath "//URL" | select innerxml`	Displays all <URL> elements
`$doc.SelectNodes("//Website/@ID")` or `select-Xml h:\demo\powershell\xml\websites.xml -XPath "//Website/@ID" | select innerxml`	Displays all ID attributes of all <Website> elements
`$doc.SelectSingleNode("//Website[@ID=3]/URL")` or `select-Xml h:\demo\powershell\xml\websites.xml -XPath "//Website[@ID=3]/URL" | select innerxml`	Displays the <URL>-element of the <Website> elements with the attribute value 3 in the attribute ID

TIP `Select-Xml` has the advantage that easy-to-use support of XML namespaces is offered. The following command fetches the names of all bound C# source code files from a Visual Studio project file. Thereby, reference is made to the respective namespace of the command-line tool `MSBuild.exe`, which is responsible for the translation of the projects (see Figure 12.13).

```
Select-Xml "H:\demo\PowerShell\_own
➥Commandlets\PowerShell_Commandlet_Library\
➥PowerShell_Commandlet_Library.csproj" -Namespace
➥'dns=http://schemas.microsoft.com/developer/msbuild/2003'
➥-XPath "//dns:Compile/@Include"
```

Modifying XML Documents

Listing 12.5 adds an entry to an XML file by using the methods `CreateElement()` and `AppendChild()`.

This example shows that even in WPS there are some areas that can be somewhat more complicated. Because the subelements of an XML node can be presented as attributes of a .NET class processed by WPS, the attributes of the meta class `System.Xml.Node` (that is, classes derived therefrom) cannot be presented directly, to avoid name conflicts. These attributes are available only via their getters and setters. Therefore, with the WPS script, you cannot set the content of a node via `$node.Innertext = "xyz"`; instead, you must call `$node._set_Innertext("xyz")`.

```
<Project DefaultTargets="Build" xmlns="http://schemas.microsoft.com/developer/msbuild/2003">
...
  <ItemGroup>
    <Compile Include="Test-Dauer.cs" />
    <Compile Include="Get-Disk3.cs" />
    <Compile Include="Get-Computername.cs" />
    <None Include="Get-Disk2.cs" />
    <None Include="Get-Disk1.cs" />
    <Compile Include="Properties\AssemblyInfo.cs" />
    <Compile Include="PSSnapin.cs">
      <SubType>Component</SubType>
    </Compile>
  </ItemGroup>
...
</Project>
```

Figure 12.13 This fragment from a Visual Studio project file shows the elements to be selected and their namespace declaration.

Listing 12.5 Completion of an XML file

```
"Previously"
$doc = [xml] (Get-Content -Path j:\administration\websites.xml)
$doc.Websites.Website | select URL,Description
"After"
$site = $doc.CreateElement("Website")
$url = $doc.CreateElement("URL")
$url.set_Innertext("www.windows-scripting.com")
$description = $doc.CreateElement("description")
$description.set_Innertext("Community-Website for PowerShell")
$site.AppendChild($url)
$site.AppendChild($description
$doc.Websites.AppendChild($site)
$doc.Websites.Website | select URL,description
$doc.Save("h:\demo\buch\websites_neu.xml")
"Document saved!"
```

Exporting Pipeline Objects to XML

WPS uses its own XML format (CLIXML) to persist (serialize) the object pipeline in XML form (via `Export-CliXml`), so that it can be restored at a later point. The following command saves the object list of the current system services. Figure 12.14 shows the results.

```
Get-Service | Where-Object {$_.status -eq "running"} |
➥Export-CliXml j:\administration\services.xml
```


```
- <Objs Version="1.1" xmlns="http://schemas.microsoft.com/powershell/2004/04">
  + <Obj RefId="RefId-0">
  + <Obj RefId="RefId-0">
  + <Obj RefId="RefId-0">
  + <Obj RefId="RefId-0">
  + <Obj RefId="RefId-0">
  - <Obj RefId="RefId-0">
      <TNRef RefId="RefId-0" />
    - <Props>
        <B N="CanPauseAndContinue">false</B>
        <B N="CanShutdown">true</B>
        <B N="CanStop">true</B>
        <S N="DisplayName">Background Intelligent Transfer Service</S>
      - <Obj N="DependentServices" RefId="RefId-1">
          <TNRef RefId="RefId-1" />
          <LST />
        </Obj>
        <S N="MachineName">.</S>
        <S N="ServiceName">BITS</S>
      - <Obj N="ServicesDependedOn" RefId="RefId-2">
          <TNRef RefId="RefId-1" />
        - <LST>
          - <Obj RefId="RefId-3">
              <TNRef RefId="RefId-0" />
            - <Props>
                <B N="CanPauseAndContinue">false</B>
                <B N="CanShutdown">false</B>
                <B N="CanStop">true</B>
                <S N="DisplayName">COM+ Event System</S>
              - <Obj N="DependentServices" RefId="RefId-4">
                  <TNRef RefId="RefId-1" />
                - <LST>
                    <S>System.ServiceProcess.ServiceController</S>
                    <S>System.ServiceProcess.ServiceController</S>
                    <S>System.ServiceProcess.ServiceController</S>
                    <S>System.ServiceProcess.ServiceController</S>
                  </LST>
                </Obj>
```


Figure 12.14 Clipping from a serialization of a WPS pipeline

The equivalent to restoring the pipeline is `Import-CliXml` (see Figure 12.15).

```
Import-CliXml j:\administration\services.xml | Get-Member
```

WARNING After the deserialization of the objects, all attributes of the objects can again be used, but not the methods of the objects!

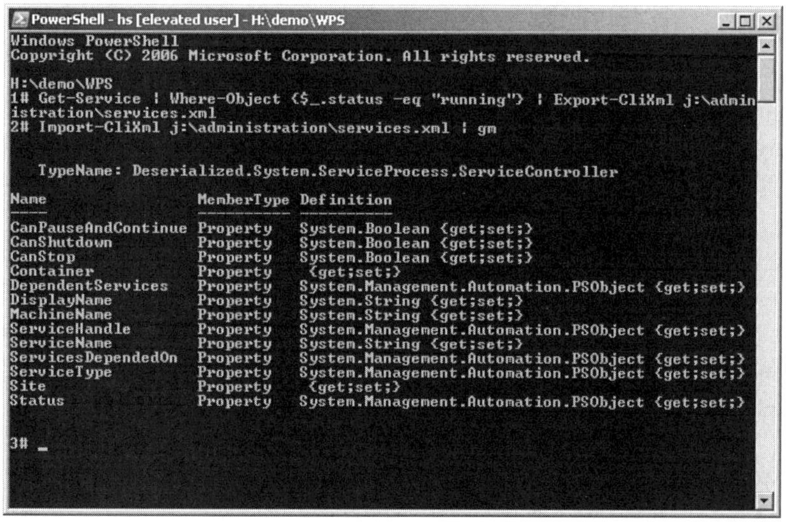

Figure 12.15 Pipeline content after serialization and deserialization with `Export-CliXml` and `Import-CliXml`

Transforming XML Documents

In PSCX, the commandlet `Convert-Xml` is provided for the application of the W3C standard XSLT (XML Stylesheet Transformations). Alternatively, you can use the .NET class `System.Xml.Xsl.XslCompiledTransform`.

The following example demonstrates how the XML file `Websites.xml` can be converted into an XHTML file with the help of the XSLT file, shown in Figure 12.16. The result is saved as `Websites.html` (see Figure 12.17).

```
Convert-Xml j:\administration\websites.xml -XsltPath
➥j:\administration\WebsitesToHTML.xslt |
➥Set-content j:\administration\websites.html
```

TIP You can get help for developing and testing XSLT files within Studio 2005/2008.

```
<?xml version="1.0" ?>
<xsl:stylesheet xmlns:xsl="http://www.w3.org/1999/XSL/Transform" version="1.0">
 <!-- Transformation -->
 <xsl:template match="Websites">
  <HTML>
   <body>
    <h2>Websites</h2>
    <ul>
     <xsl:for-each select="/Websites/Website">
      <li>
       <xsl:value-of select='Description'/>
       <br>
        <a>
         <xsl:attribute name="href">
          <xsl:value-of select="URL"/>
         </xsl:attribute>
         <xsl:value-of select="URL"/>
        </a>
       </br>
      </li>
     </xsl:for-each>
    </ul>
    <hr></hr>
    Converted from XML
   </body>
  </HTML>
 </xsl:template>
</xsl:stylesheet>
```

Figure 12.16 XSLT file

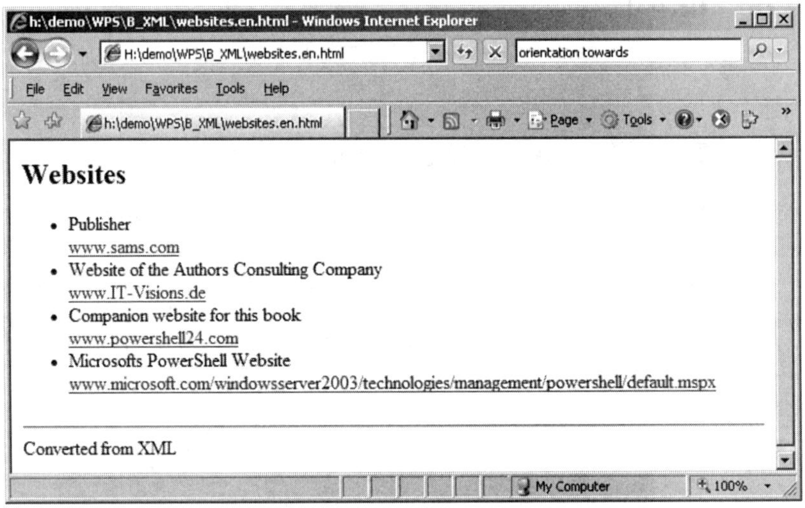

Figure 12.17 This HTML file was generated from the XML file.

HTML Files

The commandlet `Convert-Html` converts the objects of the pipeline into an HTML table.

The following command saves the list of the Windows system services as an HTML file (see Figure 12.18).

```
Get-Service | ConvertTo-Html name,status -title
➥"Servicelist" -body "List of services" |
➥Set-Content j:\administration\services.htm
```

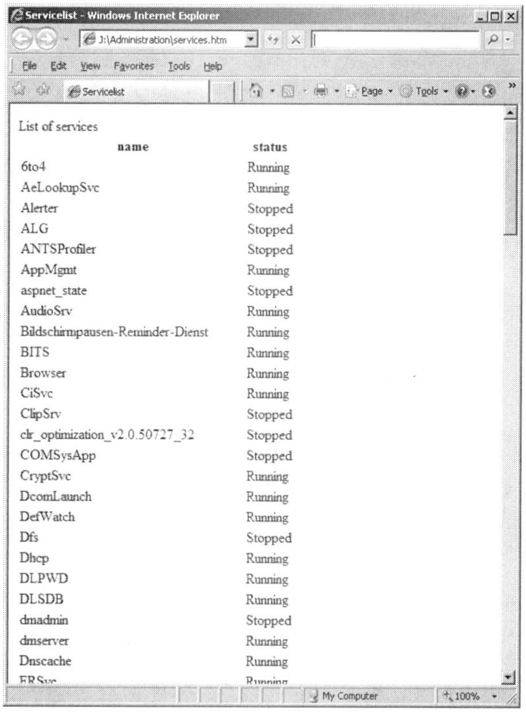

Figure 12.18 Result of converting into an HTML table

Summary

In this chapter, we looked at the handling of different document types: unstructured text files and binary files as well as three structured text file types (CSV, XML, and HTML).

WPS provides at lot of helpful commandlets such as `Get-Content`, `Set-Content`, `Export-Csv`, and `Import-Csv`. In addition, there is good support for access to XML files through the XML WPS object adapter, which allows direct access to XML nodes as if they were properties of a .NET class. You can find additional commandlets for XML handling within the PSCX (for example, `Select-Xml`, `Format-Xml`, and `Convert-Xml`).

CHAPTER 13

REGISTRY AND SOFTWARE

In this chapter:

This chapter covers accessing the registry and the administration of MSI-based and non-MSI-based installations. Examples in this chapter include

- Reading keys and values
- Creating and deleting keys and values
- Enumeration of installed software
- Installation and uninstallation of software

Registry

For accessing and manipulation of the Windows registry, Windows PowerShell (WPS) provides a PowerShell Provider. This means that the navigation commandlets (`Set-Location`, `Get-ChildItem`, `New-Item`, `Get-ItemProperty`, and so on) are available in the registry.

Reading Keys

The subkeys of a registry key are as follows (alias `dir hklm:\software`):

```
Get-ChildItem hklm:\software
```

You can also move the current path to the registry

```
Set-Location hklm:\software
```

(alias `cd hklm:\software`), and start the listing of the content of that registry key with `Get-ChildItem`.

You get access to a single registry key with

```
Get-Item www.it-visions.de
```

or with the absolute path:

```
Get-Item hklm:\software\www.it-visions.de
```

This results in .NET objects of the type `Microsoft.Win32.RegistryKey`. `Get-Item` always delivers a single instance of this class. `Get-ChildItem` delivers either no, one, or several instances.

Creating and Deleting Keys

A key in the registry is created with

```
New-Item -path hklm:\software -name "www.IT-visions.de"
```

or

```
md -path hklm:\software\www.IT-visions.de
```

NOTE `New-Item` is also available as `md`. `md`; however, it is not an alias but a built-in function.

You can also copy whole keys with `Copy-Item`:

```
Copy-Item hklm:\software\www.it-visions.de
➥hklm:\software\www.IT-Visions.de_Backup
```

You can delete a registry key together with all its values as follows:

```
Remove-Item "hklm:\software\www.it-visions.de" -Recurse
```

Defining Drives

By defining a new WPS drive, you can also define a shortcut to have quicker access to the keys:

```
New-PSDrive -Name ITV -PSProvider Registry -Root
➥hklm:\software\www.it-visions.de
```

instead of

```
Get-Item hklm:\software\www.it-visions.de
```

You can then type the following:

```
Get-Item itv:
```

Two such shortcuts are already predefined (see Table 13.1).

Table 13.1 Defined Shortcuts for Registry Main Keys

HKLM	HKEY_LOCAL_MACHINE
HKCU	HKEY_CURRENT_USER

Reading Values

Entries and their values in a registry key are listed with the following:

```
Get-ItemProperty -Path "hklm:\software\www.it-visions.de"
```

You get the content of a single entry with

```
(Get-Item "hklm:\software\www.it-visions.de").
➥GetValue("owner")
```

or

```
(Get-ItemProperty  "hklm:/software/www.it-visions.de").owner
```

Creating and Deleting Values

You can create new entries (for example, a new string value) with the following:

```
New-Itemproperty -path "hklm:\software\www.it-visions.de"
➥-name "Owner" -value  "Dr. Holger Schwichtenberg"
➥-type string
```

A numeric value is created with this:

```
New-Itemproperty -path "hklm:\software\www.it-visions.de" -name
"Foundation" -value  1996 -type DWord
```

A multistring to a key is created with the following:

```
$Websites = "www.IT-Visions.de", "www.IT-Visionen.de",
➥"hs.IT-Visions.de"
new-itemproperty -path "www.IT-visions.de" -name
➥"Websites" -value $Websites -type multistring
```

A binary value to a key is created with this:

```
$Values = Get-Content H:\demo\PowerShell\Registry\
➥www.IT-Visions.de_Logo.jpg -encoding byte
new-itemproperty -path "www.IT-visions.de" -name
➥"Logo" -value $Values -type binary
```

Figure 13.1 shows the result of all the previous registry operations.

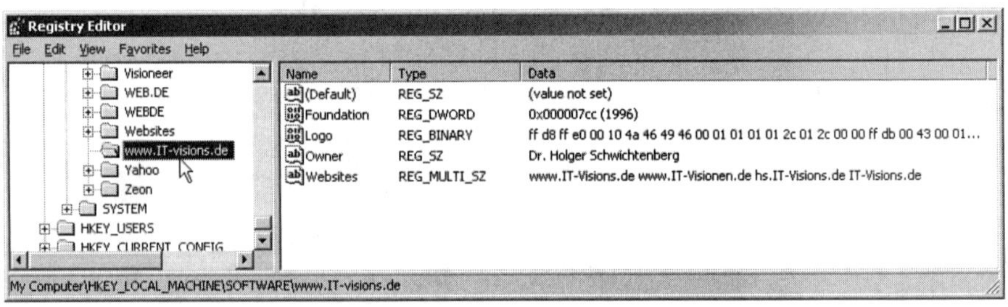

Figure 13.1 Result of registry operations

Table 13.2 shows all kinds of possible data types and their use in WPS.

Table 13.2 Data Types in the Registry

Registry Data Type	Meaning	Type Indicator	Processing in WPS
REG_BINARY	Array of byte	Binary	Byte[]
REG_DWORD	Number	DWord	Int
REG_EXPAND_SZ	String with placeholders	Multistring	String[]
REG_MULTI_SZ	Several strings	ExpandString	String
REG_SZ	Simple string	String	String

You can change an existing value with `Set-ItemProperty`:

```
# change value
$Websites = "www.IT-Visions.de", "www.IT-Visionen.de",
➥"hs.IT-Visions.de", "IT-Visions.de"
Set-Itemproperty -path "www.IT-visions.de" -name
➥"Websites" -value $Websites -type multistring
```

To delete a value of a registry key, use the commandlet `Remove-ItemProperty`:

```
Remove-ItemProperty -path "hklm:\software\www.it-visions.de"
➥-name "owner"
```

Example

Listing 13.1 stores data of multiple website configurations in the registry. The input data is shown in Figure 13.2, and the result in Figure 13.3.

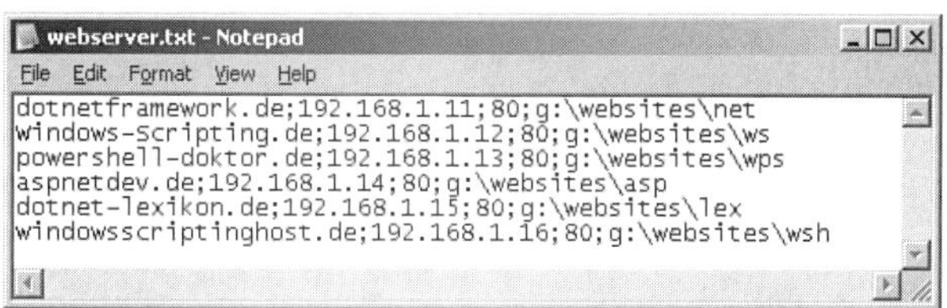

Figure 13.2 Parameters

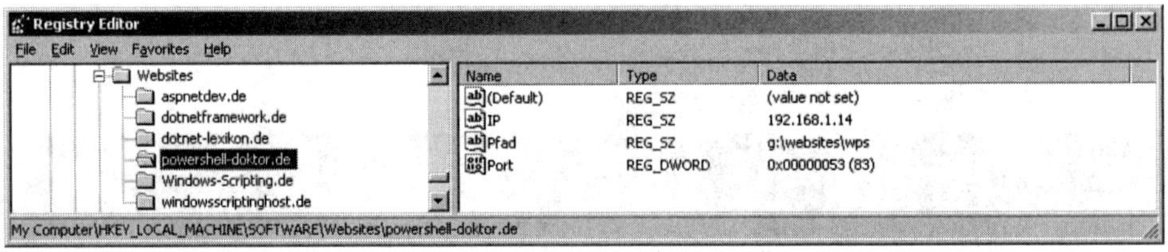

Figure 13.3 Result (created website keys in the Registry)

Listing 13.1 Storing Values from a CSV File in the Registry Software Installations

```
# Create a registry key from CSV-data

$Path = "hklm:/software/Websites"

if (Test-Path $Path) { del $Path -recurse -force }
if (!(Test-Path $Path )) { md $Path  }

$Websiteliste = Get-Content "j:\administration\webserver.txt"

foreach($Website in $WebsiteListe)
{
$WebsiteData = $Website.Split(";")
md ($Path + "\" + $WebsiteData[0])
New-Itemproperty -path ($Path + "\" + $WebsiteData[0])
➥-name "IP" -value $WebsiteData[1] -type String
New-Itemproperty -path ($Path + "\" + $WebsiteData[0])
➥-name "Port" -value $WebsiteData[2] -type dword
New-Itemproperty -path ($Path + "\" + $WebsiteData[0])
➥-name "Path" -value $WebsiteData[3] -type String
$WebsiteData[0] + " created!"
}
```

Software Administration

Software administration requires the following:

- Inventory of all installed applications
- Installation of new applications
- Uninstallation of installed applications

WPS does not offer special commandlets for software administration; therefore, you have to use WMI.

The WMI class `Win32_Product` contains information about the installed Windows Installer (alias Microsoft Installer; short, MSI) packages.

WARNING This WMI class is available only if the WMI Provider for Windows Installer has been installed. Under some versions of Windows, this provider is an installation option of Windows and not part of the standard installation.

Also, Win32_Product is valid only in applications that have been installed with Windows Installer. All applications you can see in system control can be accessed via the registry key *HKLM:\SOFTWARE\Microsoft\Windows\CurrentVersion\Uninstall.*

Software Inventory

The class `Win32_Product` delivers the installed MSI packages:

```
Get-Wmiobject Win32_Product
```

Of course, you can filter. The following command lists only those MSI packages whose names start with the letter *A*:

```
Get-Wmiobject Win32_Product | where-object { $_.name
➥-like "a*" }
```

The second filter extracts all MSI packages with Microsoft as producer:

```
Get-Wmiobject Win32_Product | where-object { $_.vendor
➥-like "microsoft*" }
```

You can also find out whether a certain application has been installed:

Listing 13.2 Checking Whether QuickTime Version 7.2.0.240 Is Installed on a Specific Computer

```
###########################################
# The PowerShell script checks if a certain software is installed
# (C) Dr. Holger Schwichtenberg
###########################################

function Get-IsInstall($Application, $Computer, $Version)
{
$a = (Get-WmiObject -Class Win32_Product -Filter
➥"Name='$Application' and Version='$Version'"
➥-computername $Computer)
return ($a -ne $null)
}

$e = Get-IsInstall "QuickTime" "E01" "7.2.0.240"

if ($e) { "Software is installed!" }
else { "Software is not installed!" }
```

In a pipeline command, you can also write a complete inventory resolution, which consecutively, according to a list in a text file, calls several computers and then exports the found applications to a CSV file:

```
get-content "computername.txt" |
foreach { get-wmiobject win32_product -computername $_ } |
where { $_.vendor -like "*Microsoft*" } |
export-csv "Softwareinventory.csv" -notypeinformation
```

You can even refine the inventory resolution by checking, before accessing the computer, with a ping whether it is even accessible to prevent the long timeout of WMI.

Because a pipelining command is not sufficient for this task and you need a script, you can instead parameterize the solution directly (see Listing 13.3).

Listing 13.3 Software Inventory via WPS Script

```
########################################
# The PowerShell script inventories the installed software
# of a producer on n computer systems
# (C) Dr. Holger Schwichtenberg
########################################

$Producer = "*Microsoft*"
$Entryfilename = "computernames.txt"
$Outputfilename = "Softwareinventory.csv"

# Import of computer names
$Computernames = Get-Content "computernames.txt"
$Computernames | foreach {

if (Ping($_))
{
Write-Host "Inventorize software for computer $_ ..."
# Fetching of installed MSI packages on all computers
$Software = foreach { get-wmiobject win32_product
➥-computername $_ } | where { $_.vendor -like $Producer }

# Export in CSV
$Software | export-csv "Softwareinventar.csv" -notypeinformation
}
else
{
Write-Error "Computer not accessible!"
}
}

# Execute Ping
function Ping
{
$status = Get-WmiObject Win32_PingStatus -filter
➥"Address='$args[0]'" | select StatusCode
return $status.Statuscode -eq 0
}
```

Additional Information about Software

You get a list of all installed software updates (patches, hotfixes) with the following:

```
Get-Wmiobject Win32_Quickfixengineering
```

You can view the installed audio-/video codecs with this:

```
Get-Wmiobject Win32_CodecFile | select group,name
```

Non-MSI Applications

`Win32_Product` is valid only for applications that have been installed with Windows Installer. All applications that you can see in the system control can be displayed only via the registry key *HKLM:\SOFTWARE\Microsoft\Windows\CurrentVersion\Uninstall:*

```
Get-ChildItem HKLM:\SOFTWARE\Microsoft\Windows\CurrentVersion\
➥Uninstall
```

The access can be simplified by defining a new WPS drive:

```
New-PSDrive -Name Software -PSProvider RegistrierungsDatabank
➥-Root HKLM:\SOFTWARE\Microsoft\Windows\
➥CurrentVersion\Uninstall
```

Thereafter, you only have to write the following:

```
Get-ChildItem Software:
```

When filtering, you have to keep in mind that the properties (for example, `DisplayName`, `Comments`, and `UninstallString`) are not properties of the object of the type `Microsoft.Win32.RegistryKey`, but subelements of this object (see Figure 13.4). Thus, `GetValue()` has to be used for the access to this data:

```
Get-ChildItem Software: | Where-Object -FilterScript
➥{ $_.GetValue("DisplayName") -like "a*"} |
➥ForEach-Object -Process {$_.GetValue("DisplayName") ,
➥$_.GetValue("Comments"), $_.GetValue("UninstallString") }
```

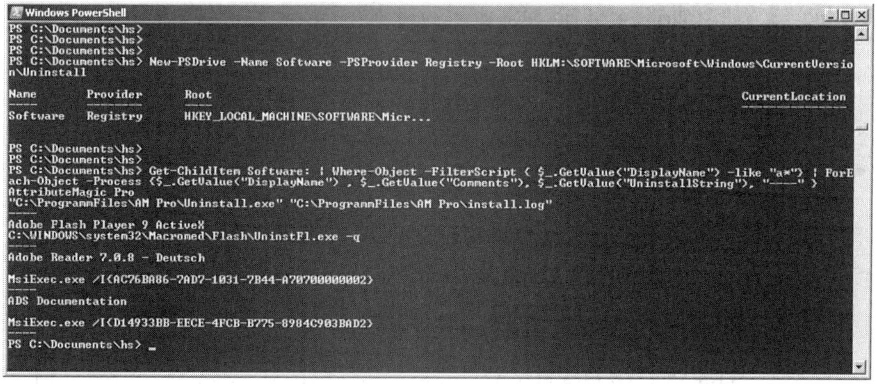

Figure 13.4 Listing of installed software starting with the letter *A*

Autostart Applications

Programs that start automatically when the operating system is started can be found in the instances of the WMI class `Win32_StartupCommand`:

```
Get-Wmiobject Win32_StartupCommand
```

Installing Software

A script-based installation is possible for many applications; the processing, however, depends on the installation technology used. Microsoft in WMI supplies installation support for installation packages based on MSI.

WMI permits the call of Microsoft Installer to install any MSI package (see Listing 13.4). The class `Win32_Product` offers the method `Install()` for this purpose. The method expects three parameters:

- The path to the MSI package
- Command-line parameters that are to be transferred to the package
- Whether an application will be installed for all users (`True`) or for the logged-in user only (`False`)

Keep in mind, however, that the `Install()` method is a static method of the WMI class `Win32_Product`. A remote installation is possible.

13. Registry and Software

Listing 13.4 Installation of an MSI package

```
$Application = "H:\demo\PS\Setup_for_HelloWorld_VBNET.msi"
"Install application..." + $Application
(Get-WmiObject -ComputerName E01 -List | Where-Object -FilterScript
➥{$_.Name -eq "Win32_Product"}).Install($Application)
"Finished!"
```

Uninstalling Software

The WMI class `Win32_Product` also offers an `Uninstall()` method for uninstalling MSI packages.

Note that to identify the application to be uninstalled, you don't have to write the name of the installation package, just the application name (`Name` or `Caption`) or the GUID (`IdentifyingNumber`). In the case of `Setup_for_HelloWorld_VBNET.msi`, the name is Hello World VB.NET (see Listing 13.5).

Listing 13.5 Uninstallation of an MSI Package

```
$Name = "Hello World VB.NET"
"Start Uninstallation..."
$Result = (Get-WmiObject -Class Win32_Product -Filter
➥"Name='$Name'" -ComputerName E01).Uninstall().Returnvalue
if ($Result -ne 0) { Write-Error "Uninstallation Error: $Result";
➥Exit }
"Uninstallation finished!"
```

For each application, a so-called uninstall string is implemented in the registry. This uninstall string tells you what to execute to uninstall the application. This also works for non-MSI-based applications.

The following command lists the uninstall commands for all applications whose name starts with the letter *A*:

```
Get-ChildItem -Path HKLM:\SOFTWARE\Microsoft\Windows\
➥CurrentVersion\Uninstall
| Where-Object -FilterScript { $_.GetValue("DisplayName")
➥-like "a*"} | ForEach-Object -Process
{$_.GetValue("DisplayName"),
➥$_.GetValue("UninstallString") }
```

Testing Installations

For a test, Listing 13.6 installs an application and then immediately uninstalls it. At the beginning, after the installation, and at the end, there will be checks whether the application has been installed (see Figure 13.5).

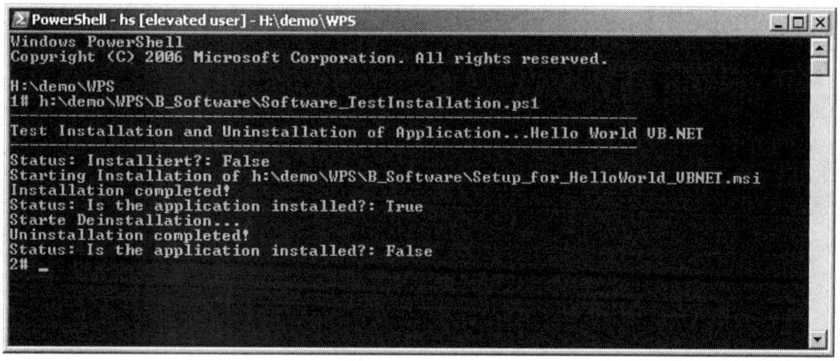

Figure13.5 Output of the scripts

Listing 13.6 Testing Software Install and Uninstall

```
function Get-IsInstall($Application, $Computer)
{
$a = (Get-WmiObject -Class Win32_Product -Filter
➥"Name='$Application'" -Computer $Computer)
return ($a -ne $null)
}

$Name = "Hello World VB.NET"
$Computer = "E01"
$Paket = "H:\demo\PowerShell\Software and
Processes\Setup_for_HelloWorld_VBNET.msi"

"-------------------------------------------------------------------"
"Testinstallation and uninstallation of the application..." + $Name
"-------------------------------------------------------------------"

"Initial condition: Installed?: " + (Get-IsInstall $Name $Computer)

"Start installation of the package " + $Package
```

(continues)

Listing 13.6 Testing Software Install and Uninstall *(continued)*

```
$Result = ([WMIClass] "Win32_Product").Install($Paket).Returnvalue
if ($Result -ne 0) { Write-Error "Installation error:
➥$Result"; Exit }
"Installation finished!"

"Intermediate result: Installed?: " + (Get-IsInstall $Name $Computer)

"Start uninstallation..."
$Result = (Get-WmiObject -Class Win32_Product -Filter
➥"Name='$Name'" -ComputerName E01).Uninstall().Returnvalue
if ($Result -ne 0) { Write-Error "Uninstallation error: $Result";
➥Exit }
"Uninstallation finished!"

"Final condition: Installed?: " + (Get-IsInstall $Name $Computer)
```

Summary

This chapter covered two topics: the registry and software.

The Windows registry is one of the data stores that are by default included in the navigation concept of WPS. In this chapter, you learned that you can access the registry like a file system, using well-known commands from the DOS age (for example, `cd`, `md`, and `rd`).

WPS provides commandlets for reading and writing keys and values: `Get-Item`, `Get-ItemProperty`, `Set-ItemProperty`, and `Remove-ItemProperty`.

In this chapter, you also learned that the administration of software installations in WPS is possible through the use of the WMI class `Win32_Product`. First, you have to make sure the class is available on your operating system because the WMI MSI Provider is not installed by default on all operating systems.

You saw how to create an inventory of the installed software on your local machine and on remote systems. In addition, you learned how to install and uninstall MSI packages.

Software that is not installed through MSI is listed in the registry and can be accessing using the command you learned in the first part of this chapter.

CHAPTER 14

PROCESSES AND SERVICES

In this chapter:

This chapter covers the management of process and covers the administration of Windows services (also known as Windows NT services). Examples in the chapter include the enumeration of process and services, starting and stopping process and services, installation of services, and changing service configuration.

Processes

The commandlet `Get-Process` (alias `ps` or `gps`) has already been used quite often in this book. This chapter discusses `Get-Process` in more depth and examines complementary commandlets.

Enumerating Processes

You get a list of all processes with the following:

```
Get-Process
```

`Get-Process` gets instances of the .NET classes `System.Diagnostics.Process`.

If the list is long, it is a good idea to group the output with the parameter `groupby` in the `Format-Table` commandlet:

```
gps | Format-Table -GroupBy Name
```

Figure 14.1 shows the results.

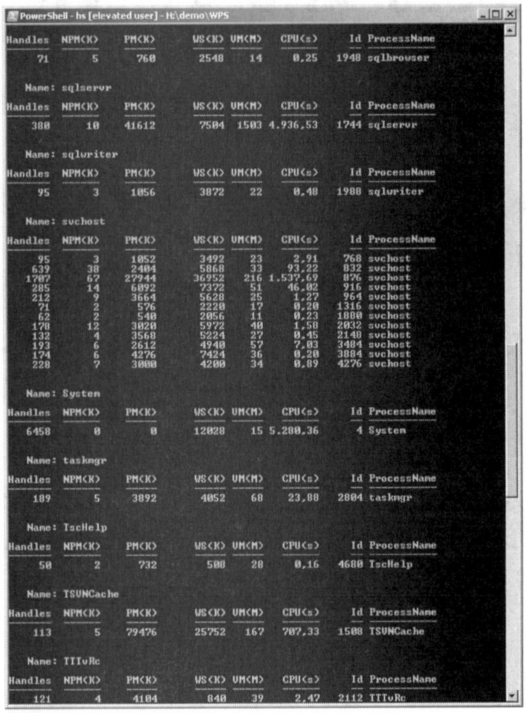

Figure 14.1 Grouped list of processes

Filtering

The following command delivers information all instances of a specific process:

```
Get-Process iexplore
```

You receive a list of all processes whose names start with the letter *I* as follows:

```
Get-Process i*
```

You can also address a process by its process ID:

```
Get-Process -id 7012
```

Starting Processes

When you call a commandlet or a command-line application in Windows PowerShell (WPS), it will start a process in WPS. When you call a Windows application (for example, `Notepad.exe`), it starts in its own process. In any case, the external process runs under the same user account as the called process.

With the commandlet `Start-Process` from PSCX, you have more control over the process behavior. You can, for instance, transfer an object of the type `PSCredential` with different login information via the parameter `-Credential`. You get an object of the type `PSCredential` via `Get-Credential`.

To start a second WPS window under another user account, you thus have to enter the following:

```
Start-Process powershell.exe -Credential (Get-Credential)
```

This is documented in Figures 14.2 and 14.3.

Figure 14.2 Call of `Start-Process` by a regular user

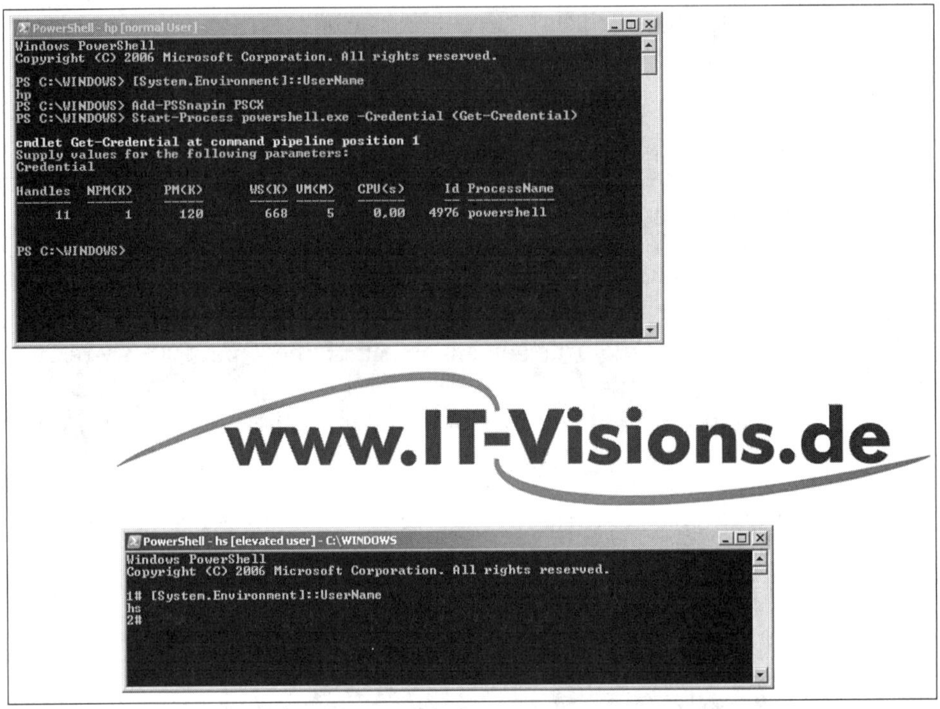

Figure 14.3 After typing the login information, you get a second WPS window for a user who belongs to the Administrators group

Further parameters of `Start-Process` include the following:

- `-WorkingDirectory` Setting of the working directory of the new process
- `-Priority` Setting of a priority class for the process

Ending Processes

To end a process, you have two options. You can call the `Kill()` of the `Process` class method:

```
Get-Process | Where-Object { $_.name -eq "iexplore" } |
➥Foreach-Object { $_.Kill() }
```

Or, even more concise, you can use the commandlet `Stop-Process`:

```
Stop-Process -name iexplore
```

`Stop-Process` usually expects the process number to be a parameter. If you want to indicate the process name, you have to use the parameter `-name`.

Other examples include the following:

- End all processes whose names start with the letter *P*

  ```
  Get-Process p* | Stop-Process
  ```

- End all processes that need more than 10MB of RAM

  ```
  Get-Process | where { $_.WS -gt 10MB } | stop-
  process
  ```

Waiting for Process Ending

The following commands make WPS wait for the closing of Microsoft Outlook.

Listing 14.1 Waiting for the End of a Process

```
$p = Get-Process outlook

if ($p)
{
$p.WaitForExit()
"Outlook has been ended!"
}
else
{
"Outlook has not been started!"
}
```

Windows Services

This section covers the administration of Windows System Services (also known as Windows NT services).

Enumerating Services

A list of system services in the form of instances of the .NET class `System.ServiceProcess.ServiceController` is displayed by the commandlet `Get-Service` (alias `gsv`).

You get a list of the running system services with the following:

```
Get-Service | Where-Object {$_.status -eq "running"}
```

Thus, a list of the ended services is delivered by the following:

```
Get-Service | Where-Object {$_.status -eq "stopped"}
```

If you want the output to be grouped by status (see Figure 14.4), you first have to sort by status:

```
Get-Service | sort Status | Format-Table -GroupBy Status
```

You can check in each script whether a service is installed (see Listing 14.2).

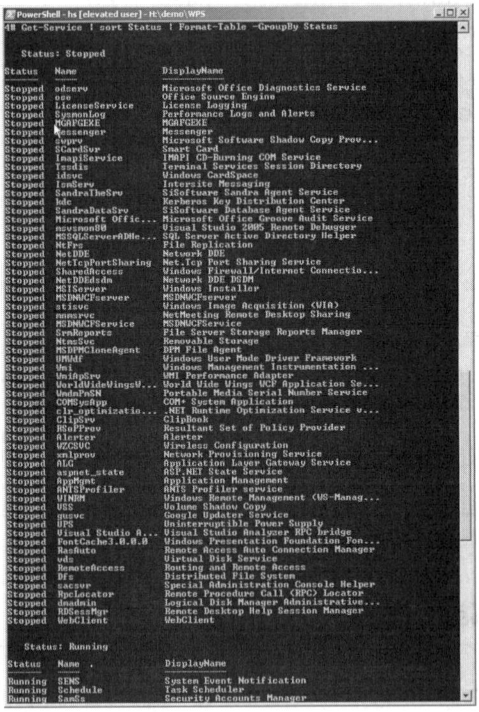

Figure 14.4 List of services grouped by status

Listing 14.2 Checking Whether IIS Is Installed

```
$service = Get-Service -name iisadmin
if ( ! $service ) { "IIS is not installed on this computer." }
else
{ "SQL Server is " + $service.Status }
```

Unfortunately, the remote query of another system with `Get-Service`, as well as with the other built-in commandlets of WPS, is not possible. This might be regarded as one of the greatest limitations of WPS 1.0. Only the detour via Windows Management Instrumentation (WMI) enables access to other systems. For this procedure, the commandlet `Get-WmiObject` is available. The following command fetches the running system services of the computer named ServerEssen04:

```
Get-WmiObject Win32_Service -computer ServerEssen04
➥-filter "State='running'"
```

Remember that the result of the operation now no longer contains instances of the .NET class `System.ServiceProcess.ServiceController`, but instead instances of the WMI class `root\cimv2\Win32_Service`, which have been packed into the .NET class `System.Management.ManagementObject`. The commandlet `Get-Member` shows this complex type as follows:

```
"System.Management.ManagementObject#root\cimv2\Win32_Service"
```

`Get-WmiObject` has another filter syntax (here, the equals sign [=] has to be used rather than `-eq`), and furthermore, the status of a service in the WMI class is indicated in the property `State` and not, as in the .NET class in status. Beginners easily get confused here.

Figures 14.5 and 14.6 show where in the MSDN documentation you can find information about these two classes.

Dependent Services

If you want to display the dependent services of a service, you have to access the attribute `DependentServices` of the .NET object `System.ServiceProcess.ServiceController`:

```
get-service iisadmin | % { $_.DependentServices }
```

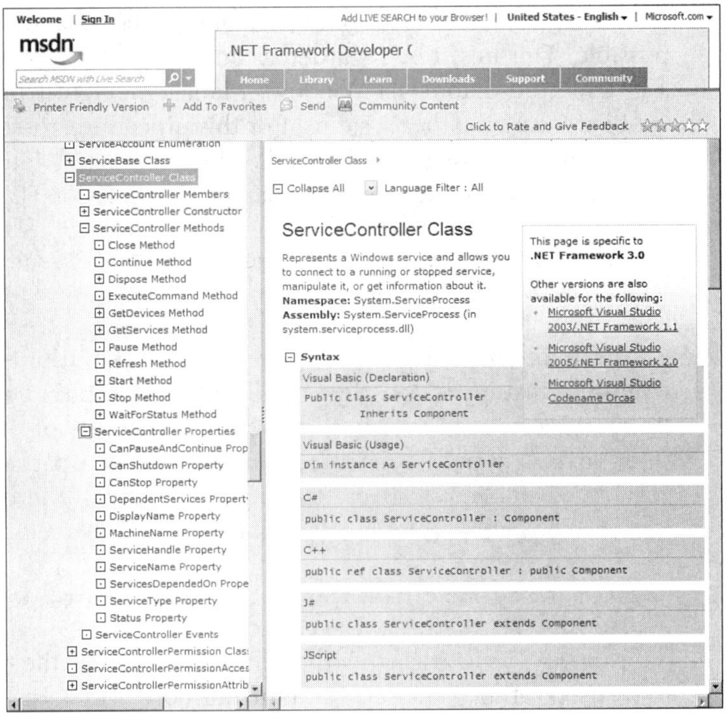

Figure 14.5 Documentation for the .NET class `System.ServiceProcess.ServiceController` in the .NET Framework class library documentation [MSDN01]

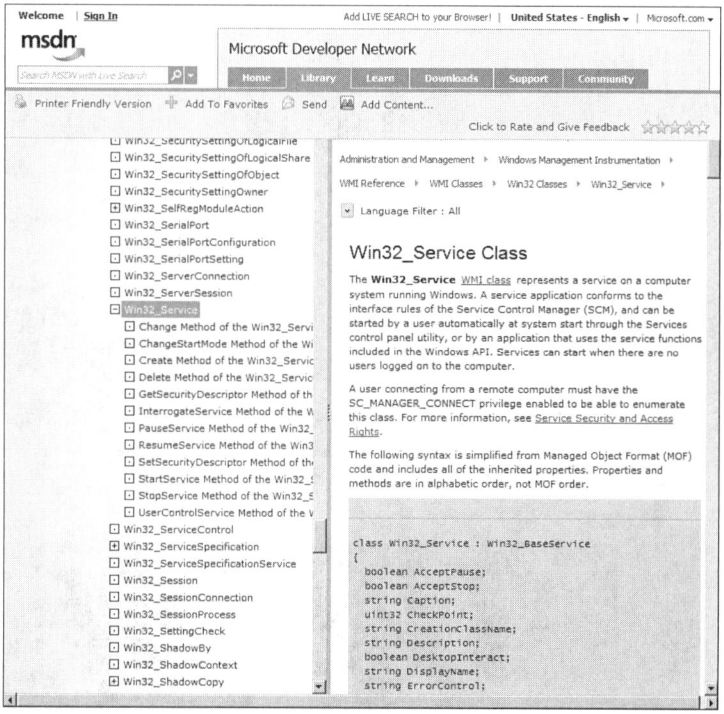

Figure 14.6 Documentation for the WMI class `Win32_Service` in the WMI schema class reference [MSDN05]

The result for Windows Server 2003 Release 2 is shown in Figure 14.7.

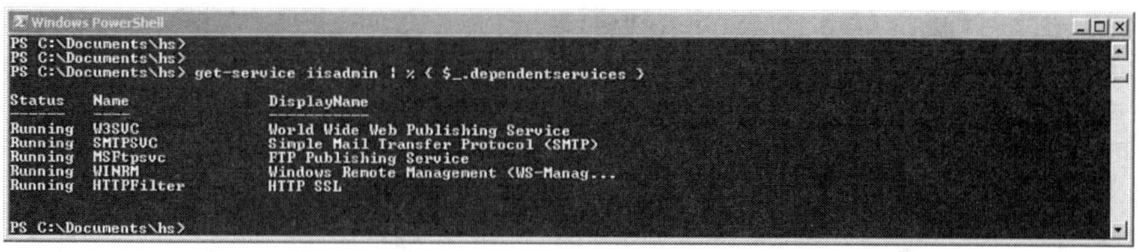

Figure 14.7 The dependent services of IISAdmin

The dependent services of a system service can alternatively be displayed in WMI, via the method `GetRelated()` in the class `ManagementObject` in the .NET class library. The following command displays the services that depend on the service `IISAdmin`:

```
(get-wmiObject win32_service -filter "Name =
➥'iisadmin'").PSBase.GetRelated("Win32_Service")
➥| select name
```

The same object volume can be displayed via a WQL query with relation to the fixed expression `AssocClass` (see Figure 14.8):

```
([wmiSearcher]"Associators of {Win32_Service.Name='iisadmin'}
➥Where AssocClass=Win32_DependentService
➥Role=Antecedent").get()
```

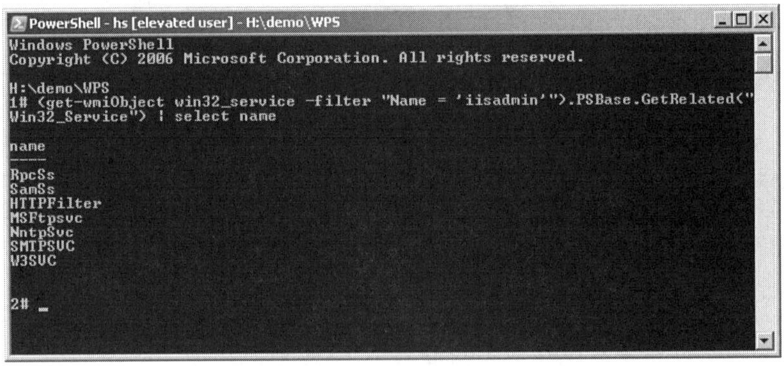

Figure 14.8 Displaying the dependent services

Starting and Stopping Services

If you want to change the service status, you can use the following commandlets:

```
Suspend-Service        Start-Service
Resume-Service         Restart-Service
Stop-Service
```

Here, the service names have to be indicated as parameters.

The following command also starts the service `IISAdmin`:

```
Start-Service IISADMIN
```

If you want to stop system services with dependent services, you have to add the parameter `-force` (see Figure 14.9):

```
Stop-Service IISADMIN -force
```

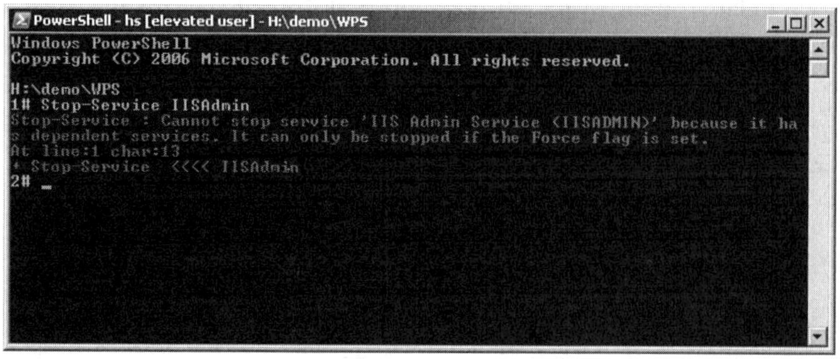

Figure 14.9 `Stop-Service` without `-force` will not work if the service has dependent services.

Because the commandlet `Start-Service` is valid only for the local computer, you have to get back to the WMI class `Win32_Service` to start a service on a remote system. The following command starts a system service on another computer:

```
Get-WmiObject -computer E02 Win32_Service -Filter
➥"Name='Alerter'" | Start-Service
```

TIP The commandlet `Restart-Service` executes the reboot of a service (end first, then start). If the service hasn't been started before, it will get started now.

Changing Service Attributes

You can influence the attributes of services, such as its booting, with `Set-Service`:

```
Set-Service IISADMIN -startuptype "manual"
```

Installation of New Windows Services

Executables that implement Windows services can be registered on your system by using the commandlet `New-Service`, as follows:

```
New-Service -Name "WWWAppServer"
-binaryPathName j:\software\wcf_server.exe
-Description "Application Server for World Wide
-DisplayName "World Wide Wings Application Server"
```

The execution of this command will create a new entry in the registry:

```
HKEY_LOCAL_MACHINE\SYSTEM\CurrentControlSet\Services
```

After that, the service will be visible in the Service Manager in the Control Panel. Then, you can start the service using `Start-Service`:

```
Start-Service WWWAppServer
```

Change Service Configuration

As with many other WMI classes, the properties of a `Win32_Service` objects are read-only. To change the configuration, you need to call the `Change()` method. Figure 14.10 shows the available parameters, and Figure 14.11 shows an example.

You don't need to pass values for all parameters; if you want a property to stay unchanged, just pass `$null` (see Listing 14.3).

Listing 14.3 Change Service Configuration

```
"Before:"
Get-WmiObject Win32_Service -filter "name='WWWAppServer'" |
➥select startname, startmode
```

```
$service = Get-WmiObject Win32_Service -filter "name='WWWAppServer'"
$service.change($null,$null,$null,$null,"Manual",$null,"itv\hs",
➥"secret+123")

"After:"
Get-WmiObject Win32_Service -filter "name='WWWAppServer'"
➥| select startname, startmode
```

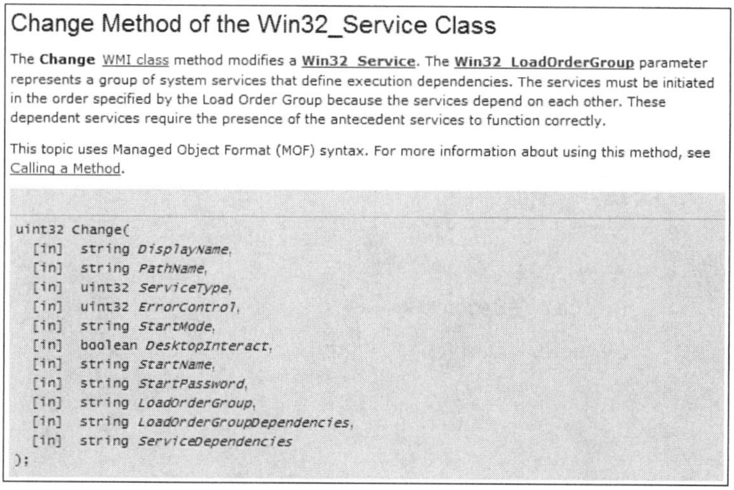

Change Method of the Win32_Service Class

The **Change** WMI class method modifies a **Win32_Service**. The **Win32_LoadOrderGroup** parameter represents a group of system services that define execution dependencies. The services must be initiated in the order specified by the Load Order Group because the services depend on each other. These dependent services require the presence of the antecedent services to function correctly.

This topic uses Managed Object Format (MOF) syntax. For more information about using this method, see Calling a Method.

```
uint32 Change(
  [in]  string DisplayName,
  [in]  string PathName,
  [in]  uint32 ServiceType,
  [in]  uint32 ErrorControl,
  [in]  string StartMode,
  [in]  boolean DesktopInteract,
  [in]  string StartName,
  [in]  string StartPassword,
  [in]  string LoadOrderGroup,
  [in]  string LoadOrderGroupDependencies,
  [in]  string ServiceDependencies
);
```

Figure 14.10 Description of the `Change()` method in the `Win32_Service` class

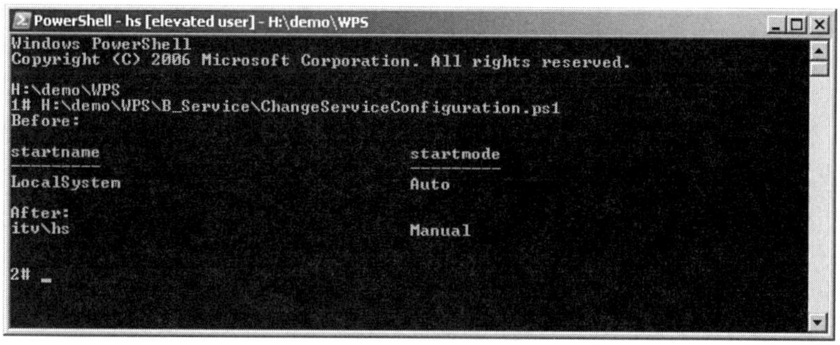

Figure 14.11 Changing a Windows service from Localsystem and Auto to a specific account and manual start

Summary

The administration of processes and services is one of the core tasks of Windows administration. WPS provides easy-to-use commandlets for both tasks, including the following:

`Get-Process`

`Stop-Process`

`Start-Process` (from PowerShell Community Extensions, PSCX)

`Set-Service`

`Suspend-Service`

`Resume-Service`

`Stop-Service`

`Start-Service`

`Restart-Service`

`Set-Service`

CHAPTER 15

COMPUTERS AND HARDWARE

In this chapter:

This chapter covers computer settings (for example, operating system versions, BIOS settings, boot configuration, environment variables), installed hardware, the management of print jobs, Windows event logs, and performance counters. Examples in the chapter include:

- Read computer settings
- Enumerate hardware devices and their properties
- Enumerate the available event logs
- Read event log entries
- Read data from performance counters
- Enumerate printers
- Administration of print jobs (pause, resume, cancel)

Computer Settings

There is no special commandlet for the displaying of information about the computer. You can get important information about the computer and the installed software with the WMI classes `Win32_Computersystem` and `Win32_OperatingSystem`:

```
Get-WmiObject Win32_Computersystem
Get-WmiObject Win32_OperatingSystem
```

The serial number of the computer is displayed with the following:

```
Get-WmiObject Win32_OperatingSystem | select serialnumber
```

You can get the version number of the software with the property `Version` in the WMI class `Win32_OperatingSystem` or with the .NET class `System.Environment`:

```
Get-WmiObject Win32_OperatingSystem | select Version
System.Environment]::OSVersion
```

The WMI class `Win32_Bios` delivers information about BIOS:

```
Get-WmiObject win32_Bios
```

The boot configuration can be found in the WMI class `Win32_BootConfiguration`:

```
Get-WmiObject Win32_BootConfiguration
```

The Windows system directory is again in the .NET class `System.Environment`:

```
"System Directory: "+ [System.Environment]::SystemDirectory
```

You will find the status of the Windows product activation in the following:

```
Get-WmiObject Win32_WindowsProductActivation
```

There is also data about the selected recovery options of the Windows software:

```
Get-WmiObject Win32_OSRecoveryConfiguration
```

You can display the environment variables via the Windows PowerShell (WPS) drive `env` (see Figure 15.1):

```
dir env:
```

Information about a single environment variable can be fetched by adding the name of the environment variable to the path, as follows:

```
dir env:/Path
```

If you want to know only the content of an environment variable, you can use `Get-Content`:

```
Get-Content env:/Path
```

The value fetched by `Get-Content` can be saved in a variable and then used by this; for example, for splitting a path string with the help of the `Split()` method from the .NET class `System.String`:

```
$Pathe = Get-Content env:/Path
$Pathe.Split(";")
```

If you want to find out how many files there are in the search paths of Windows, the following command is available:

```
(Get-Content env:/Path).Split(";")  | Get-ChildItem |
➥measure-object
```

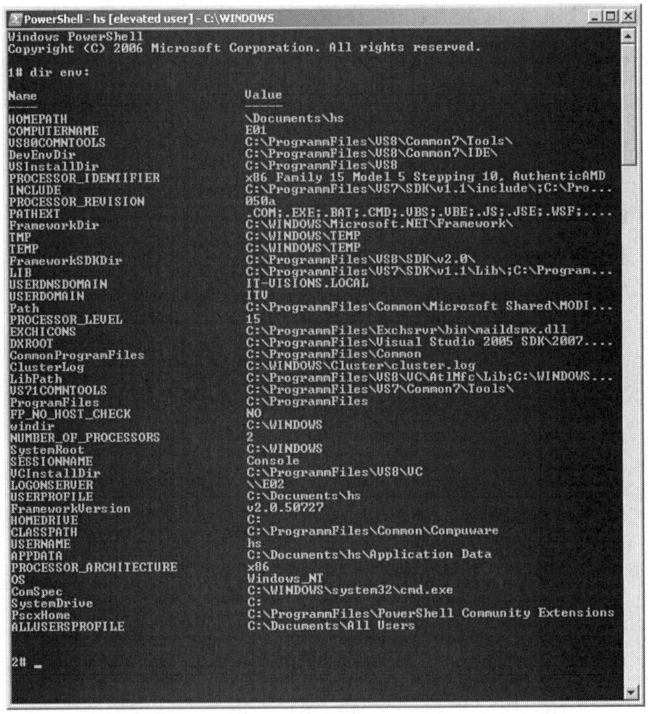

Figure 15.1 Listing of environment variables

Hardware

WPS 1.0 does not offer any commandlets for accessing hardware information. Nevertheless, you can still refer to WMI. Alternatively, you can access some functions via the www.IT-Visions.de PowerShell Extensions (These were introduced Chapter 10, "Tips, Tricks, and Troubleshooting.")

Within WPS, you can get information about installed hardware via WMI (that is, by using the commandlet `Get-WmiObject` together with the respective WMI class; see Table 15.1).

Table 15.1 Call of Hardware Information in WPS

Hardware Module	WPS Command (Standard)	www.IT-Visions.de PowerShell Extensions
Processors	`Get-WmiObject Win32_Processor`	`Get-Processor`
Main memory	`Get-WmiObject Win32_MemoryDevice`	`Get-MemoryDevice`
Video controller	`Get-WmiObject Win32_VideoController`	`Get-Videocontroller`
Sound device	`Get-WmiObject Win32_SoundDevice`	`Get-SoundDevice`
Disks	`Get-WmiObject Win32_Diskdrive`	`Get-Disk`
Tape drives	`Get-WmiObject Win32_Tapedrive`	`Get-Tapedrive`
CD/DVD drives	`Get-WmiObject Win32_CDRomdrive`	`Get-CDRomdrive`
Network adapters	`Get-WmiObject Win32_NetworkAdapter`	`Get-Networkadapter`
USB controller	`Get-WmiObject Win32_USBController`	`Get-USBController`
Keyboard	`Get-WmiObject Win32_Keyboard`	`Get-Keyboard`
Pointing device	`Get-WmiObject Win32_PointingDevice`	`Get-PointingDevice`

The number of processors on one system can also be obtained via the .NET class `System.Environment`:

```
"Number of processors: " +
➥ [System.Environment]::ProcessorCount
```

Printers and Print Jobs

The command

```
Get-WmiObject Win32_Printer
```

displays a list of all available printers on the local system. You can use the `-computername` parameter to access a remote computer (see Figure 15.2). Printers that are mapped through a terminal services session have the text "from... in session..." in their name.

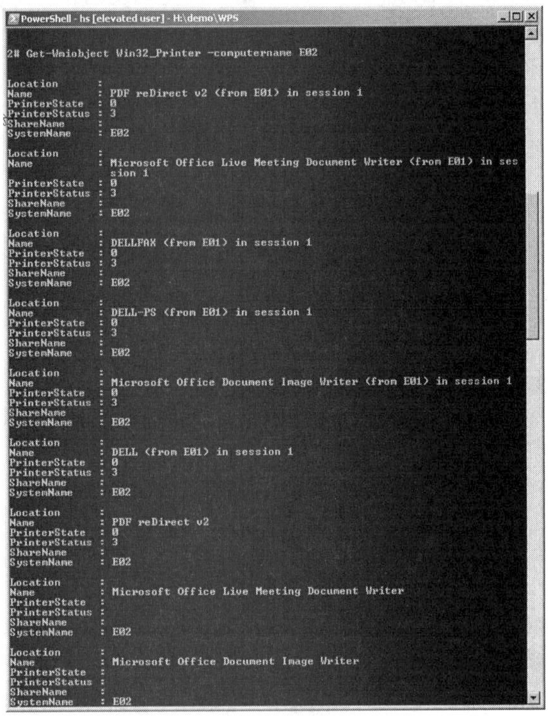

Figure 15.2 Listing of all installed printers from a remote computer

If you want to check the status of a printer, you should read `printer-status` and `detectederrorstate`:

```
Get-WmiObject win32_printer | select name,
➥printerstatus, detectederrorstate
```

In Figure 15.3, we have the following values: 3 = ready, 1 = other, 5 = low toner.

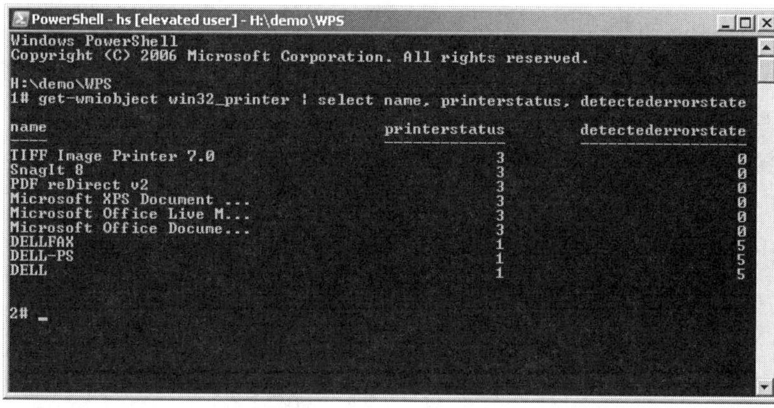

Figure 15.3 Checking the printer status

Printer Connections

If you want to install a network printer, you can use the static method `AddPrinterConnection()` in the `Win32_Printer` class:

```
$printer = [WMIClass]"\\.\root\cimv2:Win32_Printer"
$printer.AddPrinterConnection("\\E02\Dell")
```

The method will return the value of `0` if the installation is successful.

Print Jobs

To transfer information to the printer, you use the commandlet `Out-Printer` (alias `lp`) in WPS. This commandlet has already been discussed in this book (see Chapter 3, "Pipelining").

With

```
Get-WmiObject Win32_Printjob
```

you get all current print jobs on your local system (see Figure 15.4). Of course, you can use the `-computer` parameter to query a remote system.

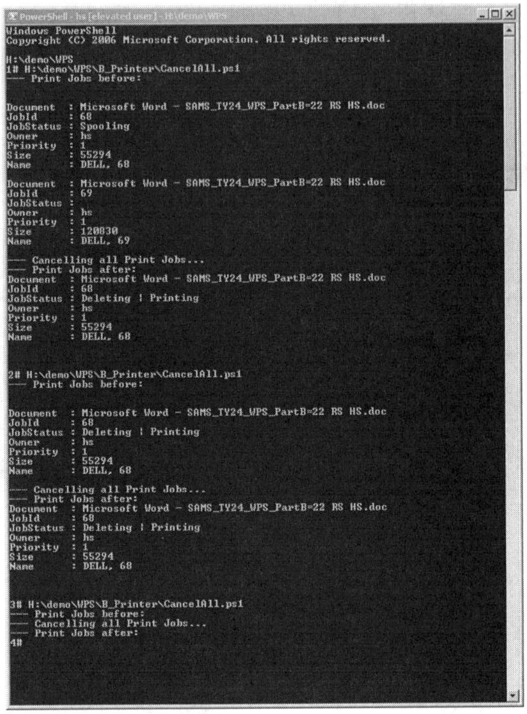

Figure 15.4 Using the print job script

You can pause all print jobs for a distinct printer with the following command:

```
Get-WmiObject Win32_Printjob -Filter
➥"Drivername='Dell 3115'" | Foreach-Object { $_.Pause() }
```

You can resume them later by calling the method `Resume()`.

To cancel all jobs, you have to call the `Delete()` method (see Listing 15.1).

Listing 15.1 Canceling All Print Jobs for a Certain Printer on a Specific Print Server

```
"--- Print Jobs before:"
Get-WmiObject Win32_Printjob -computer E01 -Filter
➥"Drivername='Dell MFP Laser 3115cn PCL6'"

"--- Canceling all Print Jobs..."
```

```
Get-WmiObject Win32_Printjob -computer E01 -Filter "Drivername='Dell
➥ MFP Laser 3115cn PCL6'" | Foreach-Object { $_.Delete() }

"--- Print Jobs after:"
Get-WmiObject Win32_Printjob -computer E01 -Filter
➥"Drivername='Dell MFP Laser 3115cn PCL6'"
```

TIP You could also call the `CancelAllJobs()` method of the `Win32_Printer` object.

MORE INFORMATION For additional information about printer administration, look at the WMI classes with the word *`Printer`* in their name (see Figure 15.5).

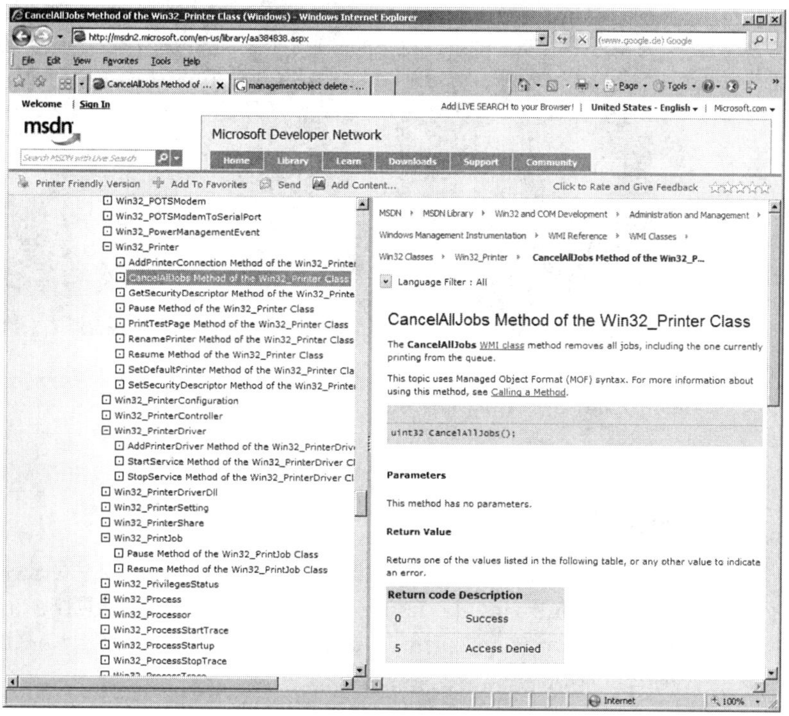

Figure 15.5 "Printer" classes in WMI documentation

Event Logs

Information about existing event logs and the entries in the event logs are provided by the commandlet `Get-EventLog`.

Event Log Names

A list of all event logs available on the local system is delivered via the following (see Figure 15.6):

```
Get-EventLog -list
```

The result contains instances of the class `System.Diagnostics.EventLog`.

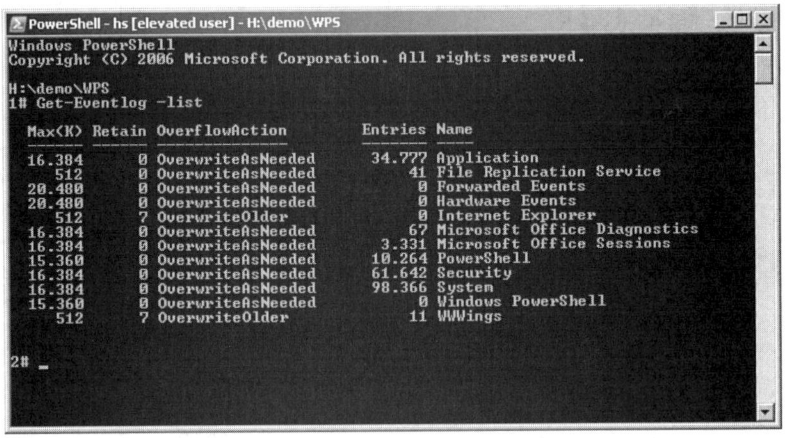

Figure 15.6 List of available event logs

Event Log Entries

However, if you call the commandlet `Get-EventLog` without the parameter `-list` but with the name of an event log instead, the commandlet displays all entries in form of objects of the type `System.Diagnostics.EventLogEntry`.

```
Get-EventLog Application
```

In this case, a limitation makes sense, because the operation would otherwise take too long. The commandlet `Get-EventLog` has a built-in filter function:

```
Get-EventLog Application -newest 30
```

With a little help routine, it's possible to limit the protocol entries to the entries of the present day:

Listing 15.2 Protocol Entries of Today

```
function isToday ([datetime]$date)
{[datetime]::Now.Date  -eq  $date.Date}

Get-EventLog Application -newest 2048 | where {isToday $_.TimeWritten}
```

Or you can fetch all entries of the past three days:

Listing 15.3 Protocol Entries of the Past Three Days

```
function isWithin([int]$days, [datetime]$Date)
{
    [DateTime]::Now.AddDays($days).Date -le $Date.Date
}

Get-EventLog Application | where {isWithin -3 $_.TimeWritten}
```

It might be of interest to group the entries according to the event identifier to identify recurring problems (see Figure 15.7):

```
Get-EventLog Application | Group-Object eventid |
➥Sort-Object Count
```

NOTE To access event logs on remote computer, you need to use the WMI class `Win32_NTLogEvent`. The following command enumerates all reboot events (event code 6009) from Server "E02":

```
Get-WmiObject -Query "select TimeWritten from
Win32_NTLogEvent where Logfile = 'System' and
SourceName = 'EventLog' and EventCode = '6009'" -computer E02
```

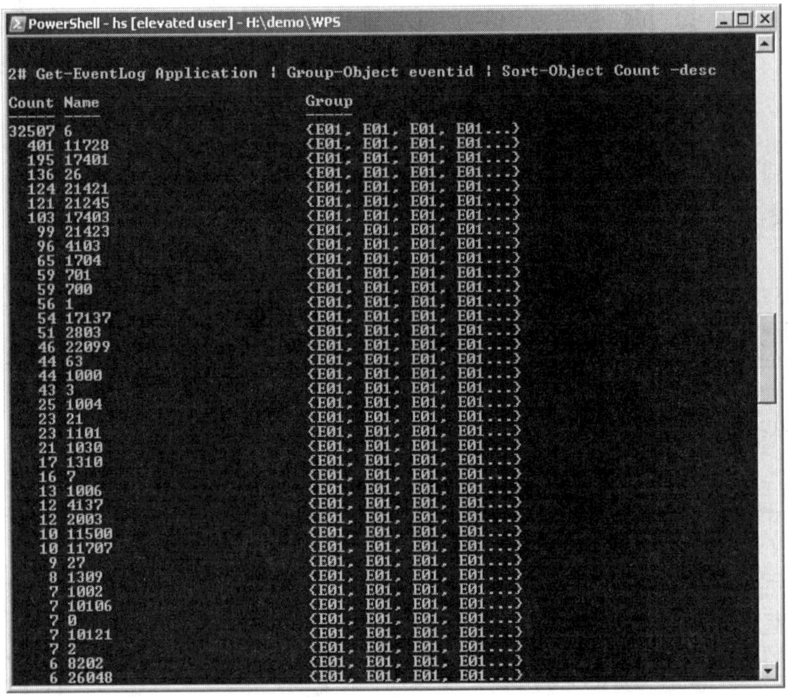

Figure 15.7 The vast majority of events in this log have the event ID 6 (which is a warning from the installed virus scanner).

Performance Counters

WMI enables access to performance data of the Windows system via the WMI Performance Counters Provider. The classes start with the string `Win32_PerfRawData`.

TIP If you don't find these classes, start the WMI service manually at the command line with `Winmgmt /resyncperf`.

Information about the used memory of running processes is displayed by the following:

```
Get-WmiObject Win32_PerfRawData_PerfProc_Process |
➥select Name,Workingset
```

Data about the available main memory is available here:

```
Get-WmiObject Win32_PerfRawData_PerfOS_Memory
```

The performance of a processor can be fetched with the following:

```
Get-WmiObject Win32_PerfRawData_PerfOS_Processor
```

WARNING `Win32_PerfRawData` is the abstract base class for all performance data classes. However, you want to refrain from the command

```
Get-WmiObject Win32_PerfRawData
```

because otherwise you just get a heap of objects.

Summary

In this chapter, you learned about a few interesting areas of administration. The available hardware can be queried thought WMI classes such as `Win32_Processor`, `Win32_DiskDrive` and `Win32_SoundDevice`. WMI also provides classes for managing printers (`Win32_Printer`) and print jobs (`Win32_Printjob`). The WPS commandlets `Get-EventLog` provides access through the local event log and WMI for remote event logs (`Win32_NTLogEvent`). WMI provides classes for performance counters.

CHAPTER 16

NETWORKING

In this chapter:

This chapter covers networking administrative tasks, including network configuration, name resolution, and the use of application-level networking protocols such as HTTP and SMTP.

This chapter also covers the administration of Exchange Server 2007 and Internet Information Server.

Pinging Computers

You can use the WMI class `Win32_PingStatus` to check the accessibility of a computer on your local network or the Internet:

```
Get-WmiObject Win32_PingStatus -filter "Address='www.Windows
➥Scripting.de'" | select protocoladdress, statuscode,
➥responsetime
```

PowerShell Community Extensions (PSCX) also offer a commandlet, `Ping-Host`, that displays a data structure of the type `Pscx.Commands.Net.PingHostStatistics` (see Figure 16.1):

```
Ping-Host 'www.Windows Scripting.de'
```

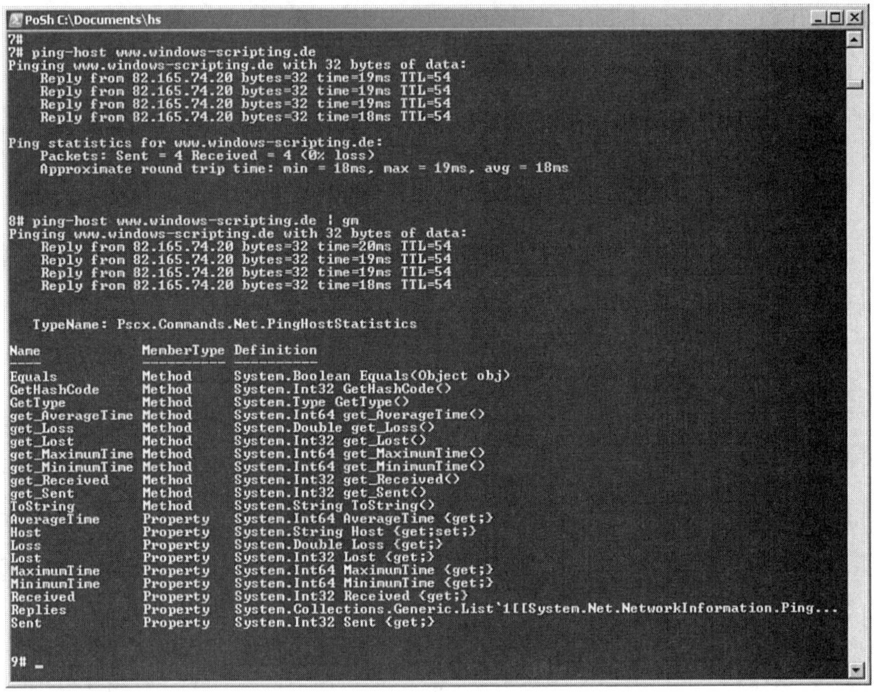

Figure 16.1 Use of `Ping-Host`

Network Configuration

WMI provides access to the network configuration through the class `Win32_NetworkAdapterConfiguration`. In `Win32_NetworkAdapterConfiguration`, the IP addresses are saved as arrays in `IPAddress`:

```
Get-WmiObject Win32_NetworkAdapterConfiguration -Filter
➥"IPEnabled=true" | select Description,IPAddress
```

The WMI class `Win32_NetworkAdapterConfiguration` enables numerous settings for network devices.

The Windows PowerShell (WPS) script in Listing 16.1 changes a network device from a static IP address to a dynamic one (DHCP). Figure 16.2 shows the output.

Listing 16.1 Change of Network Configuration

```
#######################################
# PowerShell Script
# Switch between static and dynamic IP
# (C) Dr. Holger Schwichtenberg
# http://www.windows-scripting.com
########################################

# -- Subroutines

function PrintStatus
{
$ada = Get-WmiObject Win32_Networkadapter | where
➥$_.DeviceID -eq $ADAPTERINDEX }
"Adapter: " + $ada.Caption
"Index: " + $ADAPTERINDEX
$config = Get-WmiObject Win32_Networkadapterconfiguration | where
➥{ $_.index -eq $ADAPTERINDEX }
"Description: " + $Config.Description
"IP active: " + $Config.ipenabled
"DHCP Status: " + $Config.dhcpenabled
"IP addresses: " + $Config.IPAddress
#Get-WmiObject Win32_Networkadapterconfiguration | where
➥{ $_.index -eq $ADAPTERINDEX } | select ip
}

# --- Parameters
$ADAPTERINDEX = 1
$COMPUTER = "."
```

(continues)

Listing 16.1 Change of Network Configuration *(continued)*

```
[array] $IP =    "192.168.1.15"
[array] $SUBNET = "255.255.255.0"
[array] $GATEWAYS = "192.168.1.16"
[array] $METRIC = 1

# --- Script
PrintStatus

$config = Get-WmiObject Win32_Networkadapterconfiguration
➥| where { $_.index -eq $ADAPTERINDEX }

if (!$Config.dhcpenabled)
{
  "--> Activate DHCP..."
  $Config.EnableDHCP() | Select-Object returnvalue | format-list
}
else
{
  "--> Activate Static IP Address..."
  $Config.EnableStatic($ip, $subnet) | Select-Object returnvalue
➥ | format-list
  $Config.SetGateways($Gateways, $Metric) | Select-Object
➥ returnvalue | format-list
}

PrintStatus
```

WARNING The WMI method `EnableStatic()` works only when the network device is activated.

You can display the current DHCP server with the commandlet `Get-DHCPServer` from PSCX.

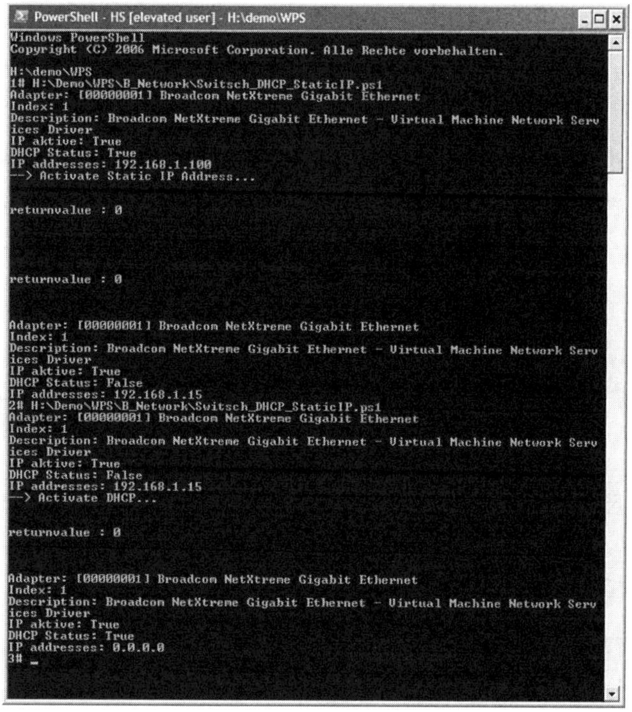

Figure 16.2 Output of the example when called twice

Name Resolution

In PSCX, the commandlet `Resolve-Host` supports name resolution. The result is an instance of the .NET class `System.Net.IPHostEntry`. You can see the result of the following three examples in Figure 16.3:

```
Resolve-Host E02
Resolve-Host E02 | fl
Resolve-Host www.IT-Visions.de
```

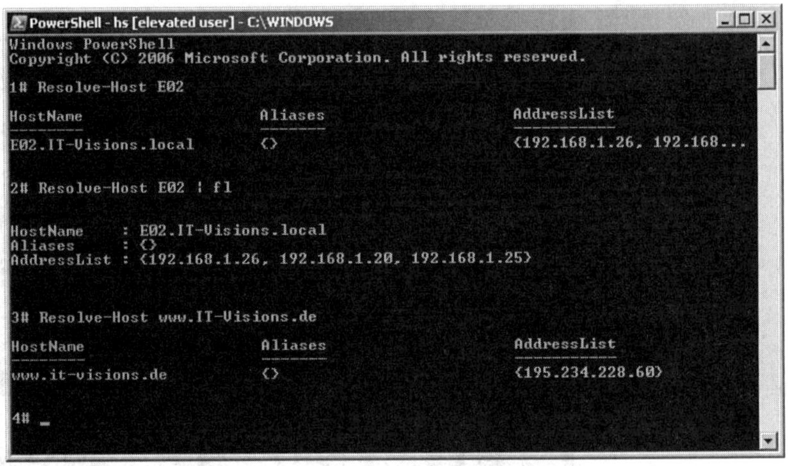

Figure 16.3 Use of `Resolve-Host`

Retrieving Files from an HTTP Server

Listing 16.2 shows how an HTML page can be retrieved from a web server. For this purpose, the class `System.Net.WebClient` from the .NET class library is used. This class offers a method that displays the content of the indicated URL in a string: `DownloadString()`. With the help of the commandlet `Set-Content`, the string is then stored in the local file system. The last four rows contain the error processing, which is responsible for issuing a report in the script whenever an error occurs.

Listing 16.2 Downloading of a File via HTTP

```
# --- Parameters
$url = "http://www.windows-scripting.com"
$target = "c:\temp\page.htm"

# --- Script
Write-Host "Downloading Webpage " $url "..."
$html = (new-object System.Net.WebClient).DownloadString($Url)
$html | Set-Content -Path $target
Write-host "Downloaded page stored under " $target
```

```
trap [System.Exception]
 {
    Write-host "Error downloading URL: `"$url`"" `n
    exit
 }
```

The next example demonstrates how you can retrieve the titles of the most recent eight news stories from an RSS feed (see Listing 16.3 and Figure 16.4). In this case, too, the script uses `DownloadString()` from the class `System.Net.WebClient`. Because the content is in XML form, you can use the WPS XML adapter to access the content (see Chapter 12, "Managing Documents").

```
  <?xml version="1.0" encoding="utf-8" ?>
- <rdf:RDF xmlns:rdf="http://www.w3.org/1999/02/22-rdf-syntax-ns#"
    xmlns="http://my.netscape.com/rdf/simple/0.9/">
  - <channel>
      <title>iX Blog - Der Dotnet-Doktor</title>
      <link>http://www.heise.de/ix/blog/1/</link>
      <description>Aktuelle Artikel im iX-Blog</description>
    </channel>
  - <item>
      <title>Fachbücher zu ASP.NET 2.0 erschienen</title>
      <link>http://www.heise.de/ix/blog/artikel/77803/from/rss09</link>
      <description>Mein Buch zu ASP.NET 2.0 gibt es jetzt sowohl in einer Variante
        mit Visual Basic 2005 als auch C# 2005.</description>
    </item>
  - <item>
      <title>Release Candidate 1 für Windows Vista und das .NET Framework
        3.0</title>
      <link>http://www.heise.de/ix/blog/artikel/77660/from/rss09</link>
      <description>Microsoft hat einen "Release Candidate" für das neue
        Betriebssystem Vista und für das Microsoft .NET Framework 3.0
        veröffentlicht.</description>
    </item>
  - <item>
      <title>Visual Studio 2005 für .NET 1.1 nutzen mit MSBee</title>
      <link>http://www.heise.de/ix/blog/artikel/77534/from/rss09</link>
      <description>Mit dem kostenlosen Add-On MSBuild Extras – Toolkit for .NET
        1.1 (MSBee) kann man mit Visual Studio 2005 Projekte auch in .NET-1.1-
        Code übersetzen lassen.</description>
    </item>
```

Figure 16.4 Example of an RSS document

Listing 16.3 Downloading and Filtering of RSS Feeds

```
Write-Host "Weblog of Dr. Holger Schwichtenberg:"
$Url = "http://www.heise.de/ix/blog/1/blog.rdf"
$blog = [xml](new-object System.Net.WebClient).DownloadString($Url)
$blog.RDF.item | select title -first 8
```

E-Mail

To send an e-mail via Simple Mail Transfer Protocol (SMTP), you can use the .NET classes `System.Net.Mail.MailMessage` and `System.Net.Mail.SmtpClient` or, even simpler, the commandlet `Send-SmtpMail` from PSCX:

Listing 16.4 Using the Commandlet `Send-SmtpMail`

```
# --- Parameters
$Subject = "PowerShell Script"
$Body = "Your daily script executed successfully!"
$From = "script@E01.Fbi.net"
$To = "hs@E01.Fbi.net"
$MailHost = "E01.Fbi.net"

# ---  Send Mail
Send-SmtpMail -SmtpHost $MailHost -To $To -From $from
➥-Subject $subject  -Body $body
```

TIP When an authentication at the SMTP server is necessary, you can retrieve this with the parameter `-Credential` and the commandlet `Get-Credential`. If you do this, however, Windows always asks for a user account via a login dialog box; an interactive execution is no longer possible.

Microsoft Exchange Server 2007

As mentioned in Chapter 10, "Tips, Tricks, and Troubleshooting," Microsoft Exchange Server 2007 has its own set of commandlets and a special version of the WPS shell called the *Exchange Management Shell.*

Basic Operations

After the start of the Exchange Management Shell, the command

```
Get-ExCommand
```

displays a list of Exchange Server–specific commandlets.

Reading Information

You get a list of all mailboxes with the following:

```
Get-Mailbox
```

The list of all databases is displayed as follows:

```
Get-Mailboxdatabase
```

And the storage groups are delivered with the following:

```
Get-Storagegroup
```

You can test the functionality of an Exchange Server with this:

```
Test-ServiceHealth
```

Managing Mailboxes

A storage group can be created with the following command. The command creates a new storage group named `"AuthorsStorageGroup"` on server `"E12"`:

```
New-Storagegroup "AuthorsStorageGroup" -server "E12"
```

You can create a database for mailboxes as follows. The commandlet `New-MailboxDatabase` needs the name for the database as well as the name of an existing storage group:

```
New-MailboxDatabase "AuthorsMailboxDatabase"
➥ -storagegroup "AuthorsStorageGroup"
```

To create a mailbox, you can use the following command:

```
New-Mailbox -alias "HSchwichtenberg" -name
HolgerSchwichtenberg -userprincipalname HS@IT-Visions.de
-database "E12\AuthorsStorageGroup\
AuthorsMailboxDatabase" -org users
```

Should the user already exist in the Active Directory, the command is shorter:

```
Enable-Mailbox hs@IT-Visions.de -database
➥ "E12\AuthorsStorageGroup \AuthorsMailboxDatabase"
```

After creating the mailbox, you can access its attributes with `Get-Mailbox` or `Set-Mailbox`. If you later add a new e-mail address, the new setting works with the attribute `EMailAddresses` with regard to the former addresses:

```
Set-Mailbox HS@IT-Visions.de -EmailAddresses
➥ ((get-Mailbox hs@IT-Visions.de).EmailAddresses
➥ + "HSchwichtenberg@IT-Visions.de ")
```

You can add the mailbox to a distribution list by mentioning the name of a list and an email address:

```
Add-DistributionGroupMember "Authors" -Member
➥ "hs@IT-Visions.de"
```

You can move the mailbox to another database:

```
Move-Mailbox hs@IT-Visions.de -targetdatabase
➥ "authorsmailboxdatabase"
```

Or you can limit the disk space consumption:

```
Get-Mailbox hs@IT-Visions.de | Set-Mailbox
➥ -UseDatabaseQuotaDefaults:$false
➥ -ProhibitSendReceiveQuota 100MB
➥ -ProhibitSendQuota 90MB -IssueWarningQuota 80MB
```

You can also limit the size of incoming e-mails for a distribution list:

```
Set-DistributionGroup "Authors" -MaxReceiveSize 5000KB
```

There is also a commandlet for deactivating a mailbox:

```
Disable-Mailbox "hs@IT-Visions.de"
```

Managing Public Folders

A database for public folders is created with the following:

```
New-PublicFolderDatabase "authorsfolderdatabase"
➥-storagegroup "authorsstoragegroup "
```

A public folder is created with this:

```
New-PublicFolder "\books" -Path \pubfolders -Server "E12"
```

Access rights to a folder are granted as follows:

```
Add-PublicFolderPermission "\books" -User hs
➥ -AccessRights "CreateItems"
```

You can set storage limitations for a public folder as follows:

```
Set-PublicFolder "\books" -PostStorageQuota 20MB
➥ -MaxItemSize 2MB
```

MORE INFORMATION You can find more WPS scripts for Exchange administration on the website [TNET02].

Internet Information Services

Internet Information Services (IIS) can be accessed through the WMI classes in the WMI namespace `root\MicrosoftIISv2` (see Figure 16.5).

The most important classes in this namespace are as follows:

- `IIsComputer` The root of the object hierarchy
- `IIsWebService` The HTTP service of the IIS
- `IIsWebServer` A virtual web server within the `IIsWebService`
- `IIsWebVirtualDir` A virtual directory within an `IIsWebServer`
- `IIsApplicationPool` An application pool in IIS (6.0 and later)

NOTE Each of these classes is read-only. However, each has a corresponding configuration class that enables you to change settings (see Figure 16.6).

```
IIsComputer > IIsComputerSetting
IIsWebService > IIsWebServiceSetting
IIsWebVirtualDir > IIsWebVirtualDirSetting
```

And so on.

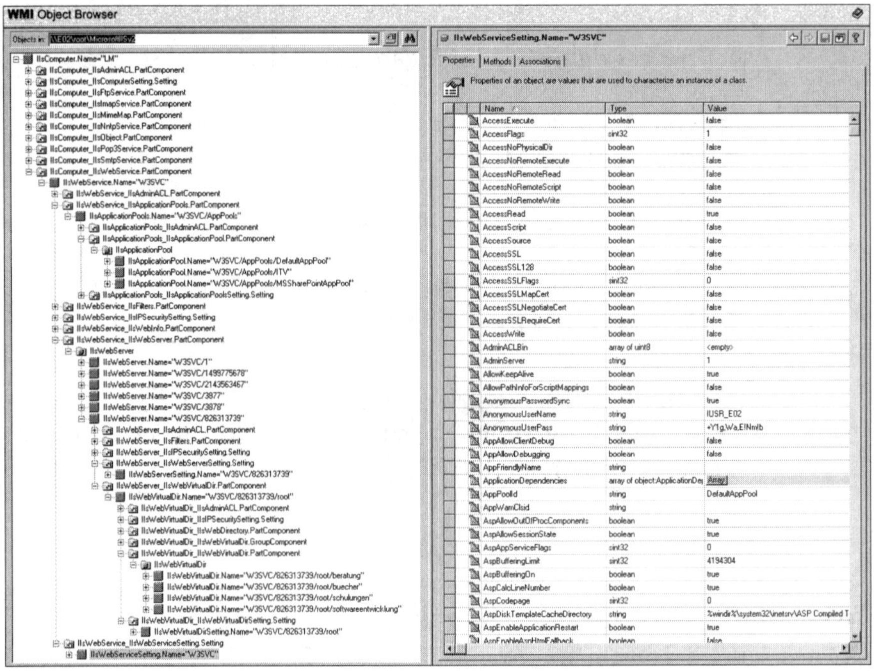

Figure 16.5 The object hierarchy of IIS seen from the WMI object browser

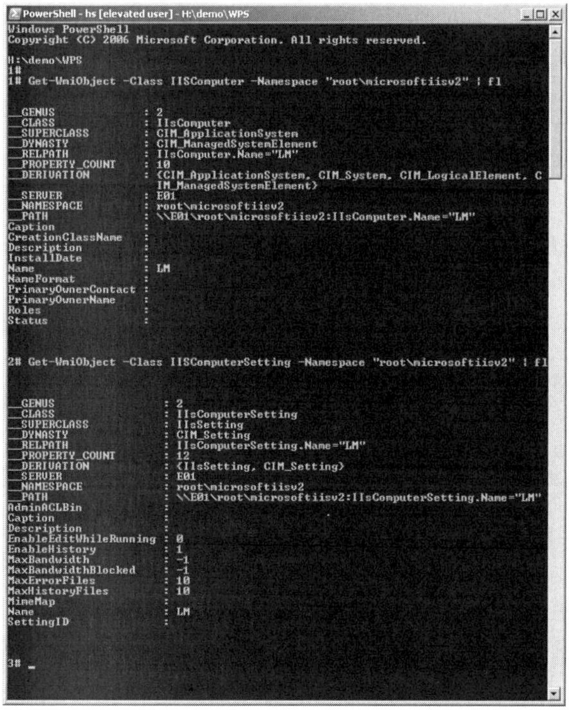

Figure 16.6 Displaying the attributes of the classes `IISComputer` and `IIsComputerSetting`

List of All Virtual Web Servers

The separation between the classes `IISWebserver` and `IIsWebServer Settings` can get a bit annoying; for example, if you want to perform an easy task such as enumerating all web servers with their internal name and state and the display name (attribute `Servercomment`). The internal name and the state are stored in instances of `IIsWebserver`, whereas the display name is stored in `IIsWebserverSetting` because it can be changed.

Therefore, executing the command

```
Get-WmiObject -Class IISWebserver -Namespace
➥"root\microsoftiisv2" | ft name, serverstate, servercomment
```

is not the right solution because `Servercomment` would be empty in all cases.

The solution is to execute a query for the associated settings object for each instance of IIsWebserver:

Listing 16.5 Get the Internal Name, the Display Name, and the Status of Each Virtual Web Server

```
# Get the internal name, the display name and the status
➥ of each virtual webserver

$Webservers = Get-WmiObject -Class IISWebserver
➥-Namespace "root\microsoftiisv2"

foreach ($Webserver in $Webservers)
{
# Get all associated Settings
$name = $WebServer.Name
$query = "ASSOCIATORS OF {IIsWebServer.Name='$name'} WHERE
➥ResultClass=IIsWebServerSetting"
$Settings = Get-WmiObject -Query $query -Namespace
➥"root\microsoftiisv2"
# However, we know for sure that there is only one object in the list!
$Setting = @($Settings)[0]
$WebServer.Name + ";" + $Setting.Servercomment+ ";" +
➥$Webserver.ServerState
}
```

Add New Virtual Web Servers

Listing 16.6 enables you to create a bunch of new websites according to the content of a CSV file (see Figure 16.7).

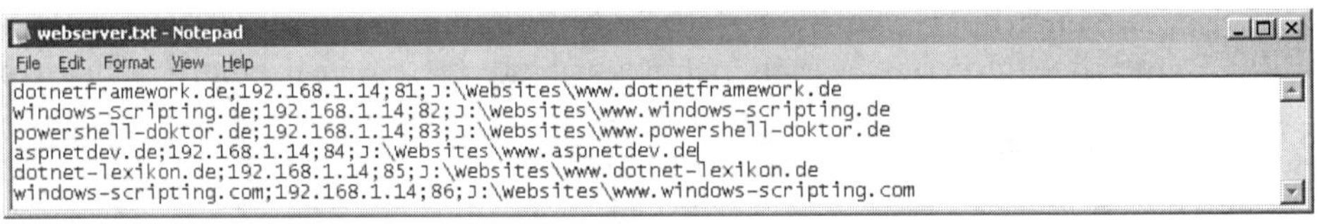

```
dotnetframework.de;192.168.1.14;81;J:\Websites\www.dotnetframework.de
windows-Scripting.de;192.168.1.14;82;J:\Websites\www.windows-scripting.de
powershell-doktor.de;192.168.1.14;83;J:\Websites\www.powershell-doktor.de
aspnetdev.de;192.168.1.14;84;J:\Websites\www.aspnetdev.de
dotnet-lexikon.de;192.168.1.14;85;J:\Websites\www.dotnet-lexikon.de
windows-scripting.com;192.168.1.14;86;J:\Websites\www.windows-scripting.com
```

Figure 16.7 A CSV text file describes the websites to be created.

To create a new virtual web server, you must follow these steps (see Listing 16.6 and Figure 16.8):

1. Create a new instance of the WMI class `ServerBinding`.
2. Fill the instance with the IP address and the port number.
3. Create a new instance of the WMI class `IIsWebService` with a reference to the binding.

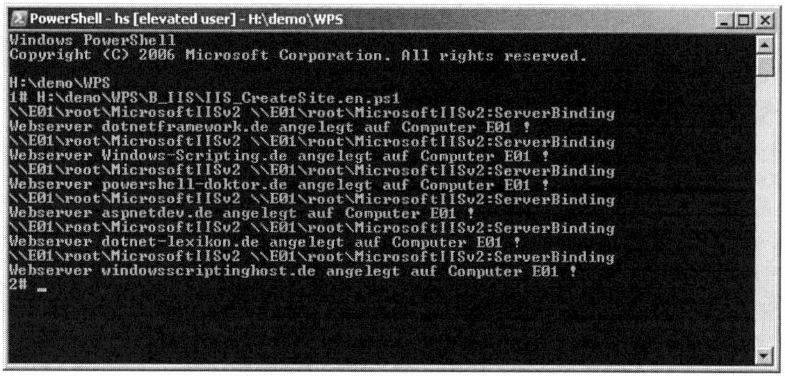

Figure 16.8 Successful creation of six websites

However, the following listing is much longer than expected. The reason is the encryption of the WMI communication that is required for access to the IIS configuration store since Windows Server 2003 Service Pack 1. Because the commandlet `Get-WmiObject` does not support the activation of the DCOM encryption, this has to be implemented with explicit use of .NET classes from the namespaces `System.Management`.

Listing 16.6 Create IIS Websites from a CSV File

```
# === Get WMI Object with DCOM encryption
Function Get-WMIObjectEx($Namespace, $Path)
{
#Write-Host $Namespace $Path
$connection = New-Object System.Management.ConnectionOptions
$connection.Authentication =
[System.Management.AuthenticationLevel]::PacketPrivacy
```

(continues)

Listing 16.6 Create IIS Websites from a CSV File *(continued)*

```
$scope = New-Object System.Management.ManagementScope($Namespace,
➥$connection)
$path = New-Object System.Management.ManagementPath($Path)
$GetOptions = New-Object System.Management.ObjectGetOptions
$WMI = New-Object
System.Management.ManagementObject($scope,$path,$GetOptions)
return $WMI
}

# === Get WMI class with DCOM encryption
Function Get-WMIClassEx($Namespace, $Path)
{
Write-Host $Namespace $Path
$connection = New-Object System.Management.ConnectionOptions
$connection.Authentication =
➥[System.Management.AuthenticationLevel]::PacketPrivacy
$scope = New-Object System.Management.ManagementScope($Namespace,
➥$connection)
$path = New-Object System.Management.ManagementPath($Path)
$GetOptions = New-Object System.Management.ObjectGetOptions
return New-Object
➥System.Management.ManagementClass($scope,$path,$GetOptions)
}

# === Create Site
function New-IISVirtWeb ([string]$Computer, [string]$Name,
➥[string]$IP, [string]$Port, [string]$Hostname, [string]$RootDir)
{
$Namespace = "\\" + $Computer + "\root\MicrosoftIISv2"
$Path1 = $Namespace + ":IIsWebService='W3SVC'"
$Path2 = $Namespace + ":ServerBinding"

# Create Binding
$class = Get-WMIClassEx $Namespace ($Namespace + ":ServerBinding")
$binding = $class.CreateInstance()
$binding.IP = $IP
$binding.Port = $Port
$binding.Hostname = $Hostname
[array] $bindings = $binding
```

```
# Create Site
$Webservice = Get-WMIObjectEx $Namespace  $Path1
$Website = $Webservice.CreateNewSite($Name, $bindings, $RootDir)

Write-Host "Webserver" $Name "created on Computer" $Computer "!"
}


# --- Parameters
$InputFile = "H:\demo\WPS\B_IIS\webserver.txt"
$Computer = "E01"

# Read textfile and create a new webserver for each line
Get-Content $InputFile | Foreach-Object {
$a = $_.Split(";")
New-IISVirtWeb $Computer  $a[0]  $a[1] $a[2] "" $a[3]
}
```


Delete Virtual Web Servers

You can delete a web server through the method `Delete()` in the WMI class `IIsWebserver`. The following command deletes all virtual web servers that are currently stopped:

```
Get-WmiObject -Class IISWebserver -Namespace
➥"root\microsoftiisv2" | where { $_.serverstate -eq 4 }
➥| foreach-object { $_.Delete() }
```

Microsoft has announced that in WPS 2.0 it will support WMI authentication in the commandlet `Get-WmiObject`. However, at the time of this writing, WPS 2.0 is still a very early pre-release version without a confirmed release date.

Summary

The WPS core system does not contain any commandlets for network protocols. However, you learned in this chapter that you can use the PSCX or a few classes (WMI and .NET) for such.

Pinging is available through the commandlet `Ping-Host` or the WMI class `Win32_PingStatus`. Network configuration is possible by using `Win32_NetworkAdapterConfiguration`. For name resolution, the easiest way is the commandlet `Resolve-Host`. HTTP downloads can be performed through the .NET class `System.Net.WebClient`. To send an e-mail, use `Send-SmtpMail`.

The beginning of this chapter discussed the administration of Exchange Server and Internet Information Services. Exchange Server has its own complete set of commandlets, whereas IIS can be accessed through WMI.

TIP Additional commandlets for a wide variety of protocols (including SNMP, SSH, POP, IMAP, TFTP, RCP, SOAP, REST, RSS, DNS) can be bought from a company called /n software, as part of its product NetCmdlets [NSOFT].

CHAPTER 17

DIRECTORY SERVICES

In this chapter:

Access to the local user database and Active Directory is one of the most common tasks for administrators in medium and large companies. This chapter and the following three chapters cover this important topic. First, in this chapter, you learn the basic concepts of Directory Services programming within Windows PowerShell (WPS). Chapter 18, "User and Group Management in the Active Directory," covers user and group management in the Active Directory. Chapter 19, "Searching in the Active Directory," covers searching. And Chapter 20, "Additional Libraries for Active Directory Administration" covers advanced features such as group policy management.

Overview of Directory Services Access

WPS 1.0 does not provide any commandlets to access the Windows user database (SAM) or the Active Directory or any other directory services. During the beta phase of WPS, there was an Active Directory navigation provider, but that had been removed before WPS 1.0 was finished. Such a provider for navigation through the Active Directory is currently available within the PowerShell Community Extensions (PSCX) [CODEPLEX01].

There also exists the commandlet `Get-ADObject` for searching in the Active Directory.

With WPS 1.0 (without PSCX) access to directory services is possible only with the classic programming techniques. Here you should use the .NET classes from the namespace `System.Directoryservices` of the .NET class library, and also the COM component Active Directory Service Interfaces (ADSI). Some functions are also available with WMI.

NOTE This chapter uses the domain FBI.net as an example. This example deals with an Active Directory for the TV series *The X Files*. The domain is called FBI.net, with the NETBIOS name FBI. The domain controllers are named XFilesServer1 and XFilesServer2. The PCs are named AgentPC01 to AgentPC99. The following organization units and users exist or will be created in this and the following chapter:

- Organizational unit "Agents" with users Fox Mulder, Dana Scully, John Doggett, and Monica Reyes
- Organizational unit "Directors" with users Walter Skinner and Alvin Kersh
- Organizational unit "Conspirators" with users Smoking Man and Deep Throat
- Organizational unit "Aliens" with numerous aliens

Managing Users and Groups Using WMI

The options for user administration with WMI are unfortunately rather limited. ADSI or `System.Directoryservices` offer a lot more, as you will see in the following chapters. However, for the sake of completeness, this chapter discusses the options you have within WMI.

The following command displays an object list of the local users and groups:

```
Get-WmiObject Win32_Account
```

Only user accounts are displayed with the following:

```
Get-WmiObject Win32_UserAccount
```

Only groups are displayed with this:

```
Get-WmiObject Win32_Group
```

Of course, you can also filter objects distinctly:

```
# Name and domain of those user accounts whose password never
➥expires
Get-WmiObject Win32_useraccount | Where-Object
{$_.Passwordexpires -eq 0 } | Select-Object Name,Domain
```

Alternatively, you can use this form:

```
Get-WmiObject Win32_Useraccount -filter
➥"Passwordexpires='false'" | Select-Object Name,Domain
```

The WMI class `Win32_Desktop` contains settings by the users. With the following command, you will get to know whether user FBI\FoxMulder has activated a screensaver on computer AgentPC04:

```
Get-WmiObject Win32_Desktop -computer AgentPC04 |
➥where { $_.Name -eq "DBI\FoxMulder" } |
➥select screensaveractive
```

You can access Active Directory entries using the WMI classes in the WMI namespace *root\directory\ldap*. For example, the following command lists all groups whose name starts with the letter *M:*

```
Get-WmiObject -Class ds_group
➥-Namespace root\directory\ldap  -Filter
➥"DS_name like 'm%'"
```

`System.DirectoryServices` and the ADSI Adapter

The classes of the .NET namespace `System.Directoryservices` are an encapsulation of ADSI. ADSI is a Component Object Model (COM) component introduced in the era of Windows 2000. Unfortunately, not all functions in the .NET library are encapsulated, and therefore ADSI still plays a role in WPS.

NOTE The classes in the namespace `System.DirectoryServices` work only when the ADSI COM component has been installed, too.

In the following text, the ADSI COM component is referred to as *classic ADSI.*

The classes in the .NET namespace `System.Directoryservices` offer only very general mechanisms for the access to directory services. There are no longer specific classes for single directory services as they exist in classic ADSI. Certain operations (for example, changing the password in a user object) therefore must be called directly or indirectly via classic ADSI.

Architecture

Figure 17.1 shows the architecture of ADSI under .NET. A .NET program (managed code) has three options to access a directory service:

- Use of objects in the namespace `System.Directoryservices` to execute directory service operations
- Use of objects in the namespace `System.Directoryservices` to call operations in classic ADSI
- Direct use of classic ADSI via COM interoperability

Integration with ADSI

That all calls in `System.Directoryservices` are executed in ADSI can be proved by error messages of the .NET class library. For example, the class `DirectoryEntry` delivers the following error message referring to the COM interface `Interop.IADS` when calling `CommitChanges()`, if the object to be created already exists:

```
System.Runtime.InteropServices.COMException (0x80071392):
The object already exists.
at System.Directoryservices.Interop.IAds.SetInfo()
at System.Directoryservices.DirectoryEntry.CommitChanges()
```

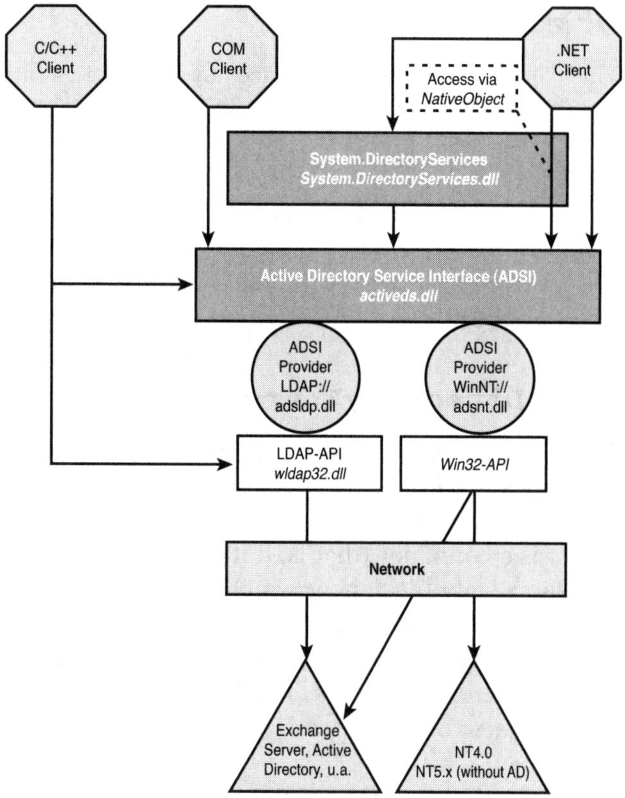

Figure 17.1 Programming interfaces for Active Directory

This does not mean anything other than that the calling of `CommitChanges()` in the class `DirectoryEntry` has internally been transferred to the method `SetInfo()` in the interface `System.Directoryservices.Interop.IADs`. `SetInfo()` is the well-known method from classic ADSI used to return the property cache to the directory service and thus to make all changes persistent.

WARNING The namespace `System.Directoryservices.Interop` is not documented and is displayed in the object browser of Visual Studio. In this namespace, the interfaces `IADs`, `IADsContainer`, and so on (well known from classic ADSI) are defined. Because an instancing of interfaces is no longer possible in .NET, the interfaces had to be combined with classes.

Object Model

The classes in the namespace `System.Directoryservices` can be divided into two groups:

- General classes for the access to leaves and containers
- Classes for the execution of LDAP search queries (see Chapter 19)

The two central classes in the namespace are `DirectoryEntry` and `DirectoryEntries`.

Class `DirectoryEntry`

The class `DirectoryEntry` represents any directory entry regardless of whether it is a leaf or a container. This class owns the property `Children` of the type `DirectoryEntries`. This object volume is filled only when the object is a container (that is, if it has subobjects). The object volume also exists in a leaf object; however, it is empty.

In the attribute `Property`, the `DirectoryEntry` class has an object volume of the type `PropertyCollection`, which represents the volume of the directory attributes. The `PropertyCollection` has three subordinated object volumes:

- `PropertyNames` points to a `KeysCollection` object that contains strings with the names of all directory attributes.
- `Values` points to `ValuesCollection`, which in turn contains single object volumes of the type `PropertyValueCollection`. This is necessary because each directory attribute can have several values. The `ValuesCollection` represents the volume of values of all directory attributes; `PropertyValueCollection`, on the other hand, stands for the single values of a directory attribute.
- The attribute `Item(ATTRIBUTNAME)` delivers the respective `PropertyValueCollection` for an attribute name that is to be transferred as parameter.

WARNING Access to the attribute `Values` generally is not executed because usually the values are needed without the attribute names. The common process is either the direct use of `Item()`, when the attribute name is known, or the iteration via `PropertyNames` and, subsequently, the use of `Item()`, if all attributes will be listed with their respective values.

Each DirectoryEntry object (see Figure 17.2) owns an attribute named NativeObject, which refers to the respective object. This enables a quick change to classic ADSI programming.

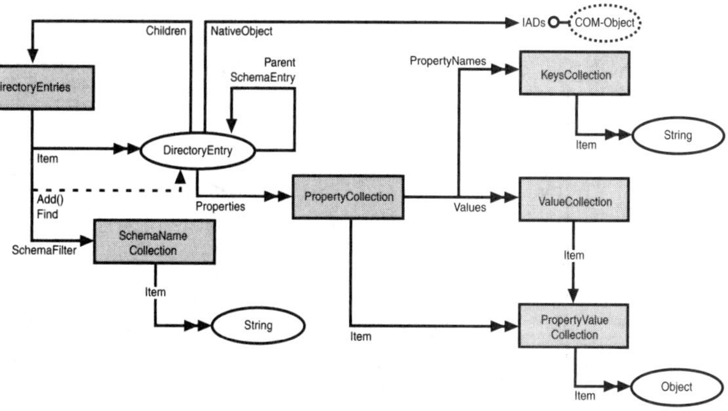

Figure 17.2 Object model of the classes in the namespace System.Directoryservices, Part 1

Class DirectoryEntries

The class DirectoryEntries supports the interface IEnumerable and thus enables the enumeration of its members via a foreach loop. The volume can be filtered by specifying a volume of directory service classes via SchemaNameCollection, which will be selected. The method Find() displays a DirectoryEntry object. If the object specified by name does not exist in this container, there is an InvalidOperationException.

The class DirectoryEntries cannot be instanced. You can retrieve a DirectoryEntries object only via the attribute Children of a DirectoryEntry object.

Class for the Execution of Search Queries

Search queries have been executed in ADSI via ActiveX Data Objects (ADO) (that is, an OLEDB provider). In .NET, there are now proper classes for the execution of LDAP search queries, which are independent of ADO.NET and can access the LDAP implementation of Windows directly.

Whereas the OLEDB provider supports LDAP query syntax and SQL commands for ADSI queries, classes built in to the .NET class library can process only LDAP query syntax.

With the OLEDB provider and with the .NET classes, only LDAP-capable directory services can be queried. The LDAP query syntax is a standard ([RFC1960] and [RFC2254]), and therefore nothing other than the COM implementation (see Figure 17.3).

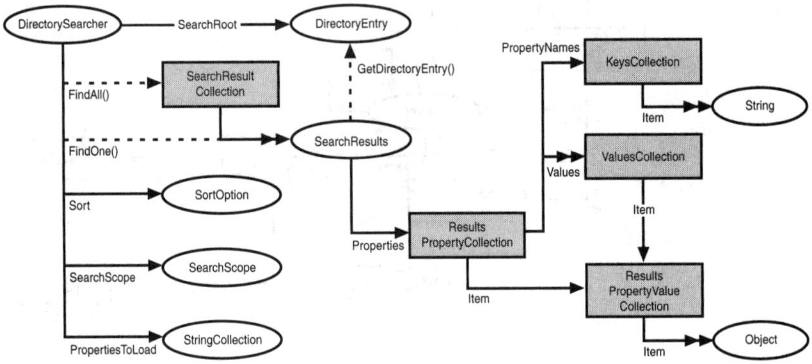

Figure 17.3 Object model of the class in the namespace `System.Directoryservices`, Part 2

Comparison of `System.Directoryservices` and ADSI

Table 17.1 shows that for many interfaces from classic ADSI there are no longer respective specific classes in `System.Directoryservices`.

Table 17.1 System.Directoryservices versus ADSI

Directory Object Class in Active Directory	ADSI in COM	ADSI in .NET (`System.Directoryservices`)
Leaf *classes*	Interface `IADs`	Class `DirectoryEntry`
Container *classes*	Interface `IADsContainer`	Class `DirectoryEntries`
Class `User`	Interface `IADsUser`	N/A (`DirectoryEntry`)
Class `Computer`	Interface `IADsComputer`	N/A (`DirectoryEntry`)
Class `Group`	Interface `IADsGroup`	N/A (`DirectoryEntry`)
N/A	Class `ADODB.Connection`	Class `DirectorySearcher`
Any classes	Class `ADODB.RecordSet`	Class `SearchResultCollection`

Deficiencies in the ADSI Adapter

Microsoft performed a fundamental shift in direction regarding directory services programming between Release Candidate 1 and Release Candidate 2 of WPS. This shift in direction was not only unexpected, it also led in the wrong direction; thus, this is the point where severe criticism toward Microsoft is appropriate.

Up to Release Candidate 1, you had to directly use a .NET class from the .NET namespace `System.Directoryservices` for these scripting jobs. As mentioned previously, these classes are internally based on COM interfaces of ADSI, and in some cases you had access to these interfaces underlying the scripting.

Starting with Release Candidate 2, Microsoft intended to introduce a simplification with the proper WPS type `[ADSI]`. The intention was good; the realization, however, was an absolute catastrophe.

There are six problems:

- The built-in WPS type `[ADSI]` instances the type `System.Directoryservices.DirectoryEntry`, but offers only attributes and no methods of this class. The methods are hidden by the WPS Adapter.
- The created WPS object offers the methods of the underlying classic ADSI interfaces instead.
- The important commandlet `Get-Member` shows neither one nor the other method.
- Also in direct instancing of `System.Directoryservices.DirectoryEntry`, the previously mentioned method chaos is effective.
- The methods of the class `System.Directoryservices.DirectoryEntry` are available only via the subobject `PSBase`.
- `DirectoryEntry` objects cannot be processed in the WPS pipeline with the common commandlets `Select-Object`, `Format-Table`, and so forth. Only the object-based style is possible.

This is a really illogical and distracting implementation. Already in the Windows Script Host (WSH), directory services scripting wasn't easy to learn; now it becomes even more difficult.

Figure 17.4 documents the chaos:

- An entry in a directory service possesses only attributes (that is, data) and no methods (that is, operations). These attributes are encapsulated in COM classes.
- Directory service operations are provided by the respective protocol (for example, LDAP). The classic ADSI encapsulates these operations in methods that are provided as part of the COM classes.

A .NET object of the type `DirectoryEntry` encapsulates the ADSI COM object, but also offers other methods at the same time (which internally rely on ADSI). The object `DirectoryEntry` offers direct access to the ADSI methods via the subobject `NativeObject`.

The WPS object, which in turn represents a capsule around the `DirectoryEntry` object, now does not use the methods of `DirectoryEntry`, but the methods of the inner ADSI objects instead.

The WPS object offers access to the methods of the `DirectoryEntry` object via the subobject `PSBase`.

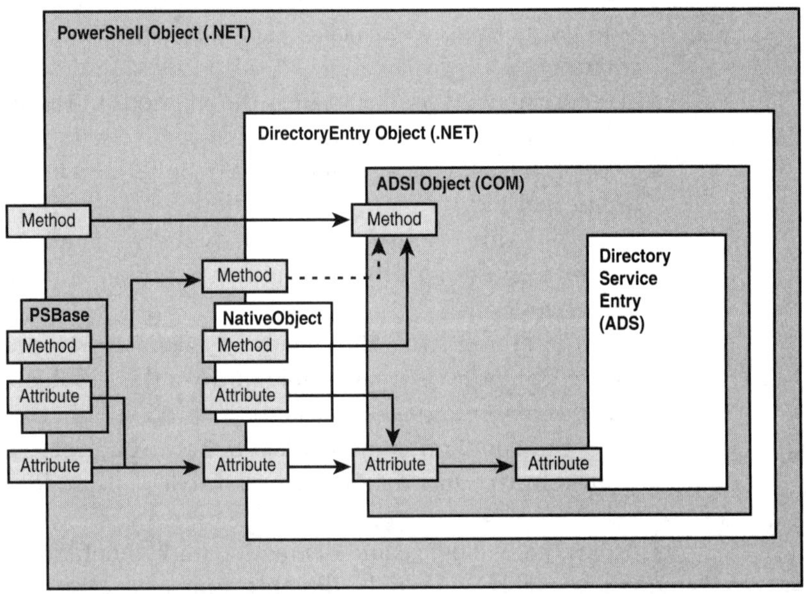

Figure 17.4 Chaos in the directory service operations

Aruk Kumaravel, Windows PowerShell Development Manager at Microsoft, admits in [Kumaravel01] that it had been unwise to hide methods: "In retrospect, maybe we should have exposed these."

Furthermore, a critical note has to be made that Microsoft implements such a fundamental change between a RC1 and a RC2. All WPS scripts written for the Active Directory until then had to go down the drain. Such a decision can be expected in the beta phase, but certainly not shortly before launching.

Microsoft has announced that in WPS 2.0 they will improve the ADSI object adapter by exposing all the members of `DirectoryEntry`, especially `Parent`, `Path`, `Children`, `SchemaClassName`, and `SchemaEntry`. However, at the time of this writing, WPS 2.0 is still an early prerelease version, and there is not yet a confirmed release date.

Object Identification in Directory Services (Directory Services Paths)

To program with directory services, you must be able to identify the entries in the directory service.

ADSI also uses the so-called COM monikers for path names under .NET to identity entries in different directory services and to get a pointer to the meta object. The moniker has the following form:

```
<Namespace ID>:<Provider-Specific Part>
```

And it is called the *directory path* (or *ADSI path*) in this context.

WARNING Be careful: The namespace IDs are case sensitive. However, the rest of the path is not case sensitive.

The provider-specific part of the directory service path contains the distinguished name (DN) of the directory object and a server name (see Table 17.2).

Table 17.2 Sample Paths in Different Directory Services

Namespace	Directory Path
Active Directory (via LDAP)	*LDAP://server/cn=Agents,dc=FBI,dc=NET* *LDAP://XFilesServer1.FBI.net/cn=Fox Mulder, OU=Agents,dc=FBI,dc=NET*
NT 4.0-domains and local Windows user databases ("SAM")	*WinNT://Domain/Computer/User* *WinNT://Computername/Groupname* *WinNT://Domain/User*
Novell 3.x	*NWCOMPAT://NWServer/printername*
Novell 4.x (NDS)	*NDS://Server/O=FBI/OU=Washington/cn=Agents*
IIS	*IIS://ComputerName/w3svc/1*

Object Identification in the Active Directory

For addressing the entries in an Active Directory, LDAP directory paths in the form *LDAP://server:port/DN* are used. In this path, all components are optional.

If there is no server name, the so-called *Locator Service* is used. Regarding serverless connections, the Active Directory locator service, with help from the Domain Name Service (DNS), looks for the best domain controller for the indicated directory entry. Domain controllers with a good connection are preferred.

Without a designated port, the standard LDAP port 389 is used.

Without a DN, the *default naming context* is called in the current domain.

TIP Regarding Active Directory, you should always use the name of the domain controller closest by as server name. You can retrieve the server name of the domain controller via the commandlet `Get-DomainController` (contained in PSCX). Connecting without indicating a server (serverless connection) is possible, but for performance reasons not recommendable.

When addressing a directory entry with such a path, there is the danger that directory objects have been renamed in the meantime. Some directory services thus enable connecting via a GUID, which remains unchangeable for a directory object:

```
LDAP://XFilesServer1/<GUID=228D9A87C30211CF9AA400AA004A5691>
```

For standard containers in an Active Directory, there is special support. For these so-called *well-known objects*, there is a predefined GUID (well-known GUID), which is the same in each Active Directory:

```
LDAP://<WKGUID=a9d1ca15768811d1aded00c04fd8d5cd,dc=fbi,dc=net>
```

Note that here `WKGUID=` is to be used, and that the GUID indicated thereafter is not the real GUID of the object. The standard containers get an individual GUID when Active Directory is installed; the WKGUID is a generally valid alias.

Table 17.3 List of Well-Known Objects

Well-Known Object	GUID
cn=Deleted Objects	18E2EA80684F11D2B9AA00C04F79F805
cn=Infrastructure	2FBAC1870ADE11D297C400C04FD8D5CD
cn=LostAndFound	AB8153B7768811D1ADED00C04FD8D5CD
cn=System	AB1D30F3768811D1ADED00C04FD8D5CD
ou=Domain Controllers	A361B2FFFFD211D1AA4B00C04FD7D83A
cn=Computers	AA312825768811D1ADED00C04FD8D5CD
cn=Users	A9D1CA15768811D1ADED00C04FD8D5CD

Overview of the Common Programming Tasks

This section documents the most important mechanisms of directory service programming with `System.DirectoryServices`.

Binding to Directory Entries

Precondition for access to entries in the directory service is the binding of a meta object to a directory entry (see Figure 17.5). Whereas under the classic ADSI the binding process was executed via the method `GetObject()`, in `System.DirectoryServices` this happens via a parameter during the instancing of the class `DirectoryEntry`.

For example

```
$o = new-object system.directoryservices.directoryEntry
➥("LDAP://XFilesServer1")
$u = new-object system.directoryservices.directoryEntry
➥("LDAP://XFilesServer1/CN=Fox Mulder,OU=Agents,DC=FBI,DC=net")
```

For this purpose, there also exists a shortcut via the built-in WPS data type `[ADSI]`, for example

```
$o = [ADSI] "LDAP://XFilesServer1"
$u = [ADSI] "LDAP://XFilesServer1/CN=Fox
➥Mulder,OU=Agents,DC=FBI,DC=net"
```

After this operation, the variable `$o` contains the instance of the class `DirectoryEntry`. When you access `$o`, the relative path appears on the console.

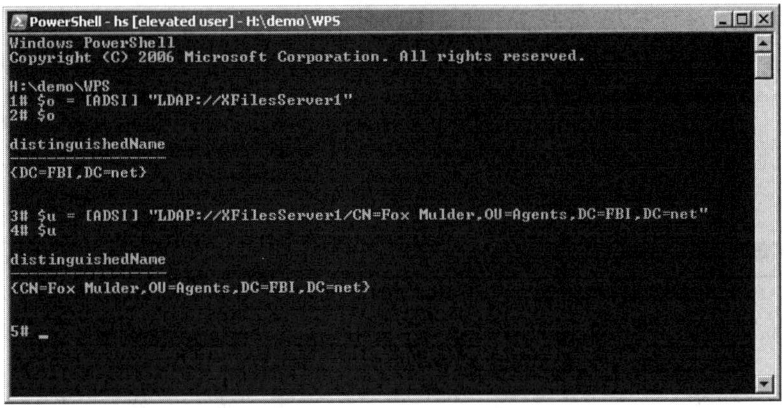

Figure 17.5 Access to an Active Directory entry

If there is no indication for an LDAP path, `DirectoryEntry` will set up a connection to the default naming context of the Active Directory to which the computer belongs when instanced:

```
New-Object System.DirectoryServices.DirectoryEntry
```

Impersonation

By default, the class `DirectoryEntry` logs in to the Active Directory under the user account that originally started the script. When you apply impersonation, however, it is possible to use another user for the communication with the Active Directory, if the starting user does not have sufficient privileges.

The class `DirectoryEntry` uses the ADSI impersonation mode by indicating a username and a password when instancing the class `DirectoryEntry` as second and third parameters (see Figure 17.6):

```
$o = new-object system.directoryservices.directoryEntry
➥("LDAP://XFilesServer1/CN=Fox
➥Mulder,OU=Agents,DC=FBI,DC=net", "FoxMulder",
➥"I+love+Scully")
```

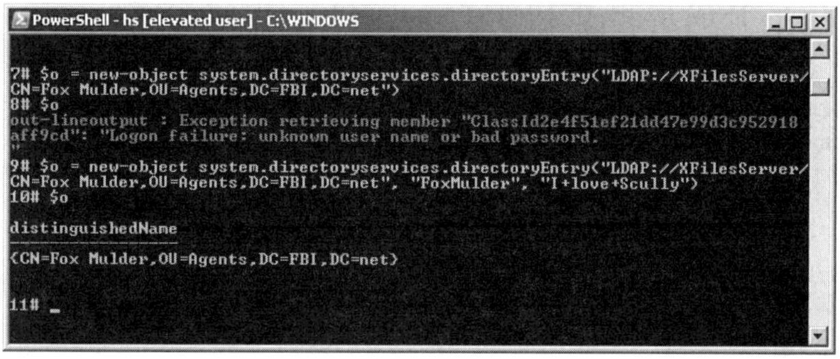

Figure 17.6 Access with and without impersonation

Checking the Existence of Directory Entries

The classic ADSI did not have a built-in method to check the existence of a directory object. You had to rely on time-consuming "trial and error" [WPE01]. Under .NET, the class `DirectoryEntry` offers the static method `Exists()` to check whether a directory object, specified by means of its ADSI path, really exists:

```
$YesNo = [system.directoryservices.directoryEntry]::Exists
➥("LDAP://XFilesServer1/CN=Fox
➥Mulder,OU=Agents,DC=FBI,DC=net")
```

You can shorten this as follows:

```
$YesNo = [ADSI]::Exists("LDAP://XFilesServer1/CN=Fox
➥Mulder,OU=Agents,DC=FBI,DC=net")
```

Reading Directory Entry Attributes

Actually, the object model of `System.Directoryservices` is complicated. In a `DirectoryEntry` object, the single values are convoluted and are accessible only via the volumes `Properties` and `PropertyValue ObjectCollection`. However, the WPS ADSI adapter makes it easier for the user. You can just write the following:

```
$xy = $obj.AttributeName
```

Even multivalued attributes can be retrieved in this way.

In Listing 17.1, data about a user is retrieved.

Listing 17.1 Fetching a Directory Object

```
new-object
system.directoryservices.directoryEntry("LDAP://XFilesServer1/
➥CN=Fox Mulder,OU=Agents,DC=FBI,DC=net")
"Name: "+ $o.sn
"City: " + $o.l
"Telephone Number: " +$o.Telephonenumber
"Other Telephone Numbers: " +$o.OtherTelephone
```

WARNING The access to a directory attribute that does not exist does not cause an error. Therefore, be careful of the syntax!

To fetch the directory path of a directory entry, which is already accessible for you in form of a variable, you have to use `.psbase.path` (for example, `$o.psbase.path`).

ADSI Property Cache

Because ADSI objects are only placeholders for directory entries, attribute values are administered in a property cache. When an attribute is accessed for the first time, ADSI downloads all attribute values in the property cache. Write accesses are possible via assignments to the attributes.

All write accesses have to be concluded by calling the method `CommitChanges()` (`SetInfo()` under classic ADSI). Only then will the property cache be transferred to the underlying directory service. Therefore, transaction security can be guaranteed: Either all changes will be effected or none. There is also a method for the import of attributes into the property cache: `RefreshCache()` (complies with `GetInfo()` under classic ADSI). The program should explicitly call it when there are doubts that the values in the property cache are not up to date. With `RefreshCache()`, changes can also be discarded, if there is no `CommitChanges()` between the changes and the `RefreshCache()`. Before a first access to an attribute is executed, single values can be imported in the property cache by indicating an array with attribute name in `RefreshCache(ARRAY_OF_STRING)`, to diminish the network use by preventing a transfer of all attributes.

In contrast to classic ADSI, `System.Directoryservices` offers the possibility to switch off the property cache. To do this, you need the following command after instancing the `DirectoryEntry` object:

```
$o.PSBase.UsePropertyCache = 0
```

NOTE The switching off of the property cache does not work with creating directory objects of directory classes that possess mandatory attributes, because the directory service creates an entry only after all mandatory attributes have been transferred.

Writing Directory Entry Attributes

Writing to a directory attribute is nearly as simple as reading. You only have to assign a value or an array of values (if a multivalued attribute is concerned) to the relevant directory attribute.

It's important, however, that in the end the property cache is written to the directory service. Because of the already mentioned method chaos, there are now two options:

- Calling the COM method `SetInfo()`
- Calling the .NET method `CommitChanges()` via the subobject `PSBase`

In the .NET world, the method is not named `SetInfo()`, but `CommitChanges()`:

Listing 17.2 Changing a Directory Object

```
$o.Telephonenumber = "+49 201 7490700"
$o.OtherTelephone = "+01 111 222222","+01 111 333333","+49 111 44444"
$o.SetInfo()
# oder:
$o.PSBase.CommitChanges()
```

Common Properties

The meta class `DirectoryEntry` possesses a few attributes that contain basic properties of a directory object (see Listing 17.3), including the following:

- `Name` Relative distinguished name of the object
- `Path` Distinguished name of the object
- `SchemaClassName` Name of the directory service class in the diagram of the directory service
- `Guid` Global unique identifier (GUID) of the meta object
- `NativeGuid` The GUID for the directory service object
- `Children` List of the subordinate objects
- `UsePropertyCache` Flag, which indicates whether the property cache will be used

WARNING Unfortunately, you cannot call these general attributes directly in the current final version of WPS, but only via `PSBase`.

Listing 17.3 Accessing Basic Properties of a Directory Object

```
$o = new-object system.directoryservices.directoryEntry
➥("LDAP://XFilesServer1/CN=Fox Mulder,OU=Agents,
➥DC=FBI,DC=net", "FoxMulder", "I+love+Scully")
"Class: " + $o.PSBase.SchemaClassName
"GUID: " + $o.PSBase.Guid
```

Accessing Container Objects

Binding to container objects and access to their directory attributes is affected completely identically to the access to leaf objects (that is, via the class `DirectoryEntry`). If you want to have the subobjects of the container listed, however, you must call the subobject `Children`, which displays a `DirectoryEntries` object (see Listing 17.4). The `DirectoryEntries` object contains an instance of the class `DirectoryEntry` for each subordinated directory entry.

Again, keep in mind that the subobject `Children` is not available directly, but only via `PSBase`.

Listing 17.4 List of the Subobjects of a Container

```
$Path= "LDAP://XFilesServer1/OU=Agents,DC=FBI,DC=net"
$con = new-object system.directoryservices.directoryEntry($Path)
$con.PSBase.Children
```

Actually, the `DirectoryEntries` collection does not possess a numeric index. Nevertheless, WPS allows numeric access to the elements with a trick (that is, encapsulating the collection into a hash table with the @ sign; see Chapter 5, "The PowerShell Navigation Model"):

```
"The second element is " +
➥@($con.PSBase.Children)[1].distinguishedName
```

Alternatively, you can search for an element in the container by means of its CN with the method `Find()`:

```
"Search for an element " +
➥$con.PSBase.Children.find("cn=Fox Mulder").distinguishedName
```

Creating Directory Entries

A directory entry is created via the parent container because only this container knows whether it is at all prepared to accept a certain directory class as subobject. The method `Add()` of the .NET class `DirectoryEntries` expects in the first parameter the relative distinguished name (RDN) of the new entry, and in the second parameter the name of the directory service class, which will be used as schema for the entry. After setting of potential mandatory attributes, you have to call `CommitChanges()`:

Listing 17.5 Creating an Organizational Unit

```
"Creating a OU..."
$Path= "LDAP://XFilesServer1/DC=FBI,DC=net"
$con = new-object system.directoryservices.directoryEntry($Path)
$ou = $con.PSBase.Children.Add("ou=Directors","organizationalUnit")
$ou.PSBase.CommitChanges()
$ou.Description = "FBI Directors"
$ou.PSBase.CommitChanges()
"OU has been created!"
```

Deleting Directory Entries

A directory entry is either deleted via a method call to itself (`DeleteTree()`) or via the execution of the method `Remove()` on a parent container entry. In this case, you have to indicate the `DirectoryEntry` object, which represents the directory entry that is to be deleted, as parameter. The call of `CommitChanges()` is not necessary:

Listing 17.6 Deleting an Organizational Unit

```
$ouPath= "LDAP://XFilesServer1/ou=Directors,DC=FBI,DC=net"
$ou = new-object system.directoryservices.directoryEntry($ouPath)
if ([system.directoryservices.directoryEntry]::Exists($ouPath))
{
"OU already exists and will now be deleted!"
$ou.PSBase.DeleteTree()
}
```

TIP `DeleteTree()` has the advantage that it recursively also deletes all subobjects.

Summary

Unfortunately, WPS 1.0 includes no commandlets for the administration of directory services. Also, WMI is not helpful here. In this lesson, you learned how to use the Active Directory Service Interface (ADSI) and its .NET-based API `System.DirectoryServices` to access LDAP- and non-LDAP-based directory services.

You learned about object identification with paths, binding from a `DirectoryEntry` object to the real directory entry, impersonation when using a directory service, and all basic operations such as reading and writing entries and the creation of new entries and the deletion of entries.

In the next chapter, you use this as the necessary basic knowledge for the administration of user accounts and groups in the Active Directory.

CHAPTER 18

USER AND GROUP MANAGEMENT IN THE ACTIVE DIRECTORY

In this chapter:

This chapter provides some examples of the use of classes of the namespace `System.Directoryservices` to access Microsoft Active Directory. Specifically, you will learn how to manage user accounts, groups, and organizational units.

Directory Class `User`

A user entry in the Active Directory (AD class `user`) possesses numerous directory attributes. A mandatory attribute, owned by all user entries, is `SAMAccountName`, which contains the Windows NT 3.51/NT 4.0-compatible login name.

Table 18.1 shows further directory attributes of user entries in the Active Directory. There are some amazingly short names, such as `l` for city, and extremely long ones, such as `physicalDeliveryOfficeName` for office.

Table 18.1 Selected Attributes of the Active Directory Class User

Name	Mandatory	Multivalued	Data Type (Length)
cn	Yes	No	DirectoryString (1-64)
nTSecurityDescriptor	Yes	No	ObjectSecurityDescriptor (0-132096)
objectCategory	Yes	No	DN
objectClass	Yes	Yes	OID
ObjectSid	Yes	No	OctetString (0-28)
SAMAccountName	Yes	No	DirectoryString (0-256)
accountExpires	No	No	INTEGER8
accountNameHistory	No	Yes	DirectoryString
badPwdCount	No	No	INTEGER
comment	No	No	DirectoryString
company	No	No	DirectoryString (1-64)
createTimeStamp	No	No	GeneralizedTime
department	No	No	DirectoryString (1-64)
description	No	Yes	DirectoryString (0-1024)
desktopProfile	No	No	DirectoryString
displayName	No	No	DirectoryString (0-256)
displayNamePrintable	No	No	PrintableString (1-256)
DistinguishedName	No	No	DN
division	No	No	DirectoryString (0-256)
employeeID	No	No	DirectoryString (0-16)
EmployeeType	No	No	DirectoryString (1-256)
expirationTime	No	No	UTCTime
FacsimileTelephoneNumber	No	No	DirectoryString (1-64)
givenName	No	No	DirectoryString (1-64)
homeDirectory	No	No	DirectoryString
HomeDrive	No	No	DirectoryString
homeMDB	No	No	DN
Initials	No	No	DirectoryString (1-6)
internationalISDNNumber	No	Yes	NumericString (1-16)

Name	Mandatory	Multivalued	Data Type (Length)
l	No	No	DirectoryString (1-128)
lastLogoff	No	No	INTEGER8
LastLogon	No	No	INTEGER8
logonCount	No	No	INTEGER
LogonHours	No	No	OctetString
logonWorkstation	No	No	OctetString
manager	No	No	DN
middleName	No	No	DirectoryString (0-64)
Mobile	No	No	DirectoryString (1-64)
name	No	No	DirectoryString (1-255)
objectGUID	No	No	OctetString (16-16)
ObjectVersion	No	No	INTEGER
otherFacsimile TelephoneNumber	No	Yes	DirectoryString (1-64)
OtherHomePhone	No	Yes	DirectoryString (1-64)
physicalDeliveryOfficeName	No	No	DirectoryString (1-128)
PostalAddress	No	Yes	DirectoryString (1-4096)
postalCode	No	No	DirectoryString (1-40)
PostOfficeBox	No	Yes	DirectoryString (1-40)
profilePath	No	No	DirectoryString
SAMAccountType	No	No	INTEGER
scriptPath	No	No	DirectoryString
street	No	No	DirectoryString (1-1024)
streetAddress	No	No	DirectoryString (1-1024)
TelephoneNumber	No	No	DirectoryString (1-64)
title	No	No	DirectoryString (1-64)
userWorkstations	No	No	DirectoryString (0-1024)
whenChanged	No	No	GeneralizedTime
whenCreated	No	No	GeneralizedTime
wWWHomeLeaf	No	No	DirectoryString (1-2048)

Some multivalued fields from the dialog boxes of the MMC snap-in Active Directory User and Computer are stored in Active Directory in more than one attribute. A good example for this is the list of telephone numbers. The main telephone number is stored in the single-valued attribute `telephoneNumber`, whereas the other telephone numbers are persisted in the multivalued attribute `otherTelephone`. Additional cases of this kind include the following:

```
mobile/otherMobile
mail/otherMailbox
logonWorkstation/otherLoginWorkstations.
```

NOTE By the way, the preceding named attributes are not typos by the author (login–logon), but inconsistencies within the Active Directory; the persons responsible for this can be found in Redmond.

You can gather a complete list of all directory attributes in the documentation of the Active Directory schema [MSDN09]. In the script, use the LDAP names of the attributes, indicated in the documentation as "LDAP Display Name" (see Figure 18.1).

Unfortunately, the LDAP attribute name is partly located very far away from the names in the MMC console. The document "User Object User Interface Mapping" [MSDN10] helps to find the right LDAP names. Another option is to take a look at the "raw" directory and search for the LDAP names with the tool ADSI Edit from the Support Tools for Windows Server.

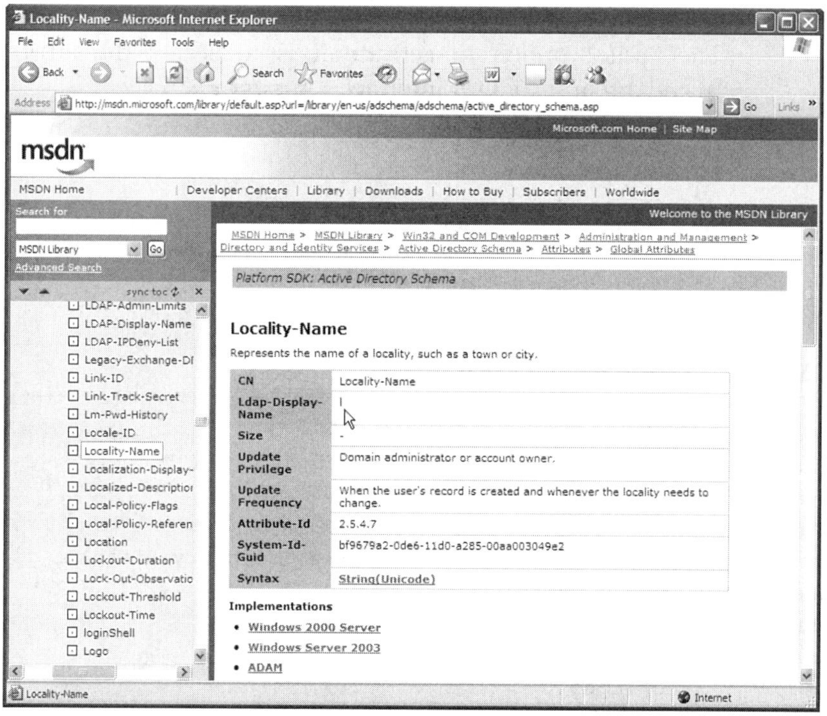

Figure 18.1 Documentation of the Active Directory schema

Creating a User Account

Because the creation of an object is initiated by the parent container, the first step is to bind the container to `DirectoryEntry`. The creation of a new entry is effected with a call to the method `Add()`, by indicating the RDN of the new entry in the first parameter and the Active Directory class name `user` in the second parameter.

The setting of the attribute `SAMAccountName` is mandatory. If the property cache has not been switched off, `CommitChanges()` has to be executed after all attributes have been set; otherwise, the user entry will not be created.

By default, a new user account is deactivated in the Active Directory. The easiest option to activate it is to access the attribute `Account Disabled` in the COM interface `IADsUser`.

Example

In Listing 18.1, a user account, Walter Skinner, with the login name WalterSkinner is created. As optional attributes, only city (`l`) and description (`Description`) are set.

Listing 18.1 Creating a User Object in Active Directory

```
# Create ADS-user
$Path= "LDAP://XFilesServer1/OU=Directors,DC=FBI,DC=net"
$name = "Walter Skinner"
$NTname = "WalterSkinner"
$ou = New-Object Directoryservices.DirectoryEntry($Path)
$user = $ou.PSBase.Children.Add("CN=" + $name,'user')
$user.PSBase.CommitChanges()
$user.SAMAccountName = $NTname
$user.l = "Washington"
$user.Description = "FBI Director"
$user.PSBase.CommitChanges()

"User has been created: " + $user.PBase.Path
$user.SetPassword("secret-123")
"Password is set"
$user.Accountdisabled = $false
"User has been activated!"
```

Setting the Password

The password of a user account can be set only after the user account has been created in the directory service. Also in this operation, the impersonation is necessary under .NET. Listing 18.2 shows setting a password.

You can now take advantage from the fact that Windows PowerShell (WPS) publishes ADSI methods rather than COM methods, because the method for the setting of a password (`SetPassword()`) does not exist on the .NET level. Being a parameter, the new password has to be transferred in form of a string; it cannot be encrypted! After the setting of a password, the user can be activated.

Listing 18.2 Setting a Password for an AD User Account

```
"User has been created: " + $user.PBase.Path
$user.SetPassword("secret-123")
"Password has been set"
$user.userAccountControl = 512
$user.PSBase.CommitChanges()
```

Authentication

Unfortunately, there is no built-in method that enables an authentication with username and password against Active Directory. To realize this, you can only use the trial-and-error method [WPE01]. You try to access the Active Directory by applying the impersonation with the login data to be checked. If access to the attribute `NativeGuid` is successful, the data is correct. If the data is not correct, you receive an error message. This is realized in the following helper routine, `Authenticate-User()` (see Listing 18.3).

Listing 18.3 Authentication with Active Directory

```
Function Authenticate-User {
trap [System.Exception] { "Error!"; return $false; }
"Try, user " + $args[1] + " with the password " + $args[2] +
➥" to authenticate " + $args[0] + "..."
$o = new-object
system.directoryservices.directoryEntry([string]$args[0],
➥[String]$args[1], [String]$args[2])
$o.PSBase.NativeGUID
return $true
}

#$o = new-object system.directoryservices.directoryEntry("LDAP://E02")
#$o.get_NativeGUID()
$e = Authenticate-User "LDAP://XFilesServer1"
➥"fbi\foxmulder" "I+love+Scully"
$e
if ($e) { "User could be authenticated!" }
else { "User could NOT be authenticated!" }
```

Deleting Users

To remove a user account, you can apply the method `DeleteTree()`, even if the user is a leaf entry (that is, if he has no subentries):

Listing 18.4 Deleting a User

```
$Path= "LDAP://XFilesServer1/CN=Walter Skinner,OU=Agents,DC=FBI,DC=net"
$user = new-object system.directoryservices.directoryEntry($Path)
if ([system.directoryservices.directoryEntry]::Exists($Path))
{
"User already exists and will be deleted now!"
$user.PSBase.DeleteTree()
}
else
{
"User does not exist!"
}
```

Renaming User Accounts

With the method `Rename()`, the class `DirectoryEntry` offers a quite simple procedure for the renaming of a directory entry. Under classic ADSI, you had to use the `IADsContainer` method `MoveHere()` to accomplish this.

Example

In Listing 18.5, the user account "Walter Skinner" is renamed to "Walter S. Skinner."

Listing 18.5 Renaming an AD User Account

```
# Rename user
$Path= "LDAP://XFilesServer1/CN=Walter
Skinner,OU=Directors,DC=FBI,DC=net"
$user = new-object system.directoryservices.directoryEntry($Path)
$user.PSBase.Rename("cn=Walter S. Skinner")
"User has been renamed!"
```

Moving User Accounts

In the .NET class `DirectoryEntry`, there is an equivalent to the COM method `IADSContainer.MoveHere()` with the method `MoveTo()`. This method moves a directory entry to another container. The target container has to be transferred as parameter in form of a second `DirectoryEntry` object.

Example for Moving a User Account

In Listing 18.6, the user account Fox Mulder from the organization unit Agents is moved to the standard user container Users.

Listing 18.6 Moving an AD User Account

```
# Move user
$Path= "LDAP://XFilesServer1/CN=Walter Fox
Mulder,OU=Agents,DC=FBI,DC=net"
$target = "LDAP://XFilesServer1/CN=Users,DC=FBI,DC=net "
$user = new-object system.directoryservices.directoryEntry($Path)
$user.PSBase.MoveTo($target)
"Object has been moved!"
```

Group Management

In a directory object of the type `group`, there exists an attribute `Member` with LDAP paths to the group members. To display the members of a group, you therefore only need a one-liner. The following command shows the members of the group of all FBI agents:

```
(new-object  directoryservices.directoryentry
("LDAP://XFilesServer1/CN=All Agents,DC=FBI,DC=net")).member
```

Nevertheless, this command displays only the direct members. When a group contains another group, however, there are also indirect members. The following function, `Get-Members`, which is implemented in Listing 18.7, fetches recursively all direct and indirect members of a group in the Active Directory. Figure 18.2 shows the result.

Listing 18.7 Listing of Indirect Group Members

```
########################################
# PowerShell Script
# Display all direct and indirect members of a group
# (C) Dr. Holger Schwichtenberg
# http://www.windows-scripting.com/
#########################################

#(new-object  directoryservices.directoryentry
➥("LDAP://xfilesserver/CN=All FBI
➥Employees,DC=FBI,DC=net")).member

"Direct Group Members:"
$group = New-Object directoryservices.directoryentry
➥("LDAP://xfilesserver/CN=All FBI Employees,DC=FBI,DC=net")
$group.member

function Get-Members ($group){
  if ($group.objectclass[1] -eq 'group') {
   "-- Group $($group.cn)"
    $Group.member | foreach-object {
      $de = new-object
directoryservices.directoryentry("LDAP://xfilesserver/" + $_)
      if ($de.objectclass[1] -eq 'group') {
        Get-Members $de
      }
      Else {
        $de.distinguishedName
      }
    }
  }
  Else {
    Throw "$group is not a group."
  }
}

"--- Listing of Group Members:"
"All Members (including non-direct):"
Get-Members(new-object directoryservices.directoryentry(
➥"LDAP://xfilesserver/CN=All Employees,DC=FBI,DC=net"))
```

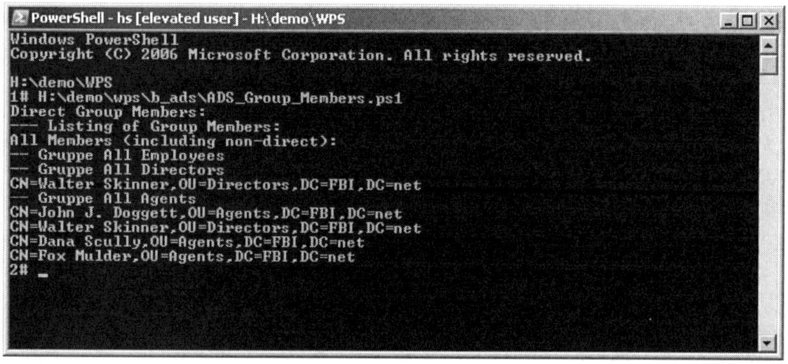

Figure 18.2 Listing of Direct and Indirect Group Members

Creating and Filling a Group

You create a group in the same way as you create a user. When creating groups, however, note the different class name (`group`) used, as compared to creating users:

Listing 18.8 Creating a Group

```
"Creating a group..."
$Path= "LDAP://XFilesServer1/DC=FBI,DC=net"
$con = new-object system.directoryservices.directoryEntry($Path)
$ou = $con.PSBase.Children.Add("cn=All Directors","group")
$ou.PSBase.CommitChanges()
$ou.samaccountname = "AllDirectors"
$ou.Description = "Group for FBI Directors"
$ou.PSBase.CommitChanges()
""Group was created!"
```

Assigning Group Members

There are no specific methods for the assignment of users to groups in the class `DirectoryEntry`. Here, a WPS object once again enables access to the methods `Add()` and `Remove()` defined in the COM interface `IADsGroup` (see Listings 18.9 and 18.10).

Listing 18.9 Adding Users to Groups

```
# Add a group member
$Path= "LDAP://XFilesServer1/cn=All Directors,DC=FBI,DC=net"
$gr = new-object system.directoryservices.directoryEntry($Path)
$User = "LDAP://XFilesServer1/CN=Walter
➥Skinner,OU=Directors,DC=FBI,DC=net"
$ou.Add($User)
"User " + $User + " have been added to the goup " + $ou + "
```

Listing 18.10 Deleting Users from Groups

```
# Deleting a group member
$Path= "LDAP://XFilesServer1/cn=All Directors,DC=FBI,DC=net"
$gr = new-object system.directoryservices.directoryEntry($Path)
$User = "LDAP://XFilesServer1/CN=Walter
Skinner,OU=Directors,DC=FBI,DC=net"
$ou.Remove($User)
"User " + $User + " have been deleted from group " + $ou + "
```

Organizational Units

How organization units (directory service class `organizationalUnit`) are created and deleted has already been demonstrated in Chapter 17, "Directory Services."

When creating organization units, note the different class name (`organizationalUnit`) in the first parameter and the different attribute name (`OU`) in the first parameter of `Add()`, as compared to the creation of users or groups (see Listing 18.11).

Listing 18.11 Script to Create an OU

```
# Script to create an OU (The OU will be deleted if it already
➥exists!)

$ouPath= "LDAP://XFilesServer1/ou=Directors,DC=FBI,DC=net"
$ou = new-object system.directoryservices.directoryEntry($ouPath)
if ([system.directoryservices.directoryEntry]::Exists($ouPath))
{
"OU already exists and will be deleted!"
$ou.PSBase.DeleteTree()
}

"Creating an OU..."
$Path= "LDAP://XFilesServer1/DC=FBI,DC=net"
$con = new-object system.directoryservices.directoryEntry($Path)
$ou = $con.PSBase.Children.Add("ou=Directors","organizationalUnit")
$ou.PSBase.CommitChanges()
$ou.Description = "FBI Directors"
$ou.PSBase.CommitChanges()
"OU has been created!"
```

Summary

In this chapter, you learned the most common operations for user and group administration in the Active Directory. Specifically, you saw how to create users and groups through calls of the `Add()` method. This chapter also covered deleting, renaming, and moving with the methods `DeleteTree()`, `Rename()`, and `MoveTo()`.

CHAPTER 19

Searching in the Active Directory

In this chapter:

In the Active Directory, just like in other LDAP-based directory services, entries that adhere to certain criteria can be searched in several containers simultaneously using the LDAP query syntax.

LDAP Query Syntax

For LDAP queries, there exists a special syntax according to [RFC1960] and [RFC2254]:

To execute an LDAP query, you need four parameters:

- **Path.** An LDAP path, including LDAP://. The path can be indicated in Little Endian form as well as in Big Endian form.
  For example, `LDAP://XFilesServer1/dc=FBI,dc=net`
- **Filter.** A condition in Inverted Polish notation (UPN or Postfix notation). This notation is unique by the fact that the operators are set at the beginning, not between the operands. Valid operations are

`&` (and), | (or), and `!` (not). For comparison, =, <=, and >= are available, but not < and >.
For example, `(&(objectclass=user)(name=h*))`

- **Properties.** An attribute list of the desired directory attributes that will be built in to the table. This indication is not optional. The star operator (`*`), which can be used in SQL to query databases, is not valid.
For example, `AdsPath,Name,SAMAccountname`
- **Scope.** One of the constants named in Table 19.1.

Table 19.1 Search Levels in ADSI Queries

Constant (LDAP Syntax)	Explanation
`BASE`	Only the level of the indicated entry is searched. The result volume comprises one or no datasets.
`ONELEVEL`	Only those entries are searched that are subordinated to the entry indicated.
`SUBTREE`	All underlying levels are searched.

Starting with Windows Server 2003, there is a new branch, Stored Queries, in the Active Directory MMC `User and Computer` snap-in that can be used to design and execute LDAP queries (see Figure 19.1).

Example for an LDAP Query

The following query searches the complete Active Directory for all user accounts whose names start with the letter *H:*

- **Path.** `LDAP://XFilesServer1/DC=FBI,DC=net>`
- **Filter.** `&(objectclass=user)(name=h*));`
- **Properties.** `adspath,SAMAccountname`
- **Scope.** `subtree`

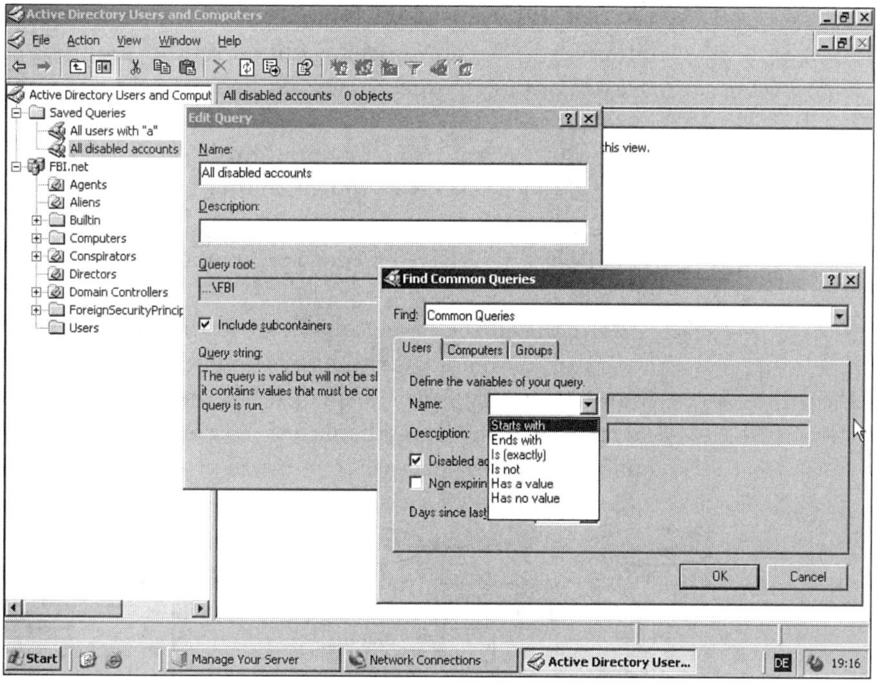

Figure 19.1 Saved queries in the MMC

LDAP Queries in PowerShell

An LDAP query is executed with .NET classes as follows (see Figure 19.2):

1. Create an instance of the class `DirectorySearcher`.
2. Set the root of the query by assigning a pointer to a `DirectoryEntry` object, which is bound to the root, to the attribute `SearchRoot`.
3. Set the filter part of the LDAP query in the attribute `Filter`.
4. Set the attributes by filling the object volume `PropertiesToLoad`.

5. Set the scope in the attribute `SearchScope`. You can define this either by the appropriate enumeration member (`[System.DirectoryServices.SearchScope]::Subtree`) or just a string (`"subtree"`).
6. Run the query via the method `FindAll()`. The method `FindAll()` retrieves an object volume of the type `SearchResultCollection`.
   The `SearchResultCollection` contains single `SearchResult` objects.
7. A `SearchResult` object enables you to either access the queried attributes by reading or to have a `DirectoryEntry` object for the found directory entry displayed by the method `GetDirectoryEntry()`. The thus displayed `DirectoryEntry` object also enables a writing access.

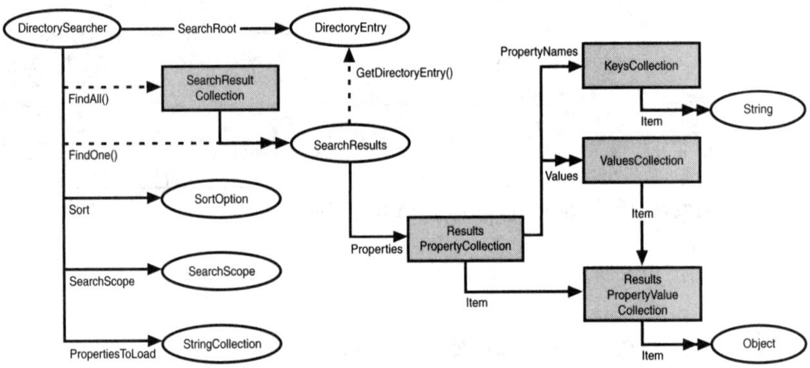

Figure 19.2 Object model for LDAP search

Example for an LDAP Query in PowerShell

In Listing 19.1, all user accounts are searched throughout the whole Active Directory for those whose directory names start with the letter *A*. Figure 19.3 shows the results.

Listing 19.1 Executing an LDAP Search in AD

```
$Root = new-object system.directoryservices.directoryEntry
➥("LDAP://XFilesServer/DC=FBI,DC=net")
$Filter = "(&(objectclass=user)(name=a*))"
```

```
$Attribute = "CN","ObjectClass","ObjectCategory","distinguishedName",
➥"lastLogonTimestamp","description","department","displayname"

# Compile search
$Searcher = New-Object Directoryservices.DirectorySearcher($Root)
$searcher.PageSize = 900
$searcher.Filter = $Filter
$searcher.Searchscope =
➥[System.DirectoryServices.SearchScope]::Subtree
$Attribute | foreach {[void]$searcher.PropertiesToLoad.Add($_)}
# Execute search
$result = $searcher.findAll()
"Number of results: " + $result.Count
$result
```

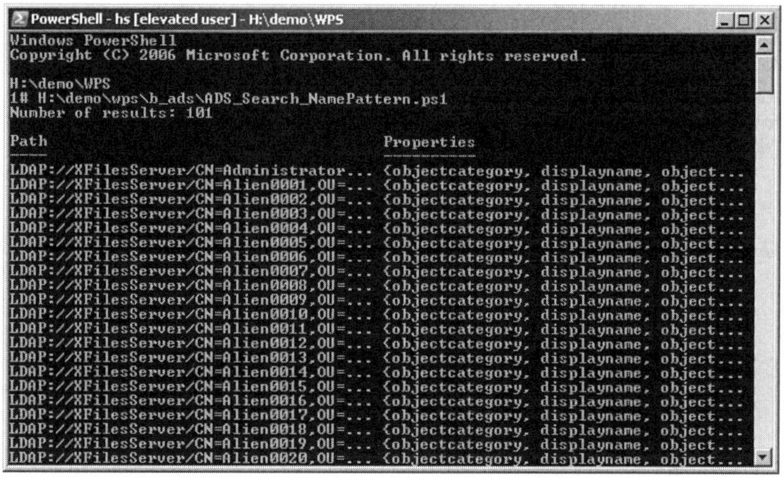

Figure 19.3 Search results

Searching a User with Its Login Name

When only the Windows NT 4.0–compatible login name of a user is known, but not the path of the directory service entry, you can execute the search in the Active Directory only with an ADSI query via the attribute `SAMAccountName` (see Listing 19.2). It is important to note that here that only the username has to be indicated, and not the Windows NT 4.0–compatible domain name.

Listing 19.2 Search Directory Service Entry for a User Whose `SAMAccountName` Is Known

```
$username = "FoxMulder"
"Search user " + $username + "..."
$root = new-object system.directoryservices.directoryEntry
➥("LDAP://XFilesServer1/DC=FBI,DC=net")
$Filter = "(SAMAccountName=" + $username +")"
$Attribute = "CN","ObjectClass","ObjectCategory","distinguishedName",
➥"lastLogonTimestamp","description","department","displayname"

# Compile search
$Searcher = New-Object Directoryservices.DirectorySearcher($root)
$searcher.PageSize = 900
$searcher.Filter = $Filter
$searcher.SearchScope = "subtree"
$Attribute | foreach {[void]$searcher.PropertiesToLoad.Add($_)}
# Execute search
$searcher.findAll()
```

Search Tips and Tricks

This section contains tips and tricks for effective and well-performing searches in the Active Directory.

Use Indexed Attributes

You should use as many indexed attributes in queries as possible. In the documentation of the Active Directory, you will learn which attributes are indexed. Figure 19.4 shows where you can find the documentation for Active Directory attributes in the Active Directory schema in the MSDN library. The entry `Is Indexed: True` shows indexed attributes.

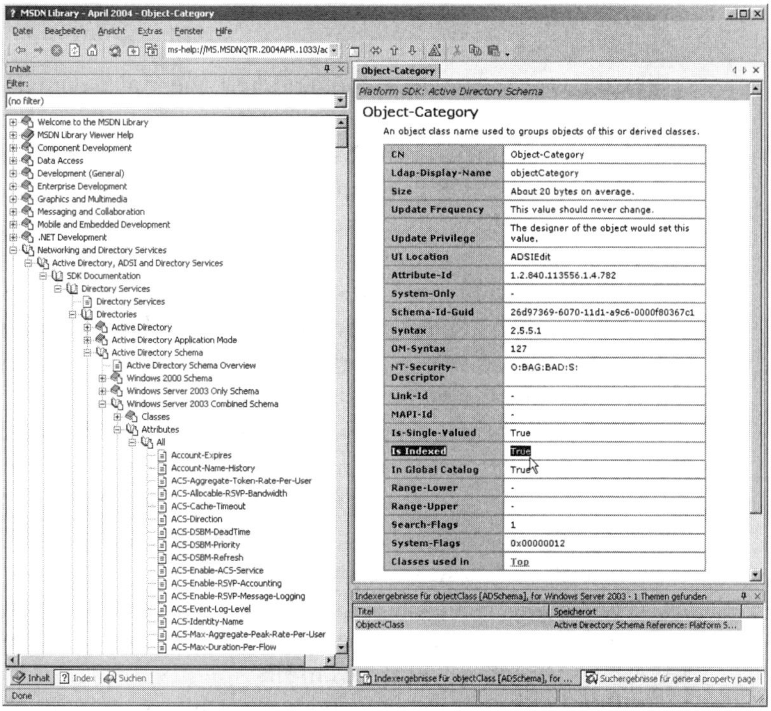

Figure 19.4 Documentation of AD attributes in the MSDN developer library

Avoid Multivalued Attributes

Although the following the query is correct

- **Path.** `LDAP://XFilesServer1/dc=FBI,dc=net>`
- **Filter.** `(&(objectClass=user)(name=a*))`
- **Properties.** `name,adspath`

for performance reasons it is not optimal. It is better to use the following:

- **Path.** `LDAP://XFilesServer1/dc=FBI,dc=net>`
- **Filter.** `(&(objectCategory=person)(objectClass=user)(name=a*));`
- **Properties.** `name,adspath`

When executing in a large directory service, you will notice that the second query is executed much faster.

Besides `objectClass`, the modified query also contains a reference to the attribute `objectCategory`. The reason for this is that `objectClass` is a multivalued attribute that shows the complete inheritance hierarchy of the directory class. For example, there is a `user` object "top, person, organizationalPerson, user" stored. It's interesting that a `computer` object indicates that a computer is a specialization of the user, because `objectClass` contains the following for a computer: "top, person, organizationalPerson, user, computer." A search via a multivalued attribute is very time-consuming. Unfortunately, no attribute in the Active Directory contains the class name in a single-valued attribute.

Besides the class, there also exists a categorization of the directory objects. Categories are `person`, `group`, `computer`, and `organizational Unit`. `Person` contains the classes `user` and `contact`. The category of a directory object is stored in `objectCategory`, and `objectCategory` is an indexed attribute that enables a quick search. For this reason, it makes sense to add `objectClass` and `objectCategory` to the conditions.

The sequence of the attributes in the condition, however, is optional; the Active Directory optimizes itself.

The following list shows the correct filters for a quick search for different directory classes:

- **Contacts.** `(&(objectclass=contact) (objectcategory= person)`
- **User.** `(&(objectclass=user) (objectcategory=person)`
- **Groups.** `(&(objectclass=group) (objectcategory=group)`
- **Organizational units.** `(&(objectclass=organizational Unit) (objectcategory=organizationalUnit)`
- **Computer.** `(&(objectclass=user) (objectcategory= computer)`

Avoid the Star Operator

Another tip for the optimization of Active Directory queries is that you should avoid the use of placeholders (star operator, `*`) at the beginning of a string.

Search Results Restrictions

In standard configuration, the Active Directory limits the number of search results to 1,000. You can change this setting in the domain policies, as shown in Listing 19.3 and Figue 19.5.

Listing 19.3 Changing Domain Policies for Search Results Restrictions Using `Ntdsutil.Exe`

```
C:\> ntdsutil
ntdsutil: ldap policies
ldap policy: connections
server connections: connect to server SERVERNAME
Connected to SERVERNAME using credentials of locally logged on user
server connections: q
ldap policy: show values

Policy                      Current(New)

...MaxPageSize                 1000...

ldap policy: set maxpagesize to ##### (for example, 50000)
ldap policy: commit changes
ldap policy: q
ntdsutil: q
Disconnecting from SERVERNAME ...
```

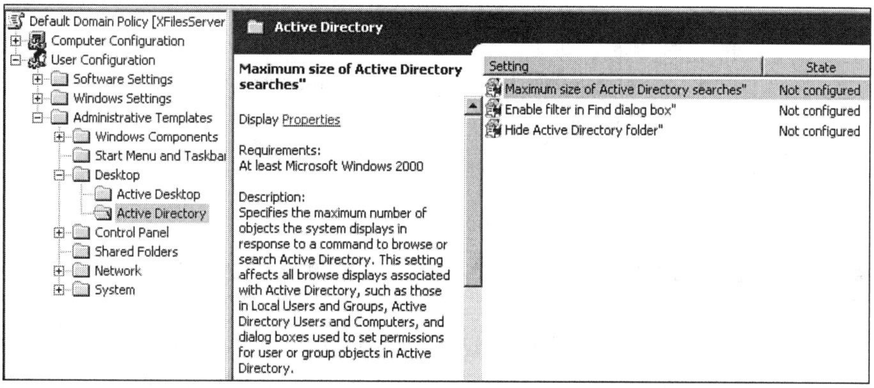

Figure 19.5 Changing the domain policies for the search restriction using the MMC

LDAP Query Examples

The following list contains further examples for possible filters for the search for user accounts:

- All users whose name starts with *S*
  `(&(objectCategory=person)(objectClass=user)(name=s*))`
- All users without a description
  `(&(objectCategory=computer)(!description=*))`
- All deactivated users
  `(&(objectCategory=person)(objectClass=user)`
  `(userAccountControl:1.2.840.113556.1.4.803:=2))`
  In this case, the challenge is that the deactivation information is stored in a single bit in `userAccountControl`. A comparison with a fixed value with the equals sign would not lead to the desired result. A bitwise AND is necessary. Unfortunately, this is a rather complicated expression in LDAP query syntax: `1.2.840.113556.1.4.803`. A bitwise OR would be the value `1.2.840.113556.1.4.804`.
- All users with the Password Does Not Expire setting
  `(&(objectCategory=person)(objectClass=user)`
  `(userAccountControl:1.2.840.113556.1.4.803:=65536))`
- All users created after 2004/10/11
  `(&(objectCategory=person)(objectClass=user)`
  `(whenCreated>=20041110000000.0Z))`

WARNING A query that consists only of the condition `class=*` does not work. To retrieve all directory objects, the star operator has to be applied to another attribute.

Using the Commandlet `Get-ADObject`

The PowerShell Community Extensions contain the commandlet `Get-ADObject`, which is able to apply the LDAP filter. Output objects are of the type `System.Directoryservices.DirectoryEntry`.

Table 19.2 Using the `Get-ADObject` Commandlet

`Get-ADObject -Class user`	Fetches all user accounts (instances of the directory service class `user`)
`Get-ADObject -value "*domain*"`	Fetches all directory service objects whose names contain the word *domain*
`Get-ADObject -Filter "(&(objectCategory=person)(objectClass=user)(userAccount Control:1.2.840.113556.1.4.803:=2))"`	Fetches all deactivated user accounts
`Get-ADObject -Server E02 -SizeLimit 10`	Fetches the first ten directory entries of domain controller E02
`Get-ADObject -Server E02 -Scope subtree -DistinguishedName "CN=Users,DC=IT-Visions,DC=local"`	Fetches all entries in the Users container and its subcontainers

Summary

In this chapter, you learned how to use the power of LDAP search queries to find entries in an LDAP-based directory service that match certain criteria. LDAP queries contain a root path, a filter, a list of properties and a search scope. LDAP queries can be executed through the .NET class `System. Directoryservices.DirectorySearcher` or the commandlet `Get-ADObject` from the PowerShell Community Extensions. If you want to write well-performing queries, however, keep in mind the special structure of the Active Directory, especially the inheritance, multivalued attributes, and indexed attributes.

CHAPTER 20

ADDITIONAL LIBRARIES FOR ACTIVE DIRECTORY ADMINISTRATION

In this chapter:

A few advanced Active Directory administrative tasks can be performed only through an additional library (for example, access to group policies). In this chapter, you are introduced to three Add-On libraries that ease the Active Directory administration within Windows PowerShell (WPS).

Navigating the Active Directory Using the PowerShell Community Extensions

As soon as the PowerShell Extensions (PSCX) [CODEPLEX01] are installed, the Active Directory can be used as a navigation container. When WPS is started, PSCX automatically creates a new drive for the Active Directory to which the computer belongs. The drive is named according to the Windows NT 4.0–compatible domain name (that is, FBI:, for the domain with the DNS name fbi.net).

The following command selects all groups that have the word *domain* in their names from the `Users` container of the Active Directory and displays this list sorted according to name:

```
dir FBI:/users | where { ($_.name -match "domain") -and
➥($_.Type -match "group") } | sort name
```

To create a new organizational unit with the OU Directors, you need only one command using the commandlet `New-Item`:

```
New-Item -path FBI://Directors -type organizationalunit
```

However, the capabilities of this provider are limited.

Using the www.IT-Visions.de Active Directory Extensions

The commandlet library of www.IT-Visions.de provides some commandlets for the directory service administration that make the work much easier, including the following:

- `Get-DirectoryEntry` Access to a single directory object
- `Get-DirectoryChildren` Access to the content of a container object (lists the subelements)
- `Add-User` Access to a user account with password
- `Add-DirectoryEntry` Creation of a directory object that does not need a password
- `Remove-DirectoryEntry` Deleting a directory object
- `Get-DirectoryValue` Fetching a value for a directory attribute
- `Set-DirectoryValue` Setting a value for a directory attribute

NOTE The commandlets support the commandlet-based programming style

```
Add-User -name $Name -Container ("WinNT://" +
➥$Computer) -Password "secret"
Set-DirectoryValue -Path ("WinNT://" +
➥$Computer +"/" + $Name) -Name "Fullname"
➥-Value "Dr. Holger Schwichtenberg"
```

and the object-based style, because the commandlets transfer the relevant objects to the pipeline:

```
$u = Add-User -Password "secret" -RDN $Name
➥-Container ("WinNT://" + $Computer)
$u.Fullname
$u.PSBase.CommitChanges()
```

Example

Listing 20.1 shows the application of the directory services commandlets, applicable to a local Windows user database (tested on a Windows Server 2003 member server) or an Active Directory (tested on a Windows Server 2003 domain controller). Figure 20.1 shows a sample of the output.

Listing 20.1 Various Directory Service Operations via WinNT-Provider (available through www.IT-Visions.de commandlets)

```
##########################################
## Test script for directory service access with
## the www.IT-Visions.de PowerShell commandlets
## Dr. Holger Schwichtenberg 2007
##########################################

Add-PSSnapin ITVisions_PowerShell_extensions

# --- Parameters

$Name = "cn=FoxMulder"
$Container = "LDAP://XFilesServer/OU=Agents,DC=FBI,DC=net"

# --- Write

Write-Host "Access to Container" -ForegroundColor yellow
Get-DirectoryEntry $Container | select name

Write-Host "Create user" -ForegroundColor yellow
$u = Add-User -Name $Name -Container $Container -Password
➥"secret-123" -verbose
```

(continues)

Listing 20.1 Various Directory Service Operations via WinNT-Provider (available through www.IT-Visions.de commandlets) *(continued)*

```
Write-Host "Set attribute - Commandlet Style" -ForegroundColor yellow
Set-DirectoryValue -Path $u.psbase.path -Name "Description"
➥-Value "Agent"

Write-Host "Set attribute - Object Style" -ForegroundColor yellow
$u.l = "Washington DC"

$u.PSBase.CommitChanges()

# --- Read

Write-Host "Read attribute - Object Style" -ForegroundColor yellow
$u = Get-DirectoryEntry $u.psbase.path
"Name: " + $u.Description

Write-Host "Read attribute - Commandlet style" -ForegroundColor yellow
Get-DirectoryValue -Path $u.psbase.path  -Name "Description"

Write-Host "Delete user" -ForegroundColor yellow
Remove-DirectoryEntry $u.psbase.path

Write-Host "List container content" -ForegroundColor yellow
Get-DirectoryChildren $Container | Select name
```

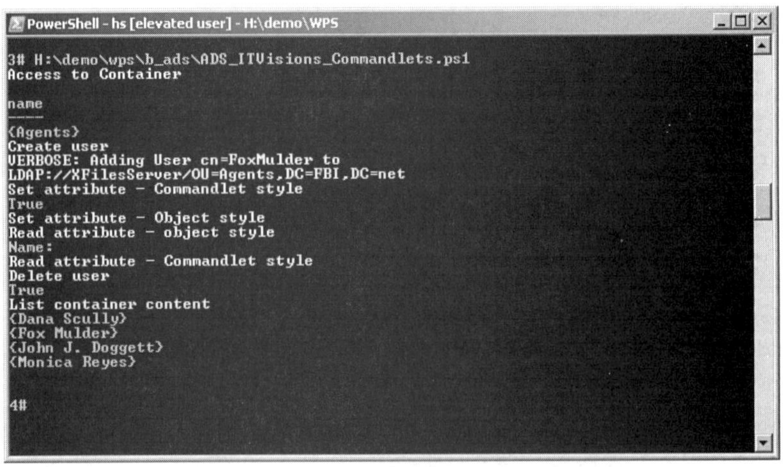

Figure 20.1 Clipping from the output of Listing 20.1

Using the Quest Active Directory Extensions

The company Quest provides commandlets for Active Directory administration (for example, `Get-QADComputer`, `Get-QADUser`, `New-QADObject`, `Set-QADObject`) and as an adapted PowerShell console (Quest Management Shell for Active Directory); see Figure 20.2.

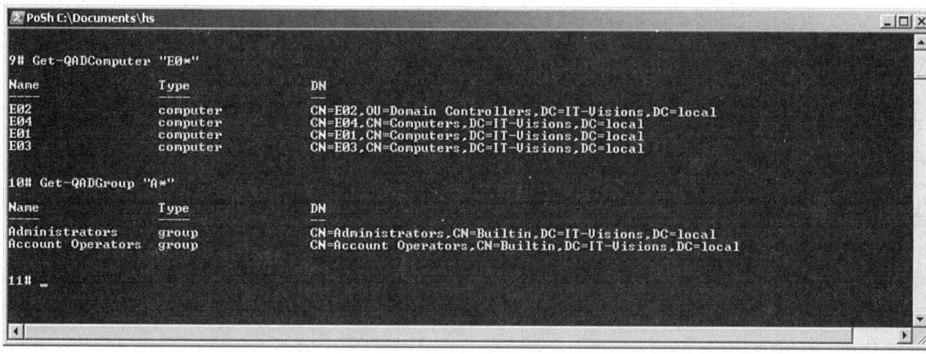

Figure 20.2 Quest Management Shell for Active Directory

Getting Information about the Active Directory Structure

In addition to the namespace `System.Directoryservices`, which contains general classes for the programming of directory services, there is the subnamespace `System.Directoryservices.ActiveDirectory` (also called Active Directory Management Objects, ADMO) in .NET, starting with version 2.0. This namespace contains some Active Directory–specific functions that are not applicable to other directory services.

In particular, this namespace offers classes for the administration of the complete structure of an Active Directory (for example `Forest`, `Domain`, `ActiveDirectoryPartition`, `DomainController`, `GlobalCatalog`, and `ActiveDirectorySubnet`). Some classes specially designed for the Active Directory Application Mode (ADAM, a function-reduced version of the Active Directory for use as data storage for some applications) are supported with classes such as `ADAMInstanceCollection` and `ADAMInstance`.

Example 1: Domains and Forests

Listing 20.2 gives information about the domain to which the computer belongs and about the forest to which this domain belongs.

Listing 20.2 Information about the Domain and the Forest

```
# Display current domain
$d = [System.Directoryservices.ActiveDirectory.Domain]
➥::GetCurrentDomain();

# Information about current domain
"Name: " + $d.Name
"Domain Mode: " + $d.DomainMode
"Owner of InfrastructureRole: " + $d.InfrastructureRoleOwner.Name
"Owner of PdcRole: " + $d.PdcRoleOwner.Name

# Information about forest of current domain
$f = $d.Forest;
"Name of forest: " + $f.Name
"Mode of forest: " + $f.ForestMode
```

Example 2: Domain Controllers and Roles

In Listing 20.3, all domain controllers (and their roles) of a special domain are listed.

Listing 20.3 Information about the Domain Controllers and Their Roles

```
# Display current domain
$d =
[System.Directoryservices.ActiveDirectory.Domain]::GetCurrentDomain()
$DCs = $d.DomainControllers
# Loop over all domain controllers
foreach ($DC in $DCs)
{
    "Name: " + $DC.Name
    "IP: " + $DC.IPAddress.ToString()
    "Time: " + $DC.CurrentTime.ToString()
```

```
    "Roles:"
   # Loop over all roles of DC
    foreach ($R in $DC.Roles)
    {
     "- " + $R.ToString()
    }
}
```

Group Policies

Group policies cannot be accessed through ADSI or `System.DirectoryServices`. Group policies can be managed by the COM component GPMGMT, which is part of the Group Policy Management Console (GPMC) [MS04].

WARNING Confirm that the GPMC is installed on your system before running any of the scripts in this chapter.

Note that via the GPMGMT component you can attach and detach group policies to Active Directory containers. However, it does not enable you to create new group policies or change settings within an existing group policy.

Classes

Figure 20.3 shows the object model of the GPMGMT component. As the root class, `GPMGMT.GPM` is the only instantiable class; all scripts start by creating an instance of this class.

Enumerating Policies

Listing 20.4 lists the display name and creation time for all group policies in a specific domain. After instantiation of the root class, you have to access the domain through the method `GetDomain()`. After that, you can use the method `SearchGPO()` on the domain object to search for Group Policy objects. In this case, no filters are used.

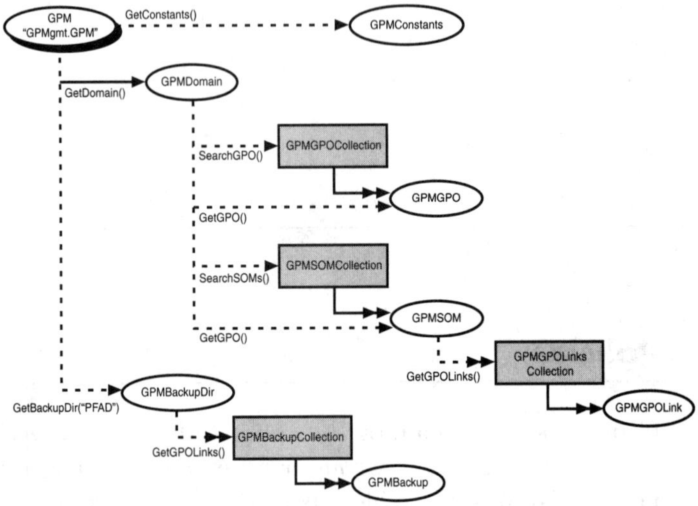

Figure 20.3 Object model of the GPMGMT component for Group Policy Management

Listing 20.4 Enumerate Group Policies

```
# Parameters
$Domain = "fbi.net"

# Create root object
$gpm = New-Object -ComObject "GPMGMT.GPM"

# Access Domain
$Domain = $GPM.GetDomain($Domain, "", $GPM.GetConstants().UseAnyDC)

# Filter Object
$Filter = $gpm.CreateSearchCriteria()

# Get GPOs
$GPOList = $Domain.SearchGPOs($Filter)

# Display GPOs
$GPOList | Select Displayname, CreationTime
```

If you want to enumerate all group policies that are linked to a certain organizational unit, you can use the script shown in Listing 20.5. `GetSOM()` retrieves a container in the Active Directory, and `GetGPOLinks()` retrieves a list of links. Each link contains the global unique identifier of the linked group policy.

Listing 20.5 Enumerating All Group Policies Linked to a Container

```
# Parameters
$Domain = "fbi.net"
$Container = "ou=agents, dc=fbi, dc=net"

# Create root object
$gpm = New-Object -ComObject "GPMGMT.GPM"

# Access Domain
$Domain = $GPM.GetDomain($Domain, "", $GPM.GetConstants().UseAnyDC)

# Container
$Container = $Domain.GetSOM($Container)

# Get GPOs
$Links = $Container.GetGPOLinks()

# Display GPOs
foreach ($link in $Links)
{
$GPO = $Domain.GetGPO($link.GPOID)
$GPO | Select Displayname, CreationTime
}
```


Create a New Group Policy Link

To link a group policy to a container, complete these steps (see Listing 20.6 and Figure 20.4):

1. Create an instance of the root object.
2. Access the domain through `GetDomain()`.
3. Access the container through `GetSOM()`.

4. Get a reference to the Group Policy object using the GUID of the group policy through `GetGPO()`.
5. Call the method `CreateGPOLink()` on the container.

Listing 20.6 Create a GPO Link

```
trap {
      Write-Error ("ERROR: " + $_.Exception.Message)
      if ($_.Exception.InnerException -ne $null) { Write-Error
➥("ERROR: " + $_.Exception.InnerException.Message) }
      exit
}

# Parameters
$Domain = "fbi.net"
$Container = "ou=agents, dc=fbi, dc=net"
$GPOID = "{063751AF-8CBD-4F04-B889-196840B99D2E}"

# Create root object
$gpm = New-Object -ComObject "GPMGMT.GPM"

# Access Domain
$Domain = $GPM.GetDomain($Domain, "", $GPM.GetConstants().UseAnyDC)

# Container
$Container = $Domain.GetSOM($Container)

# Get GPO Object
$GPO = $Domain.GetGPO($GPOID)

# Create Link
$Link = $Container.CreateGPOLink(-1, $GPO)

"Link created!"
```

Delete a Group Policy Link

The script in Listing 20.7 deletes all Group Policy links for a given container in the Active Directory. To delete a link, call the `Delete()` method of the appropriate `GPMGPOLink` object.

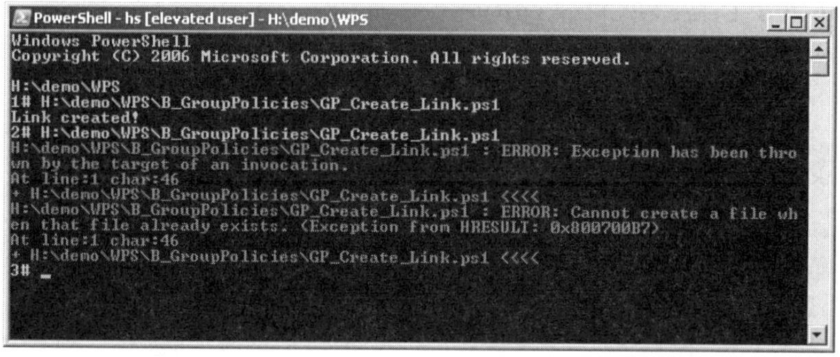

Figure 20.4 A container can contain only one link to each policy.

NOTE Note that the script will delete only the links. The group policies will remain, even if they are not linked to a container any more. If you want to delete the group policy, call `Delete()` on the Group Policy object itself.

20. ADDITIONAL LIBRARIES

Listing 20.7 Delete GPO Links

```
# Parameters
$Domain = "fbi.net"
$Container = "ou=agents, dc=fbi, dc=net"

# Create root object
$gpm = New-Object -ComObject "GPMGMT.GPM"

# Access Domain
$Domain = $GPM.GetDomain($Domain, "", $GPM.GetConstants().UseAnyDC)

# Container
$Container = $Domain.GetSOM($Container)

# Get GPOs
$Links = $Container.GetGPOLinks()

# Display GPOs
foreach ($link in $Links)
```

(continues)

Listing 20.7 Delete GPO Links *(continued)*

```
{
$GPO = $Domain.GetGPO($link.GPOID)
"Deleting Link..."  + $GPO.Displayname
$link.Delete()
}
```

Summary

The first topic in this chapter concerned simplifications for Active Directory handling that are provided in different PowerShell extension libraries.

Second, you got to know the classes of the `System.Directoryservices.ActiveDirectory` library that deliver information about the Active Directory domain structure.

Third, you saw how to use the COM component GPMGMT to link and unlink group policies to Active Directory containers.

CHAPTER 21

DATABASES

In this chapter:

In this chapter, you learn how to access databases through ADO.NET, which is a class library within the .NET Framework. You also learn to use the commandlets from the www.IT-Visions.de PowerShell Extensions, which encapsulate a lot of the complexity of ADO.NET.

NOTE Chapter 23, "Security Settings," continues the topic data access, focusing on some advanced features.

Introducing ADO.NET

Windows PowerShell (WPS) has no commandlets for database access and no navigation provider either, although it would be convenient to include databases in the concept of navigation providers. As far as database access is concerned, you can use ADO.NET in WPS. After all, WPS supports the access of single tables by offering column names as attributes of the table object (in this case, an automatic figure occurs, similar to what happens with WMI objects).

This chapter teaches some necessary basics about ADO.NET. Figure 21.1 shows the ADO.NET architecture.

Just like its predecessor concepts ODBC and OLEDB, ADO.NET also uses database-specific drivers, which are called *ADO.NET Data*

Provider, *.NET Data Provider*, and *Managed Provider*. Data Provider for OLEDB and ODBC provide the backward compatibility of ADO.NET for those data sources that don't (yet) have a specific ADO.NET data provider.

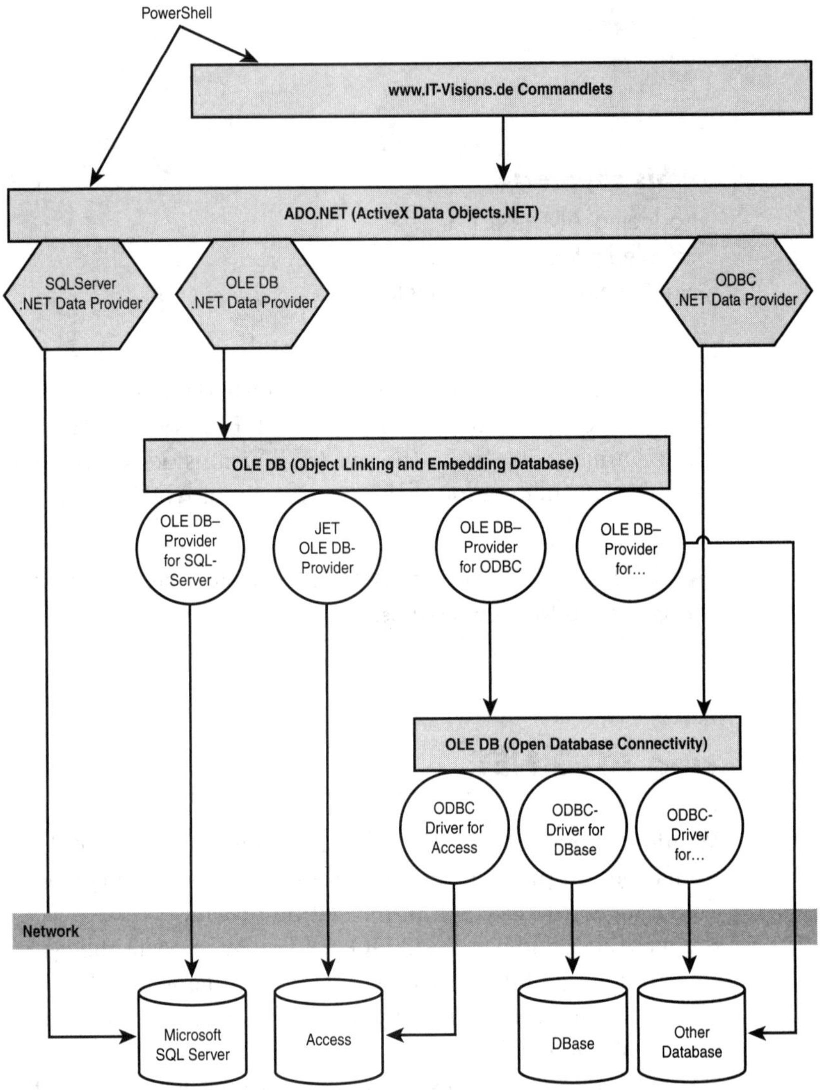

Figure 21.1 ADO.NET driver architecture

Data Providers

The .NET Framework 2.0, 3.0, and 3.5 are delivered with the following data providers (.NET Data Provider or Managed Data Provider):

- `System.Data.SqlClient` Special driver for Microsoft SQL Server 7.0/2000 and 2005
- `System.Data.SqlServerCe` Special driver for Microsoft SQL Server CE
- `System.Data.OracleClient` Special driver for Oracle databases
- `System.Data.OLEDB` Bridge to OLEDB providers
- `System.Data.Odbc` Bridge to ODBC drivers

Additional providers (for example, for MySQL, DB2, Sybase, Informix, and Ingres) are delivered from different producers, a list of which can be found under www.dotnetframework.de/tools.aspx [DOTNET02].

Enumerating the Installed Providers

The ADO.NET data providers existing on a system can be enumerated via the static method `System.Data.Common.DbProviderFactories.GetFactoryClasses()`.

Access to this method in WPS looks like this (see Figure 21.2):

```
[System.Data.Common.DbProviderFactories]::GetFactoryClasses()
```

NOTE The installed providers are not stored in the registry, but in the central XML configuration file of .NET Framework (`machine.config`) in the section `<system.data> <DbProviderFactories>`.

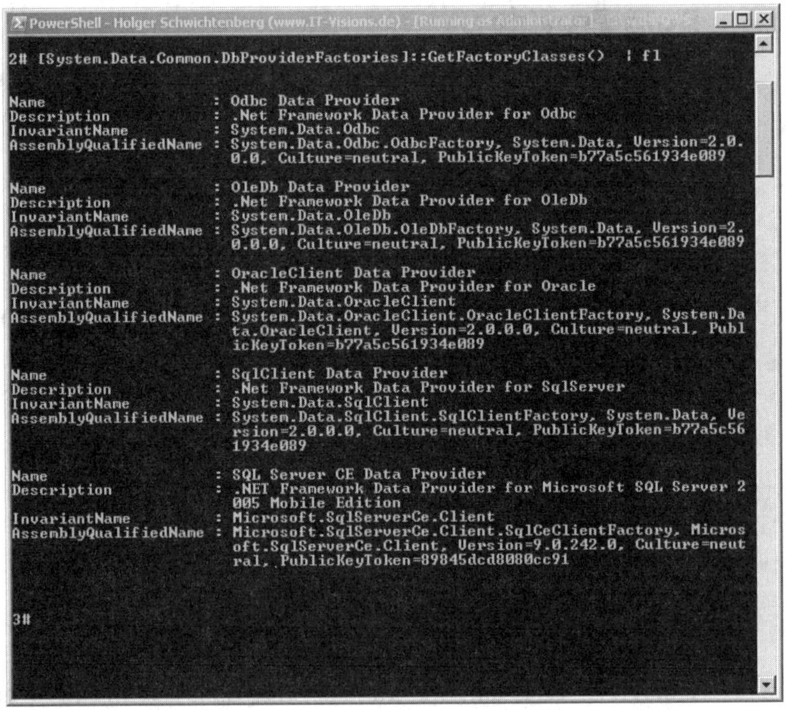

Figure 21.2 Enumeration of the installed ADO.NET drivers

List of Available SQL Servers

If you want to know which instances of Microsoft SQL Server are active in your domain, you can use the .NET class `SqlDataSourceEnumerator` (see Figure 21.3):

```
[System.Data.Sql.SqlDataSourceEnumerator]
➥::Instance.GetDataSources()
```

DataReader versus DataSet

Figure 21.4 shows different ways of receiving data from a data source in ADO.NET. Data can be received by the data user via a provider-independent `DataReader` object or via a provider-independent `DataSet` object. The `DataSet` object needs a `DataAdapter` object (not to be confused with a WPS object adapter) to get the data, which, in turn, has to be implemented separately in each data provider.

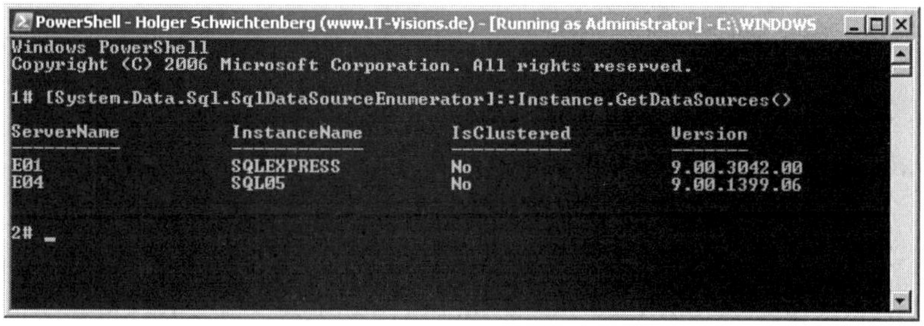

Figure 21.3 List of available SQL servers

Starting with .NET 2.0, .NET also provides so-called data source control elements, which make it easier for the developer to bind data to a control element. These data source control elements are part of the libraries for graphic user interfaces (Windows Forms and ASP.NET) and are not discussed in this book.

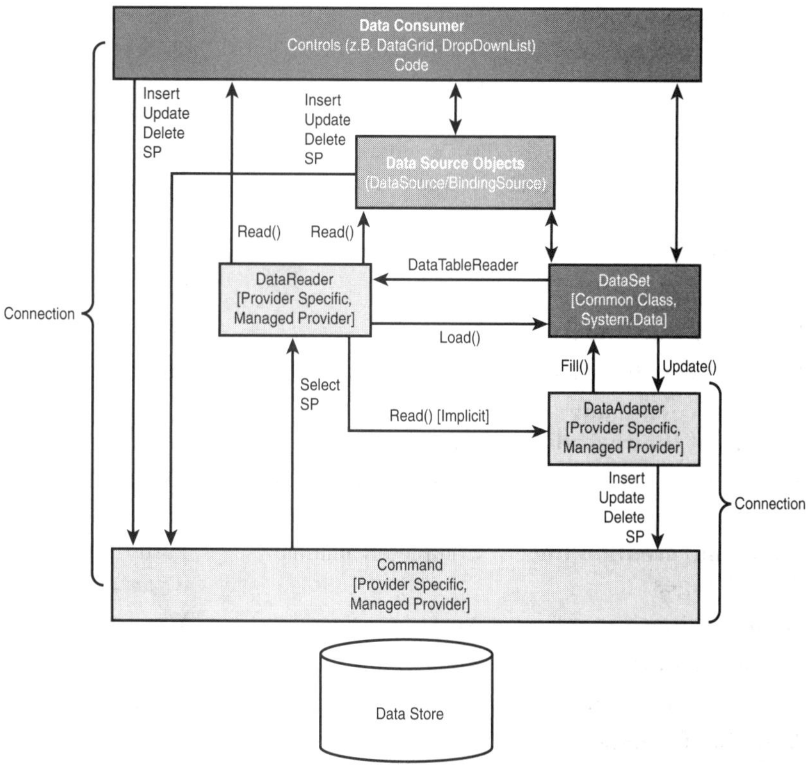

Figure 21.4 Data paths in ADO.NET 2.0

TIP It is possible, although somewhat more difficult, to program the access to a data source in such a way that the database can easily be exchanged.

In the description of the data paths, `DataReader` and `DataSet` were mentioned. Table 21.1 and Figure 21.5 compare both data access method in detail. As you can see from the table, the `DataSet` provides more options, but also has a higher memory consumption. However, because most scripting solutions do not use large sets of data, the `DataSet` is appropriate in most cases within WPS.

Table 21.1 `DataReader` versus `DataSet`

	`DataReader`	`DataSet`
Model	Server Cursor	Client Cursor
Implemented in	Each ADO.NET Data Provider	`System.Data`

Basic classes	`DbDataReader`
	`MarshalByRefObject`
	`Object`
		`MarshalByValueComponent`
		`Object`

Interfaces	`IDataReader`, `IDisposable`, `IDataRecord`, `IEnumerable`	`IListSource`, `IXmlSerializable`, `ISupportInitialize`, `ISerializable`
Read data	Yes	Yes
Read data forward	Yes	Yes
Read data backward	No	Yes
Direct access to any row	No	Yes
Direct access to any column of the record	Yes	Yes
Modify data	No, only via separate command objects	Yes (via data adapter)
Command creation for data changes	Completely manually	Partly automatic (`CommandBuilder`)
Data caching	No	Yes
Change history	No	Yes
Memory consumption	Low	High
Available for data transport between levels	No	Yes

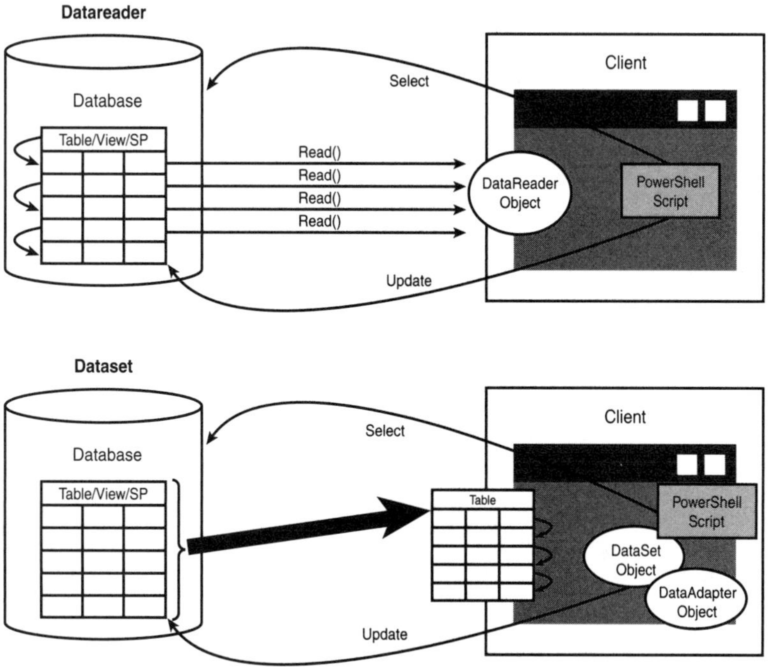

Figure 21.5 Comparing `DataReader` and `DataSet`

Example Database

The example database is taken right out of the everyday life of system administration. It contains a list of user accounts that was either exported from a Windows system or that might serve to create a series of users per script (see Figure 21.6).

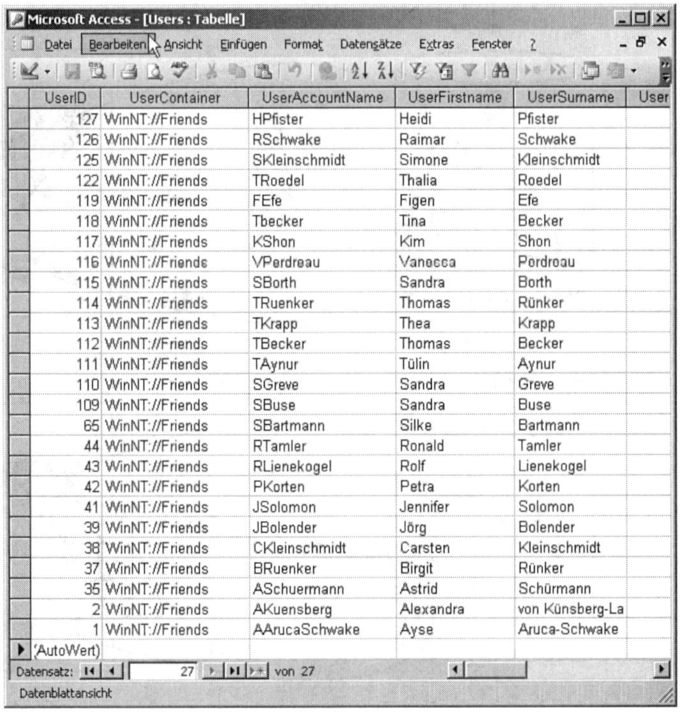

UserID	UserContainer	UserAccountName	UserFirstname	UserSurname	User
127	WinNT://Friends	HPfister	Heidi	Pfister	
126	WinNT://Friends	RSchwake	Raimar	Schwake	
125	WinNT://Friends	SKleinschmidt	Simone	Kleinschmidt	
122	WinNT://Friends	TRoedel	Thalia	Roedel	
119	WinNT://Friends	FEfe	Figen	Efe	
118	WinNT://Friends	Tbecker	Tina	Becker	
117	WinNT://Friends	KShon	Kim	Shon	
116	WinNT://Friends	VPerdreau	Vanessa	Perdreau	
115	WinNT://Friends	SBorth	Sandra	Borth	
114	WinNT://Friends	TRuenker	Thomas	Rünker	
113	WinNT://Friends	TKrapp	Thea	Krapp	
112	WinNT://Friends	TBecker	Thomas	Becker	
111	WinNT://Friends	TAynur	Tülin	Aynur	
110	WinNT://Friends	SGreve	Sandra	Greve	
109	WinNT://Friends	SBuse	Sandra	Buse	
65	WinNT://Friends	SBartmann	Silke	Bartmann	
44	WinNT://Friends	RTamler	Ronald	Tamler	
43	WinNT://Friends	RLienekogel	Rolf	Lienekogel	
42	WinNT://Friends	PKorten	Petra	Korten	
41	WinNT://Friends	JSolomon	Jennifer	Solomon	
39	WinNT://Friends	JBolender	Jörg	Bolender	
38	WinNT://Friends	CKleinschmidt	Carsten	Kleinschmidt	
37	WinNT://Friends	BRuenker	Birgit	Rünker	
35	WinNT://Friends	ASchuermann	Astrid	Schürmann	
2	WinNT://Friends	AKuensberg	Alexandra	von Künsberg-La	
1	WinNT://Friends	AArucaSchwake	Ayse	Aruca-Schwake	
(AutoWert)					

Figure 21.6 Database with user accounts

Data Access with PowerShell

This section first discusses the creation of a connection. After that, access is executed.

Connections

No matter which data access form is chosen, and no matter which action is to be executed, communication with the database management system always requires a connection.

Each data provider has its own implementation of the connection class: `SqlConnection`, `OracleConnection`, `OleDbConnection`, and so on. During the instantiating of theses objects, the connection string can be transferred. After that, the call `Open()` is executed. A connection has to be closed by `Close()`.

Examples

Listings 21.1 through 21.3 show the creation and closing of a connection to three different kinds of databases, respectively:

- A dynamically loaded Microsoft Access database file (Listing 21.1)
- A statically bound Microsoft SQL Server database (Listing 21.2)
- A dynamically loaded Microsoft SQL Server database file (only works with Microsoft SQL Server Express) (Listing 21.3)

Listing 21.1 Creating and Closing a Connection to a Microsoft Access Database

```
# parameters
$Conn = "Provider=Microsoft.Jet.OLEDB.4.0;Data
Source=H:\demo\WPS\B_Database\users.mdb;"
$SQL = "Select * from users order by UserSurname"

# Open databses
"Open the database..."
$conn = New-Object System.Data.OleDb.OleDbConnection($Conn)
$conn.open()
"Status of database: " + $conn.State

# Close database
$Conn.Close()
"Status of database: " + $conn.State
```

Listing 21.2 Creating and Closing a Connection of a Statically Bound Microsoft SQL Server Database

```
# parameters
$Connstring = "Data Source=.\SQLEXPRESS;Initial catalog=Users;Integrated
Security=True;"
$SQL = "Select * from users order by UserSurname"

# Open database
"Open the database..."
$conn = New-Object System.Data.SqlClient.SqlConnection($Connstring)
$conn.open()
```

(continues)

Listing 21.2 Creating and Closing a Connection of a Statically Bound Microsoft SQL Server Database *(continued)*

```
"Status of database: " + $conn.State

# Close database
$Conn.Close()
"Status of database: " + $conn.State
```

Listing 21.3 Creating and Closing a Connection to a Dynamically Bound Microsoft SQL Server Express Database File

```
# Parameters
$Connstring = "Data Source=.\SQLEXPRESS;AttachDbFileName=
➥H:\demo\PowerShell\data bases\users.mdf;Integrated Security=True;"
$SQL = "Select * from users order by UserSurname"

# Open database
"Open the database..."
$conn = New-Object System.Data.SqlClient.SqlConnection($Connstring)
$conn.open()
"Status of database: " + $conn.State

# Close database
$Conn.Close()
"Status of database: " + $conn.State
```

Provider-Independent Data Access

In the previous examples, different classes were used, depending on which database provider (Microsoft Access or Microsoft SQL Server) was used. This is not ideal an ideal scenario (when you have to access different databases or if you intend to change the database later). ADO.NET also supports the provider-independent data access (see Listing 21.4).

When you access data provider independence, you don't instantiate the connection class directly, but via a so-called provider factory. You get the provider factory from the .NET class `System.Data.Common.DbProviderFactories` by indicating the so-called provider invariant name as a string, as follows:

- **For Microsoft Access.** `"System.Data.OleDb"`
- **For Microsoft SQL Server.** `"System.Data.SqlClient"`
- **For Oracle.** `"System.Data.OracleClient"`

WARNING Provider-independent data access is executed without the translation of SQL commands. If you use database-specific commands, you lose the provider independence.

Listing 21.4 Provider-Independent Establishment of a Connection

```
# Parameters
$PROVIDER = "System.Data.SqlClient"
$CONNSTRING = "Data Source=.\SQLEXPRESS;AttachDbFileName=
➥H:\demo\WPS\B_Database\users.mdf;Integrated Security=True;"
$SQL = "Select * from FL_Flights"

# Create factory
$provider =
[System.Data.Common.DbProviderFactories]::GetFactory($PROVIDER)

# Create and fill connecting object
$conn = $provider.CreateConnection()
$conn.ConnectionString = $CONNSTRING;

# Establish connection
$conn.Open();
"Status of database: " + $conn.State

# Close database
$Conn.Close()
"Status of database: " + $conn.State
```


Executing Commands

Each database provider provides a provider-specific command object (`SqlCommand`, `OracleCommand`, `OleDbCommand`, and so on). Moreover, there also exists a provider-neutral command object of the type `DbCommand`.

The command object offers the following functions:

- `ExecuteNonQuery()` for the execution of DML (for example, `Insert`, `Update`, `Delete`) and DDL (for example, `Create Table`) commands, which do not retrieve data rows. As long as these commands retrieve the number of the affected rows, this result is received through the return value of the method. Otherwise, the return value is `-1`.
- `ExecuteRow()` delivers the first row of the result set in the form of a `SqlRecord` object (only SQL Server).
- `ExecuteScalar()` fetches the first column of the first row of the result set.
- `ExecuteReader()` delivers a `DataReader` object (see next paragraph).

Provider factories also enable you to work provider independently with the command object, as the next example demonstrates. In this case, the command object has to be created by the provider factory via `CreateCommand()`.

Example

In Listing 21.5, first the number of users is counted, then a new user is created, and then the number of users is counted again. In the end, the newly created user is deleted, and another counting is executed. (Figure 21.7 shows the execution.)

Listing 21.5 Executing Commands with Provider-Independent Command Objects

```
# Parameters
$PROVIDER = "System.Data.SqlClient"
$CONNSTRING = "Data Source=.\SQLEXPRESS;AttachDbFileName=
➥H:\demo\WPS\B_Database\users.mdf;Integrated Security=True;"
$SQL1 = "Select count(*) from users"
$SQL2 = "insert into users ( UserFirstName, UserSurname)
➥values ('Hans', 'Meier')"
$SQL3 = "delete from users where UserSurname='Meier'"

# Create factory
$provider =
➥[System.Data.Common.DbProviderFactories]::GetFactory($PROVIDER)
```

```
# Create connection object
$conn = $provider.CreateConnection()
$conn.ConnectionString = $CONNSTRING

# Open connection
$conn.Open();
"Status of database: " + $conn.State

# create command #1
[System.Data.Common.DbCommand] $cmd1 = $provider.CreateCommand()
$cmd1.CommandText = $SQL1
$cmd1.Connection = $conn
# execute command #1
$e = $counter = $cmd1.ExecuteScalar()
"Count before insert: " + $Counter

# create command #2 (INSERT)
[System.Data.Common.DbCommand] $cmd2 = $provider.CreateCommand()
$cmd2.CommandText = $SQL2
$cmd2.Connection = $conn
# execute command #2
$e = $cmd2.ExecuteNonQuery()

# execute command #1
$counter = $cmd1.ExecuteScalar()
"Count after insert: " + $Counter

# create command #3 (DELETE)
[System.Data.Common.DbCommand] $cmd3 = $provider.CreateCommand()
$cmd3.CommandText = $SQL3
$cmd3.Connection = $conn
# execute command #2
$e = $cmd3.ExecuteNonQuery()

# execute command #1
$counter = $cmd1.ExecuteScalar()
"Count after delete: " + $Counter

# Close database
$Conn.Close()
"Status of database: " + $conn.State
```

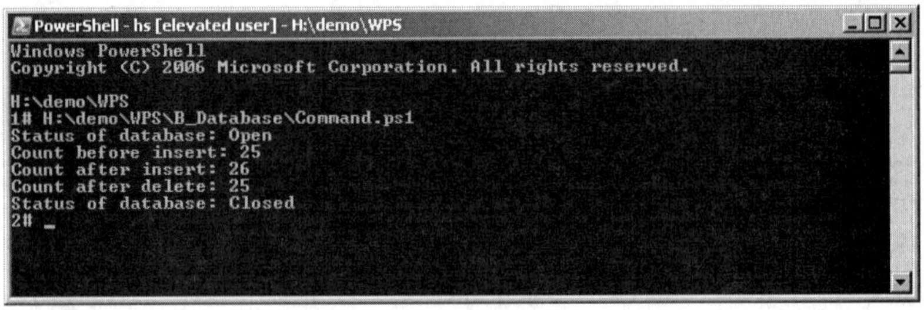

Figure 21.7 Execution of the script `Command.ps1`

Data Access Using a Data Reader

A `DataReader` object is a server-side cursor that allows only unidirectional reading access (only forward) to the result of a `SELECT`-application (`Resultset`). A change of the data is not possible. In contrast to `DataSet`, `DataReader` supports only a flat presentation of the data. Data retrieval is executed only row-wise, and therefore you have to iterate via the result volume. Compared with the classic COM-based ActiveX Data Objects (ADO), an ADO.NET `DataReader` is the equivalent to a "read-only/forward-only `Recordset`."

Each ADO.NET data provider contains its own `DataReader` implementation, so there are numerous different `DataReader` classes in .NET Framework (for example, `SqlDataReader`, `OLEDBDataReader`, and `OracleDataReader`). The `DataReader` classes derive from `System.Data.ProviderBase.DbDataReaderBase` and implement `System.Data.IDataReader`.

To fetch the data, a `DataReader` needs a command object that is just as provider specific (for example, `SqlCommand`, `OLEDBCommand`, and `OracleCommand`). The connection to the database itself requires a provider-specific connection object (for example, `SqlConnection` or `OleDbConnection`). Figure 21.8 demonstrates the connection of these objects by the example of the data provider for SQL Server. The object model is similar for OLEDB—just replace `Sql` in the class name with `OleDb`. The provider for SQL Server (`SqlClient`) has, starting with .NET 2.0, an additional class, `SqlRecord`, which represents a single dataset as result of a command.

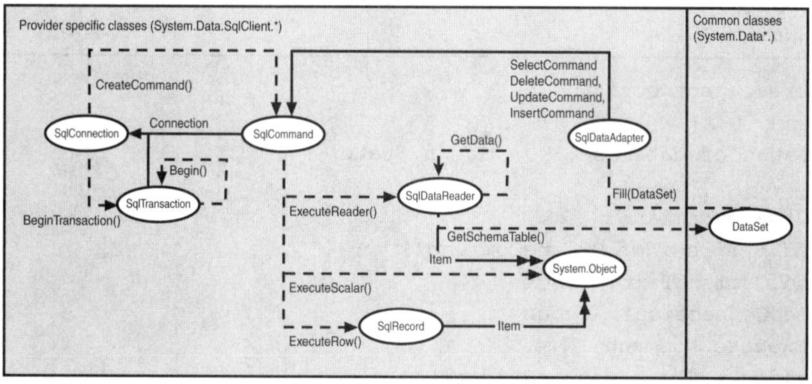

Figure 21.8 Connecting objects by the example of the data provider for SQL Server

The `DataReader` can also be used provider independently via an instance of the class `System.Data.Common.DbDataReader`, retrieved from a provider-independent command object via `ExecuteReader()`.

Example for Using a Data Reader

Listing 21.6 fetches all users from the user table.

Listing 21.6 Fetching of a Database Table with a Provider-Independent `DataReader`

```
# Parameters
$PROVIDER = "System.Data.SqlClient"
$CONNSTRING = "Data Source=.\SQLEXPRESS;AttachDbFileName=
➥H:\demo\WPS\B_Database\users.mdf;Integrated Security=True;"
$SQL = "Select * from users"

# Create factory
$provider =
➥[System.Data.Common.DbProviderFactories]::GetFactory($PROVIDER)

# Create and fill connection object
$conn = $provider.CreateConnection()
$conn.ConnectionString = $CONNSTRING
```

(continues)

Listing 21.6 Fetching of a Database Table with a Provider-Independent `DataReader` *(continued)*

```
# Create connection
$conn.Open();
"Status of database: " + $conn.State

# Create command
$cmd = $provider.CreateCommand()
$cmd.CommandText = $SQL
$cmd.Connection = $conn
# Execute command
$reader = $cmd.ExecuteReader()

# Loop over all data rows
while($reader.Read())
{
$reader.Item("UserID").ToString() + ": " + $reader.Item("UserFirstName")
➥ + " " + $reader.Item("UserSurname")
}

# Close database
$Conn.Close()
"Status of database: " + $conn.State
```

Summary

There are no commandlets for the access to databases in WPS 1.0. However, you learned in this chapter all the necessary basics to use the ADO.NET library from the .NET Framework. ADO.NET has a provider model with a few providers included in the .NET Framework, and more providers are available from third-party vendors. ADO.NET enables you to connect to a database (classes such as `SqlConnection` or `OleDbConnection`), to execute commands (`SqlCommand or OleDbCommand`), and read data through a data reader (`OleDbDataReader` or `SqlDataReader`). Don't forget to close a connection as soon as possible, at the latest at the end of your script.

The next chapter covers an important advanced feature: the `DataSet`. In addition, the next chapter covers commandlets from the www.IT-Visions.de PowerShell Extension Library that facilitate data access.

CHAPTER 22

Advanced Database Operations

In this chapter:

This chapter contains advanced database access techniques (specifically, using an ADO.NET `DataSet`). This chapter provides examples on how to read and change data and convert between tabular data and XML documents. You also learn that using the commandlets within the www.IT-Visions.de Commandlet Library makes data access a lot easier.

Data Access Using a `DataSet`

A `DataSet` contains a collection of data tables that are presented by single `DataTable` objects. The `DataTable` objects can be filled from any data sources without a relation existing between object and data source; the `DataTable` object does not know where the data comes from. The `DataTable` objects can also be filled with data without a database in the backend.

A `DataSet` offers, in contrast to the `DataReader`, all kinds of access (that is, also adding, deleting, and changing `DataSets`). You can also view hierarchic relations between single tables and store them in a `DataSet`. This enables a processing of hierarchic data volumes. By the way, in the background, `DataSet` uses a `DataReader` to fetch the data.

A `DataSet` is a client-side cache. A `DataSet` does not lock any rows in the database, but uses the so-called optimistic locking (that is, conflicts caused by concurrent changes arise only when you try to write the data).

WARNING A `DataSet` consumes much more memory than a self-defined data structure. The fetching of data with a `DataReader`, the storing in a self-defined data structure, and the saving of changes with SQL commands are more work-intensive during developing, but they are much more efficient in the execution. This is especially important for server-based applications. It is not important for most WPS applications.

`DataSet` Object Model

A `DataSet` object consists of a number of `DataTable` objects in the `DataTableCollection`. Each `DataTable` object owns a link to the `DataSet` to which it belongs via the attribute `DataSet` (see Figure 22.1).

The `DataTable` object also contains a `DataColumnCollection` with `DataColumn` objects for each column of the table and a `DataRowCollection` with `DataRow` objects for each row. Within a `DataRow` object, you can call the contents of the cells via the indexed attribute `Item`. `Item` alternatively expects the column name, the column index, or a `DataColumn` object.

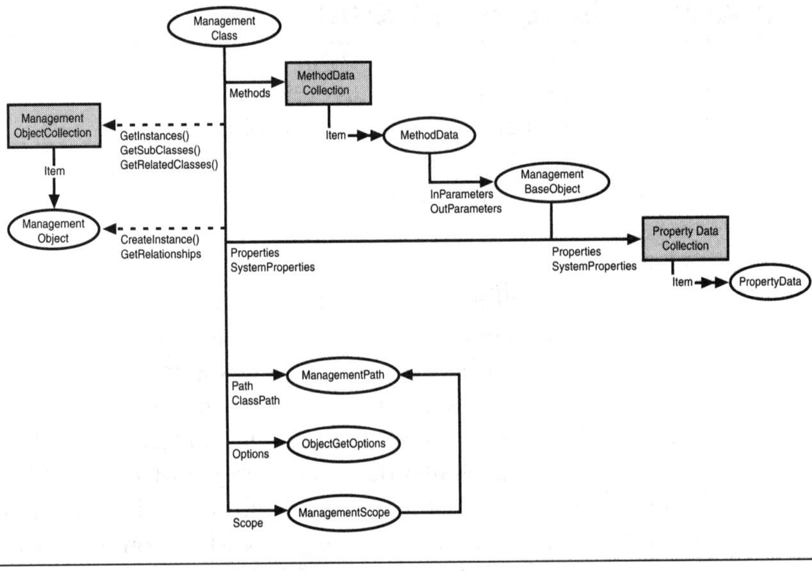

Figure 22.1 Object model of the `DataSet` class

Data Adapter

To fetch data, a `DataSet` needs a data adapter. Reading data with a `DataSet` is executed in the following steps:

1. Creation of a connection to the database with a `Connection` object. During the instantiating of the object, the string can be transferred.
2. Instantiating of the command class and connecting the object to the `Connection` object via the attribute `Connection`.
3. Setting of a SQL command that displays data (for example, `SELECT` or a stored procedure) in the `OLEDBCommand` object in the attribute `CommandText`.
4. Instantiating of the data adapter based on the command object.
5. Instantiating of the `DataSet` object (without parameter).
6. The execution of the method `Fill()` in the `DataSet` object copies the complete data in form of a `DataTable` objects in the `DataSet`. You can set the alias name for the `DataTable` object as second parameter when using `Fill()` within the `DataSet`. Without this setting, the `DataTable` object is named Table.
7. Optionally, further tables can be fetched and connected with each other in the `DataSet`.

Thereafter, the connection can be closed immediately.

Provider-Specific Example

Listing 22.1 retrieves all `DataSets` sorted from a Microsoft Access database. In this case, the OLEDB provider for ADO.NET is used. Implementation is provider specific. Figure 22.2 shows the result.

The script consists of the following steps:

1. Setting of the connection string and the SQL command to be executed
2. Instantiating of a connecting object (`OleDbConnection`) with the help of the connection string, and opening of the connection to the database
3. Creation of a command object (`OleDbCommand`) by indicating the connection object and the SQL command

4. Creation of a data adapter (`OleDbDataAdapter`) for the command
5. Instantiating of an empty data container (`DataSet`) to be filled with data
6. Filling of the data container by the data adapter with help of the method `Fill()`
7. Access to the first table in the data container (counting starts with 0)
8. Output of the data through pipelining of the table

NOTE It is not possible to access the contents of the table with `$Table.Columnname`, analogical to XML documents. According to the ADO.NET object model, the `DataTable` object does not contain the columns directly, but `DataRow` objects instead. WPS, however, can split `DataTable` objects in rows and columns when pipelining them. With single `DataRow` objects, access to the columns via their names can be executed by the automatic mapping, as follows:

```
$Table | % { $_.UserSurname }
```

You can also use two other syntax forms if the column name contains a blank:

```
$Table | % { $_["User Surname"] }
$Table | % { $_."User Surname" }
```

Listing 22.1 Database Access with a `DataSet` via a Provider-Specific Data Adapter to an Access Database

```
# Parameters
$CONNSTRING = "Provider=Microsoft.Jet.OLEDB.4.0;
➥Data Source=H:\demo\WPS\B_Database\users.mdb;"
$SQL = "Select * from users order by UserSurname"

# Open database
"Open the database..."
$conn = New-Object System.Data.OLEDB.OLEDBConnection($CONNSTRING)
$conn.open()
"Status of database: " + $conn.State
```

```
# Execute SQL command
"Execute command: " + $SQL
$cmd = New-Object System.Data.OLEDB.OLEDBCommand($sql,$conn)
$ada = New-Object System.Data.OLEDB.OLEDBDataAdapter($cmd)
$ds = New-Object System.Data.DataSet
$ada.Fill($ds, "user") | Out-null
"Number of tables in dataset: " + $ds.Tables.Count
"Number of datasets in table 1: " + $ds.Tables[0].Rows.Count

# Access to table
$Table = $ds.Tables["user"]

# Output
"Output of the data:"
$Table | Select UserFirstName, UserSurname, userid
```

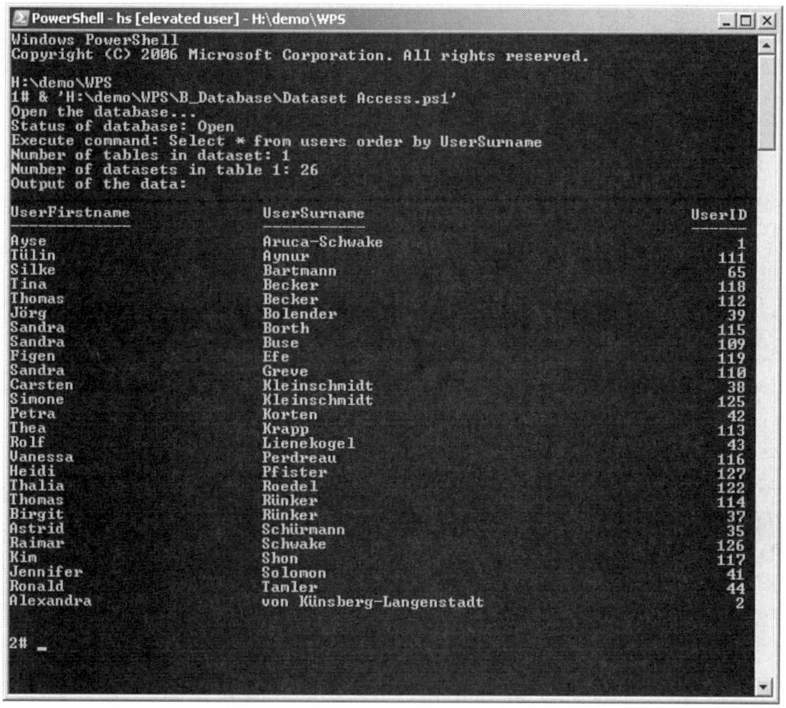

Figure 22.2 Output of the script

Provider-Independent Example

In Listing 22.2, the database adapter is created by the provider factory.

Listing 22.2 Database Access with a `DataSet` via a Provider-Neutral Data Adapter to a Microsoft SQL Server Database

```
# Parameters
$PROVIDER = "System.Data.SqlClient"
$CONNSTRING = "Data Source=.\SQLEXPRESS;AttachDbFileName=
➥H:\demo\wps\b_database\users.mdf;Integrated Security=True;"
$SQL = "Select * from users"

# Create Factory
$provider =
[System.Data.Common.DbProviderFactories]::GetFactory($PROVIDER)

# Create Connection
$conn = $provider.CreateConnection()
$conn.ConnectionString = $CONNSTRING

# Open Connection
$conn.Open();
"Status of database: " + $conn.State

# Create Command
$cmd = $provider.CreateCommand()
$cmd.CommandText = $SQL
$cmd.Connection = $conn

# Create Adapter
[System.Data.Common.DbDataAdapter] $ada =
➥$provider.CreateDataAdapter()
$ada.SelectCommand = $cmd

# Create Dataset
$ds = New-Object System.Data.DataSet
```

```
# Retrieve data
$e = $ada.Fill($ds, "User")

# Close database
$Conn.Close()
"Status of database: " + $conn.State

# Output
"Number of Tables: " + $ds.Tables.Count
"Number of Rows in Table 1: " + $ds.Tables[0].Rows.Count

# Access table
$Table = $ds.Tables[0]

# Print all rows
"Rows:"
$Table | Select UserFirstName, UserSurname, userid
```


XML Export and Import

Single data tables or whole DataSets with multiple tables can be exported to XML files:

```
...
# Export to XML
$Table.WriteXml("H:\demo\WPS\B_Database\users.xml")
$Table.WriteXmlSchema("H:\demo\WPS\B_Database\users.xsd")
```

The export of the XML Schema (XSD) is useful for the later re-import of the XML document to a DataSet:

```
# Import DataSet XML
$Table = New-Object System.Data.DataTable
$Table.ReadXmlSchema("H:\demo\WPS\B_Database\users.xsd")
$Table.ReadXml("H:\demo\WPS\B_Database\users.xml")
$Table | ft
```

Data Access with the www.IT-Visions.de PowerShell Extensions

Data access through ADO.NET classes is somewhat "gossip" because of the necessary handling of connections, commands, and adapters. However, in most cases, only standard options are required.

The www.IT-Visions.de PowerShell extensions provide the following commandlets to facilitate data access:

- `Test-DbConnection` Shows (`True/False`), if a connection can be created.
- `Invoke-DbCommand` Executes an SQL command on the data source. The return value is a number indicating how many rows were affected.
- `Get-DataTable` Displays a data volume according to an SQL command from a data source in form of a volume of `DataRow` objects (see Figure 22.3).
- `Get-DataRow` Delivers a row from a data source in the form of an ADO.NET `DataRow` object. If the indicated SQL command retrieves more than one row, only the first row is displayed (see Figure 22.4).
- `Set-DataTable` Saves changes in a `DataTable` object in the data source.
- `Set-DataRow` Saves changes in a `DataRow` object in the data source.

All commandlets are based on provider-neutral programming. As long as commandlets expect a connecting string, they also allow the setting of a provider (parameter `-Provider`). The setting of a provider is the optional, standard setting `"MSSQL"`. Other possible values are `"OLEDB"`, `"ODBC"`, `"ORACLE"`, and `"ACCESS"`. Note that these short forms are expected, not the full provider-invariant name.

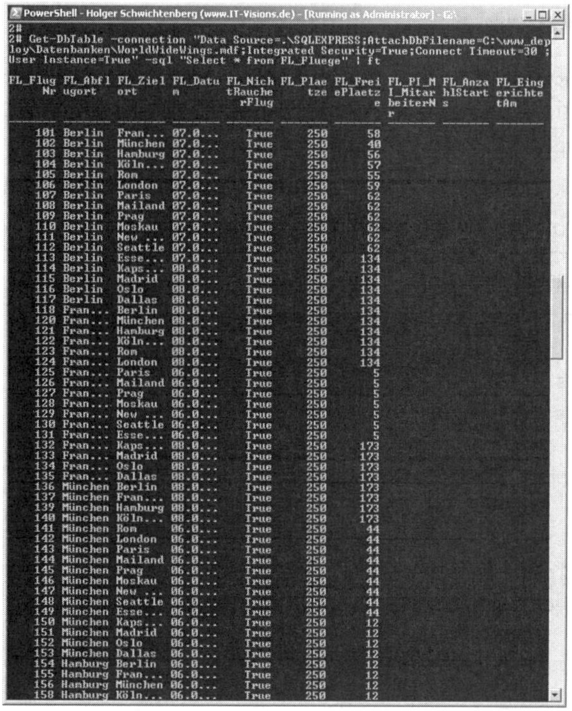

Figure 22.3 Use of `Get-DataTable` to access a Microsoft SQL Server table containing flight data

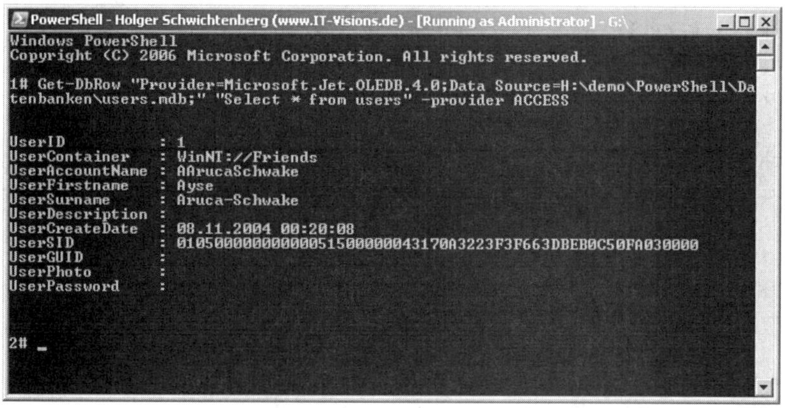

Figure 22.4 Use of `Get-DataRow` to access the first dataset in an Access table

Example

The script in Listing 22.3 shows the previously discussed commandlets in action. The script executes all jobs of the prior scripts, but much more concisely! (Figure 22.5 shows the output.)

Listing 22.3 Database Access with the PowerShell Extensions of www.IT-Visions.de

```
# Requirements: www.IT-Visions.de Commandlet Extension Library
# http://www.PowerShell doctor.de

# Parameters
$SQL = "Select * from users order by UserSurname"
$Conn = "Provider=Microsoft.Jet.OLEDB.4.0;Data
Source=H:\demo\PowerShell\B_Databases\users.mdb;"
$Provider = "ACCESS"

"----------Test database connections:"
test-dbconnection -connection $Conn  -provider $Provider

"---------- Execute Commands:"

$SQL1 = "Select count(*) from users"
$SQL2 = "insert into users ( UserFirstName,
➥UserSurname) values ('Hans', 'Meier')"
$SQL3 = "delete from users where UserSurname='Meier'"

invoke-ScalarDbCommand -connection $Conn
➥-sql $SQL1 -provider $Provider
invoke-DbCommand -connection $Conn
➥-sql $SQL2 -provider $Provider
invoke-ScalarDbCommand -connection $Conn
➥-sql $SQL1 -provider $Provider
invoke-DbCommand -connection $Conn
➥-sql $SQL3 -provider $Provider
invoke-ScalarDbCommand -connection $Conn
➥-sql $SQL1 -provider $Provider

"---------- Get Data "
$table = Get-DbTable -connection $Conn
➥-sql $SQL -provider  $Provider
$table | ft
```

```
"---------- Select Row "
$row = $table | where  { $_.usersurname -eq "Pfister" }
$Row

"---------- Change Row "
$row.UsercreateDate = [DateTime] "11/11/2005"
$Row

"---------- Update Data "
$table | Set-DbTable -connection $Conn -sql $sql
➥-provider  $Provider  -verbose

"---------- Get Row"
$SQL = "Select * from users where usersurname = 'Pfister'"
$row = Get-DbRow $Conn $SQL $Provider
$row
```

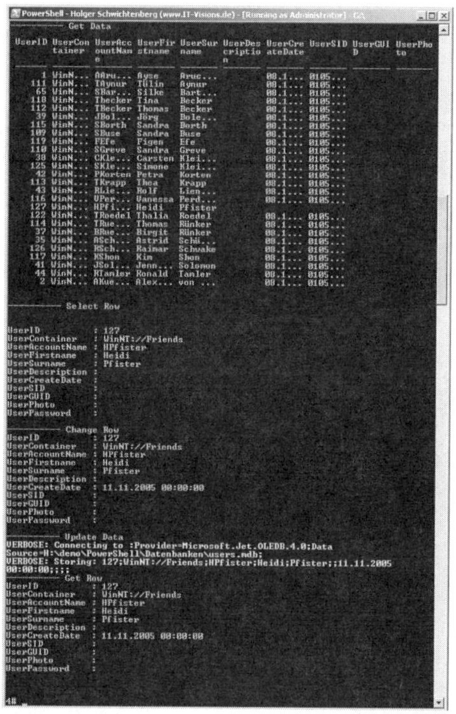

Figure 22.5 Output of the script in Listing 22.3

Summary

In this chapter, you learned how to use the `DataSet` as a disconnected offline cache for data. This use, in contrast to the `DataReader`, allows changing data and writing the changes back to the database through the use of a data adapter.

However, you saw that a few steps are necessary each time you work with a `DataSet`. This can be shortened a lot by the use of the www.IT-Visions.de PowerShell Extension Library, which provides easy-to-use commandlets such as the following:

```
Test-DbConnection
Invoke-DbCommand
Get-DataTable
Get-DataRow
Set-DataTable
Set-DataRow
```

CHAPTER 23

Security Settings

In this chapter:

This chapter covers the management of access control lists for files, directories, and registry keys. The access control list is a crucial concept of Windows that controls access to resources. Resources such as file system objects and registry entries are protected by access control lists (ACLs). Windows PowerShell (WPS) offers two built-in commandlets for working with ACLs:

- `Get-Acl` Read the ACL of a resource
- `Set-Acl` Write the ACL of a resource

They include the basic functions of downloading and saving an ACL, depending on the displayed resource path. With WPS 1.0, however, only the file system and the registry are supported.

NOTE Besides the previously named commandlets, you need some knowledge from the .NET namespace `System.Security.AccessControl` for the manipulation of ACLs.

Windows Security Basics

For a better understanding using and changing security settings, the basics of Windows security are presented here.

Accounts

User and groups are entities that can have rights on resources. There are three different ways to describe an account:

- Account name (for example, \\itv\hs)
- Security identifier, SID (for example, S-1-5-32-544)
- SDDL security identifier (for example, "BA")

A SID is a number array in variable length. In text form, the SID is indicated with a starting *S*.

Security Descriptors

Each resource (for example, a file, a folder, an entry in the Active Directory, a registry key) possesses a so-called *security descriptor* (SD) for the saving of the access controls. An SD consists of three parts:

- The owner's security identifier (SID) of the account
- The discretionary ACL (DACL), which describes the access control
- The system ACL (SACL), which contains the auditing settings

Access Control Lists

An access control list (ACL) (DACL and SACL) consists of access control entries (ACEs). In turn, an ACE contains the following information:

- **Identity (trustee).** The SID of the user or the group of users.
- **Access mask.** The access mask defines the rights for the trustee. For each object type (for example, file system entry, registry entry, Active Directory entry), there are different possible rights a trustee can receive. Each right is a bit of a combination of bits with a 32-bit integer value. As a rule, an access mask consists of an addition of several single access rights.

- **Access control type.** The type is either `ALLOW` or `DENY`.
- **Inheritance flags.** Inheritance of rights is controlled via the inheritance flags. `ObjectInherit` means that subordinated leaf objects (for example, files in the file system) derive their setting from the ACE. `ContainerInherit` means that subordinated container objects derive their setting from the ACE (for example, folder in the file system). `ObjectInherit` and `ContainerInherit` can be combined. Alternatively, you can define that no inheritance takes place (`NONE`).
- **Propagation flags.** Inheritance is further controlled via the propagation flags. `InheritOnly` means that the ACE is derived only, but does not work on the current object itself. `NoPropagateInherit` means that the ACE is derived but cannot be derived again by the deriving objects.

Access Masks

Table 23.1 contains the possible rights for entries in the file system.

NOTE The following table is quoted unchanged from the MSDN documentation [MSDN01]. The author of the table is Microsoft.

Table 23.1 Access Rights on the Windows File System

Right	Description
`AppendData`	Specifies the right to append data to the end of a file.
`ChangePermissions`	Specifies the right to change the security and audit rules associated with a file or folder.
`CreateDirectories`	Specifies the right to create a folder. This right requires the `Synchronize` value. Note that if you do not explicitly set the `Synchronize` value when creating a file or folder, the `Synchronize` value will be set automatically for you.

(continues)

Table 23.1 Access Rights on the Windows File System *(continued)*

Right	Description
`CreateFiles`	Specifies the right to create a file. This right requires the `Synchronize` value. Note that if you do not explicitly set the `Synchronize` value when creating a file or folder, the `Synchronize` value will be set automatically for you.
`Delete`	Specifies the right to delete a folder or file.
`DeleteSubdirectoriesAndFiles`	Specifies the right to delete a folder and any files contained within that folder.
`ExecuteFile`	Specifies the right to run an application file.
`FullControl`	Specifies the right to exert full control over a folder or file, and to modify access control and audit rules. This value represents the right to do anything with a file and is the combination of all rights in this enumeration.
`ListDirectory`	Specifies the right to read the contents of a directory.
`Modify`	Specifies the right to read, write, list folder contents, delete folders and files, and run application files. This right includes the `ReadAndExecute` right, the `Write` right, and the `Delete` right.
`Read`	Specifies the right to open and copy folders or files as read-only. This right includes the `ReadData` right, `ReadExtendedAttributes` right, `ReadAttributes` right, and `ReadPermissions` right.
`ReadAndExecute`	Specifies the right to open and copy folders or files as read-only, and to run application files. This right includes the `Read` right and the `ExecuteFile` right.
`ReadAttributes`	Specifies the right to open and copy file system attributes from a folder or file. For example, this value specifies the right to view the file creation or modified date. This does not include the right to read data, extended file system attributes, or access and audit rules.

Right	Description
`ReadData`	Specifies the right to open and copy a file or folder. This does not include the right to read file system attributes, extended file system attributes, or access and audit rules.
`ReadExtendedAttributes`	Specifies the right to open and copy extended file system attributes from a folder or file. For example, this value specifies the right to view author and content information. This does not include the right to read data, file system attributes, or access and audit rules.
`ReadPermissions`	Specifies the right to open and copy access and audit rules from a folder or file. This does not include the right to read data, file system attributes, and extended file system attributes.
`Synchronize`	Specifies whether the application can wait for a file handle to synchronize with the completion of an I/O operation. The `Synchronize` value is automatically set when allowing access, and automatically excluded when denying access. The right to create a file or folder requires this value. Note that if you do not explicitly set this value when creating a file, the value will be set automatically for you.
`TakeOwnership`	Specifies the right to change the owner of a folder or file. Note that owners of a resource have full access to that resource.
`Traverse`	Specifies the right to list the contents of a folder and to run applications contained within that folder.
`Write`	Specifies the right to create folders and files, and to add or remove data from files. This right includes the `WriteData` right, `AppendData` right, `WriteExtendedAttributes` right, and `WriteAttributes` right.
`WriteAttributes`	Specifies the right to open and write file system attributes to a folder or file. This does not include the ability to write data, extended attributes, or access and audit rules.

(continues)

Table 23.1 Access Rights on the Windows File System *(continued)*

Right	Description
`WriteData`	Specifies the right to open and write to a file or folder. This does not include the right to open and write file system attributes, extended file system attributes, or access and audit rules.
`WriteExtendedAttributes`	Specifies the right to open and write extended file system attributes to a folder or file. This does not include the ability to write data, attributes, or access and audit rules.

Classes

The namespace `System.Security.AccessControl` contains numerous classes for the administration of rights (ACLs). For each kind of resource whose ACLs can be administered, the namespace `AccessControl` offers one class derived from `System.Security.AccessControl.ObjectSecurity`. For example, `System.Security.AccessControl.FileSecurity` is used to read and process the ACLs of a file in the file system.

Figure 23.1 shows these classes in the inheritance tree of the .NET class library. The other resources indicated there (for example, Active Directory) cannot yet be called via `Get-Acl`. A direct call via the .NET class library, however, is possible.

Members of the Class Object Security

The basic class `ObjectSecurity` derives, among others, the following members, so that they are provided in all subordinate classes:

- `GetOwner()` Displays the owner of the resource.
- `SetOwner()` Sets the owner of the resource.
- `GetAccessRules()` Displays a list of ACEs. The return value has the type `AuthorizationRuleCollection`. The contained objects are dependent on the resource type (for example, `FileSystemAccessRule` or `RegistryAccessRule`).

- `GetAuditRules()` Displays the entries of the system ACL (SACL).
- `IsSddlConversionSupported` Indicates, whether the ACL can be expressed in SDDL.
- `GetSecurityDescriptorSddlForm()` Delivers the ACL as an SDDL string.

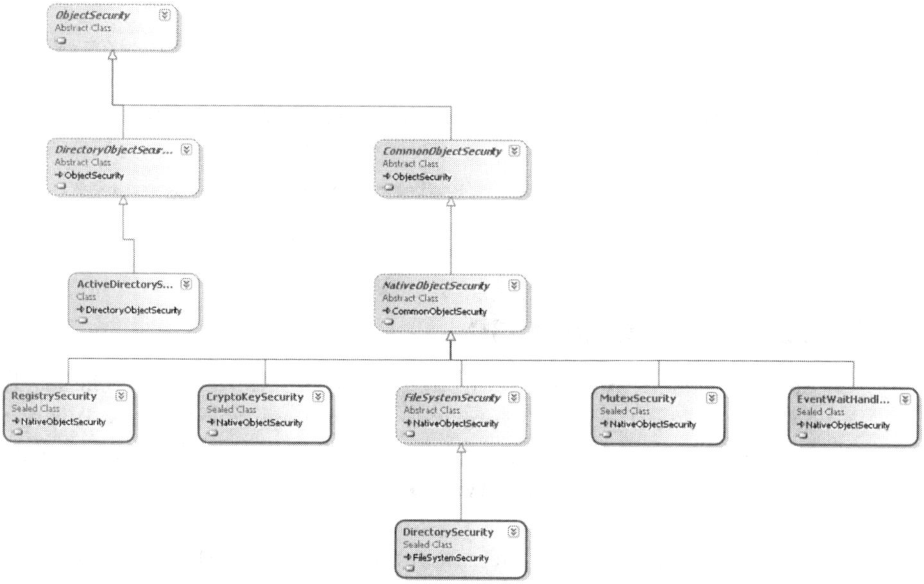

Figure 23.1 Inheritance hierarchy of the classes used for the saving of the ACL

Resource Classes

Throughout the whole .NET class library, you will find classes that possess a method `GetAccessControl()` and display an object derived from the class `ObjectSecurity` (see Table 23.2).

Table 23.2 Security Classes for Different Resources

Resource Class	Class for ACL	Class for ACE	Enumeration for Rights
`System.IO.File`	`FileSystemSecurity`	`FileSystemAccessRule`	`FileSystemRights`
`System.IO.Directory`	`DirectorySecurity`	`FileSystemAccessRule`	`FileSystemRights`
`System.IO.FileInfo`	`FileSystemSecurity`	`FileSystemAccessRule`	`FileSystemRights`
`System.IO.DirectoryInfo`	`DirectorySecurity`	`FileSystemAccessRule`	`FileSystemRights`
`Microsoft.Win32.RegistryKey`	`RegistrySecurity`	`RegistryAccessRule`	`RegistryRights`

User Accounts and SIDs

The namespace `System.Security.AccessControl` uses classes from `System.Security.Principal` to present control holders (users and groups). `System.Security.Principal` supports the two indicators known for control holders in Windows:

- Account name (for example, ITVisions\hs) via the class `System.Security.Principal.NTAccount`
- Security Identifier (for example, S-1-5-21-565061207-3232948068-1095265983-500) via the class `System.Security.Principal.SecurityIdentifier`

Reading ACLs

`Get-Acl` provides instances of the following .NET classes, depending on the resource type:

- `System.Security.AccessControl.DirectorySecurity` (for directories)
- `System.Security.AccessControl.FileSecurity` (for files)

- `System.Security.AccessControl.RegistrySecurity` (for registry keys)

`Get-Acl` expects as a parameter the path of the resource whose ACL will be displayed, as follows:

```
Get-Acl hklm:/software/www.IT-visions.de
Get-Acl j:\projects
Get-Acl j:\projects\content.csv
```

Standard output is executed with `Format-Table`. The output with `Format-List` is obvious, and the output is thus easier to read.

Figure 23.2 demonstrates the application of `Get-Acl` to a directory in the file system. Figure 23.3 shows the same ACL in Windows Explorer.

NOTE Note that `Access` is not an attribute of the .NET class `ObjectSecurity`; instead it is a PowerShell code property that calls `GetAccessRules()` internally. The return value is in both cases an `AuthorizationRuleCollection`.

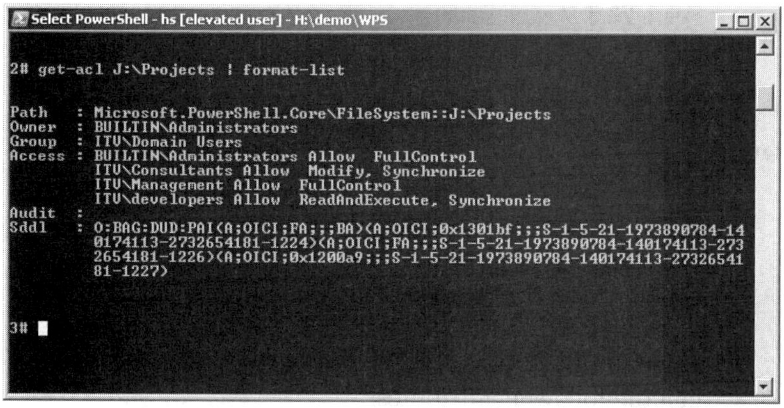

Figure 23.2 Fetching an ACL

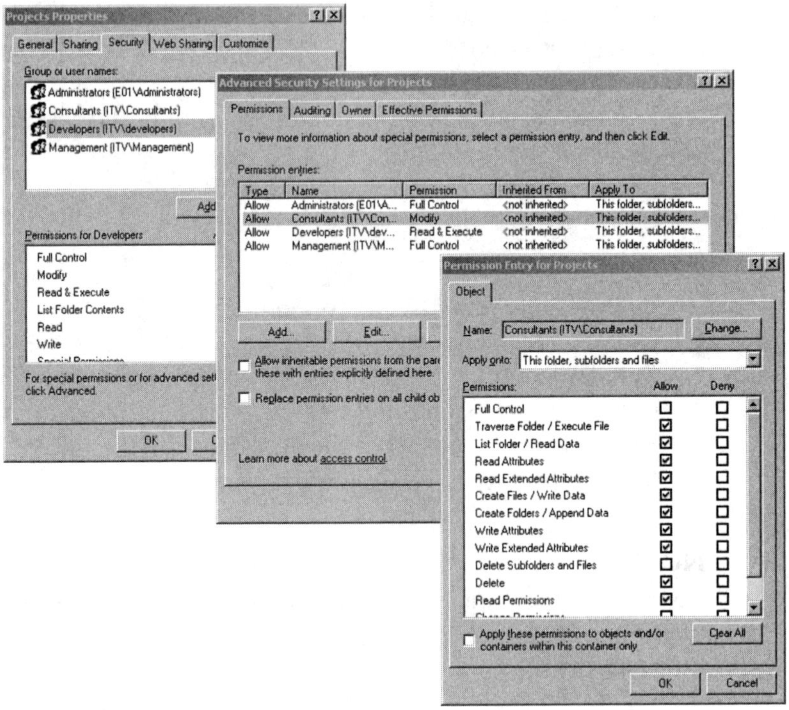

Figure 23.3 Actual settings

Reading ACEs

If you want to take a closer look at the single ACEs of a system module, you should iterate via the ACL yourself. The list of the type `AuthorizationRuleCollection` displayed by `Access` or `GetAccessRules()` contains, as far as the file system is concerned, objects of the type `FileSystemAccessRule`. These objects, in turn, contain the following attributes:

- `IdentityReference` Subject (user or group) holding access control
- `FileSystemRights` Rights
- `AccessControlType` Control type (allowed or denied)
- `IsInherited` Indicates, whether the rule is inherited
- `InheritanceFlags` Indicates the kind of downward derivation

User accounts can be expressed in two ways: in clear text or via SIDs. When you use `GetAccessRules()`, you have to indicate how you want to view the user: `[System.Security.Principal.NTAccount]` (clear text) or `[System.Security.Principal.SecurityIdentifier]` (SID). Before this, the method has two parameters that enable you to control which rules you want to look at: the rules set explicitly on the object (first parameter) and the inherited rules (second parameter). Explicit ACEs always hold the first place in the list.

Code property access is equivalent to `GetAccessRules($true, $true, [System.Security.Principal.NTAccount])`. If you want to get other information, you have to use `GetAccessRules()` explicitly. In Listing 23.1, the second output of the list (see Figure 23.4) shows only the inherited rules in SID form.

Listing 23.1 Display Details from the ACEs

```
$a = Get-Acl "j:\projects\"
$aces =$a.access
# or: $aces =$a.GetAccessRules($true, $true,
➥[System.Security.Principal.NTAccount])

Write-Host "All ACEs, account name form:" -F yellow
foreach ($ace in $aces)
{
write-host $ace.IdentityReference.ToString() " has "
➥$ACE.FileSystemRights $ACE.AccessControlType " Inherited?"
➥$ACE.IsInherited
}

# --------
$a = Get-Acl j:\projects
$aces =$a.GetAccessRules($true, $false,
[System.Security.Principal.SecurityIdentifier])
Write-Host  "Only explicit rules, SID form:"  -F yellow
foreach ($ace in $aces)
{
write-host $ace.IdentityReference.ToString() " has "
➥$ACE.FileSystemRights $ACE.AccessControlType " Inherited?"
➥$ACE.IsInherited
}
```

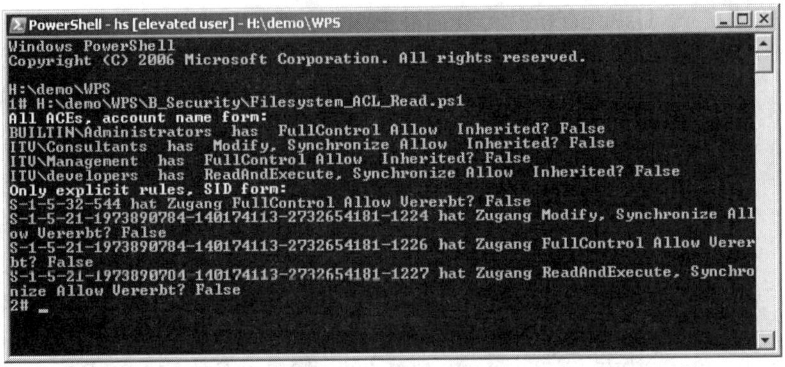

Figure 23.4 Output of the script in Listing 23.1

Summary

The programmatic access to security settings is one of the most difficult areas of system administration. In this chapter, you learned about the use of the commandlets `Get-Acl` and `Set-Acl` in connection with the .NET classes from the `System.Security.AccessControl` library. You learned how to display ACLs and how to access each ACE within the list.

CHAPTER 24

ADVANCED SECURITY ADMINISTRATION

In this chapter:

This last chapter covers all the write operations that can be performed on access control lists (ACLs) and access control entries (ACEs). Examples in this chapter include

- Reading the owner of a resource
- Adding a new access control entry to access control lists
- Removing an access control entry from an access control list
- Transferring access control lists from one resource to another
- Setting access control lists using the Security Descriptor Definition Language (SDDL)

Account Identifier Translation

As we prepare to modify ACLs, you learn in this section three different ways of representing accounts and about the conversion between them.

Converting between Username and Security Identifier

If you want to display the security identifier (SID) of any user (see Listing 24.1), you can also create an instance of `System.Security.Principal.NtAccount` by indicating the username in text form and calling `Translate()` afterward.

Listing 24.1 Displaying the SID

```
# Translate account name to SID
$Account = new-object system.security.principal.ntaccount("itv\hs")
$SID =
➥$Account.Translate([system.security.principal.securityidentifier]).value
➥$SID

# Translate SID to account name
$Account = new-object system.security.principal.securityidentifier
➥("S-1-5-32-544")
$Name = $Account.Translate([system.security.principal.ntaccount]).value
$Name
```

Using Well-Known SIDs

Besides users and groups, Windows also knows pseudo-groups such as Everybody, Interactive User, and System. These groups are called *well-known security principals*. To change the security settings, you need the SIDs shown in Table 24.1. (Listing 24.2 shows access via an SID.) In the Active Directory, the well-known security principals are saved in the `ConfigurationNamingContext` in the container `cn=Well Known Security Principals`. However, you will not find these users in the `DefaultNamingContext`.

WARNING Do not confuse the well-known security principals with the built-in accounts (for example, Guests, Administrators, Users). You will find the latter in the Active Directory in the `DefaultNamingContext` in `cn=BuiltIn`.

Table 24.1 SIDs of the Well-Known Security Principals

Well-Known Security Principal	SID
Anonymous logon	1;1;0;0;0;0;5;7;0;0;0
Authenticated users	1;1;0;0;0;0;5;11;0;0;0
Batch	1;1;0;0;0;0;5;3;0;0;0
Creator group	1;1;0;0;0;0;3;1;0;0;0
Creator owner	1;1;0;0;0;0;3;0;0;0;0
Dialup	1;1;0;0;0;0;5;1;0;0;0
Enterprise domain controllers	1;1;0;0;0;0;5;9;0;0;0
Everyone	1;1;0;0;0;0;1;0;0;0;0
Interactive	1;1;0;0;0;0;5;4;0;0;0
Network	1;1;0;0;0;0;5;2;0;0;0
Proxy	1;1;0;0;0;0;5;8;0;0;0
Restricted	1;1;0;0;0;0;5;12;0;0;0
Self	1;1;0;0;0;0;5;10;0;0;0
Service	1;1;0;0;0;0;5;6;0;0;0
System	1;1;0;0;0;0;5;18;0;0;0
Terminal server user	1;1;0;0;0;0;5;13;0;0;0

The .NET class library provides an enumeration `System.Security.Principal.WellKnownSidType` that you can use for the instancing of the class `SecurityIdentifier`. You can thus avoid the language-specific differences of the operating system (for example, the English Guests is named Gäste on German operating systems).

Listing 24.2 Access to an Account via the SID

```
# Well-Known Security Identifier
$SID = [System.Security.Principal.WellKnownSidType]::
➥BuiltinAdministratorsSid
$Account = new-object system.security.principal.securityidentifier
➥($SID, $zero)
$Name = $Account.Translate([system.security.principal.ntaccount]).value
$Name
```

Some built-in users and groups contain the SID of the domain within their own SID. In this case, when an instancing of the class `SecurityIdentifier` is executed, the domain SID has also to be indicated. Unfortunately, the documentation remains silent with regard to how the domain SID can be fetched with .NET methods. Even on the World Wide Web, there is not yet an example for this.

SDDL Names

Another possibility for an access to built-in users and groups is the use of the abbreviations for built-in users and groups (see Table 24.2 and Listing 24.3) as defined in the Security Descriptor Definition Language (SDDL).

Listing 24.3 Displaying a SID from an SDDL Abbreviation

```
# SDDL name
$Account = new-object System.Security.Principal.SecurityIdentifier("BA")
$Account.Value
```

Table 24.2 SDDL Abbreviations for Built-In Users and Groups

SDDL Abbreviation	Meaning
"AO"	Account operators
"AN"	Anonymous logon
"AU"	Authenticated users
"BA"	Built-in administrators
"BG"	Built-in guests
"BO"	Backup operators
"BU"	Built-in users
"CA"	Certificate server administrators
"CG"	Creator group
"CO"	Creator owner
"DA"	Domain administrators
"DC"	Domain computers
"DD"	Domain controllers
"DG"	Domain guests

SDDL Abbreviation	Meaning
"DU"	Domain users
"EA"	Enterprise administrators
"ED"	Enterprise domain controllers
"WD"	Everyone
"PA"	Group Policy administrators
"IU"	Interactively logged-on user
"LA"	Local administrator
"LG"	Local guest
"LS"	Local service account
"SY"	Local system
"NU"	Network logon user
"NO"	Network configuration operators
"NS"	Network service account
"PO"	Printer operators
"PS"	Personal self
"PU"	Power users
"RS"	RAS servers group
"RD"	Terminal server users
"RE"	Replicator
"RC"	Restricted code
"SA"	Schema administrators
"SO"	Server operators
"SU"	Service logon user

Reading the Owner

You can read the owner of a system module via the code property `Owner` from the object derived from `ObjectSecurity` and extended by Windows PowerShell (WPS), which `Get-Acl` retrieves. Alternatively, you can use `GetOwner()` and choose again which form is to be used (see Listing 24.4). Conversion between the two forms of the user presentation is also possible with the method `Translate()`.

Listing 24.4 Read User Information

```
"owner information:"
$a = Get-Acl j:\projects
$a.Owner
$a.GetOwner([System.Security.Principal.NTAccount]).Value
$a.GetOwner([System.Security.Principal.SecurityIdentifier]).Value

# Converting between account name and SID
$account = $a.GetOwner([System.Security.Principal.NTAccount])
$account.Translate([system.security.principal.securityidentifier]).value

# Converting between SID and account name
$account = $a.GetOwner([System.Security.Principal.SecurityIdentifier])
$account.Translate([system.security.principal.NTAccount]).value
```

Adding a New ACE to an ACL

Listing 24.5 demonstrates the adding of an ACE to an ACL of a file in the file system. New ACEs of the type `FileSystemAccessRule` need five indications:

- Account object (`NTAccount` object or `SecurityIdentifier` object)
- Access control rights to be granted (values from the `FileSystemRights` enumeration)
- Targets of the inheritance (values from the `InheritanceFlags` enumeration)
- Type of inheritance (values from the `PropagationFlags` enumeration)
- Type of rule: Allow or deny (values from the `AccessControlType` enumeration)

The following script grants a user reading rights to a directory (see Figures 24.1 and 24.2).

Listing 24.5 Add an ACE

```
# Adding an ACE to an ACL: Set read permissions for a user

# Parameters
$DIR = "j:\projects"
$USER = "HS"

# Get ACL
$ACL = Get-Acl  $DIR

"ACL before:"
$acl | format-list

# Define ACE
$Rights = [System.Security.AccessControl.FileSystemRights]
➥"ReadData, ReadExtendedAttributes, ReadAttributes, ReadPermissions"
$Access=[System.Security.AccessControl.AccessControlType]::Allow
$Inherit=[System.Security.AccessControl.InheritanceFlags]::
➥ContainerInherit `
        -bor [System.Security.AccessControl.InheritanceFlags]::
➥ObjectInherit
$Prop=[System.Security.AccessControl.PropagationFlags]::InheritOnly
$AccessRule =
➥new-object System.Security.AccessControl.FileSystemAccessRule `
($USER,$Rights,$Inherit,$Prop,$Access)

# Add ACL to ACE
$ACL.AddAccessRule($AccessRule)

# Save ACL
Set-Acl -AclObject $ACL -Path $DIR

# Controle
$ACL = Get-Acl  $DIR

"ACL afterwards:"
$acl | format-list
```

TIP When several flags have to be set in a parameter, they have to be linked together through an OR (operator `-bor` in WPS language):

```
$Rights= [System.Security.AccessControl.FileSystemRights]::
➥Read `
-bor [System.Security.AccessControl.FileSystemRights]::
➥ReadExtendedAttributes `
-bor [System.Security.AccessControl.FileSystemRights]::
➥ReadAttributes `
-bor [System.Security.AccessControl.FileSystemRights]::
➥ReadPermissions
```

To be more concise, you can also write the enumeration values in a string, separated by commas:

```
$Rights = [System.Security.AccessControl.FileSystemRights]
➥"ReadData, ReadExtendedAttributes, ReadAttributes,
➥ReadPermissions"
```

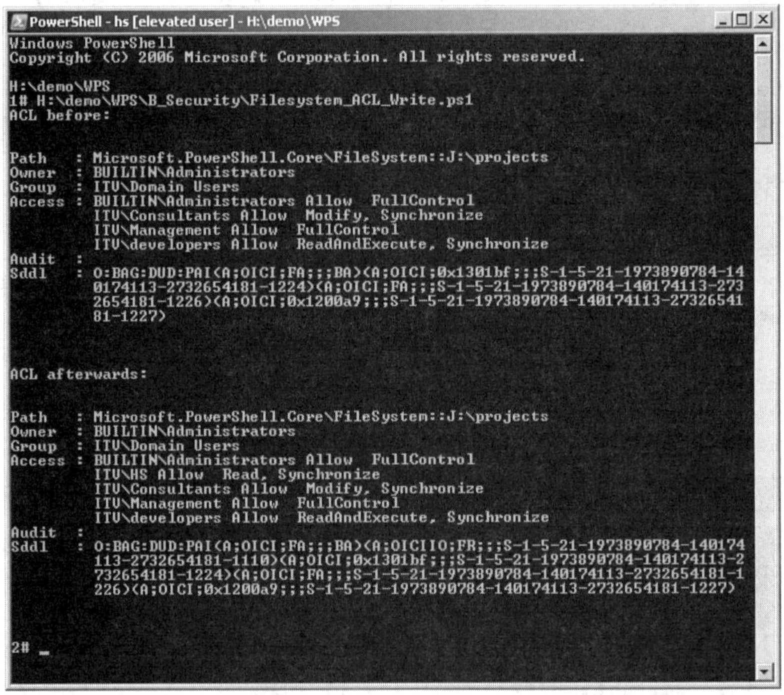

Figure 24.1 Execution of a script that grants reading rights to a user

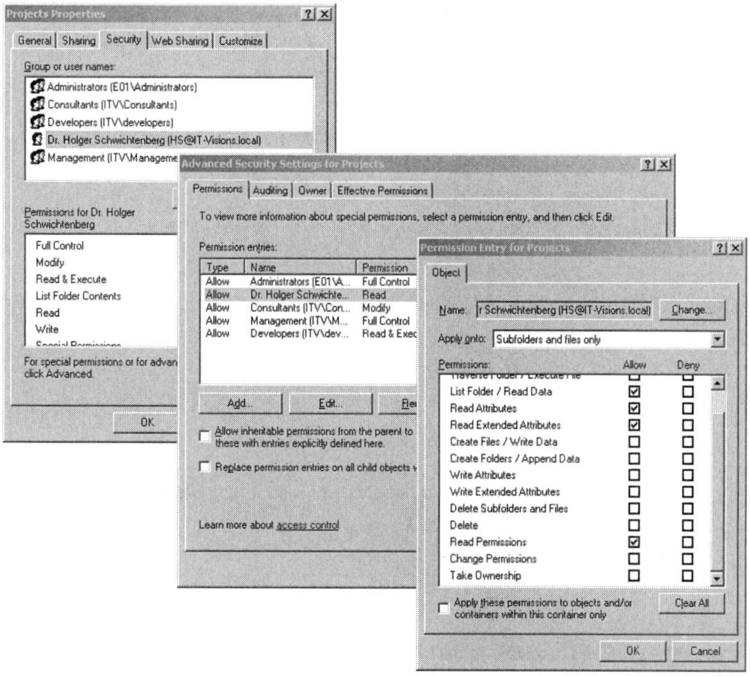

Figure 24.2 View of the rights in Windows Explorer

Removing an ACE from an ACL

To remove an ACE from the ACL, you can use the method `RemoveAccessRule()`, which is inherited from `NativeObjectSecurity` by all access control classes. The method expects an object of the type `AccessContolEntry` as a parameter.

In case you want to remove all entries belonging to a user, you can use `PurgeAccessRules()` and indicate a user account object (not the account name).

Example 1

The script in Listing 24.6 deletes all ACEs belonging to a certain user from the ACL.

Listing 24.6 Write ACL: Delete All ACEs of a User

```
# Parameters
$DIR = "j:\projects"
$USER = "itv\HS"
$Count = 0

# Control output
$acl = Get-Acl  $DIR
"ACL previously:"
$acl | format-list

# Get ACL
$acl = Get-Acl j:\projects

$Account = new-object system.security.principal.ntaccount("itv\hs")
$acl.PurgeAccessRules($Account)
set-acl -AclObject $ACL -Path $DIR

# Save ACL
set-acl -AclObject $ACL -Path $DIR

# Check output
$acl = Get-Acl  $DIR
"ACL afterwards:"
$acl | format-list
```

Example 2

The script in Listing 24.7 deletes all ACEs from the ACL in which the right to read and write has been granted (`"ReadAndExecute"`). Figure 24.3 shows the result.

Listing 24.7 Deleting ACEs from an ACL

```
# Write ACL: Delete all access control entries from an access control
➥list, which contain the right to read and execute ("ReadAndExecute")

# Parameters
$DIR = "j:\projects"
```

```
$USER = "itv\HS"
$Count = 0

# Control output
$acl = Get-Acl  $DIR
"ACL previously:"
$acl | format-list

# Get ACL
$acl = Get-Acl j:\projects

# Access to ACEs
$aces =$acl.GetAccessRules($true, $true,
➥[System.Security.Principal.NTAccount])

# Loop over all ACEs
foreach ($ace in $aces)
{
Write-host $ace.IdentityReference.ToString() " has right "
➥$ACE.FileSystemRights $ACE.AccessControlType " Inherited?"
➥$ACE.IsInherited
# Selectively deleting
if ($ace.FileSystemRights.ToString() -match "ReadAndExecute")
 {
  "...will be removed..."
  $Result = $acl.RemoveAccessRule($ace)
if ($REsult) { echo "Has been removed!"; $Count++ }
 }
}

# Save ACL
set-acl -AclObject $ACL -Path $DIR

echo ($Count.ToString() + " ACEs have been removed!")

# Control output
$acl = Get-Acl  $DIR
"ACL afterwards:"
$acl | format-list
```

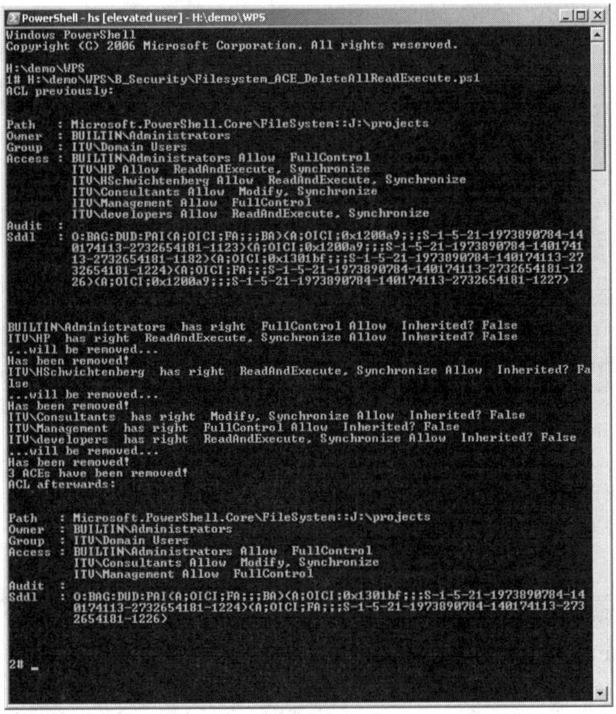

Figure 24.3 Three ACEs have been removed.

Transferring ACLs

The combination of `Get-Acl` and `Set-Acl` enables an easy transfer of an ACL from one file system object to another:

Listing 24.8 `File System_ACL_transfer.ps1`

```
# Transfer an ACL from one folder to another
Get-Acl j:\projects | Set-Acl j:\customers

# Transfer an ACL from one file to a volume of files
$acl = Get-Acl j:\projects
Get-ChildItem g:\data | foreach-object { Set-Acl $_.Fullname $acl;
➥"transfer to $_" }
```

Setting ACLs Using SDDL

The Security Descriptor Definition Language (SDDL) is a text format for the description of ACLs with single ACEs in Windows (introduced with Windows 2000).

An example for a SDDL string is as follows:

```
O:BAG:DUD:PAI(A;;FA;;;BA)(A;OICI;0x1600a9;;;S-1-5-21-
➥1973890784-140174113-2732654181-1188)
➥(A;OICI;0x1200a9;;;S-1-5-21-1973890784-
➥140174113-2732654181-1189)
```

Example

The script in Listing 24.9 uses SDDL to transfer an ACL from one directory to another. In the meantime, the ACL is stored in the file system (`acl.txt`) so that reading and setting are independent from each other, as regards timing (see Figures 24.4 and 24.5).

Listing 24.9 Transfer of Permissions Using SDDL

```
# Transferring an ACL via SDDL

$SOURCE = "j:\projects"
$TARGET = "j:\software"

function replace-acl
{
Param (
  $Object,
  $SDDL
  )
  $acl = Get-Acl $Object
  $acl.SetSecurityDescriptorSddlForm($SDDL)

  Set-Acl -aclObject $acl $Object
}

# Read and save SDDL in a text file
```

(continues)

Listing 24.9 Transfer of Permissions Using SDDL *(continued)*

```
(Get-Acl $SOURCE).SDDL > h:\demo\wps\b_security\acl.txt

# Read SDDL from text file
$sddl = Get-Content h:\demo\wps\b_security\acl.txt
replace-acl $TARGET $sddl

"The following rights have been transferred: " + $sddl
```

Figure 24.4 Successful export and import of rights using SDDL

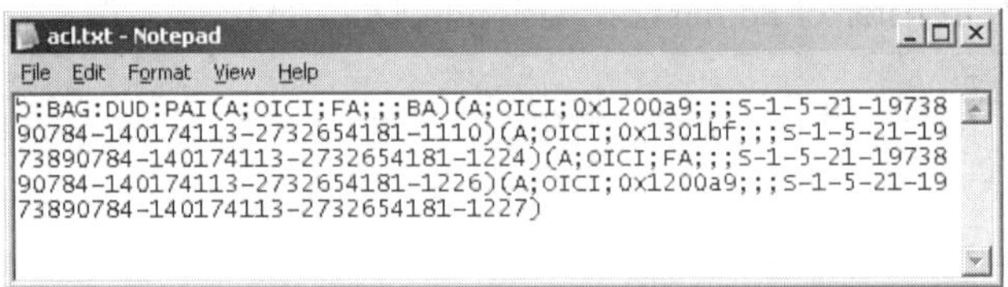

Figure 24.5 Saved ACL in SSDL form

Summary

In this last chapter of this book, you learned how to work with different security account identifiers (account name, SID, well-known security identifiers), how to read ACEs, and how to remove them from an ACL.

Also, this chapter covered the transfer of an ACL from one resource to another. The SDDL is a text representation of an ACL. This enables you to save an ACL to a file and later write the ACL back to the same or another resource.

PART III

APPENDICES

APPENDIX A

PowerShell Commandlet Reference

This appendix contains a list of all commandlets that are part of Windows PowerShell (WPS) 1.0, PowerShell Community Extensions Version 1.1.1 (PSCX), and www.IT-Visions.de PowerShell Extensions Version 2.0.

Commandlet	Description	Product/Version
`Add-Content`	Adds content to the specified item(s).	WPS 1.0
`Add-DirectoryEntry`	Adds a directory entry to a container.	www.IT-Visions.de PowerShell Extensions 2.0
`Add-History`	Appends entries to the session history.	WPS 1.0
`Add-Member`	Adds a user-defined custom member to an instance of a WPS object.	WPS 1.0
`Add-PSSnapin`	Adds one or more WPS snap-ins to the current console.	WPS 1.0
`Add-User`	Adds a new user to a directory service.	www.IT-Visions.de PowerShell Extensions 2.0
`Clear-Content`	Deletes the contents of an item, such as deleting the text from a file, but does not delete the item.	WPS 1.0
`Clear-Item`	Deletes the contents of an item, but does not delete the item.	WPS 1.0
`Clear-ItemProperty`	Deletes the value of a property, but it does not delete the property.	WPS 1.0
`Clear-Variable`	Deletes the value of a variable.	WPS 1.0

Commandlet	Description	Product/Version
`Close-DBConnection`	Closes an ADO.NET database connection.	www.IT-Visions.de PowerShell Extensions 2.0
`Compare-Object`	Compares two sets of objects.	WPS 1.0
`ConvertFrom-Base64`	Converts base64 encoded string to byte array.	PSCX 1.1.1
`ConvertFrom-SecureString`	Converts a secure string into an encrypted standard string.	WPS 1.0
`Convert-Path`	Converts a path from a WPS path to a WPS provider path.	WPS 1.0
`ConvertTo-Base64`	Converts byte array or specified file contents to base64 string.	PSCX 1.1.1
`ConvertTo-Html`	Creates an HTML page that represents an object or a set of objects.	WPS 1.0
`ConvertTo-MacOs9LineEnding`	Converts the line endings in the specified file to Mac OS9 and earlier style line endings `\r`.	PSCX 1.1.1
`ConvertTo-SecureString`	Converts encrypted standard strings to secure strings. It can also convert plain text to secure strings. It is used with `ConvertFrom-SecureString` and `Read-Host`.	WPS 1.0
`ConvertTo-UnixLineEnding`	Converts the line endings in the specified file to UNIX line endings `\n`.	PSCX 1.1.1
`ConvertTo-WindowsLineEnding`	Converts the line endings in the specified file to Windows line endings `\r\n`.	PSCX 1.1.1
`Convert-Xml`	Performs XSLT transforms on the specified XML file or `XmlDocument`.	PSCX 1.1.1
`Copy-Item`	Copies an item from one location to another within a namespace.	WPS 1.0
`Copy-ItemProperty`	Copies a property and value from a specified location to another location.	WPS 1.0
`Disconnect-TerminalSession`	Disconnects a specific remote desktop session on a system running Terminal Services/Remote Desktop.	PSCX 1.1.1

Commandlet	Description	Product/Version
`Export-Alias`	Exports information about currently defined aliases to a file.	WPS 1.0
`Export-Bitmap`	Exports bitmap objects to various formats.	PSCX 1.1.1
`Export-Clixml`	Creates an XML-based representation of an object or objects and stores it in a file.	WPS 1.0
`Export-Console`	Exports the configuration of the current console to a file so that you can reuse or share it.	WPS 1.0
`Export-Csv`	Creates a comma-separated values (CSV) file that represents the input objects.	WPS 1.0
`ForEach-Object`	Performs an operation against each of a set of input objects.	WPS 1.0
`Format-Byte`	Displays numbers in multiples of byte units.	PSCX 1.1.1
`Format-Custom`	Uses a customized view to format the output.	WPS 1.0
`Format-Hex`	Displays the contents of files or byte streams in hex format and optionally ASCII.	PSCX 1.1.1
`Format-List`	Formats the output as a list of properties in which each property appears on a new line.	WPS 1.0
`Format-Table`	Formats the output as a table.	WPS 1.0
`Format-Wide`	Formats objects as a wide table that displays only one property of each object.	WPS 1.0
`Format-Xml`	Pretty print for XML files and `XmlDocument` objects.	PSCX 1.1.1
`Get-Acl`	Gets the security descriptor for a resource, such as a file or registry key.	WPS 1.0
`Get-ADObject`	Search for objects in the Active Directory/Global Catalog.	PSCX 1.1.1

Commandlet	Description	Product/Version
Get-Alias	Gets the aliases for the current session.	WPS 1.0
Get-AuthenticodeSignature	Gets information about the Authenticode signature in a file.	WPS 1.0
Get-BIOS	Gets information about the BIOS on a local or remote computer	www.IT-Visions.de PowerShell Extensions 2.0
Get-CDRomdrive	Gets information about the CD-ROM drives on a local or remote computer	www.IT-Visions.de PowerShell Extensions 2.0
Get-ChildItem	Gets the items and child items in one or more specified locations.	WPS 1.0
Get-Clipboard	Gets data from the clipboard.	PSCX 1.1.1
Get-Command	Gets basic information about cmdlets and about other elements of WPS commands.	WPS 1.0
Get-ComputerInfo	Gets information about the local computer.	www.IT-Visions.de PowerShell Extensions 2.0
Get-Computername	Gets the name of the local computer.	www.IT-Visions.de PowerShell Extensions 2.0
Get-Content	Gets the content of the item at the specified location.	WPS 1.0
Get-Credential	Gets a credential object based on a username and password.	WPS 1.0
Get-Culture	Gets information about the regional settings on a computer.	WPS 1.0
Get-CurrentUser	Gets information about the current user.	www.IT-Visions.de PowerShell Extensions 2.0
Get-Date	Gets the current date and time.	WPS 1.0
Get-DbConnection	Opes a database connection.	www.IT-Visions.de PowerShell Extensions 2.0

Commandlet	Description	Product/Version
`Get-DbRow`	Gets a single row from a database table.	www.IT-Visions.de PowerShell Extensions 2.0
`Get-DbTable`	Gets a database table.	www.IT-Visions.de PowerShell Extensions 2.0
`Get-DhcpServer`	Gets a list of authorized DHCP servers.	PSCX 1.1.1
`Get-DirectoryChildren`	Gets the child items of a directory service container.	www.IT-Visions.de PowerShell Extensions 2.0
`Get-DirectoryEntry`	Gets a single entry in a directory service.	www.IT-Visions.de PowerShell Extensions 2.0
`Get-DirectoryValue`	Gets a value from an entry in a directory service.	www.IT-Visions.de PowerShell Extensions 2.0
`Get-Disk`	Gets objects about all disks on a local or remote computer.	www.IT-Visions.de PowerShell Extensions 2.0
`Get-DomainController`	Gets a list of available domain controllers in the current forest/ domain.	PSCX 1.1.1
`Get-EventLog`	Gets information about local event logs or the entries stored in those event logs.	WPS 1.0
`Get-ExecutionPolicy`	Gets the current execution policy for the shell.	WPS 1.0
`Get-ExportedType`	Displays public types for a given `AssemblyName` by loading the associated assembly into a reflection-only context and dumping all publicly accessible `Type` objects to the pipeline.	PSCX 1.1.1
`Get-FileVersionInfo`	Gets a `FileVersionInfo` object for the specified path.	PSCX 1.1.1

Commandlet	Description	Product/Version
`Get-ForegroundWindow`	Returns the `hWnd` or handle of the window in the foreground on the current desktop. See also `Set-ForegroundWindow`.	PSCX 1.1.1
`Get-Hash`	Gets the hash value for the specified file or byte array via the pipeline.	PSCX 1.1.1
`Get-Help`	Displays information about WPS cmdlets and concepts.	WPS 1.0
`Get-History`	Gets a list of the commands entered during the current session.	WPS 1.0
`Get-Host`	Gets a reference to the current console host object. Displays WPS version and regional information by default.	WPS 1.0
`Get-Item`	Gets the item at the specified location.	WPS 1.0
`Get-ItemProperty`	Retrieves the properties of a specified item.	WPS 1.0
`Get-ITVisions`	Displays information about this extension and checks for updates using a web service.	www.IT-Visions.de PowerShell Extensions 2.0
`Get-Keyboard`	Gets information about the key-board on a local or remote computer.	www.IT-Visions.de PowerShell Extensions 2.0
`Get-Location`	Gets information about the current working location.	WPS 1.0
`Get-Member`	Gets information about objects or collections of objects.	WPS 1.0
`Get-MemoryDevice`	Gets information about the RAM on a local or remote computer.	www.IT-Visions.de PowerShell Extensions 2.0

Commandlet	Description	Product/Version
`Get-Metadata`	Gets metadata about the objects in the pipeline.	www.IT-Visions.de PowerShell Extensions 2.0
`Get-MountPoint`	Returns all mount points defined for a specific root path.	PSCX 1.1.1
`Get-Networkadapter`	Gets objects about all network adapters on a local or remote computer.	www.IT-Visions.de PowerShell Extensions 2.0
`Get-PEHeader`	Gets the Portable Header information from an executable file.	PSCX 1.1.1
`Get-PfxCertificate`	Gets information about PFX certificate files on the computer.	WPS 1.0
`Get-PipelineInfo`	Gets type information about the objects in the pipeline.	www.IT-Visions.de PowerShell Extensions 2.0
`Get-PointingDevice`	Gets objects about mouse devices on a local or remote computer.	www.IT-Visions.de PowerShell Extensions 2.0
`Get-Privilege`	Lists privileges held by the session and their current status.	PSCX 1.1.1
`Get-Process`	Gets the processes that are running on the local computer.	WPS 1.0
`Get-Processor`	Gets objects about all processors on a local or remote computer	www.IT-Visions.de PowerShell Extensions 2.0
`Get-PSDrive`	Gets information about WPS drives.	WPS 1.0
`Get-PSProvider`	Gets information about the specified WPS provider.	WPS 1.0
`Get-PSSnapin`	Gets the WPS snap-ins on the computer.	WPS 1.0
`Get-PSSnapinHelp`	Generates an XML file containing all documentation data.	PSCX 1.1.1
`Get-Random`	Returns a random number or a byte array.	PSCX 1.1.1
`Get-ReparsePoint`	Gets NTFS reparse point data.	PSCX 1.1.1
`Get-Service`	Gets the services on the local computer.	WPS 1.0

Commandlet	Description	Product/Version
`Get-ShortPath`	Gets the short, 8.3 name for the given path.	PSCX 1.1.1
`Get-SoundDevice`	Gets objects about all sound devices on a local or remote computer.	www.IT-Visions.de PowerShell Extensions 2.0
`Get-TabExpansion`	Gets matching tab expansions.	PSCX 1.1.1
`Get-Tapedrive`	Gets objects about all tape drives on a local or remote computer.	www.IT-Visions.de PowerShell Extensions 2.0
`Get-TerminalSession`	Gets information on terminal services sessions.	PSCX 1.1.1
`Get-TraceSource`	Gets the WPS components that are instrumented for tracing.	WPS 1.0
`Get-UICulture`	Gets information about the current user interface culture for WPS.	WPS 1.0
`Get-Unique`	Returns the unique items from a sorted list.	WPS 1.0
`Get-USBController`	Gets objects about all USB controllers on a local or remote computer.	www.IT-Visions.de PowerShell Extensions 2.0
`Get-Variable`	Gets the variables in the current console.	WPS 1.0
`Get-Videocontroller`	Gets objects about all video controllers on a local or remote computer.	www.IT-Visions.de PowerShell Extensions 2.0
`Get-WmiObject`	Gets instances of WMI classes or information about available classes.	WPS 1.0
`Group-Object`	Groups objects that contain the same value for specified properties.	WPS 1.0
`Import-Alias`	Imports an alias list from a file.	WPS 1.0
`Import-Bitmap`	Loads bitmap files.	PSCX 1.1.1
`Import-Clixml`	Imports a CLIXML file and creates corresponding objects within WPS.	WPS 1.0
`Import-Csv`	Imports CSV files in the format produced by the `Export-CSV` cmdlet and returns objects that correspond to the objects represented in that CSV file.	WPS 1.0

Commandlet	Description	Product/Version
Invoke-DbCommand	Invokes a command in a database.	www.IT-Visions.de PowerShell Extensions 2.0
Invoke-Expression	Runs a WPS expression that is provided in the form of a string.	WPS 1.0
Invoke-History	Runs commands from the session history.	WPS 1.0
Invoke-Item	Invokes the provider-specific default action on the specified item.	WPS 1.0
Invoke-ScalarDbCommand	Invokes a command in a database that returns a single value.	www.IT-Visions.de PowerShell Extensions 2.0
Join-Path	Combines a path and child path into a single path. The provider supplies the path delimiters.	WPS 1.0
Join-String	Joins an array of strings into a single string.	PSCX 1.1.1
Measure-Command	Measures the time it takes to run script blocks and cmdlets.	WPS 1.0
Measure-Object	Measures characteristics of objects and their properties.	WPS 1.0
Move-Item	Moves an item from one location to another.	WPS 1.0
Move-ItemProperty	Moves a property from one location to another.	WPS 1.0
New-Alias	Creates a new alias.	WPS 1.0
New-Hardlink	Creates file system hard links. The hardlink and the target must reside on the same NTFS volume.	PSCX 1.1.1
New-Item	Creates a new item in a namespace.	WPS 1.0
New-ItemProperty	Sets a new property of an item at a location.	WPS 1.0
New-Junction	Creates NTFS directory junctions.	PSCX 1.1.1
New-Object	Creates an instance of a .NET or COM object.	WPS 1.0

Commandlet	Description	Product/Version
`New-PSDrive`	Installs a new WPS drive.	WPS 1.0
`New-Service`	Creates a new entry for a Windows service in the registry and the service database.	WPS 1.0
`New-Shortcut`	Creates shell shortcuts.	PSCX 1.1.1
`New-Symlink`	Creates file system symbolic links. Requires Microsoft Windows Vista or later.	PSCX 1.1.1
`New-TimeSpan`	Creates a `TimeSpan` object.	WPS 1.0
`New-Variable`	Creates a new variable.	WPS 1.0
`Out-Clipboard`	Formats text via `Out-String` before placing in the clipboard.	PSCX 1.1.1
`Out-Default`	Sends the output to the default formatter and the default output cmdlet. This cmdlet has no effect on the formatting or output. It is a placeholder that lets you write your own `Out-Default` function or cmdlet.	WPS 1.0
`Out-File`	Sends output to a file.	WPS 1.0
`Out-Host`	Sends output to the command line.	WPS 1.0
`Out-Null`	Deletes output instead of sending it to the console.	WPS 1.0
`Out-Printer`	Sends output to a printer.	WPS 1.0
`Out-String`	Sends objects to the host as a series of strings.	WPS 1.0
`Ping-Host`	Sends ICMP echo requests to network hosts.	PSCX 1.1.1
`Pop-Location`	Changes the current location to the location most recently pushed onto the stack. You can pop the location from the default stack or from a stack that you create by using `Push-Location`.	WPS 1.0
`Push-Location`	Pushes the current location onto the stack.	WPS 1.0
`Read-Host`	Reads a line of input from the console.	WPS 1.0
`Remove-DirectoryEntry`	Removes a directory entry from a directory service.	www.IT-Visions.de PowerShell Extensions 2.0
`Remove-Item`	Deletes the specified items.	WPS 1.0
`Remove-ItemProperty`	Deletes the property and its value from an item.	WPS 1.0

Commandlet	Description	Product/Version
`Remove-MountPoint`	Removes a mount point, dismounting the current media if any. If used against the root of a fixed drive, removes the drive letter assignment.	PSCX 1.1.1
`Remove-PSDrive`	Removes a WPS drive from its location.	WPS 1.0
`Remove-PSSnapin`	Removes WPS snap-ins from the current console.	WPS 1.0
`Remove-ReparsePoint`	Removes NTFS reparse junctions and symbolic links.	PSCX 1.1.1
`Remove-Variable`	Deletes a variable and its value.	WPS 1.0
`Rename-Item`	Renames an item in a WPS provider namespace.	WPS 1.0
`Rename-ItemProperty`	Renames a property of an item.	WPS 1.0
`Resize-Bitmap`	Resizes bitmaps.	PSCX 1.1.1
`Resolve-Assembly`	Resolves and optionally imports assemblies by partial name with optional version.	PSCX 1.1.1
`Resolve-Host`	Resolves host names to IP addresses.	PSCX 1.1.1
`Resolve-Path`	Resolves the wildcard characters in a path and displays the path contents.	WPS 1.0
`Restart-Service`	Stops and then starts one or more services.	WPS 1.0
`Resume-Service`	Resumes one or more suspended (paused) services.	WPS 1.0
`Select-Object`	Selects specified properties of an object or set of objects. It can also select unique objects from an array of objects or it can select a specified number of objects from the beginning or end of an array of objects.	WPS 1.0
`Select-String`	Identifies patterns in strings.	WPS 1.0
`Select-Xml`	Selects elements in XML files and `XmlDocument` objects with XPath expressions.	PSCX 1.1.1
`Send-SmtpMail`	Sends e-mail via specified SMTP server to specified recipients.	PSCX 1.1.1

Commandlet	Description	Product/Version
`Set-Acl`	Changes the security descriptor of a specified resource, such as a file or a registry key.	WPS 1.0
`Set-Alias`	Creates or changes an alias (alternate name) for a cmdlet or other command element in the current WPS session.	WPS 1.0
`Set-AuthenticodeSignature`	Uses an Authenticode signature to sign a WPS script or other file.	WPS 1.0
`Set-Clipboard`	Puts the specified object into the system clipboard.	PSCX 1.1.1
`Set-Content`	Writes or replaces the content in an item with new content.	WPS 1.0
`Set-Date`	Changes the system time on the computer to a time that you specify.	WPS 1.0
`Set-DbTable`	Saves the updated data of a data table.	www.IT-Visions.de PowerShell Extensions 2.0
`Set-DirectoryValue`	Sets a value in a directory entry.	www.IT-Visions.de PowerShell Extensions 2.0
`Set-ExecutionPolicy`	Changes the user preference for the execution policy of the shell.	WPS 1.0
`Set-FileTime`	Sets a file or folder's created and last accessed/write times.	PSCX 1.1.1
`Set-ForegroundWindow`	Given an `hWnd` or window handle, brings that window to the foreground. Useful for restoring a window to uppermost after an application that seizes the foreground is invoked. See also `Get-ForegroundWindow`.	PSCX 1.1.1
`Set-Item`	Changes the value of an item to the value specified in the command.	WPS 1.0
`Set-ItemProperty`	Sets the value of a property at the specified location.	WPS 1.0

Commandlet	Description	Product/Version
`Set-Location`	Sets the current working location to a specified location.	WPS 1.0
`Set-Privilege`	Adjusts privileges held by the session.	PSCX 1.1.1
`Set-PSDebug`	Turns script debugging features on and off, sets the trace level and toggles strict mode.	WPS 1.0
`Set-Service`	Changes the display name, description, or starting mode of a service.	WPS 1.0
`Set-TraceSource`	Configures, starts, and stops a trace of WPS components.	WPS 1.0
`Set-Variable`	Sets the value of a variable. Creates the variable if one with the requested name does not exist.	WPS 1.0
`Set-VolumeLabel`	Modifies the label shown in Windows Explorer for a particular disk volume.	PSCX 1.1.1
`Sort-Object`	Sorts objects by property values.	WPS 1.0
`Split-Path`	Returns the specified part of a path.	WPS 1.0
`Split-String`	Splits a single string into an array of strings.	PSCX 1.1.1
`Start-Process`	Starts a new process.	PSCX 1.1.1
`Start-Service`	Starts one or more stopped services.	WPS 1.0
`Start-Sleep`	Suspends shell, script, or runspace activity for the specified period of time.	WPS 1.0
`Start-TabExpansion`	Initializes the tab expansion caches.	PSCX 1.1.1
`Start-Transcript`	Creates a record of all or part of a WPS session in a text file.	WPS 1.0
`Stop-Process`	Stops one or more running processes.	WPS 1.0
`Stop-Service`	Stops one or more running services.	WPS 1.0
`Stop-TerminalSession`	Logs off a specific remote desktop session on a system running Terminal Services/Remote Desktop.	PSCX 1.1.1
`Stop-Transcript`	Stops a transcript.	WPS 1.0

Commandlet	Description	Product/Version
`Suspend-Service`	Suspends (pauses) one or more running services.	WPS 1.0
`Tee-Object`	Pipes object input to a file or variable, and then passes the input along the pipeline.	WPS 1.0
`Test-Assembly`	Tests whether the specified file is a .NET assembly.	PSCX 1.1.1
`Test-DbConnection`	Tests the availability of a database.	www.IT-Visions.de PowerShell Extensions 2.0
`Test-Path`	Determines whether all elements of a path exist.	WPS 1.0
`Test-Xml`	Tests for well formedness and optionally validates against XML Schema.	PSCX 1.1.1
`Trace-Command`	Configures and starts a trace of the specified expression or command.	WPS 1.0
`Update-FormatData`	Updates and appends format data files.	WPS 1.0
`Update-TypeData`	Updates the current extended type configuration by reloading the `*.types.ps1xml` files into memory.	WPS 1.0
`Where-Object`	Creates a filter that controls which objects will be passed along a command pipeline.	WPS 1.0
`Write-BZip2`	Creates BZIP2 format archive files from pipeline or parameter input.	PSCX 1.1.1
`Write-Clipboard`	Writes objects to the clipboard using their string representation, bypassing the default WPS formatting.	PSCX 1.1.1
`Write-Debug`	Writes a debug message to the host display.	WPS 1.0
`Write-Error`	Writes an object to the error pipeline.	WPS 1.0
`Write-GZip`	Creates GNU Zip (Gzip) format files from pipeline or parameter input.	PSCX 1.1.1
`Write-Host`	Displays objects by using the host user interface.	WPS 1.0

Commandlet	Description	Product/Version
`Write-Output`	Writes objects to the success pipeline.	WPS 1.0
`Write-Progress`	Displays a progress bar within a WPS command window.	WPS 1.0
`Write-Tar`	Creates Tape Archive (TAR) format files from pipeline or parameter input.	PSCX 1.1.1
`Write-Verbose`	Writes a string to the verbose display of the host.	WPS 1.0
`Write-Warning`	Writes a warning message.	WPS 1.0
`Write-Zip`	Creates Zip format archive files from pipeline or parameter input.	PSCX 1.1.1

APPENDIX B

POWERSHELL 2.0 PREVIEW

At their TechEd Europe 2007 conference, Microsoft announced Windows PowerShell 2.0 and made available a very early prerelease version. WPS 2.0 will be compatible with WPS 1.0 and will include some major advances and a lot of minor advances.

Major advances in WPS 2.0 include the following:

- A graphical user environment for WPS, including a script editor with syntax highlighting and IntelliSense (see Figure B.1).
- Remote execution of commands and scripts (on a remote computer or a few remote computers at the same time)
- Asynchronous operations (background execution in a different thread)
- Script debugging (console based, not graphical)
- Constrained runspaces (shells restricted to certain commands)
- An event system that informs about any changes in objects (for example, start of a process)
- Packaging of scripts and additional files

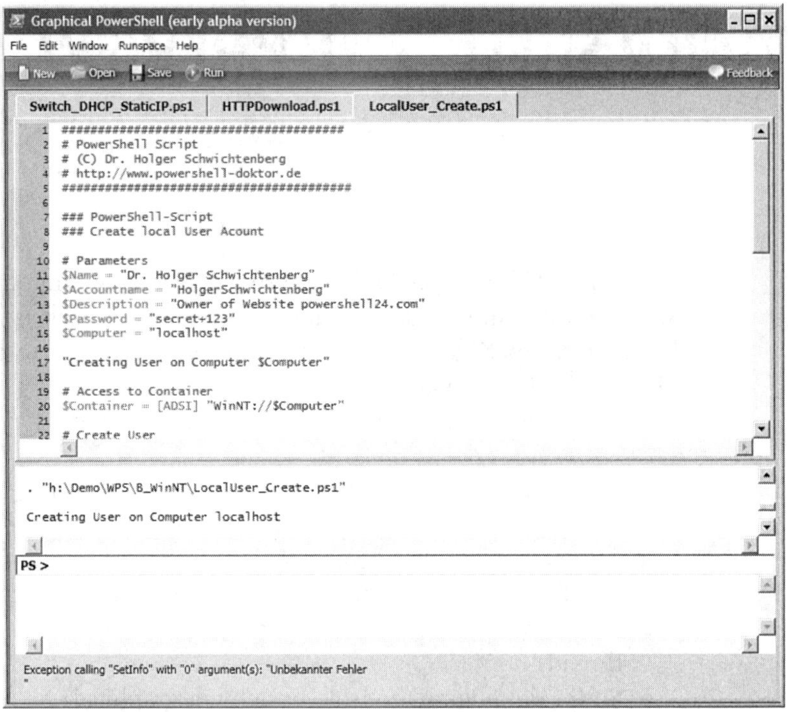

Figure B.1 The "Graphical WPS" is still basic at this early stage in the WPS 2.0 product development.

At this point, only a few of the minor advances that will be available in WPS 2.0 are public:

- Enhancements to `Get-Member` (display of intrinsic members such as `PSBase`)
- New operators for string splitting and joining
- New syntax for data declarations, including internationalization
- Script commandlets now as powerful as .NET-based commandlets (including `-confirm`, `-whatif`, `-debug`, and `-verbose`)
- Improvements to the ADSI object adapter (members of the `DirectoryEntry` class such as `Parent`, `Path`, `Children`, `SchemaClassName`, and `SchemaEntry` no longer hidden)
- Additional commandlets for WMI (`Invoke-WmiMethod`, `Remove-WmiObject`)

- Support for WMI authentication in `Get-WmiObject`
- New data type `[ADSISearcher]` for the definition of LDAP queries
- Hash tables that can be used as parameter lists for commandlets (a feature called *splatting*)
- New commandlet `Out-GridView` for viewing pipeline content in a table, including grouping and search support (see Figure B.2)

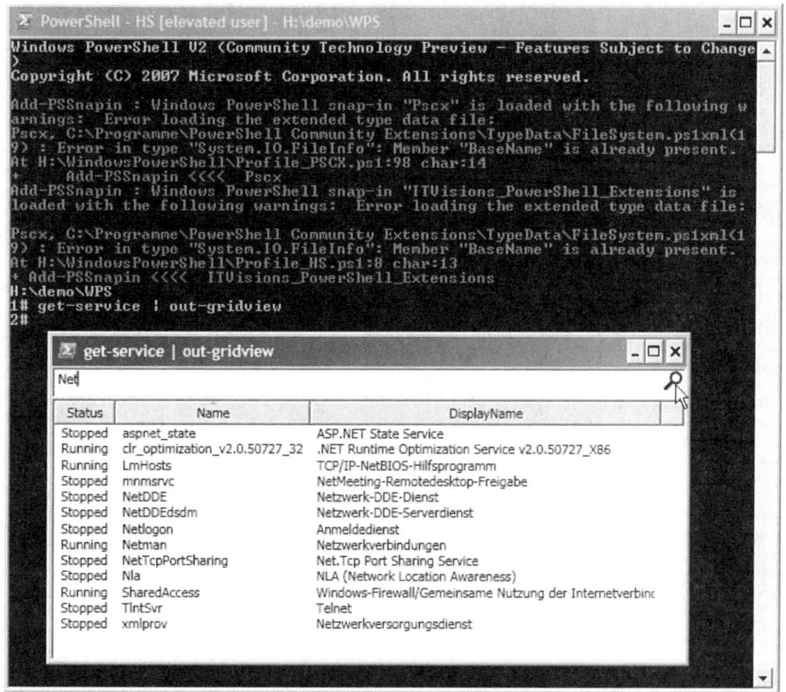

Figure B.2 The WPS 2.0 CTP has some problems with `Add-PsSnapIn`. The `Out-GridView` commandlet, however, is already quite nice.

WARNING Most features of WPS 2.0 are based on .NET Framework 2.0, but some (for example, the editor and the commandlet `Out-GridView`) will require .NET Framework 3.0 or later.

APPENDIX C

BIBLIOGRAPHY

[CODEPLEX01]	PowerShell Community Extensions	www.codeplex.com/PowerShellCX/
[CODEPLEX02]	PowerShell SharePoint Provider	www.codeplex.com/PSSharePoint
[DOTNET01]	.NET Framework Community Website	www.dotnetframework.de
[DOTNET02]	.NET Tools and Software Components Reference	www.dotnetframework.de/tools.aspx
[FAY01]	PowerShell Help Editor	www.wassimfayed.com/PowerShell/CmdletHelpEditor.zip
[Gotdotnet01]	PowerShell remoting	www.codeplex.com/powershellremoting
[Kumaravel01]	AD Access Change/Break in RC2	groups.google.de/group/microsoft.public.windows.powershell/browse_thread/thread/7cf4b1bb774dfb90/17ad75cae89a341d?lnk=st&q=%22Folks%2C+I+know+that+many+of%22&rnum=6&hl=de#17ad75cae89a341d
[MS01]	PowerShell download	www.microsoft.com/windowsserver2003/technologies/management/powershell/download.mspx
[MS02]	PowerShell Documentation	www.microsoft.com/downloads/details.aspx?familyid=B4720B00-9A66-430F-BD56-EC48BFCA154F&displaylang=en
[MS03]	Windows PowerShell Graphical Help File	www.microsoft.com/downloads/details.aspx?familyid=3b3f7ce4-43ea-4a21-90cc-966a7fc6c6e8&displaylang=en

[MS04]	Group Policy Management Console with Service Pack 1	www.microsoft.com/downloads/details.aspx?familyid=0a6d4c24-8cbd-4b35-9272-dd3cbfc81887&displaylang=en
[MSDN01]	.NET Framework Class Library documentation for `FileSystemRights`-Enumeration	msdn2.microsoft.com/library/system.security.accesscontrol.filesystemrights(VS.80).aspx
[MSDN02]	How to Write Cmdlet Help	msdn2.microsoft.com/en-us/library/aa965353.aspx
[MSDN03]	PowerShell Software Development Kit (SDK)	msdn2.microsoft.com/en-us/library/aa139691.aspx
[MSDN04]	Windows PowerShell Extended Type System (ETS)	msdn2.microsoft.com/en-us/library/ms714419.aspx
[MSDN05]	WMI Schema Class Reference	msdn2.microsoft.com/en-us/library/Aa394554.aspx
[MSDN06]	Documentation for the .NET Namespace `System.Management`	msdn2.microsoft.com/en-us/library/system.management.aspx
[MSDN07]	Cmdlet Development Guidelines	msdn2.microsoft.com/en-us/library/ms714657.aspx
[MSDN08]	.NET Framework Regular Expressions	msdn2.microsoft.com/en-us/library/hs600312(VS.80).aspx
[MSDN09]	Active Directory-Schema	msdn.microsoft.com/library/en-us/adschema/adschema/active_directory_schema.asp
[MSDN10]	User Object User Interface Mapping	msdn.microsoft.com/library/default.asp?url=/library/en-us/ad/ad/user_object_user_interface_mapping.asp
[MSSec01]	Malicious Software Encyclopedia: Worm:MSH/Cibyz.A	www.microsoft.com/security/encyclopedia/details.aspx?name=Worm:MSH/Cibyz.A
[NSOFT]	NetCmdlets from nsoftware	www.nsoftware.com/powershell/
[RFC1960]	A String Representation of LDAP Search Filters	www.ietf.org/rfc/rfc1960.txt
[RFC2254]	The String Representation of LDAP Search Filters	www.rfc-editor.org/rfc/rfc2254.txt

[TNET01]	Documentation for the Exchange Management Shell	technet.microsoft.com/en-us/library/bb124413.aspx
[TNET02]	Exchange Server Scripts for the PowerShell	www.microsoft.com/technet/scriptcenter/scripts/message/exch2007/default.mspx?mfr=true
[TNET03]	Converting VBScript Commands to Windows PowerShell Commands	www.microsoft.com/technet/scriptcenter/topics/winpsh/convert/default.mspx
[W3C01]	XML Path Language (XPath) Version 1.0 W3C Recommendation 16 November 1999	www.w3.org/TR/xpath
[WPE01]	Definition of "trial and error"	en.wikipedia.org/wiki/Trial_and_error
[WS01]	Companion website for this book	www.windows-scripting.com

Index

B–C

H

M

S

Addison-Wesley